Persianate Selves

PERSIANATE SELVES

Memories of Place and Origin Before Nationalism

Mana Kia

STANFORD UNIVERSITY PRESS
Stanford, California

STANFORD UNIVERSITY PRESS
Stanford, California

Printed in the United States of America on acid-free, archival-quality paper

Library of Congress Cataloging-in-Publication Data
Names: Kia, Mana, author.
Title: Persianate selves : memories of place and origin before nationalism /
    Mana Kia.
Description: Stanford, California : Stanford University Press, [2020] |
    Includes bibliographical references and index.
Identifiers: LCCN 2019037226 (print) | LCCN 2019037227 (ebook) | ISBN
    9781503610682 (cloth) | ISBN 9781503611955 (paperback) | ISBN
    9781503611962 (epub)
Subjects: LCSH: Iranians—Ethnic identity—History—18th century. |
    Nationalism—Iran—History—18th century. | Iran—History—16th-
    18th centuries.
Classification: LCC DS268 .K53 2020 (print) | LCC DS268 (ebook) |
    DDC 305.891/55009033—dc23
LC record available at https://lccn.loc.gov/2019037226
LC ebook record available at https://lccn.loc.gov/2019037227

Cover design: Susan Zucker

Typeset by Kevin Barrett Kane in 10.25/15 Adobe Caslon Pro

For Rassa June, light of my eyes

Contents

Acknowledgments

This book has been written in fits and starts over a number of years. It should have been finished much sooner, but births, relocations, separations, unions, continuing duties, and new challenges punctuated its completion. In substance, it has been expanded and revised almost unrecognizably beyond its first iteration, but first thanks are due to my early mentors. From the very beginning Afsaneh Najmabadi was quick to respond to questions and messy drafts, and kept me conceptually accountable. In addition to being an amazing scholar from whom I had the honor of learning a great deal, she gave me the freedom to follow my interests, which wended their way across time and space. Over the years Engseng Ho challenged me to keep the big picture in mind and to take my thinking in new directions. With good humor and integrity Paul Losensky has provided guidance and feedback, both general and pinpointed, as well as most gracious support. Sunil Sharma literally spent years reading these and other Persian texts with me; I owe an incalculable debt to him for his generosity as a teacher and a friend.

My sense of being in the world is one in which connection to friends and family is crucial. My grandmother Betty Parviz's stories first set me on this path and I still miss her every day. I am grateful for my extended maternal family (especially Hamid, Shahnaz, Mojdeh, Omid, Mandana, Rodolphe, Arash, Mona), who act as an anchor in my life. My mother, Soosan Yeganegi, and my cousin, Farbod Mirfakhrai, were especially supportive and encouraging. My aunt, Zohreh Sullivan, encouraged my love of books and writing from the very beginning. Mowgli Holmes and Tara Nolan have always felt like family, and their friendship has been a refuge for over two decades. Bahareh Mahdi has loved me with amazing generosity for over thirty years, even during my most annoying and sanctimonious phases.

Talking things through is a large part of my thinking process, and over the years I have benefited from the engagement and advice of many mentors, friends, and colleagues from my student days: Sebouh Aslanian, Kathryn Babayan, Alireza Doostdar, Philip Grant, Rajeev Kinra, Darryl Li, Derek Mancini-Lander, Dan Sheffield, Nick Smith, Naghmeh Sohrabi, and Mohamad Tavakoli. In particular, I would not have survived Cambridge without Eric Beverley, Sarah Waheed, Nicole Brown, and Sam Bayard.

I am also grateful for the funding and professional opportunities that supported this project. I began preliminary research with an Arthur Lehman Merit Fellowship in fall 2006 from Harvard University. In 2007–2008, I went to London, Delhi, and Tehran with a Frederick Sheldon Travelling Fellowship from Harvard. I would never have survived the mean streets of Delhi without the friendship of Neichu Angami and Sarah Waheed. Once in India, I was able to travel to Patna with a Tata Study Grant from the South Asia Initiative at Harvard. Dr. Imtiyaz Ahmad at the Khuda Bakhsh Library provided me with instrumental assistance. In Tehran, Drs. Susan Ghahremani and Hossein Doostdar graciously hosted and guided me during my stay. I am also grateful to Saiedeh Karimi for her assistance and friendship. I wrote most of the chapters on which this book is based with a dissertation completion fellowship from the American Council of Learned Societies (ACLS), before putting it aside. I then spent two years of education and engagement on what has come to be a second project at the Max Planck Institute for Human Development's Center for the History of Emotions. I picked this book up again during my time at Columbia, during which I was fortunate to have presented various parts in a number of different forums: the Jordan Center for Persian Studies at UC Irvine, South Asia Colloquium at University of Pennsylvania, the workshop on Local History in the Persianate Cosmopolis at SOAS, and the Center for Middle Eastern Studies at University of Chicago. These opportunities helped me refine my arguments. I did additional research in London and Berlin with a Provost's

Faculty Diversity Grant from Columbia University. Final revisions were begun and ended with two Junior Faculty Summer Research Grants from Columbia and sustained in between with the support of an SSRC/Andrew Mellon Transregional Junior Scholars Fellowship: InterAsian Contexts and Connections.

At Columbia, I benefited from the intellectual stimulation and guidance of my colleagues, especially Allison Busch, Partha Chatterjee, Patricia Dailey, Mamadou Diouf, Najam Haider, Gil Hochberg, David Lurie, Mahmood Mamdani, Brinkley Messick, Tim Mitchell, Debashree Mukherjee, Sheldon Pollock, Anupama Rao, and Emmanuelle Saada. Tenure track is quite the mental health Olympics, and the support of Manan Ahmed and Eric Beverley has been crucial. I have also benefited from engagement with and support of various other friends and colleagues: Orit Bashkin, Purnima Dhavan, Roy Fischel, Barry Flood, Behrooz Ghamari, Nile Green, Katharina Ivanyi, Arash Khazeni, Dipti Khera, Julie Livingston, Afshin Marashi, Matt Melvin-Koushki, Durba Mitra, Margrit Pernau, Christine Philliou, Robert Pluma, Sholeh Quinn, Ali Raza, Sadia Shirazi, Kamran Sullivan, and Farzin Vejdani.

Additional thanks are due to Kate Wahl at Stanford University Press for guiding me with extraordinary editorial skill to pull this book out of a manuscript nearly twice its size, as well as her efficiency in seeing it through the review and revision process. Debra Osnowitz and David Horne's editorial skills helped me polish this manuscript into something more readable.

I am especially thankful for (and to) my beloved companion, Gil Anidjar, whose brilliance, thoughtfulness, and ferocious engagement have been a singular joy. Though we have parted ways, I must also thank my former husband, A. Seth Young, for the years we spent together and for our daughter, Rassa June. It is to her that this book is dedicated, with love and the deepest gratitude. I was a single parent the last year that I worked on this book, and she helped me remember what is really important.

Notes on Dates and
Transliteration

NOTE ON DATES: For the most part I have listed only Gregorian dates (AD). When I deemed it necessary or significant, I have included Hijri dates as well (AH). They are duly marked when both dates are present. In the bibliography, works published in Iran follow the solar (shamsi) Hijri calendar (SH).

NOTE ON TRANSLITERATION: I have used IJMES transliteration conventions with some modifications. In the running text I have used diacritic marks only for the long vowels, hamza, and 'ayn, except for titles, personal names, and place names. Diacritic marks are used in the initial rendition of names in the "Dramatis Personae," in citations within endnotes, and in the bibliography, to facilitate research.

Dramatis Personae
(Major Figures and Works)

Sirāj al-Dīn ʿAlī Khān "Ārzū"
(1689–1756 AD/1101–69 AH)

Born to a lineage of learned men descended from Shaykh Chiragh Dihlavi and Shaykh Muhammad Ghaws Gwaliori Shattari, Arzu was raised and educated in Gwalior and Agra. In 1719–20 AD/1132 AH, he moved to Delhi, where he was at the center of scholarly and literary circles. An illustrious scholar, teacher, and poet, he wrote literary treatises, commentaries, poetic collections (*dīvāns*), and the voluminous commemorative biographical compendium (*tazkirih*), *Majmaʿ al-Nafāʾis* (1750–51 AD/1164 AH) centered on Timurid Hindustan. He was teacher to many Persian and Urdu poets, and his position on proper idiomatic innovation was central to the development of north Indian Urdu poetic culture. Arzu's main patron was Muhammad Shah's khān-i sāmān, Muʿtamin al-Dawlih Ishaq Khan Shushtari, and then his eldest son, Najam al-Dawlih Ishaq Khan. Through Ishaq Khan's second son, Salar Jang, Arzu moved to Lucknow under Shujaʿ al-Dawlih's patronage in 1754–55, as part of the migration of literati seeking patronage in the regional courts after Muhammad Shah's death. Arzu died soon after in 1756, and his body was transported back to Delhi for burial.

Mīr Ghulām ʿAlī "Āzād" Bilgrāmī
(1704–86 AD/1116–1200 AH)

He was a noted poet, teacher, and scholar (of Persian and Arabic). Born into
a scholarly family of sayyids in the Awadhi town of Bilgram, his initial education was with his father and his grandfather, Mir ʿAbd al-Jalil Bilgrami. In
his youth he traveled between Bilgram and Sindh (via Lahore and Delhi)
in the employ of his uncle, the imperial chronicler (*vaqāʿ nigār*) of Sihvan.
In 1738 Azad went to the Hijaz for hajj and to study hadith. After his return in 1739, he settled in Aurangabad. There he was a participant of the
Nakhshbandi Sufi lodge (*takiyyih),* initially patronized by Nizam al-Mulk's
second son. He authored hadith commentaries, literary treatises, and poetry
in both Arabic and Persian. During his time in Aurangabad, he was at the
center of *tazkirih* production. Besides his own three *tazkirih*s, *Yad-i Bayza*
(1732 AD/1145 AH); *Maʾasir al-Kiram* (1752–53 AD/1166 AH), the second part of
which is *Sarv-i Azad*; and *Khizanih-yi ʿAmirih* (1763–64 AD/1176 AH), he also
rescued and completed his friend Shahnavaz Khan Aurangabadi's *tazkirih* of
Timurid office holders, the well-known *Maʾasir al-Umara*, after the author's
death. Azad trained a number of students, including Shafiq Aurangabadi.
He eventually relocated to Dawlatabad, where he continued his scholarly
pursuits until his death. He was buried in Khuldabad.

Lutf ʿAlī "Āzar" Baygdilī
(1722–80 AD/1134–95 AH)

Born in Isfahan, Azar fled with his Shāmlū family to Qum for fourteen years
after the Afghan invasion, which occurred in the year of his birth. In 1736,
Azar's father was appointed governor of Lar (in place of the governor whose
murder caused Hazin to flee to Hindustan) and then Fars, bringing the family to Shiraz. After his father's death in 1738, Azar accompanied his uncle on
hajj, by way of the Shiʿa shrine cities. Nadir Shah's army was returning from
Hindustan in 1741 (with Kashmiri in tow). Azar accompanied Nadir's army
to Mazandaran, Azarbayjan, and ʿIraq-i ʿajam, eventually settling in Isfahan.
He spent the next years in service to various rulers of the city, frequenting
circles of the eloquent and learned there and in Shiraz, in particular those of
his teacher, Mir Sayyid ʿAli "Mushtaq." In the years that followed, he made

enough of a name for himself to be known in Delhi. Eventually, he retired to Qum in the 1760s, where he wrote poetry and his famed *tazkirih*, the *Atashka-dih* (begun in 1760–61 AD/1174 AH, with additions until 1779 AD/1193 AH). He died in 1780.

Āqā Ahmad **Bihbahānī**
(1777–1819)

Aqa Ahmad was descended from the late Safavid Shaykh al-Islam of Isfahan, Muhammad Baqir Majlisi, and related by descent or marriage to other great Shi'a juris-consults (*mujtahids*) of late eighteenth-century Iraq, such as Vahid Bihbahani and Sayyid 'Ali Tabataba'i. Born in Kermanshah, educated in the Iraqi shrine cities, he traveled extensively in Iran, studying and seeking patronage before traveling to Hindustan in 1805. He circulated through port cities and regional centers, such as Bombay, Hyderabad, Murshidabad (where he had relatives), Faizabad, Lucknow, and Patna, where he finally found patronage under the East India Company as Friday prayer leader. He wrote his *Mir'at al-Ahval* before returning to Iran in 1810. The text is dedicated to the Qajar prince Mohammad 'Ali Mirza Dawlatshah (1789–1821), though he purposefully left multiple copies in Patna.

Joseph **Emin**
(1726–1809)

Born in Hamadan to a merchant family, Emin circulated with his merchant family through Iran and *Iraq-i 'arab* (Hamadan, Gilan, Baghdad, Basra) before finally settling in Calcutta. He grew up largely in the care of his pious grandfather, who was also responsible for his education. He arrived in Calcutta when he was seventeen. There he began learning English, though he ultimately rejected his family's vocation and fled to England in 1751, where he charmed his way into elite circles, received military training, and made the ostensible liberation of an Armenian homeland a celebrated cause. His patrons and correspondents included Dukes of Northumberland and Cumberland, Lady Montague, and Edmund Burke. He traveled three times to the Caucasus over the next two decades to achieve his goal. After these failed attempts to inspire the Armenian Catholicos, Georgian Prince Heraclius, or most of the Armenian merchant community, Emin finally settled in New

Julfa Isfahan, where he married. When Karim Khan died in 1779, Emin returned to Calcutta, where he found himself marginalized by the East India Company's increasingly exclusionary governance policies. He wrote a memoir of his life and times in English in Calcutta (1788), which was republished in London (1792 and later reissued in 1918).

Shaykh Muhammad ʿAlī "Hazīn" Lāhījī
(1692–1766 AD/1103–80 AH)

Though born and raised in Isfahan, Hazin identified himself according to his father's birthplace of Lahijan. At the age of twenty, he traveled through *Iraq-i ʿajam* and Fars to expand his education. He lived through the Afghan siege of Isfahan, though he lost many family, friends, and possessions. Afterward, he traveled incessantly between the lands of western and central Iran (*ʿIraq-i ʿajam*), Mesopotamia (*ʿIraq-i ʿarab)* and the Hijaz, never remaining in one place for more than a couple of years. His alleged involvement in the assassination of Nadir Shah's governor in Lar resulted in his voyage to Timurid Hindustan in 1734. He spent various periods of time in Sindh and the Punjab, particularly in Lahore. After a notorious decade in Delhi, where he alienated many political and learned elites, Hazin resettled in Benares in the year of Muhammad Shah's death (1748) and lived out the rest of his days. He ostensibly wrote three *dīvān*s in Iran before migrating, though all are lost. His fourth *dīvān* was written in India, and collected by his companion and patron, Valih Daghistani, in 1742–43 AD/1155 AH. He wrote a memoir of his life and times, which came to be called *Tazkirat al-Ahval* (1742 AD/1154 AH). His narrowly focused *Tazkirat al-Muʿasirin* was completed (1752 AD/1165 AH) soon after his move to Benares, where he was warmly received by its ruler, Raja Balvant Singh. During that time he taught a number of Hindu and Muslim students, including Raja Ram Naraʾin (later governor of Patna), Sher Afgan Khan "Basiti," Kumar Chet Singh, Shaykh Gulshan ʿAli Jaunpuri, Ghulam Husayn Tabatabaʾi, and Tafazzul Husayn Khan. He is buried in Benares in a tomb of his own design.

Mirzā Abū Tālib Khān Isfahānī
(1752–1806)

Born in Lucknow to a migrant father from Isfahan and mother from a

well-established Mughal family, both in service to the second Navvab of Lucknow, Safdar Jang. Due to a change in political fortunes the family fled to
Murshidabad in 1766. After serving in an administrative capacity there, Abu
Talib returned to Lucknow after the rise of Asaf al-Dawlih and then moved
to Calcutta in 1787, where soon after he met 'Abd al-Latif Shushtari. His *tazkirih*, *Khulasat al-Afkar* (1208 AH/1793–94 AD), focuses on the genre of *masnavi*
(narrative verse). He also authored scientific treatises, a *divan*, a *masnavi*, and
historical works. In Calcutta, he entered into the employ of the East India
Company, under whose auspices he traveled to London in 1799. On his return
journey, he disembarked at Istanbul and traveled overland to the Iraqi shrine
cities. His travel text, *Masir-i Talibi*, was written after his return in 1803.

Khvājih 'Abd al-Karīm **Kashmīrī**
(d. 1784)

Originally from Kashmir, he was a resident of Delhi at the time of Nadir
Shah's conquest (1739). He accompanied Nadir's army as a functionary
(*mutasaddi*) to Iran via Turan. He parted ways from Nadir's army in Qazvin
(1741) and made his way to the Iraqi shrine cities and then onto the Hijaz to
perform hajj. He returned via ship to Bengal (1742) and resettled in Delhi.
Written soon after his return (though ongoingly added to for decades),
Bayan-i vaqi' provides an account of Nadir Shah's rise and invasion, Kashmiri's travels and pilgrimage, and the high politics of the Mughal kingdom
from the 1740s up through his death. It was among the commemorative texts
translated into English by East India Company officials in the late eighteenth century as they became a regional power in the subcontinent.

Navvāb 'Alī Ibrāhīm Khān "**Khalīl**" Banārasī
(d. 1793–94 AD/1208 AH)

Khalil was born in Patna and was initially in the service of Mir Qasim of
Lucknow. After Mir Qasim's defeat, he entered the East India Company's
service and was appointed judge (*qāzi*) of Benares. Notably, he was friendly
with Warren Hastings. In addition to a history of the Maratha wars, he authored three *tazkirih*s, *Gulzar-i Ibrahim*, on *Rikhta* (Urdu) poets; *Khulasat
al-Kalam*, on Persian *masnavi*s; and the vast *Suhuf-i Ibrahim* (1205 AH/1790–
91 AD, though he worked on it until his death), on Persian poets.

Mirzā ʿAlī "**Maftūn**" ʿAzīmābādī
(d. after 1833)

Not much is known about Maftun aside from the fact that he was born in Delhi and moved with his family to Azimabad Patna, from where he undertook the hajj in November 1825. He traveled to the Hijaz via Calcutta and the Indian Ocean. Afterward, he arrived in the port of Bushihr in November 1826, traveling through Shiraz, Isfahan, and Tehran on his way to the tomb of the eighth Shiʿa Imam in Mashhad, from where he returned overland to Hindustan (1828). His *hajjnāma*, *Zubdat al-Akhbar* (1833) also contains a great deal of his own poetry.

Mīr Muhammad Taqī "**Mīr**"
(1723–1810 AD/1135–1225 AH)

Mir was born in Agra to a family descended from migrants who had arrived to north India from the Hijaz in Akbar's time. His father died while he was young, causing the family to suffer financial hardships. Mir migrated to Delhi, initially staying with Arzu, his relative by marriage, with whom he had a difficult relationship. A poet of both Persian and Urdu, Mir is considered amongst the finest of this early generation of poets writing in *Rīkhta* in mid-eighteenth-century Delhi. His *Nikat al-Shuʿara* (1165 AH/1751–52 AD) is considered the first *tazkirih* dedicated to *Rīkhta* poets. Written while Arzu was still alive, the *Nikat* places Arzu as the third (after Amir Khusraw and Bidil) and most immediate ancestor of Mir's circle of poets. Mir completed *Zikr-i Mir* (1782–83 AH/1197 AD) after he had fled Delhi and relocated to Lucknow. The text commemorates his life and the difficult times he lived through. His poetic corpus was both prodigious and wide-ranging.

Amīn ibn Ahmad **Rāzī**
(d. 1619)

Born in Ray to a family with members in Safavid imperial service during Shah Tahmasp's reign. Razi was also related to Nur Jahan, queen to the Timurid ruler, Jahangir. Amin Razi migrated to Hindustan near the end of Akbar's reign and completed the *Haft Iqlim*, a geographically organized *tazkirih* of great men, in 1002 AH/1593–94 AD.

Lachmī Nara'in "**Shafiq**" Aurangābādī
(1745–1808)

Descended from a family of Lahori Khatri Kapuris, Shafiq's grandfather was a Persian munshi who migrated to Aurangabad with 'Alamgir's camp in the late seventeenth century. He was educated by Azad Bilgrami, who also helped advance his father's career. Shafiq wrote three *tazkirih*s: *Chamanistan-i Shu'ara*, on *Rīkhta*/Urdu poets (1761–62 AD/1175 AH); *Gul-i Ra'na*, on Persian poets born in Hindustan (1767–68 AD/1181 AH); and *Sham-i Ghariban*, on poets who came to Hindustan (1782–83 AD/1197 AH). Later, during his long career as an administrator in Hyderabad, he wrote a collection of letters, several *masnavī*s, and several histories: of the Asaf Jahis (*Ma'asir-i Asafi*), of the city of Hyderabad (*Ahval-i Haydarabad*), of the Deccan (*Tanmiq-i Shigarf*), and of the Maratha wars (*Bisat al-Ghana'im*).

Mīr 'Abd al-Latīf Khān **Shūshtarī**
(1759–1806 AD/1172–1220 AH)

Born to a family of Musavvi sayyid scholars who settled in Shushtar in the late seventeenth century, 'Abd al-Latif was educated in Shushtar and Shiraz, before migrating to Hindustan. Once there he traveled widely. In 1788, Shushtari came to Calcutta, where he met Abu Talib and benefited financially from lucrative trade with his brother, who was based in Basra. After some years he relocated to Hyderabad under the auspices of his cousin, 'Abd al-Qasim Mir 'Alam, a powerful figure in Asaf Jahi Hyderabad. The family was engulfed in a scandal involving his cousin and the East India Company resident. He was under house arrest in the aftermath when he wrote *Tuhfat al-'Alam*, a commemorative text of his life, times, and knowledge dedicated to Mir 'Alam. After the family regained its fortunes, he wrote an appendix to the text in which he mentions meeting the young Aqa Ahmad Bihbahani, newly arrived in Hyderabad in 1805.

'Alī Qulī Khān "**Vālih**" Dāghistānī
(1712–56 AD/1124–69 AH)

He was born in Isfahan to a noble family from Daghistan, titled Shamkhal, claiming descent from the 'Abbasid Caliphs. By the time Isfahan had fallen to the Afghans in 1722, his family had been several generations in imperial service. His great uncle, Fath 'Ali Khan Daghistani, vizier under Shah Sultan Husayn, was deposed in 1720, at which time the whole family were removed from their offices. This childhood in Isfahan provides the site of Valih's famous love story with his cousin, Khadijih "Sultan," set to verse later in Delhi by Mir Shams al-Din "Faqir" Dihlavi as *Masnavi-yi Valih Sultan* (1747). Valih joined the retinue of Shah Tahmasp II in Qazvin in 1729–30. When Nadir imprisoned Tahmasp in 1732 as part of consolidating his own rule, Valih returned to Isfahan to find his betrothed forcibly seized out of wedlock by Nadir, and subject to a number of forcible marriages, first to Nadir's governor of Yazd and then to a servant of Karim Khan Zand. By 1734, Valih had migrated to Hindustan with Hazin, whom he had met earlier in Lar, when its infamous governor was assassinated. In Lahore, he met Azad Bilgrami, in whose company he and Hazin traveled to Delhi. Upon his arrival in Delhi, Valih was presented to Muhammad Shah through the patronage of Burhan al-Mulk, the ruler of Awadh and a migrant from Nishapur, and was made commander of four thousand, given the post of the second Mir Tuzuk and the title Zafar Jang. In 1737–38 AD/1150 AH, Valih married a dancer and poet, Ram Jani, and had a daughter, Gunnah Baygum, who eventually married Imad al-Mulk, the notorious Timurid vizier of the 1750s. Valih remained in Timurid service in the retinue of Burhan al-Mulk and his successors, advancing steadily in position, until his death. Valih authored the voluminous *tazkirih Riyaz al-Shu'ara* (1749 AD/1162 AH) and a *dīvān* (compiled by Faqir Dihlavi in 1744–45 AD/1157 AH).

Persianate Selves

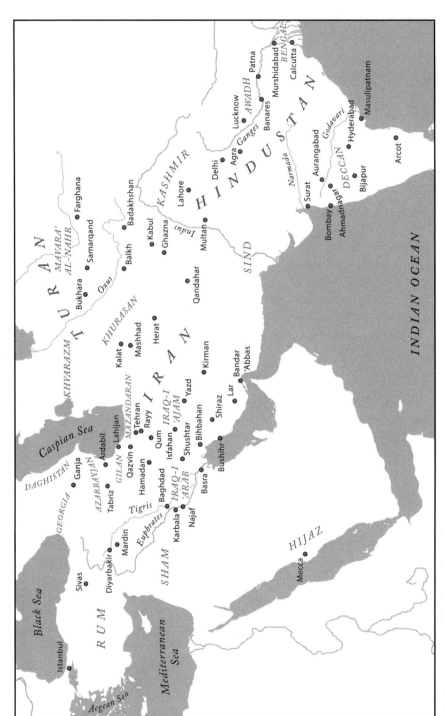

The Persianate world in the eighteenth century

The Shadow of Nationalism

دوستان در پرده میگویم سخن

گفته خواهد شد به دستان نیز هم

چون سر آمد دولت شبهای وصل

بگذرد ایام هجران نیز هم

هر دو عالم یک فروغ روی اوست

گفتمت پیدا و پنهان نیز هم [1]

Friends, though my speech is veiled
　　so too shall revelations be spoken
Just as the nights of union reach their climax
　　so too shall the days of separation fade away
I say to you, both worlds are the selfsame splendor of the beloved's face
　　so too are the manifest and the concealed

EVERY YEAR ON THE VERNAL EQUINOX, my mother opens at random a collection of poems (*dīvān*) by Hafiz of Shiraz (d. 1389) and reads the first full poem her eyes fall upon. As Persians around the world celebrate this day as the first of the new year, they join my mother in consulting Hafiz, the Voice of the Hidden World (*lisān al-ghayb*). His poems indicate what the new year holds,[2] and readers with the most refined insight can understand the poem's deepest layers of meaning as prescience. This Hidden World was where God as Truth resided, made potentially accessible through the form and substance of Hafiz's verses. Like his poetry, which can be read as the celebration of hedonism or union with the divine, this act of consultation has layers of meaning. It is simultaneously a quintessentially Persian act (poetry on the new year) and an act of hermeneutical engagement that defines Islam (supplication to God).[3] Far from contradictory, these different meanings are an enduring remnant of what it meant to be Persian before nationalism.

Growing up in a large immigrant enclave in southern California, I was often asked, "Where are you from?" It was an attempt to gain purchase on another question—"Who are you?"—and then, inevitably, "Iranian or Persian?" I was taught to respond, "I am Persian." Being Persian foregrounded the Persian language and selective elements of its culture, such as pre-Islamic political history and a "classical" poetic tradition that ended with Hafiz in the fourteenth century. This modern selection of culture elided Islam and its supposedly degrading effect on Persian. Claiming a separate identity, it also promoted distance from images of turbaned ayatollahs whipping crowds into a frenzy, of women swathed in black, or of US embassy hostages, who dominated media coverage of Iran in the years after 1979. This culture, however, had come from a place. The term "Persian" and its signifiers—lyrical poetry, epics of mythical kings, and exquisite miniatures from across Asia—became associated with the territory that is now the nation-state of Iran.[4]

Persians were proud of their culture, which made them better than everyone else. The vaunting of ancient empires and classical art forms, made national, allowed Persians to claim superiority according to a nineteenth-century European system of civilizational hierarchy.[5] This valuation, however, was informed by modern, European empires and their attendant racism, and it was structured by capitalism, which exerted the most brutal imperialism the world had ever seen.[6] Iranian nationalism revealed the tensions of this new civilizational ideal, which spoke of progress and moral stature but ruled through racial and political domination. In the midst of these tensions, nationalism posited a problematic of civilizational decline—"we" have been great, but we are no longer. In the Pahlavi era, this "we" was a Persian defined by a pure, ancient culture, separate from Islam and focused on the continuous history of the land that came to be modern Iran. These notions of place and origin produced a certain kind of Persian, one who saw those outside this narrow definition as foreign, inferior, and even dangerous.[7]

Such an articulation of Persian had been formulated over the course of the twentieth century.[8] Its most hallucinatory version conceived of Iran before Islam as "secular" by equating Zoroastrian politics and society with post-Enlightenment ideals of human rights and justice, supposedly emancipated from religion. "Classical" poets and thinkers after the advent of Islam somehow lapsed in their religion or overcame its influence, according to a European metric that narrowly equated religion with theology and law alone.[9] Hafiz's appeals to the Unseen realm of Truth bewilderingly became un-Islamic, even as he repeatedly invoked the comforts of reading *Qur'an*.[10]

Empirical truth, the most authoritative means of remembering the past, offered limited options for resolving the problem of civilizational decline. Ultimately, while modern Persians became the proud owners of an ancient and grand civilization, Islam remained integral to Iran, which was outside Europe. Persian intellectuals thus turned to European racism, seized upon its concept of Aryanism, and extended it to themselves. For Europeans, Persians had once been Aryans, but the decline of their civilization had divided them from the true heirs of Aryanism in Europe. Persians might claim this heritage, but their "dislocative nationalism" sought a vanishing horizon.[11] A relentless urge to laud Persian ways thus vied with claims to superiority based on an unbridgeable distance from those ways.

The exaltation of a pre-Islamic past served to cut Iranians off from both their western and their eastern neighbors, Shi'a Arabs and Persianate Indians and Central Asians, who were deemed unacceptably similar. This story of a pre-Islamic nation also subordinated more recent, enduring ties of language, culture, circulation, commerce, kinship, and history. Pre-Islamic Persian history was not a new feature of the historiographical tradition. But nationalism took this heritage, severed it from the Islamic history with which it had been harmoniously intertwined, and reconstituted it into a shining story of the nobility and dignity of Persians as Iranians alone. Arabs became savages, Afghans thieves, Indians smelled, and Turks were stupid. These claims to a progressive cultural superiority, based on racism, were strikingly insecure and contradictory.

The main basis of being Persian was language and, as time went on, origin, which meant Persian parents, according to the blood logic of racialized descent. Both language and origin presumed a Persian who was from Iran. What, then, did possessing the Persian language mean before modern nationalism? What did its stories, poetry, aesthetic sense, and above all its proper forms in perceiving, speaking, and acting—its *adab*—mean in an earlier period? Can we find in those meanings the resources for decolonizing ourselves, for envisioning a future outside the heritage of European colonial modernity? *Persianate Selves* considers these questions by outlining the meaning of Persian place and origin before nationalism.

Up through the early nineteenth century, Persian was the language of power and learning across Central, South, and West Asia. It was used for poetry, storytelling, government, philosophy, religious instruction, ethical literature, and historical commemoration. Persians were people who had received a particular basic education through which they understood and engaged with the world. Not everyone who lived in the land of Iran was Persian, and Persians lived in many other lands as well.[12] Iran, therefore, was not the only significant place, nor were Safavid domains, which included non-Iranian lands and excluded some Iranian lands.[13] Similarly, origin was far more expansive than birthplace or parentage.

Persianate selfhood thus encompassed a broader range of possibilities than nationalist claims to place and origin allow. This range of Persianate selves not only challenges nationalist narratives but also reveals a larger Persianate world, where proximities and similarities constituted a logic that distinguished between people while simultaneously accommodating plurality. To be a Persian was to be embedded in a set of connections with people we today consider members of different groups. We cannot grasp these older connections without historicizing our conceptions of place, origin, and selfhood. Yet our hopelessly modern analytic language remains an obstacle.

As my mother's consulting Hafiz on the new year suggests, aspects of these older possibilities for Persian selfhood remain, even as the modern nation-state has overpowered their logic. What became the Iranian nation (essentially Persian, just as Hindu became essentially Indian) was—and remains—a group of people with multiple languages, affiliations, and collective lineages (what we call ethnicities). The experience of colonial modernity and its appropriation into nationalist frameworks of thought, practice, governance, and aspiration transformed these varieties of Persian into differences and subsumed some within a single nation. Nationalism then rooted these differences in a territory and defined other shared practices and features as foreign, threatening, and in need of suppression. In the process, one kind of Persian was obliterated, and another took shape.

This new type of Persian required a previously unnecessary homogeneity. In contrast, Persians before nationalism certainly had moral hierarchies, and equality was not a vaunted goal. What was Persian remained coherent by allowing equivalences between differences. Rather than homogeneity or equality, what was Persian encompassed symbiosis, multiplicity, relationality, and similitude. Being Persian provided a way to live with, affiliate, and even understand kinship with differing people. Of course, these differences might be insurmountable. The quality of difference, however, was far from absolute and offers a compelling instance of coexistence.

The single most important concept I learned as a child was *adab*. It was the proper form of things and of being in the world. This concept—of proper aesthetic and ethical forms, of thinking, acting, and speaking, and thus of perceiving, desiring, and experiencing—provided the coherent logic of being Persian. *Adab* transcended whatever land constituted Iran as a kingdom or nation-state at any given time and sometimes even the Persian language itself.[14] Analyzing the period just before the contraction of the Persian language and the rise of modern nationalisms, *Persianate Selves* elaborates the *adab* of place and of origin, its forms of meaning, and the possibilities for selfhood that it offered.

Disjunctures: Place and Origin of Nationalism

The territorial truth of a nation has an obviousness that is deeply contingent historically and politically. Yet even studies that chart nationalism as a historically specific process assume a national territory as transhistorically and objectively identifiable in terms of the empty space of empirical geography. This results in applications of modern notions of culture, society, and geography onto earlier contexts.[15] For instance, Kashani-Sabet understands Qajar ideas of Iran, based on Safavid domains, as the latest manifestation of an already constituted Iran reaching back millennia, to pre-Islamic times.[16] Such scholarship uncritically adopts this notion from Qajar political narratives, which project an Iran originating from the Sassanian Empire to claim a legitimacy comparable to the Safavids.[17] Applying these later formulations of historical continuity to earlier periods, however, essentializes Iran as a timeless and unchanging entity. By contrast, scholars in South Asian studies often make recourse to strikingly modern conceptions of regions, connecting them to vernacular languages and political kingdoms. In arguing for the older (Indian) roots of modern nationalism, as "old patriotism" or "proto-nationalism," Bayly insists on earlier senses of "rootedness to a particular territory." He claims, as an example, that the word *vatan*, which later came to mean the territorial homeland of the nation, "began by meaning the home domain of a particular ruling dynasty."[18] In the pages that follow, I show the untenability of such a simple equivalence of *vatan* with domain, and the possible ways in which this notion was embedded in broader notions of origin. Bayly's questioning of scholarly adoptions of modernity's narrative of rupture is valuable, but his answers do not break free of the same limitations.

In thinking of premodern selves and collectives, Bayly rightly rejects ethnicity as "too imbricated with ideas of blood and race." But embracing the concept of patriotism, defined as "a historically understood community of laws and institutions fortified by a dense network of social communication generally expressing itself through a common language,"[19] reinscribes modern nationalism's restricted imagining of affiliations and connections. Bayly's patriotism creates a society's sense of attachment to a region made homeland through the people's common language, shared (local) institutions of governance, and regionally specific contingencies ("active social and ideological movements" or "a series of conflicts with outside Others" that are "given ideological meaning and memorialized for future generations").[20] *Persianate Selves* argues for a different kind of continuity, asking, What about the resolutely smaller meanings of homeland and a shared language that actively linked people across regions and polities?

Geographical essentialism also structures studies focusing on earlier periods, though they locate the national territory in larger cultural worlds or define it as a later articulation of smaller scales (like the region).[21] Implicitly, historians tend to treat these future nationalist or colonial borders as definitive notions of origin and thus of collective. Even the most sophisticated scholars, such as Tavakoli-Targhi or Alam, at pains to historicize Persianate culture and society, speak of Iranians and Indians and make reference to an "Indian world" or "Indian psyche" as if the South Asian subcontinent already formed a cohesive whole distinct from other entities such as "Iranians," "Turko-Persians," and "Islamic peoples."[22] Although using terms other than Iranian or Indian might render discussion awkward, these concepts need at least to be problematized, so that modern meanings do not structure scholarship. This lack of critical attention results in a methodological and analytic nationalism, in spite of explicitly stated intentions to the contrary.[23] Positing Iran and India as the operative categories in the early modern period obfuscates what people shared, as well as the legibility of smaller geographical entities and their ties and distinctions with one another, which could justify different understandings of regional coherence. In the Persianate world, multiple understandings of territorial and cultural boundaries defied nation-states as readily as they prefigured them. Scholars have tended to take historical meanings that resonate with modern outcomes (for example, land as the basis of belonging), separate them from their conceptual apparatus, which included other bases of belonging, and ignore the rest.[24]

The problem is that we cannot historicize without some self-reflection on our own understandings of place and origin. Modern geography distinguishes interpreted place from physical space.[25] Land, space, and territory are deemed objective and self-evident. This logic of empiricism as the sole natural ground of truth is both ubiquitous and anachronistic. It conveys a consistently empty space upon which subjectivities of place are built. In earlier times, however, what we now understand as empiricism was but one form of meaning-making that produced place. For instance, travel between places was defined by the time spent in transit (*farsakh*) rather than spatial measurement.[26] By assuming that land is empirically verifiable and ontologically consistent, with different understandings stemming only from interpretation, we reinscribe narrow, hermeneutical matrices of modern positivism as universal and transhistorical.[27] In contrast, we might consider the ways that meanings associated with place could produce materiality, both as impetus to build and as hermeneutics of perception.

Scholarly demarcation of regional fields reinforces these problems. Middle Eastern and South Asian studies reify distinctions historically unjustifiable. Challenges to presumed difference have begun in the context of Iranian and Ottoman studies,[28] but reconsideration of linkages across polities comes more easily when two realms are studied as part of the same region ("the Middle East"). Linkages between Iran and South Asia, in contrast, seem to be conceived only as fundamentally foreign influences within an otherwise "native" domain.

Separate treatment of modern Iran and South Asia also stems from the presumed definitive salience of formal colonial experience. The differences that inform national, popular, and scholarly histories, however, have obscured two important similarities. One is centuries of a shared Persianate education, sustained past the advent of colonial rule in India. The other is a shared transformation of self-understanding engendered by the power-knowledge nexus of Orientalist narratives. Though spared formal colonial rule, European colonial domination was integral to the constitution of many aspects of Iranian modernity, including the creation of its borders and the understanding of its history and culture.[29] Persian-speaking thinkers, writers, and officials engaged with a broader global dialogue, and European ideas circulating in Egypt, Ottoman domains, and British India.[30]

The scripts that underpin Iranian and Indian nationalisms are similar. Both depend on narratives about the origin of a people and the shape of a land. In some versions, a glorious ancient past forms the natural core of the nation as the basis of a pure, original culture, society, and political life.[31] With Muslim invasions and subsequent rule, this glory dimmed and degenerated. Not all nationalist narratives, even those propagated by the state, were anti-Islamic. Rather, aspects of Islamic civilization could be nationalized through recourse to indigenous ethnicities and "real" kinship.[32] Origin was thus racialized (Hindus were Aryans too!). The deleterious effects on the present—whether a result of Islam, political corruption, or societal negligence—were proven by the ease with which Europeans dominated these lands.[33] To become worthy of self-rule and national success once more, these scripts explain, Iran and India needed to recover their true national selves, ironically based on historical narratives generated by European powers and appropriated by sons of the nation. A particular understanding of a self and its connections thus engenders political visions and authorizes all manner of actions—from modernization to militarization to exigencies of the state that makes life unlivable for whole groups of people.

The Persianate

Let me put it another way. A commonsensical formulation asserts that Persian is the language of a place called Persia, which has existed since antiquity. This is the nationalist formulation of culture, based on an assumed confluence of territory, people, and language linked by modern notions of native-ness. The mirror image of this formulation holds sway in South Asia, where Persian was the language of Muslim conquerors and thus is inherently foreign. Both of these nationalist narratives rely on modern notions of what is native, what is foreign, and what "naturally" constitutes difference. The foreign-native binary coheres around an idea of home and origin that, in each case, appears empirical and thus objectively true, singular, and mutually exclusive.

Underlying this ostensible mutual exclusivity, however, is a history of commonality and intimacy. For centuries, Persians from Central, South, and West Asia read the same corpus of well-known ethical, literary, and commemorative texts.[34] These basic texts, some widely disseminated through oral recitation, gave rise to shared literary tropes, interpretive paradigms, and representational forms. These were also diversely inflected. Most educated Persians had other languages of learning, such as Arabic or Sanskrit, and other vernacular languages such as Chagatai or Braj.[35] Nevertheless, Szuppe has argued that "a clear perception of belonging to a single cultural space was maintained over this geographically vast area" (eastern Iran, or Khurasan, Central Asia, and northern India)

> for centuries after the "Empire" of Timur's descendants had disappeared in the years following 1506. This perception derives partly from the use in these regions of the Persian language as the dominant idiom of literary expression, as well as from a common adherence to the Perso-Islamicate cultural-social system of education, behavior, and good manners, or *adab*, which provided a common basis for the educational and cultural references shared in particular by the literate middle and upper classes of society.[36]

Through this basic education, a person imbibed proper forms of aesthetic style and ethical conduct (the two faces of *adab*) that made them Persian.[37] These forms changed according to geographical and temporal contingencies, producing variations that lay alongside one another with uneven degrees of comfort.

Despite differing local contexts, these meanings were shared between the educated classes of former Safavid and Timurid domains. Certain local specificities became diffused across regions through sustained circulation of people, texts, and ideas.[38] What was Persian thus remained living, breathing, and diverse, not only across religions or regions but also across types of people—courtiers, scholars, poets, merchants, mystics, military leaders, and many who combined these roles. Their perspectives and affiliations differed, even as they shared the means for expressing these differences. A shared basic education bestowed particular forms of place, origin, and proper conduct, creating modes of affiliation constituting selves and community. This commonality did not necessarily lead to agreement about the meanings of places or the relative values of particular origins. Rather, Persians shared a mutually intelligible vocabulary with which they expressed agreement or disagreement, drawn from their shared education. The sometimes conflicting views of Persians in Irani and Hindustani domains thus points to a range of possibilities for connection and affiliation, as well as distance and difference.

To understand common notions of place and origin, we must first embrace a form of meaning-making different from our own. For Persians, categorical differences did not need to be absolute or mutually exclusive. The sensibilities imparted by their basic education were governed by *adab* (proper form), whose aporetic character allowed for multiplicities of meaning and interpretation within its forms. Concepts were constituted relationally, so that the meanings of place and origin could be multiple and shifting. Elucidating these meanings reveals a different kind of Persianate self, with a range of possibilities. Before nationalism, Persianate selves could hail from many places, and their origins comprised a variety of lineages. The interrelations among these lineages render coherent their multiple modes of imagination, practice, and experience.

For the Islamic, this multiplicity has been called "coherent contradiction," reconciled through hierarchies of meaning, interdependent and part of the same truth of the unity of God (*tawhīd*).[39] The road to the more valued unseen (*bātin*) was through and connected to the manifest (*zāhir*), which was at once superficial *and* necessary.[40] Multiplicities and their tensions were thus necessary, even if ideally transcendable (for some; others could only recognize or merely follow). As Hafiz's verses in the epigraph show, the unseen and the manifest were part of one Splendor. This cosmology was simultaneously articulated in *adab*, the proper form of things, as the means and manifestation of the most harmonious, beautiful, and virtuous substance, most perfect and closest to the Truth. Historically, awareness of the multiplicity that hierarchies of meaning allowed produced an understanding of difference as overlapping gradients, rather than as mutual exclusivity. Certain categories of people, for instance, could be from Iran, even as they belonged to India.

Aporia is key here. Formulating categories with discrete borders—like the distinction between text and context or Iranian and Indian—is a way of knowing firmly rooted in modern epistemology. Another logic, however, governs our sources. Persian *adab* and its defining limits thus present to us moderns as a set of paradoxes. Instead of paradox, I use the term aporia to underline the way in which seeming contradictions appear so through the lens of our present. I borrow Jacques Derrida's formulation of aporia as a distinction that has "no limit. There is not yet or there is no longer a border to cross, no opposition between two sides: the limit is too porous, permeable and indeterminate."[41] Two categories need not be oppositional; rather "they are articulated with each other; they supplement and engender each other."[42] Thus aporetically defined distinctions create the terms by which social affiliations, their forms, and the articulation of their hermeneutical contours imbued and linked language and practice, the imaginative and the experiential.

To make room for prenationalist Persian self-understandings and their possibilities for connection, I argue against the application of modern notions of ethnicity in historicizing origins of earlier periods. Disavowing Orientalism and its narratives of stagnation and decline require us to consider the immediate premodern past as more than a prelude to modernity. This caveat applies especially to the politically fragmented eighteenth century, which has been disregarded on its own terms in the absence of political glory. More generally, standing in the way of a fresh consideration of the not-so-distant past is a set of modern ideas that have structured scholarly practice. In what follows, I outline concepts that undergird *Persianate Selves*, to open space for new discussions.

Outside the Shadow

To remove Persianate culture from the shadow of nationalisms, we need to disaggregate the Persianate from Iran.[43] *Persianate Selves* thus examines the relation between Iran and the subcontinent "as a set of mobile, circumambulatory, projectile, and always impermanent propositions," attempting a small part of what Dabashi has proposed. This relational approach relies on a hermeneutical ground more historically intelligible than a nation before nationalism. Otherwise, nationalist interpretations limit the articulation of place, origin, and selfhood and so constrain analyses from breaking beyond their epistemological borders. Accepting the premise that "a forceful nationalization of a polyfocal culture is no less colonial in its epistemic disposition and racial in its analytics" allows us to revisit the very premise of modern terms such as "Persian," "Iranian," or "Indian."[44]

Anachronistic names contribute to anachronistic interpretations of the past. When speaking of larger regional entities, therefore, I refer to Turan (for Central Asia) and Hindustan (for the South Asian subcontinent). I consider Iran a group of West Asian provinces, mostly part of Safavid domains, and Persian a language of cultural forms shared by all three regions.[45] These terms were current in the eighteenth century, and their plurivalent meanings varied depending on context. For instance, "Hindustan" might name the kingdom ruled by the Timurids, the smaller region of the Indo-Gangetic plain that was the seat of that empire, or the subcontinent as a whole.[46] "Iran" became more common as a geographic term only after the fall of the Safavids; their domains had been named with reference to the major eastern and western regions, either separately or in tandem, as *Iraq-i 'ajam* (with its counterpart, *Iraq-i 'arab*, in Ottoman domains) and *Khurasan*. Even then, "Iran" was a contextually specific term, used when discussing the Safavid kingdom or large geographical entities, and it could be a singular place or a cluster of domains. That the two *Iraq*s, a geographical pair, were split between two empires, shows the disjointed relation between polity and region, and undermines the hard distinctions of nationalist narratives.

The terms with which I begin—Iran, Turan, and Hindustan—are thus approximate, and I complicate their meanings in the course of this book. They are only once removed from modern associations in contemporary English but nevertheless provide some critical distance from methodological nationalism. Other significant geographical reference points were smaller domains or cities. I have translated the term *mamlakat* as "domain" to preserve its most common connotation as a place with a recognizable character, history, and, at times, political and social autonomy. Because of the relationality of meanings, a region is sometimes a domain (such as Bengal), a city and its environs (such as Kirman), or a kingdom. Therefore, when I use the term "transregional," it means crossing a particular scale of region, whether within Hindustan (as the Timurid kingdom, or the subcontinent) or between Hindustan and Iran (as kingdoms or larger geographical entities).

Rather than Mughals, I call the dynasty that ruled most of the subcontinent at the opening of the eighteenth century Timurids.[47] They were also Mughals, but this term was broader. Mughals were people both specific to the subcontinent and indicative of its embeddedness within the larger, transregional circulation of Persians. As I explore the meanings of place and home, origins and affiliations, and commemorations of self and community, I also introduce new terms. Some of these terms are lost to us now, but their intelligibility is central to a historicity focused less on tracking change in relation to the present and more on understanding graduated continuities and forgotten alternatives. Attending to alternatives and continuities, I argue, gives us a broader range of resources with which to remember ourselves and imagine new futures.[48]

Following Marshall Hodgson's definition of "Islamicate," I use "Persianate" to refer to social and cultural formations associated with the Persian language and to forms of expression and practice heavily inspired by Persian, largely across the Islamic east and Anatolia.[49] The past two decades have seen an increased focus on the Persianate in Iranian and South Asian studies. Much analysis, however, takes the term "Persianate" as self-evident, though often inconsistently. This lack of critical attention has resulted in studies regional in scope, national in focus, but strangely in harmony. In Iranian studies, no matter how far the reach of Persian, the font of its literary culture is still Iran. South Asian studies tells a similar study, though one of an (Indian) Persian assimilated to the "Indic" in a typically Indian story of multicultural inclusivity that reifies the link between blood, soil, and culture. The study of Islam or Persian in South Asia becomes one of "Indo-Islamic" and "Indo-Persian," terms delimited according to these indelible linkages, even in studies seeking to challenge reductive images of intolerant Muslims touted by Orientalists, self-Orientalizing reformers, and Hindu nationalists alike.[50]

The coherent contradiction that gives rise to aporia provides new purchase on the relationship between the Persianate and the Islamic without reliance on discredited binaries such as secular-religious or foreign-native. Yet at the analytical level, the notion of aporia has met remarkable resistance, even by scholars who acknowledge the aporias of Islamic or Persian *adab*. The two remain irreconcilable, or, at best, Perso-Islamic. Hodgson considers the Persianate one form of the Islamicate, with Persian merely a language used to express Islamicate concepts. Arguing against the split between religion and culture, upon which the "-cate" of Islamicate rests (with Islam a religion in the Protestant sense), Ahmed trenchantly upholds the Islamic nature of *adab*.[51] He continues, however, to treat language merely as the means of expressing a common (Islamic) lexicon.[52] Indeed, *adab* is a Muslim concept shared across a number of languages. But because *adab* is proper form, the specifics of language, articulation of concepts, and accumulated traditions are necessarily central.

Most of Ahmed's examples are drawn from the High Persianate period and from Persianate languages. He eschews the term "Persianate," however, because he understands its connotations as irretrievably ethnocentric.[53] Yet what he called the Balkans-to-Bengal-complex depends on the transregional reach of the Persian language.[54] In other words, when a premodern Persianate self is foreclosed, so too is the possibility of the Islamic. The two share a fate and are aporetically linked. *Persianate Selves* offers a supplement to Ahmed's arguments, contending that the Islamic is also the Persianate, though not always. As we see in Chapter 4, one could be a Khatri, a Lahori and Aurangabadi, a Timurid administrator, the student of a prominent sayyid scholar, and a Persian man of letters who laid claim to *adab* without laying claim to Islam. Properly historicized, the Persianate can explain how Persians could profess other faiths, or even be hostile to Islam, without necessarily being outside of it.[55]

By looking at specific meanings broadly shared among Persians, this book takes seriously the proposition that form constitutes meaning, certainly historically. The Persianate is not entirely commensurate with the Islamic, but Islam, as a set of ideas and worldviews, permeated the being of so many Persians throughout the centuries that Persian in the early modern period was partially a product of this permeation (together with other features, such as Turco-Mongol social structures).[56] Nonetheless, some features (such as profession of Islam) could be pulled out of focus as a muted background against which other concerns were brought to the fore and embraced, even celebrated, by those who did not profess Islam.[57]

The categorical reconceptualization necessary to historicize the ways in which people thought of themselves and what these ways meant for their interactions with other people requires a critical philological engagement with the primary basis of commonality between Iran and India. This reconceptualization requires self-reflexive engagement with our own time and place. The eighteenth century is the end of what is increasingly called the High Persianate period (c. fourteenth–nineteenth centuries AD). But to understand the eighteenth century as an ending, rather than a bright moment of the High Persianate's waxing, is to write history in hindsight.[58] By the start of the eighteenth century, Persian had permeated social groups and strata more deeply than ever before across regions.[59] The largest number of Persian speakers lived in the South Asian subcontinent, and many were not Muslim.[60]

Persianate Selves begins from temporal terrain startling to nationalist sensibilities, and outlines what it meant to be Persian in such a way that avoids linking language to land according to Eurocentric definitions. Persians were not people from Persia. Outside European sources, a place called Persia does not exist. Instead, Persian was a shared set of forms, acquired and circulated transregionally. This circulation depended not on a single empire or institution but on Persian as the language of Islamic universalism that made its forms available both to Muslims and others who lived with them. Persians could reconcile the universality of what was shared transregionally with particular forms of local knowledge. I intend the arguments presented in this book about shared notions of culture to be generative for further work on regional contexts or other periods. But first, we must revisit the place of Hindustan in the Persianate.

Persianate Hindustan

From its earliest moments, Persian literary culture flourished on the subcontinent. The Ghaznavid realm, one of the first places where Persian was the language of literature and political administration, spanned Khurasan to the Punjab.[61] Persians came to Hindustan for trade and material pillage, bringing the learned on the heels of conquest and rule. One eighteenth-century source put it like this: "[T]he Persian language (*zabān-i Fārsī*) has been in Hindustan from the time that Persian-speaking kings (*salātīn-i Fārsī-gū*) have accomplished the subjugation of these domains and the people of Iran and Turan settled in this land. I begin, therefore, with a description of the conquest of Hindustan at the hands of the people of Islam (*ahl-i Islam*)."[62]

These two moments, the Muslim conquest and the arrival of Persian-speaking kings (and migrants from Iran and Turan), are not the same. The Khatri author Lachmi Nara'in "Shafiq" Aurangabadi (1745–1808) inaugurates the story of Muslim conquest with the Umayyad general Muhammad bin Qasim's conquest of Sindh. The arrival of Persian-speaking kings begins later, with Mahmud of Ghazna and then the Ghurids. The migrations these latter conquests engendered are an outgrowth of the arrival of Islam.[63] The Persian-speaking migrants of Iran and Turan, also largely Muslim, stayed, intermarried, and made friends until they were not only migrants and their descendants but also locals. Memory and ongoing mobility defined the larger community.[64]

These early invaders came from Khurasan or Turan, where Persian was a vernacular language distinguishing regional sultanates still subscribed to broader Abbasid imperial legitimacy.[65] The first great wave of migration after the northern subcontinent came under Muslim rule also came from Khurasani and Turani domains, spurred by the thirteenth-century Mongol invasions of West and Central Asia.[66] These invasions gave rise to the High Persianate period. This temporal boundary must be treated as porous, however, since the circulation of literary texts connected the Caucasus to Khurasan, Turan, and Hindustan even earlier.[67] Subsequent migrations occurred during cataclysmic events in Irani and Turani domains and during periods of efflorescence in Hindustan and the Deccan. As Wheeler Thackston notes, in the wake of the Timurids, "given the extraordinary unified culture that had been produced by a century of Turco-Persian Timurid rule, the educated elite from Chinese Turkistan to Constantinople, regardless of ethnicity, communicated on a learned level in one language, Persian, read the same classics of Persian literature, and participated in one Persian culture."[68] Timurid rule, also concentrated in Khurasan and Turani domains, enjoyed the political legitimacy of royalty.[69]

The broader effects of this rule were significant; chronicles that had incorporated pre-Islamic Persian history into their narratives also incorporated Mongol and, later, Turco-Mongol (Timurid) accounts of the past and notions of political legitimacy.[70] While it is tempting to locate the center of this culture in Khurasan and Turan, other cities enjoyed their own relationships, as Shiraz did with the Deccan and Bengal.[71] Nevertheless, one minor prince, born ruler of Ferghana, won Kabul by force of arms and eventually defeated the last Lodi sultan of Delhi in 1526. Over the next several hundred years, goods, texts, and people flowed into Timurid and Deccani domains from Iran and Turan.[72]

As in other Turco-Mongol-ruled domains, the Timurids of Hindustan embraced Persian as the language of power, prestige, and administration and presided over its spread. At the heart of their rule was a careful balance of what Richards calls "ethnic and factional interests," which wove together various local groups (with both transregional and more regionally based lineages), as well as migrants from Iran and Turan who participated in ruling, adorning, and administering the empire.[73] Migrants with various skills—arts, crafts, scribing, poetry, accounting, military leadership, political and fiscal administration—were welcomed and worked alongside local Persians, both Muslim and Hindu.[74] Many of these learned individuals were from prominent backgrounds, with familial ties to well-known saintly or dynastic figures or with intellectual lineages from famous Sufis, scholars, or poets. Multiple lineages—service, natal, intellectual—provided strands that enabled each other and wove together people's connections.

These migrations were certainly spurred by the resources for patronage at the disposal of Timurid royals and their nobles, which were far greater than those in Irani and Turani domains.[75] Other important factors were upheavals in Iran and Turan, such as the Uzbeg conquest of Turan, the fall of Timurid Herat to the Safavids, ongoing Safavid conflict with the Ottomans, protracted civil war following Shah Tahmasp's death, Shah Abbas's radical overhaul of the power base of Safavid rule from a Qizilbash to a slave elite, and the changing nature of Safavid Shiʿism in the seventeenth century, which affected the position of Sufi orders.[76] Though opportunities were more limited by the late seventeenth century with the Timurid state stretched thin through military and political expansion, regional centers and noble retinues, now firmly ensconced in networks of circulation and kinship, still drew migrants and travelers.[77]

As Francis Robinson emphasizes, Persian was never so widespread throughout the subcontinent as it was in the eighteenth century.[78] Noting the decline of Timurid power, centralized patronage, and the rise of regional vernaculars and of Urdu as a poetic language, Robinson emphasizes that these challenges to Persian were only then emerging:

> Until the 1830s Persian was the language of government in most of the subcontinent. This was the case not just at provincial Muslim courts which sprang up as Mughal power ebbed—Murshidabad, Hyderabad, Arcot, Mysore, Awadh, Shahjahanpur, Rampur; it was also the case under the Sikhs and Marathas, and even under the British. All these successor governments rested on the established systems of Mughal administration and the skills of its service classes. Thus, there continued to be a substantial Persian-speaking bureaucratic class.[79]

Yet scholars have often overemphasized Urdu's importance in the eighteenth century, based on later outcomes.[80]

The British abolition of Persian as a language of power began only in 1832, when vernaculars and English replaced Persian in the Bombay and Madras presidencies, with Calcutta following suit in 1837.[81] The "Minute on Education" (1835), which amazingly does not mention Persian, heralded changes in political and education policies, and reflects British understandings of "native" culture, not of Persian's lack of importance.[82] In the century's early decades, use of Persian meant that

> [m]en from the great service families of northern India traveled to Calcutta, Hyderabad and Arcot. Men from Kashmir, Brahmin pandits and Muslims forced out by Afghan or Sikh rule, found work in northern India ... Iranians who wished to come could still find a ready outlet for their talents, while a Hindu convert to Islam who was skilled in Persian, like Mirza Qatil (d. 1817), could make a home for himself for years in Shiraz, Isfahan, Tehran and Azerbaijan.[83]

Even after Persian faded as the lingua franca of mobile communities, such communities did not disappear but rather added new languages, such as Urdu and English, to their repertoires.[84]

Assumptions about eighteenth and nineteenth-century Persian as a vernacular "native" to Iran (and thus "foreign" to Hindustan) also need scrutiny. Language in the Persian world was far from homogeneous. Common ethical and literary tropes did create similarities, but differences were important. For one, there was always regional variation.[85] Further, the Persian language permeated the societies of these regions in different ways. Deployed as a language of power and government in Hindustan, Persian was a learned language of prestige and education. In Iran, a High Persian literary education was beyond the grasp of most, but the language, and its poetry and epics, existed in oral forms through more social strata, though often not as a first language.[86] In Iran, Persian had little of the competition as a literary language evident in Hindustan, where vernacular and regional languages, as well as Sanskrit, occupied various significant positions.

But lest we imagine a "natural" link between land and language, with Persian as the language of a place we call Persia, we need to recognize the importance of Turkic to both vernacular and literary registers in Safavid Iran.[87] In the course of Timurid rule in Hindustan, Persian eclipsed the Turkic literature that had briefly flourished at the Khurasani and Turani Timurid courts, and Turkic was less prevalent as a spoken language than in Safavid domains. The vernacular of the Safavid court and military was Turkic, and much of the elite in Iran at this time spoke some form of Turkic as a first language or cultivated it as a vernacular. Turkic's prestige and prevalence are easy to overlook since "as a high-status vernacular and a widespread contact language" it influenced "spoken Persian, while written Persian, the language of high literature and civil administration, remained virtually unaffected in status and content." Perry further notes that "the semantic domains of this vocabulary include the pastoral, domestic, military, technological, and commercial—all testifying to the effects of interaction at the spoken, vernacular, practical day-to-day level of intermingled and bilingual populations."[88] Because the spoken, vernacular Persian of Iran contained many Turkic loan words that were never used in written Persian, a split in register occurred even for those whose first language was Persian.

At a broader level, more often than not, the vernacular (and certainly the first language) of the general population in Safavid domains was some form of Turkish (Azeri, Qashqai, or Eastern Turkic dialects) or a regional language such as Kurdish, Baluch, Gilaki, or Mazandarani.[89] While these regional languages were closer to learned Persian than, for instance, Bengali, Persians in Safavid domains, much like Hindustani Persians, needed education, suggesting that Persian was not a mother tongue in the modern sense. As in South Asia, individuals and whole communities across West Asia possessed "multiple first-language capacities."[90] Such differences in political, social, and cultural contexts are important for considering the diverse developments in regional styles, standards, and idioms in Iran and Hindustan.[91] *Persianate Selves* considers the shared elements within Persianate culture in the hope that when future scholarship addresses questions of difference, it will look to the possibilities of selves and collectives offered by education in the proper forms of *adab*.

Transregional Persianate Selves: Texts and Contexts

A prominent conceit of nationalism is a view of society defined by geographical rootedness and culture determined by political structures. Therefore, *Persianate Selves* is a thematic study of certain aspects of Persianate culture and societies *between* West and South Asia. The parameters delineating the book's temporal span are two events: the fall of the Safavids, in 1722, and Macaulay's "Minute on Education," in 1835. These constitute important moments, though not clear beginning and end points of a narrative history. Rather, these dates are imperfect brackets of a period just before the rise of (colonial) modernity in both Iran and Hindustan. The fall of the Safavids defined shared meanings of place, origin, and possible selves, even though these meanings display clear continuities with what came before. Similarly, the "Minute on Education" articulated the policy abolishing Persian as the language of power in the subcontinent and so led to the transformation of those shared meanings, although Persianate forms, meanings, and the overlapping societies they enabled endured through the nineteenth century. Colonial modernity spurred new constructions of the past to explain a nationalized present. A reinterpretation of the period just before its rise is thus crucial for a critical reconsideration of all that it engendered.[92]

The fall of the Safavids is also significant for our modern idea of Iran. Throughout the sixteenth and seventeenth centuries, Safavid domains were usually referred to by their main provinces of Persian Iraq (*'Iraq-i 'ajam*) and Khurasan.[93] Not until after the fall of the Safavids were the lands constituting their domains more often called Iran. Thus, after 1722, the idea of Iran increasingly became the dominant character of the domains that the Safavids had ruled. This idea of Iran was thus defined by an absence, commemorated in a way rarely seen when the dynasty still held power. Various eighteenth-century attempts to rule something understood as Iran depended on the complete possession, or lack thereof, of former Safavid domains. And it was specifically *this* idea of Iran, not a timeless conception stretching back through millennia, that was taken up by modern nationalists in their reconceptualizations of home.[94]

Through the first half of the eighteenth century, Timurid rule was also sorely tested, from within and without. Both the Deccani Sultanates and the Timurid kingdom that absorbed them had been centers of literary, social, and political patronage in the Persianate world for well over a century. With the fall of the Safavids, Hindustan was viewed, sometimes ambivalently, as the remaining center of Persianate culture. By the beginning of the nineteenth century, former Safavid domains were newly (and briefly) unified under Qajar rule, while Timurid Hindustan was politically fractured into regional kingdoms and colonial domains, resulting in ever-shrinking patronage for Persian poetry. But these changes did not entail, as is so often claimed, an end to mobility and circulation between these two regions and the disappearance of Persian from the subcontinent. Social and cultural changes are rarely tied to political events in so straightforward a way.

The following chapters draw on a constellation of texts, all broadly commemorative. Commemorative texts include poetry, histories, travel narratives, *tazkirih*s (biographical compendia), autobiographies, and the many texts that display multiple features of these flawed generic distinctions. I bring them together as a single archive, following their shared styles and conventions, as well as their common concerns, the explicit and significant work of commemoration, and their reliance, to various degrees, on biographical representation.[95] These texts are often intertextually related. To call them commemorative is far more justifiable, historically and textually, than calling, say, a group of texts, only some of which call themselves *tarīkh*, histories, while severing them from texts such as *tazkirih*s (or travelogues, biographies, and so on). Most of these texts draw on one another, use the same methods of verification, and employ similar modes of rhetoric and meaning-making for the stated purposes of commemoration.

Modern forms of biography and history are structured by the prerogatives of positivism, based on ostensibly objective documentation as full and true, mutually exclusive of all else, which is untrue. In contrast, recording what happened is only one concern of commemorative texts. The subjects of commemoration could be understood in more than one way, with their meanings presented in the manner of telling. Texts thus commemorated events, stories, and biographical subjects in a variety of styles and forms, giving rise to multiple versions of the same subject. This multiplicity stands in contrast to singular truth, the focus of "objective" history.

Among the sources to announce their commemoration most explicitly are *tazkirih*s. These are some of the richest texts for cultural and social history, in part because they are constituted by social relations and conditions. *Tazkirih*s evoke "ideas of memory and remembrance." The word is a causative verbal noun from the Arabic root *dh-k-r* meaning "to make remember" or to "remind."[96] Memorializing had moral benefits, whether as warning (*'ibrat*) or as celebration of worthy example.[97] Various modes of commemorative writing were indelibly and aporetically linked, in medieval Arabic models and later in Persian forms, so that "autobiography as a specific type of Arabic literature thus evolved mainly in the context of the Arabic biographical tradition, which in turn had emerged primarily as a branch of historical writing."[98] Thus texts generally now understood as defying genre by mixing elements of biography, autobiography, and history were previously understood as part of the same tradition, which we can broadly understand as commemorative.

These texts commemorate a group of individual subjects according to particular criteria, thereby creating a textual collective. They also stimulated social collectives in generations of readers, some of whom went on to write their own commemorative texts, drawing on those written earlier. The act of commemoration, as writing and reading, of repeating and reframing was a principal staging ground for Persianate selves. The self emerged through collective connections that maintained individual distinctions. The collective brought forth the self; the self did not consent to join (or become inducted into) the collective.

The authors of these commemorative texts form three intertwined generations (see list of dramatis personae). The first generation, such as Hazin Lahiji and even Valih Daghistani, retained memories of Safavid times or, like Khan Arzu and Azad Bilgrami, of a still functioning Timurid imperial system in transition. The next generation, including Azar Baygdili and 'Abd al-Karim

Kashmiri, came of age in the chaotic aftermath that followed, though the latter falls between the two generations. The third generation was born in the second half of the eighteenth century, into the reality of regional kingdoms, and wrote at the turn of the early nineteenth century. Ahmad Bihbahani, Abu Talib Khan Isfahani, and ʿAbd al-Latif Shushtari are all one generation removed from those who fled Iranian domains after the fall of the Safavids.

These authors were all educated Persians. They were literate in that they could read and were acquainted with well-known texts of history, ethics, and poetry—the stuff of a basic education. Yet their levels of education and focus of study varied. Not all of these authors were *fāzil* (learned), the sort of figures defined by their learning in one or more fields of knowledge. Joseph Emin's education was basic and hodgepodge, as the form of his text and his use of terms, concepts, and Persian poetry demonstrate. Valih was a well-educated Khan, learned in poetry and history, though without much knowledge of the sciences. In contrast, Shushtari prided himself on his knowledge of the sciences, and Abu Talib Isfahani and ʿAbd al-Karim Kashmiri were educated administrators and men of letters. But these individuals did not function as teachers and exemplars in the manner of Hazin Lahiji, Khan Arzu, Azad Bilgrami, Azar Baygdili, and to some extent, the aspiring arbiter of Shiʿa jurisprudence, Ahmad Bihbahani.

In their texts, authors are located within collectives, their selves birthed through the selected constellation and representation of biographical subjects with whom they affiliated. Losensky notes about poetry that the I "that speaks in the poem is as much a product of precedent and tradition as of the poet's own experiences. Far from indicating autobiographical identity, the poet's name in the final verse of the ghazal serves as a literary mask or persona, acting out one of the limited number of roles that are sanctioned by generic usage."[99] Experience was thus mediated through received forms of language and its accumulated traditions. *Persianate Selves* focuses on prose, on figural narratives woven through the representation of selves and others. These narratives mobilize ideas explored in this book. They constitute places and modes of affiliation, lineages of origin, common notions of a Persianate past, and ethical valuation in political and historical interpretations. While formal constraints determined possible form and expression, form itself was also subject to temporal and geographical contingencies.

Persianate Selves reads well-known and transregionally circulated commemorative texts alongside lesser known or regionally limited texts. This
juxtaposition highlights the remarkable continuity of the means of expression, its forms and language, in the midst of disagreement over positions and
interpretations. Yet, I argue, particular disagreements do not constitute hermeneutical ground. While noting disagreements is important, understanding
them as definitive has led to rooting culture in territory and ignoring the
larger, shared hermeneutics that constitutes Persianate culture. Rather, within
the constraints of *adab*, common threads bound together authors, even as
they exercised choices that reflected their engagement with social concerns
and cultural preoccupations of particular moments and places.

Outline

Part I addresses the meaning of places, the possible modes of place-making,
and the ways in which places were invested with meaning. Authors drew on
universal, transregionally recognizable representational practices and narratives of the past. Meaning-making had a particular form, and some places
carried their own meaning, which authors had to contend with as they situated the relationships and proximities of places according to these proper
forms. As the chapters in this section explain, these forms of Persianate
place-making are crucial for historicizing difference and similarity.

Chapter 1, "Landscapes," begins with a lexicographical discussion. It distinguishes common ways of understanding units of geographical place, such
as kingdoms and provinces, from affective notions of place, such as homelands or other sites vested with significance within the Persianate world.
The chapter then parses the different ways by which places were marked
and measured. It further examines how specific locales and regions, narrated
through universal Persianate histories, gained a transregionally recognized
character imbued with geocultural meanings.

Discussions of place often invoked narratives of the past to make
sense of the present.[100] Chapter 2, "Remembering, Lamenting," illustrates the commemoration of the near and far past in attributing meaning
to eighteenth-century presents marked by the fall of the Safavids and the
devolution of Timurid power for Persians in and between Iran and India.
Diverse interpretations of contemporary events evinced remarkably similar

understandings of lands, geographies, and their relations to other places, all with reference to proper ethical forms (learning, service, rulership, social interaction, and enactment of divine ordinances).

Chapter 3, "Place-Making and Proximity," looks at the cartographic effects of meaning-making and features of place that lent them a moral cast. Features of urbanity, learning, just rule, and the storied tradition of Persian and Islamic narrative were transregionally recognized, and connected the universal with the local and particular. Through their circulation across the Persianate world, commemorations of place created a morally imbued sense of familiarity and proximity more significant than empirical geographical contiguity. Geographical coherence itself was made up of alternative schemas and relationships between people and environments. Alongside and framing these geographical ideas, the variegated features of place created a gradient of familiarity aporetically accommodating the unfamiliar, both within and beyond Persianate and Islamic lands.

Part II examines the meaning and labor of origin among Persians in Safavid Iran and Timurid India. Modern scholarship possesses impoverished conceptual means by which to understand origins outside of mutually exclusive categories taken to be definitive of affiliation. Place is given prominence along with religion and ethnicity. The chapters in this section argue that, as with place, modern categories are either not definitive or else inappropriate entirely for understanding origin. It begins with the common assumption that a homeland in the Safavid kingdom established a primordial, proto-Iranian loyalty that marked all migrants to India. By contrast, in the heavily interlinked Persianate lands of West and South Asia, origin narratives articulated multiple lineages that were transregionally constituted, circulating, and intelligible. Natal lineages and legal ties were only some of the many genealogies of descent that told the story of a person and the meaning of that person's affiliations in the world.

Situating place in relation to origins, Chapter 4, "Lineages and Their Places," argues that the form of origin was lineage, multiply constituted. Geographic place did not constitute origin as singular location but rather as dynamic lineages; they accrued significance in the specific shape of their sedimentation. Alongside territorialized notions of origin, there were often far more important lineages, including those of service, learning, aesthetics, and practice, which call into question our understanding of meaningful connection.

Chapter 5, "Kinship Without Ethnicity," looks at premodern notions of social collectives, commonly called tribes or ethnic groups. Dispensing with these terms, I historicize social collectives through the *adab* of their telling. I find continuity rather than distinction between various lineages of birth, legal status, and other formal, socially regulated relationships. Historicized origins defy modern categories such as nation, ethnicity, or tribe and require instead a reconsideration of kinship that dispenses with anachronistic notions of biological truth.

Chapter 6, "Naming and Its Affiliations," takes the previous chapter's more expansive notion of kinship and further considers the ways in which the possibilities of affiliation were sedimented in naming practices. Particularly elaborated are the regionally specific ways in which Persians named themselves and each other, and how transregional circulation allowed them to accommodate those specificities in the lineaments of the universal. In the names given to both individuals and collectives, people were linked to groups and to each other aporetically, in ways that were relational and contextual and thus belie the discrete mutual exclusivity of modern categorization.

As empires fell and societies faced dispersal across the eighteenth century, practices of commemoration proliferated. The last chapter, "Commemorating Persianate Collectives, Selves," turns to *tazkirih* writing in the aftermath of imperial devolution, focusing on the proliferation of these texts and the insight they offer into possibilities for articulating collectives and selves. I specifically examine poetic *tazkirih*s, which commemorate aesthetically and socially constituted collectives of Persianate *adab*. They included past and contemporary poets as part of an imagined collective of ancestors and peers, in which were nested skeins of social relationships. Constituted by historically specific authorial concerns and limitations, the sheer number and diversity of such texts enable understanding of the many possible ways these collectives could be imagined and their selves brought into being.

Changing political and economic factors challenged social connections and collective affiliation, raising the stakes for commemorating communities facing fracture and dispersal. One effect was that *tazkirih*s were increasingly written outside the purview of court patronage. Correspondingly, the figural presence of the author became more defined than in earlier texts. The act of writing such a text was autobiographical, but the self of Persianate autobiography was accumulated and continually redefined in the context of social relationships over a lifetime of learning, travel, and service. These texts evince a self *in situ*, figured according to *adab*'s imperatives of moral self-fashioning, necessarily continually reiterated in conduct, in connection with the world. This was a Persian who could be affiliated with a multiplicity of places and have diverse origins that little resembled those demanded by nationalism.

Place

A person can only be born in one place. However,
he may die several times elsewhere: in the exiles and
prisons, and in a homeland transformed by occupation
and oppression into a nightmare.[1]

Appeals to the past are among the commonest of
strategies in interpretations of the present. What
animates such appeals is not only disagreement about
what happened in the past and what the past was,
but uncertainty about whether the past really is past,
over and concluded, or whether it continues, albeit in
different forms, perhaps. This problem animates all
sorts of discussions—about influence, about blame and
judgment, about present actualities and future priorities.[2]

WHEN SPACE GAINED MEANING so as to register at all, it became a
place. The following discussion of place puts aside the assumption of a self-
evident empirical territory as the ground upon which signification accrued.
Place was more than representation, imagined and cordoned off from material space. For Persians, place and space were aporetic. Place registered in
many ways but not everywhere. Forms of place-making could produce and
shape the materiality of place. The forms by which Persians made the meanings of place included what we now understand as geographical knowledge,
and their rhetoric of material verisimilitude can look to us like empiricism.
Yet this mode of place-making was one among many. It was embedded and

entangled in a continuum with other modes of place-making, which we identify as more imaginative—"myths," wonders, stories, and histories—a multiplicity that fundamentally changes the import of this seeming empiricism.

Picture a kaleidoscope with geography as material space as but one of its
colors. With every turn of the cylinder, material space merges and diverges
from the other colors to create different patterns of place. In the Persianate, these colors included stories, events, rulers, wonders, landscapes, built
features, near and far histories, sociopolitical orders, and human relationships. Weaving these colors together created the forms that manifested and
thus realized moral orders. Some places were better than others because they
contained more features that registered as moral virtues. Narratives of place
made various modes of place-making do particular moral work, but narrative encompassed more than authorial agency. Particular aspects of place
demanded accounting, while some had to remain obscured at certain times.
Place was part of belonging, but for premodern Persianate selves, it differed
from that which was possible with nationalism. Place contained multiple
meanings, only some of which resonate with modern meanings.

The first two chapters in this section foreground two iconic texts to explore lexical meanings of place and their use in explaining eighteenth-century
presents. Integral to these often conflicting accounts were Persianate narratives of the near and far past, drawn from widely known histories and stories,
which constituted place as both idea and experience. These meanings mattered because shared distinctions were the common language through which
competing accounts of the present were written, affiliations declared, and belonging articulated.[3] Some narratives were indelibly linked to lands; others,
generally from the near past, were more open to contestation. As they mapped
versions of the past onto eighteenth-century presents, therefore, these sources
had to incorporate dominant place-making narratives but could use them to
make new claims or reinforce those that were more debatable.

Both texts were written in Delhi by Persians to whom scholars have
attributed archetypal views of their respective places of origin in Iran and
India. The first, Muhammad 'Ali "Hazin" Lahiji (1692–1766), was born in Isfahan. Located in the Mughal capital but hailing from the former Safavid
imperial seat, he was preoccupied with making sense of the invasions and
usurpations of power that surrounded the violent fall of the Safavid dynasty

and transformed his homeland into a nightmare. The other writer was 'Abd al-Karim Kashmiri (d. 1784). Living in the imperial capital in connection with the court, he was concerned with the declining political fortunes of Mughal rule and the social deficiencies that he identified among its causes. Each narrates the past to make sense of his respective present. Discernable in these texts are common ways of understanding place, animated by recent and distant histories. These historical narratives, particularly dominant mean-ings, gave places their moral character, through which we can understand the geocultural landscapes of the early modern Persianate. We must, however, distinguish these established landscapes from more debatable historical map-pings that sought to challenge or shift the moral valences of places.

Hazin was born and raised in Isfahan and educated by the luminaries of Isfahan and Shiraz. He lost most of his family and wealth in the Afghan invasion (1722), after which he traveled extensively across the lands of western and central Iran ('Iraq-i 'ajam), Mesopotamia ('Iraq-i 'arab), and the Hijaz. His alleged involvement in the assassination of Nadir Shah's governor in Lar resulted in his voyage to Mughal Hindustan in 1734. After a notori-ous decade in Delhi, Hazin resettled in Benares in the year of Muhammad Shah's death (1748 AD/1161 AH) and lived out the rest of his days.[4] Schol-ars generally foreground Hazin's denigration of all things Hindustani, yet his memoir, Tazkirat al-Ahval, deals with Hindustan in less than a fifth of the text.[5] Often overlooked is that most of Hazin's memoir is concerned with and structured by the fall of the Safavid state and the rise of Nadir Shah in the ensuing turbulence. The memoir narrates a life of travels, deeply intertwined with the historical events of its time. It is ultimately a text of involuntary migration, a representation of a life lived ethically in spite of the cruelties of fate and the misery of exile.[6]

Against this memoir, I read a different kind of commemorative text, whose author was a traveler, not a migrant. 'Abd al-Karim Kashmiri, a resident of Delhi at the time of its conquest by Nadir Shah (1739), accompanied Nadir's army as a functionary (mutasaddi) to Iran via Turan (Transoxiana) on his way to the Hijaz to perform hajj. He returned to Hindustan by sea, traveling through Bengal (1742) to return to Delhi.[7] Bayan-i Vaqi' (hereafter, the Bayan) provides an account of the high politics of the Mughal kingdom from the time of Kash-miri's return to Delhi and several decades afterward.[8] The Bayan is primarily a history with an autobiographical travel narrative of pilgrimage (*hajjnāma*) nested within it.[9] Kashmiri's account is drawn from his own observations, buttressed by earlier written histories and the orally transmitted information of contemporaries he deemed reliable, such as various high-ranking officials close to Nadir.[10] Hazin's text, from which Kashmiri draws historical accounts of the fall of the Safavids and Nadir Shah's rise, is also partly comprised of others' oral and written accounts. That both texts incorporate accounts from various informants makes it difficult to call either one a discrete view from Iran or Hindustan, as if such things were mutually exclusive. Rather, these texts are products of multiple, regionally diverse voices, edited and mediated by their respective authorial voices but not reducible to them.

Scholars often interpret Hazin's views of Hindustan as iconic of Iranian proto-nationalism and so assume a modern, anachronistic signification of Iran as a place and an origin. Ascribing proto-nationalist meaning, however, grossly oversignifies Hazin's text. Tapping into the trope of the stranger, well disseminated in Islamicate literary cultures, Hazin foregrounds the inherent misery and abject state of being far from home as a narrative device. Rosenthal notes,

> Reflections on the stranger stress his utter miserableness. Constant and bitter complaining is the hallmark of his existence. Yet, the Muslim view, nourished by *adab* literature, that all matters human have a positive as well as a negative side was extended to cover the stranger. The negative aspects were expressed most frequently and most forcefully, but certain advantages were noted that could be found in breaking away from home and living in a strange environment.[11]

Narrating the migrant self as the stranger to emphasize its negative aspects so unequivocally was but one choice for self-representation. Other mid-eighteenth-century migrants from Iran narrated themselves with a more equivocal notion of the stranger, also articulating its positive aspects. Still others made themselves at home among Persianate communities in Hindustan, relegating their homes in Iran to an itinerary of origin that distinguished themselves within, but was not definitive of collective affiliations.

Ascribing proto-nationalist meaning to what was merely one option for migrant self-representation obfuscates broader, overlapping ideas of home, exile, and the importance of specific historical events that shaped Persianate belonging.[12] Though relations among them varied, Persians shared notions of home and exile, as well as geographical and political sensibilities that shaped their respective regional affiliations. However much historical changes in the eighteenth century resulted in new regional configurations and a concomitant fracturing of the Persianate world, a common cultural repository continued to make possible the textual borrowings that expressed differing, and sometimes conflicting, valuations and historical meanings. These differences, however, were mutually intelligible, contestable, and part of a dialogue among Persians.

CHAPTER I

Landscapes

MEANINGS OF PLACE ILLUSTRATE transregional commonalities while accommodating regionally specific differences. This chapter addresses the range of meanings that defined place in the Persianate, from "objective" understandings of the geographical, political, and historical to more "subjective" renderings of myths, homelands, and stories. Rather than an empirical reality divorced from imaginative ideas, these modes of meaning-making were aporetically distinct, overlapping, and concurrently constituted place in multiple ways.

Let us begin with home. In commemorative texts, home appears as a series of concepts, multiple, shifting, and only sometimes geographically rooted. Iran and Hindustan, as geographically defined polities, were only rarely the units for measuring the idea of home. Homes were small places, almost exclusively cities, towns, or parts of domains, entities with their own histories, practices, geographical characters, and administrative organizations. Kingdoms were constituted from a number of these domains. Home was also a morally rooted concept, and the absence of just rule and ethical conduct, whether by overthrow or devolution, resulted in a lament characterized by a shared understanding of an ideal society and articulated in a set of common terms. Home was the presence of friends and peers and the social comfort of such intimacies; their lack produced a sense of estrangement. A man's relationship to home was constituted differently by specific

historical events, but the common sensibilities by which these identifications were articulated endured through the eighteenth century. The political
fracturing of Persianate empires was thus a process distinct from transregional cultural dissolution.[1]

Early nineteenth-century texts also display this multiple, often nongeographically rooted conception of home, together with the importance
of history in understanding the meaning of place. But in the context of a
new present, migrants from Iran no longer perceived themselves as coming
from a ruined land. Iran had been recently unified under Qajar rule, while
Hindustan was now fragmented into various regional kingdoms and increasingly dominant British rule. After the fall of the Safavids, the idea of Iran
continued to endure as the apogee of their empire. The completeness, or lack
thereof, of various attempts to rule something understood as Iran depended
on the gain or loss of former Safavid domains. It was this Safavid-specific
idea of Iran—not a timeless, homogenous geographical Iran stretching back
through millennia—that was taken up by early nationalists in their reconceptualizations of home.

Animating and intertwined with geographical understandings were narratives that had accrued to places, to their names, environments, and material
structures. Places were an accrual of time and character, as much as of brick
and stone. Narratives were part of a continuum of knowledge about the past,
though we moderns tend to divide them into histories, myths, and fictional
stories according to our own notions of veracity. This Persianate language
of place, however, is essential to understanding the ways in which places
(and their pasts) figured in making sense of the present. While the specifics varied widely, the terms used to agree or disagree about the meaning
of place remained the same. Even conflicting accounts drew on the same
figures and relied on the same modes of meaning-making. These overlapping connections counter our modern contradistinctions between empirical
and imaginative, historical and mythical (or literary). They offer the bases of
possibility for how places signified, the work to which specific narratives of
place could be put, and what this meant for Persianate belonging. Since most
scholarship focuses on particularity and difference, this chapter focuses on
what was shared, leaving divergences for the next chapter.

Homes, Kingdoms, and the Places in Between:
A Lexicographical Note

A common lexicon of geographical domains and kingdoms had a particular relationship to home. Originating from a region or a city within a kingdom had a meaning distinct from modern notions of national identity, though not completely. Modern and premodern notions of home and origin do share a partial similitude, which scholars have often emphasized in isolation from its other meanings. It has been easier to accept that a homeland is a place subjectively constituted, imbued with affective meaning, even as it is also an objectively existing place. Its borders and significance can thus be elastic. A homeland's borders might fit around a city or, as histories of nationalism have told us, expand to encompass political kingdoms and, ultimately, states. We reach the epistemological limits of modern analytic categories when subjective homeland is separate from, secondary to, and grafted onto an objective kingdom, which is understood as a place with empirically grounded boundaries. Thus, in both subjective and objective renderings of place, homeland, or kingdom, is a "real" material space whose existence is uncontestable and which anchors any further meaning as additive. Historically, however, such a material ground was but one among a number of ways in which place took shape, some of which did not presume a ground or contained signifiers that shifted or were only relationally intelligible. These forms of place lay on a gradient continuum of veracity that constituted reality and even materiality.

In the eighteenth century, terms denoting Persianate places that did have a material ground had multiple meanings relationally dependent on context. This multiplicity extended to terms such as *mamlakat* (domain or country) and *vatan* (homeland), often presumed to have stable, definite, and singular meanings. Historically, these words sometimes appear to have modern definitions and other times defy modernity's mutually exclusive categorizations. *Vatan* meant home, a place of residence with which one identified.[2] A person could have multiple homes, distinct from birthplace, in the course of a life. A person could be from a particular city but have an original homeland. For instance, the Sufi and poet Shah Faqirullah "Afarin" was "from Lahore," but his "original homeland (*vatan-i aslash*) is not known."[3] Home might thus be distinct from origin (as Chapter 4 elaborates) and was only sometimes geographic. Moral valence and multiple affiliations textured material ground, creating a palimpsest of place unlike the singular, "natural" connection common to modern empiricism.

Given the history of the Persian language, it is unsurprising that these meanings were shared, even as they accommodated difference and conflict. Persian in Hindustan was seen as a language that came to and settled there, making a home. From the very beginning, Persian written in Hindustan contributed to larger Persianate culture, part of a shared tradition with Khurasani and Turani kingdoms, where Persian textual forms had crystallized under the Samanids and Ghaznavids in the ninth and tenth centuries. Lahore was under Ghaznavid rule for far longer than Khurasan.[4] Persianate dynasties based in Delhi, which originated in Khurasani and Turani lands, saw themselves as heirs to the Ghaznavids, who sought to meld Islam with Persian notions of kingship and ethics.[5] Most immediately, the Gurganis traced both their natal and cultural lineages to the era of Timurid rule over Turan and Iran.[6] Larger geographic designations, such as Hindustan, Turan, and Iran, however, were not congruent with kingdoms, which sometimes ruled over parts of more than one region. For example, Khurasan was sometimes ruled with or from parts of Turan, rather than the more westerly provinces, which we now associate with Iran, such as 'Iraq-i 'ajam. Timur's successors ruled Khurasan, considered a *mamlakat* of Iran, as well as Samarqand and Bukhara, major cities of Turan.[7] These smaller regions had their own histories, as parts of shifting polities with varying connections to other regions, and thus acquired their own geographical distinctions.[8]

Within these smaller domains, homelands were distinct places. For example, 'Abd al-Karim Kashmiri refers to Kalat alternately as Nadir Shah Afshar's birthplace (*mawlūd gāh*) and as his homeland (*vatan*) and notes that Nadir allows his countrymen (*ham vatanhā-yi khwud*) to overcharge him in resupplying his household.[9] Such indulgences are granted nowhere else, and such language is not used for any other part of Iran or Khurasan (the domain in which Kalat is located). Kingdoms, or else larger or smaller geographical designations, were operative only in discussions specific to them. Even in the context of transregional movement, Hazin describes both Mirza Fathullah Jawzani's place of birth and his residence as the village of Jawzan (near

Isfahan). When he returned to his *vatan* from the kingdom of Hind, he returned to "that village" [Jawzan], not to *'Iraq-i 'ajam* or Iran.[10]

There were distinctions between smaller domains within Iran and Hindustan. Hazin notes that Mulla Muhammad Taqi Ta'zim Mazandarani returned to his *vatan* (the largely rural Mazandaran) after his education in Isfahan.[11] Similarly, 'Abd al-Hakim "Hakim" Lahori, author of a mid-eighteenth-century *tazkirih*, notes that Sayyid 'Abdullah "Tajarrud" of Lahore "came to Hindustan from his homeland (*vatan*) and from there [Hindustan] he went to Burhanpur."[12] Here, Lahore and Burhanpur are both distinguished from Hindustan (as the Indo-Gangetic plain), though all were within the larger meanings of Hindustan, which referred to Timurid domains or even the whole subcontinent. These places—smaller domains, larger domain, and political kingdom—were related. In its smaller sense, Hindustan was the heartland of Timurid rule and could stand for the whole domain. Within the definition of Hindustan as political kingdom, or as a larger domain, was Burhanpur, which in this larger context was nevertheless distinguished from northern domains as part of the Deccan. Even within a smaller domain, a homeland was distinct from other cities and towns. Lutf 'Ali "Azar" Baygdili notes that Aqa Muhammad Sadiq, a sayyid from Tafrish, went to Isfahan to study. After the death of his teacher and the end of Safavid rule, he returned to his *vatan* (Tafrish).[13] Both of these locations are within the smaller domain of *Iraq-i 'ajam*.

The *vatan* of a person in another country might be a whole domain but not necessarily a kingdom. Kashmiri, writing from Delhi, calls the Marathas "the Deccani armies" when detailing their decision to cut their losses against 'Ali Vardi Khan in Bengal and return to their *vatan* before the onset of the monsoons.[14] The *vatan* to which the Marathas return is in the Deccan, a geographical region with several smaller domains and political dominions, including that of the Marathas. Though 'Alamgir had nominally incorporated the Deccan into the Timurid Empire by the end of the seventeenth century, it retained a sense of geographical distinction from Hindustan, even for Timurid writers like Kashmiri, and soon became politically autonomous in the mid-eighteenth century under the Asaf Jahi Nizams.[15]

One need not leave a *mamlakat*, a domain in the smaller sense of the word, to be in exile from one's homeland. In his memoir, titled *Zikr-i Mir*,

Mir Muhammad Taqi "Mir" (1723–1810) calls Agra his *vatan*, where his great great-grandfather had settled (*tavattun ikhtiyār kard*) after migrating from the Hijaz to the Deccan and then to Hindustan. Agra, not Hindustan, as either a small or a large domain, was his home. He explains, "not having found any opportunities for livelihood in my homeland (*vatan*), I was hastily obliged to [enter] exile (*ghurbat*). I set myself toward the toil of the road, chose the hardships of travel, and arrived at Shahjahanabad Delhi. [Though] I strove greatly, I was not shown any kindness."[16] Travel from Agra to Delhi was within the smaller domain of Hindustan but was still migration from home to a state of exile characterized by hardships (*shadā'id*) and lack of the kindnesses of intimacy (*shafīqī*). Like the more transregionally mobile Hazin and Kashmiri, Mir, who never traveled farther than Lucknow, distinguished home from both domain and kingdom. One could move from one city to another, even within a smaller geographical domain, and still be in exile from home.

That *mamlakat* could refer to domains of different scales upsets the logic of a singular, stable empirical ground as anchor for meaning. Unsurprisingly, scholarly language derived from empiricism that demands mutually exclusive categories of one-which-is-not-the-other is insufficient for capturing historical meanings. Tavakoli-Targhi claims that Russian and British pressures on Iran throughout the nineteenth century resulted in territorial border demarcations that "shifted the characterization of Iran from a confederation of territories (*mamālik*) to a cohesive entity (*mamlikat-i Iran* or *kishvar-i Iran*). The displacement of *mamālik-i Iran* with *mamlikat-i Iran* marked the transition from an empire to a modern nation-state."[17] Such a language of binary clarity obscures the simultaneous use of the two terms in eighteenth- and early nineteenth-century Persian sources in both Iran and Hindustan. Change was a process of shifting emphasis, not neat replacement. The multiple ways of referring to Iran, as a singular kingdom or a plurality of smaller domains, narrowed later as the latter's intelligibility became dominated by that of the former. Earlier, in the context of empire, the singular *mamlakat* had referred to Iran as former Safavid dominions. It was also the name for a larger geographical land known through various historical and epic literatures. Simultaneously, the term *mamlakat* referred to smaller domains with local features, practices, histories, and social structures. Iran as a political entity had thus existed before the modern nation-state, but both the Safavid Empire and the more approximate larger geographical domain of Iran were comprised of these more enduring, smaller domains.

Context determined whether a kingdom was singular or plural. When Hazin discusses Hindustan or Iran as a political dominion, he refers to each as a *mamlakat*.[18] Similarly, Kashmiri notes that Nadir "consigned the kingdom of Hindustan (*mamlakat-i Hindustan*) to Muhammad Shah" before departing Delhi to return to Iran.[19] By contrast, in describing the formal enthronement of Nadir as Shah on the plain of Mughan in Azarbayjan, Hazin notes that Nadir "summoned great men, village heads (*kad khudāyān*), elders (*rīsh sifīdān*) from all of the cities of the dominions of Iran (*jamiʿ-i bilad-i mamālik-i Iran*)."[20] The realm of Iran is here simultaneously a *mamlakat* and a region consisting of smaller parts, each also called a *mamlakat* (or, in the plural, *mamālik*). In the context of empires and larger regions, Kashmiri describes Nadir's campaigns across the span of the domains (*mamālik*) of Hindustan, Turan, and Rum.[21] Writing several decades later, Azar Baygdili (1722–80 AD/1134–1195 AH) describes Babur conquering the land of (*mamlakat-i*) Hindustan.[22] These simultaneous meanings were transregionally shared, and they endured through the eighteenth century.

Within a political domain, *mamlakat* could also be a smaller domain (or region) with a recognizable character and its own political and administrative coherence. For Kashmiri and Hazin, Khurasan is a smaller region, a *mamlakat* that was part of the Safavid *saltanat* (realm) and was among the *mamālik* (plural of *mamlakat*) of Iran.[23] Within the Safavid domains, Khurasan had its own coherence and was thus ruled as a whole by a provincial governor. Kashmiri recognizes this coherence and refers to the slaves that Nadir Shah freed in Turan as "the people of (*mardum-i*) Khurasan" who are from "the delineated areas of (*hudūd-i*) Khurasan."[24] Smaller domains were autonomously intelligible and sometimes even predominated, even when they were parts of larger entities.

Kashmiri's and Hazin's usages were shared by other Hindustani Persians. Smaller domains were distinct and prominent whether writers originated in Timurid Hindustan or were writing about it from within or afar. As Nadir leaves Ottoman dominions, Kashmiri says not that he is returning to the land of Iran but that Nadir proceeded in the direction of *ʿIraq-i ʿajam* and

Khurasan from his regional location in *'Iraq-i 'arab*.[25] Siraj al-Din 'Ali Khan
"Arzu" (1689–1756 AD/11.1–69 AH) mentions the movement of 'Alamgir's
armies from "the Deccan to Hindustan."[26] Similarly, Mir Ghulam 'Ali "Azad"
Bilgrami (1704–86 AD/1116–1200 AH) describes traveling to Delhi as "returning to the country (*kishvar*) of Hind from the domain (*mulk*) of Sindh."[27]
Here Hind is the domain of the central Indo-Gangetic plain of north India,
excluding Sindh, Punjab, Gujarat, and Bengal, not the Timurid kingdom
and certainly not the South Asian subcontinent. The term *mamlakat* did not
coincide with a modern sense of an Iranian or Indian nation-state, proto
or otherwise, since the word's meanings contained decentralized alternative
meanings that undermine any simple equivalence.

Places within a kingdom but outside one's region or city of birth or residence could be as strange as places outside a kingdom. Bengal, though within
the dominions of Timurid Hindustan, was a separate administrative and
geographical region.[28] Kashmiri's manner of describing it is similar to his
descriptions of places in Turan and Iran: "Bengal is a rich and productive (*zar
khīz*) land (*mulk*) that yields abundant income. Its climate, on account of the
severity of the rainfall and nearness of the great sea, is extremely humid."[29]
Writing for a Delhi audience, he provides information typical of another
mamlakat with a distinct climate and natural resources, not what would be
said of a familiar place.

Smaller domains had their own histories and characters, often expressed
by the epithets of their major cities, including former capitals (such as
Herat), places of pilgrimage (such as Mashhad), or abodes of learning (such
as Shiraz).[30] Referring to the fifteenth century, when the regions of Iran
were not under a single rule, Beatrice Manz notes that "cities and regions
had the political ability to decide their own fates and to separate from the
center, and if a ruler was to stay in control he required the active consent of
local forces."[31] Manz describes a period of decentralized rule under Turco-
Mongol governing structures that the Safavid Shahs tried to strengthen;
nevertheless, local forces remained important.[32] Localities and regions were
the building blocks of any imperium, and in times of imperial dissolution,
they were autonomous entities. The assassination of Nadir's governor at
Lar, a man whom Hazin describes as thoroughly unjust and disrespectful of
local notables, is an instance of upset in the necessary balance between local

benefits derived from service to a central government and that government's ability to garner support from local forces. The general breakdown in central government and its links to local elites does not mean that local structures ceased to function.

Hazin and Kashmiri share impressions of post-Safavid Iran as a wasteland and Timurid Hindustan as rapidly falling into disorder and decay (the specifics of these historically significant views are outlined in the next chapter). One basis for these similar views, despite their many differences, is their shared preoccupation with and decidedly imperial view of their respective kingdoms. Such an imperial view derived from affiliation with an imperial capital, one of the few means for affiliating with an entire realm (service to the ruler being another means). For both, without the Safavids or the Timurids reigning supreme from Isfahan and Delhi, respectively, those realms were in shambles.[33] Rather than documentary views of a singular reality at a historical moment, these accounts are one way of representing the meaning of what had recently happened. Their expression allows us to ask new questions such as how affiliations that might look like proto-nationalism are part of a different logic of home and signification of place. Regardless of these authors' imperial focus, their works, like those by authors with different affiliations, present provinces with their own political stakes, economic mainstays, mercantile flows, and social hierarchies.[34]

People were also central to the meanings of place. The relationship between place and people was multiple, defying any singular and primary relationship between language, place, and people. When relating a people to a political domain, Hazin calls the Lezgi a *jamā'at* (group of people) with Daghistan as their *vilāyat* (land). The Lezgi "in these days of interregnum (*fatrat*) turned their heads from submission to the king of Iran."[35] Hazin's description outlines a political loyalty to the Safavid king (whom the Lezgi betray, as they then begin to treat with the Ottomans) that acknowledges both their status as a people associated with the land of Daghistan and their political subservience to a larger empire. This domain of Iran, over which the Safavids rule, is an empire encompassing distinct peoples such as the Lezgi, as well as people born of slaves from the Caucasus, those of Turco-Mongol lineages, Arabic-speaking migrants, and others. All are integral to the *mamlakat* of Safavid Iran. Some were Persian speaking; some were not. Aside

from the Persianate nature of Timurid Hindustan, Persian and Iranian were
not the same thing.

Iran was the empire of the Safavids, even after their fall, and also the
standard against which subsequent rulers were measured. In the midst of
his general repugnance over Nadir's unjust rule, Hazin lauds Nadir's military
victories against the Ottomans as an act of restoration:

> [I]n both the confines (*hudūd*) of Azarbayjan and the confines of their
> own dominions, [Nadir] fought many difficult and arduous battles with the
> armies of *Rūm* and obtained victory every time. Many Ottoman (*Rūmī*)
> commanders and soldiers without number were slain in those domains
> (*mamālik*). The fort of Erivan, Ganjah and some of the dominion (*mam-
> lakat*) of Georgia and those delineated areas (*hudūd*) that had remained in
> their [the Ottoman's] possession, were wrested [back] and nothing of the
> kingdom of Iran (*mamlakat-i Iran*) remained in the control of that group
> (*ān jamā'at*).[36]

Hazin specifies the dominions once ruled by, and owing loyalty to, the Safavid throne as those that should be ruled by the throne of Iran. Though a
mamlakat of its own, therefore, Georgia is part of the larger imperial *mamlakat* of Iran. Here the idea of Iran is the recent, historically specific Iran
constituted under the Safavids, not a timeless, unchanging notion derived
from ancient or epic history.

Kashmiri demonstrates a similar notion in his "description of the four
boundaries of the dominions of Iran," stating that "under the rule of Iran
(*saltanat-i Iran*) there are domains (*mulk*) like Khurasan, 'Iraq-i 'ajam, Fars,
Azarbayjan, Mazandaran and each domain is comprised of several cities
(*balad*) and towns (*qasbih*)." This kingdom is outlined to the east by Sindh,
Kabul, *Mavara' al-nahr*, and Khvarazm (the latter two constituting Turan);
to the west by Sham and the lands of Rum; to the north by the land of
(*vilāyat-i*) Aras (Arxes river of antiquity, near Tiflis), Circassia, and the plain
of Qipchaq; and to the south by the desert of the *Najd* (central Arabian pen-
insula) and Arabistan (Nefud desert).[37] Hazin attributes slightly more than
Kashmiri to the Iranian throne's rightful territory, including disputed territories such as Qandahar. Otherwise, Kashmiri shares Hazin's Safavid-based
vision of the dominions constituting the kingdom of Iran.

Rulers' behavior gave moral meaning to political domains and, by extension, to the land.[38] Like Kashmiri, Hazin sees Nadir as an unjust ruler, despite Nadir's restoration of Safavid domains to the throne of Iran. For Hazin, Nadir's behavior in warfare defied honor and ethical governance:

> And since he was not satisfied with this [pushing the Ottomans outside Safavid borders], he stood firm against them in several conflicts (*kārzār*) in their own kingdom (*mamlakat*). The majority of those regions became utterly destroyed and ruined. From the successive defeats and the annihilation of many soldiers and renowned lords (*pāshāyān*) and at the expense of so much wealth and property, and with the destruction of most of the delineated areas (*hudūd*) the Rūmīs were in a debilitated state. No brilliance was left in their realm (*saltanat*) and a great fear and dread became predominant amongst the inhabitants of that region, from the Sultan [down] to the peasants.[39]

Even for someone so nostalgic for Safavid Iran, restoring Iran's territorial integrity must be done honorably, in accordance with a just end. By launching his own aggression into Ottoman domains and laying them to waste, Nadir demonstrates violation of ethical bounds. For Hazin, therefore, the land of Iran remains unrestored, despite its reunified territories. Without ethical governance, which Nadir lacks, Iran is broken and its throne dishonored.[40] An empirically unified political realm was thus insufficient in the face of the moral criteria of place.

Despite their different views of the Safavids and the Timurids, Hazin and Kashmiri saw Iran and Turan as geographical entities signifying within Persianate culture in similar ways. They considered both lands as part of Islamic heartlands and mapped within the geocultural landscape of universal Persianate history. By the later, High Persianate period, authors sometimes used well-known techniques to also include Hindustan in the Persianate.

Geocultural Landscapes

The storied tradition of the Persianate past characterized certain geographies. These stories were universally known, gave meaning to place, and had to be acknowledged and contended with in commemorative accounts. Well-known stories ranged from what we call fiction to what we call fact, encompassing anecdotes, romances, and chronicles. Together they saturated the land, shaped geography with meanings, and linked regions, both within the Persianate and beyond. Geocultural landscapes were one major way in which cities and domains gained meaning.[41] Stories accrued to places. The more widespread and reiterated stories had undeniable authority. Others could be discarded, their meanings open to contestation.

Though Persian *tazkirih*s in Iran would form poetic communities based on increasingly narrow aesthetics from the late eighteenth century, Kashmiri, a Hindustani Persian who was not a poet, still referred to the same broad textual corpus as Hazin in the decades before. Both Kashmiri and Hazin reference a common set of tropes as well as literary figures and past person-ages—kings, heroes, statesmen, mystics, and lovers—regardless of their texts' generic or rhetorical priorities. Kashmiri quotes verses from Sa'di, Rumi, and Hafiz (among others) and illustrates his points with stories from narrative poems such as Firdowsi's *Shahnama* and Nizami's *Khusraw and Shirin*.[42] Ethical evaluations and paradigmatic possibilities for interpretation were contained in this corpus, which also included prose texts.[43] According to Kathryn Babayan, one prominent feature of Persianate ethos is a sense of cyclical time and being, exemplified in the *Shahnama*, in which "Iranian so-ciety is portrayed as encountering similar ethical dilemmas in different ages. In each era, kings are confronted with analogous situations as they attempt to rule their dominion with justice and to deal with political realities and ethical choices regarding their sons, warriors, subjects and neighbors (Turan, Hind, Rum)."[44]

Mitchell argues that the language and the rhetorical tools of Safavid epistolary culture, often dismissed as formulaic and empty, were meant to convey or contend with meaning. Writers used "their literary skills to access a reservoir of fables, anecdotes, parables, aphorisms, dictums, and narratives about various historical and legendary figures towards sophisticated literary constructs." While this "specialized set of skills" to evoke them in Safavid epistolary forms (*inshā*) "was the purview of the Perso-Islamic *adīb*s (both poets and *munshī*s)," its reservoir was more broadly accessible across other social locations and occupational groups. Moreover, the Safavids were but one site of Persian epistolary culture; its practitioners and the reservoir they drew from was transregionally available across "those climes where Persian literature, Islamic prophetography, and Sufi-Shiʻite hagiography, dominated both elite and popular culture (Ottoman Turkey, Caucasus, Iran, Central Asia, Indian subcontinent)."[45] The stories and figures of this "corpus of images and memories" carried meanings and narratives that did not have to be explained; they served to "graft or superimpose" established meanings onto places, people, and events.[46]

In this vein, Hazin's historical narrative regarding the Safavids and Timurids conforms to a Persianate cyclical sense of time and being, which, as we see in the next chapter, he articulates in the form of a reoccurring relationship between Iran and Hindustan throughout history. Kashmiri similarly displays a sense of cyclical time in his description of current events as reoccurring events, among them the battle between Ahmad Shah Durrani and Timurid forces, which he likens to the battle between Babur and "Ibrahim Afghan Lodi" (Sultan Ibrahim Lodi) two hundred years earlier.[47] Such comparisons were ubiquitous in texts of this period. Hazin's fellow migrant to Hindustan, ʻAli Quli Khan "Valih" Daghistani (1712–56 AD/1124–69 AH), compares his patron Burhan al-Mulk's bravery in battle to the pre-Islamic Persian king Esfandiyar and the hero Rustam.[48]

Paradigmatic Persian stories, famously told in the *Shahnama* and more widely dispersed through other texts and genres, written and rewritten continuously throughout the Persianate world, underpinned the histories imbuing place with ethical meaning. In Timurid Hindustan, manuscripts of the *Shahnama*, though less often patronized, circulated widely along with more commonly produced prose texts such as universal histories. Commemorative texts of the Persianate past were characterized by a dual narrative of pre-Islamic Persian kings reconciled with pre-Islamic Qurʼanic history and brought into the ambit of Persianate Islamic history.[49] These storied figures also populated a variety of ethico-didactic texts of Persian education, such as Saʻdi's *Gulistan* and Husayn Vaʼiz Kashifi's (d. 1504–5 AD/910 AH) *Akhlaq-i Muhsini*, whose exempla (*hikāyāt*) circulated in modular form to other texts and oral contexts. Kashifi uses figures from the Islamic era, such as the Seljuk Sultan Sanjar, and pre-Islamic Persian times, such as Afrasiyab, to discuss sensibilities such as gratitude and patience.[50] In Saʻdi's *Gulistan*, stories of the prophets and pre-Islamic Persian kings such as the first Sassanian ruler, Ardashir, outline how to inhabit virtues such as contentment.[51]

Through the early nineteenth century, this dual historical narrative permeated the Persian texts produced, read, and circulated across Central, South, and West Asia, first through a shared fifteenth-century Timurid historiography and then in related later Timurid and Safavid historiographical traditions.[52] The hugely influential Timurid universal history *Rawzat al-Safa* (written in Herat, 1469 AD/873 AH) serves as a central example. Its narrative begins with pre-Islamic Qur'anic creation through the flood, to the prophets, patriarchs, and kings of Israel, and continues at length with pre-Islamic Persian kings to the arrival of Islam. "The termination of both narratives signaled Islam's moral and political superiority," beginning with the birth of the Prophet Muhammad.[53] The narrative of pre-Islamic Persian kings is a prose reinscription of the epic poem the *Shahnama*. From the time of the Abbasids, and especially after their fall, the historical narrative of Muslim domains becomes increasingly focused on the Persianate Islamic East and then entirely on Iran and Turan.[54] This format of reconciled pre-Islamic Qur'anic and Persian histories, given in parallel in *Rawzat al-Safa* and later *Habib al-Siyar* (1524 AD/930 AH), with a post-Abbasid emphasis on the Persianate East, pervaded later Timurid and Safavid histories, however much their post-early Timurid accounts diverged.[55]

These universal histories circulated widely in the libraries of Hindustani and Irani Persians, both Muslim and non-Muslim, well through the nineteenth century, as did the *Shahnama* and its many abridged prose narrative retellings.[56] Thus from the High Persianate period's inception through the eighteenth century, the dual pre-Islamic and Persianate Islamic historical narrative permeated commemorative texts such as formal historical chronicles, *tazkirih*s, and travel texts. This history was integral to the meanings of places within the Persianate world. The events, figures, and features outlined in these stories created the Persianate sense of place, the geocultural landscapes through which Persians knew the world. Stories accumulated and distinguished places. Some we understand as fiction or myth and some as history. Together, however, they were part of a tradition by which the world took shape and held meaning for Persians.

Take, for example, Azar Baygdili's *Atashkadih* (begun 1760–61 AD/1174 AH), an iconic text, a *tazkirih* generally read as heralding the start of the Iranian neoclassical (*bāzgasht*) literary movement.[57] One of the last *tazkirih*s written in Iran that at least attempts to encompass lands beyond it, the *Atashkadih* maps poets (excepting, significantly, kings, princes, mighty commanders, women, and contemporaries) onto a regionally partitioned world of poetic Persian that reflects both the accumulated dual narrative of Perso-Islamic histories and the specifics of Azar's own time and locale. Even in a text like the *Atashkadih*, in which Iran is central to the geographical mapping of Persian literary culture, perceptions of land and culture, shared with other texts of this period, contrast with modern nationalist concepts. Iran was distinct, but its meaning was contiguous with surrounding lands. The difference with nationalism lies in geocultural meanings, the ways in which significance is vested in land through a history of near and far figures and events contained in the corpus of Persianate learning. These geocultural meanings are part of a shared hermeneutical ground, a product of the textual corpus that informs and spans conflicting ethical and aesthetic valuations. Persians writing in Iran, Turan, and Hindustan shared particular meanings of geography that constituted the bases of origin and community. Holding sway from earlier periods, lands and their meanings were distinct, but they remained linked through stories that spoke of travel, contact, and relationships.

Often read as "an early expression of literary nationalism in Iran," the *Atashkadih* did link Persian culture to the land of Iran by marginalizing Persian poets originating in Central and South Asia.[58] Yet the *Atashkadih* has two aims that must be distinguished from nationalist concerns. First, it seeks to memorialize a new style of poetics (only much later called *bāzgasht*) by refuting the value of the *tāzih gūī* style (also only later called the Indian style, or *sabk-i Hindī*) of the preceding centuries.[59] Azar thus rejected many post-Timurid poets originating in the cities of Iran, as well as from Turan and Hindustan. Second, the text seeks to place Iran (specifically 'Iraq-i 'ajam) at the center of poetic culture, originating the new style at a time when Iran was perceived to be in a state of ruin relative to its Safavid past.[60]

This impulse to recenter Persian in Iran must be understood in a context in which the greatest centers of poetic patronage had been in Timurid domains, in the cities of Lahore and Delhi, for the past century and a half.

Centers of patronage were also places where poetic style developed and emanated. The *Atashkadih* was written as an intervention in the current style,
putting Azar's own *'Iraq-i 'ajam*–based poetic circle on the larger Persianate
map by linking it to the old masters originating in what came to be Safavid
lands. The very means by which the *Atashkadih* distinguishes and centers Iran
within the Persianate world, however, relies on histories—social, aesthetic,
political, and geographical—partly shared with Persians in Turan and Hindustan. Poetically and morally, the text makes Iran foremost in the Persianate
world but neither singular nor unique. Rather, Iran shares many overlapping
features with Turan and Hindustan.

The geographically organized portion of the *Atashkadih* maps poets onto
cities, ostensibly their cities of origin. Cities are listed within smaller domains, which are in turn grouped under the larger regions of Iran, Turan,
and Hindustan. No poet is directly listed under a larger geographical unit,
emphasizing that poets' homes were cities *within* larger domains and regions,
which were not themselves intelligible as homes. Azar distinguishes these
various tiered and interlocking geographies by drawing on the dual Persianate narratives of pre-Islamic and Qur'anic history. The region (*vilāyat*) of
Iran has a "distinctly temperate climate and the intellect/perception (*idrāk*)
of the inhabitants of that region (*diyār*) does not need to be made manifest"
because "all the books of histories (*siyar va tavārīkh*) speak to this point."[61]
Significantly, Azar refers to a presumably common body of historical texts to
justify his contention about the meaning of the land's climate and inhabitants. Descriptions of larger regions are brief; descriptions of smaller domains
listed under Iran—Azarbayjan, Khurasan, Tabaristan, 'Iraq-i 'arab and 'Iraq-i
'ajam, and Fars—are more substantial.[62]

Beginning with Azarbayjan, Azar contemplates the land's history, the
origin of its name, and the characteristics of its climate and people. The terms
vilāyat and *diyār* refer to Azarbayjan as well as Iran, which acts here as a
synonym for *mamlakat*, demonstrating the aporetic way that the same word
referred to both smaller and larger domains. The name Azarbayjan

> is derived from (*mansūb bih*) Azar ibn Amīr ibn Asūd ibn Sām, who was
> the son of Nūh [Noah]. Some have written that in the time of Shāpūr,
> Azar was the name of a person who claimed to be a prophet and seduced a

great number of people into accepting his claim. Shapur seized him, melted metals (*filizzat*) on his chest and he was not injured, causing the belief of people to grow. The flourishing of that region is due to him.[63]

The qualification of "some have written," which precedes the pre-Islamic Persian narrative but not the Qur'anic lineage, gives the latter greater force of certainty. Yet doubt about these stories is itself reproduced as fact, given that they come from authoritative sources such as *Rawzat al-Safa*.[64] Azar justifies their inclusion because their wide currency has its own iterative authority, the same reasoning used in *Rawzat al- Safa*.[65]

For example, his description of Mazandaran begins with the near past, with Shah Abbas, who on account of his mother's family spent much time there building gardens and palaces. In providing geographical details, Azar taps into the far more uncertain past, identifying one of its impregnable fortresses, a place where

> during the time of Afrasiyab's conquest and the defeat of the Iranis, Manuchihr was besieged. Afrasiyab was not victorious in his conquest of the fort. In the end, the great ones of Iran and Turan agreed on this condition for peace, that from the aforementioned fort an arrow should be launched and wherever it hit the ground should be the division of the holdings of Afrasiyab and Manuchihr. Arash, one of the great warriors (*pahlavānān*) of Iran, launched an arrow that, after examination, had struck the ground on the banks of the Jayhun [Oxus] river. However much the acceptance of this story is outside the pale of probability, it has been written on account of its great fame (*shuhrat*).[66]

These pre-Islamic Persian narratives are viewed with a degree of skepticism—for example, that an arrow could fly from Mazandaran to the Oxus—yet are still included in the descriptions of geographical regions because their indelible fame informs the character of these places.

Though political fragmentation, colonial encroachment, and a decided Iranization of the Persian language was occurring in both Hindustan and Iran over the nineteenth century, a Hindustani Persian could still narrate places according to this dual Islamic and pre-Islamic Persian narrative.[67] Mirza 'Ali "Maftun," a traveler from Patna through Qajar Iran in the early nineteenth century, writing after his return home, maps the geocultural meaning of Tehran beginning with a description of the older, nearby town of Rayy, figured as Tehran's ancestor:

> It is revealed to those versed in histories that the land of Rayy is in the fourth clime and one of the great old cities of 'Iraq-i 'ajam and there are differing accounts of its founding. Some give the credit of its founding to Hushang, some to the prophet Seth, son of Adam.[68] Regarding the flourishing and habitation and spaciousness of it [Rayy] they [the histories] tell stories which are not empty of strangeness (gharābat). For those who depend on proof (ahl-i khubrat) it is manifest that the aforementioned land has been wrecked and ruined several times by earthquake, massacre, and pillage.[69]

Most spectacularly, he notes devastation by Genghis Khan. Maftun demonstrates his knowledge of the dual narrative, though he also expresses skepticism about the veracity of the more distant past. He distinguishes it from more recent history, which has left material evidence, and contemporaneous chronicles, of which he can be more certain.[70] Regardless of relative reliability, however, these stranger, less verifiable stories carry authority in the weight of their repetitive citation. They require acknowledgment and mark the geocultural meaning of place.[71]

These stories connected Iran to the lands around it, even as they made these lands distinct. Through its shared pre-Islamic Persian history, Turan was linked to Iran through shared familial origins.[72] As Azar's description of the larger region of Turan commemorates,

> when Faraydun ruled, he divided up the domains (mamālik) of his empire during his life. He gave [the land] from the banks of the Jayhūn [Oxus] to Tur, which became known as Turan. He entrusted the region of Rum [one manuscript says Hind] to Salm.[73] He gave the domain (mamlakat) of Iran to Iraj, who gave his name to Iran. In the end, what happened came to happen and it is fully detailed in [the aforementioned] histories.[74]

This story appears in the *Shahnama* and was subsequently elaborated and re-narrated, along with other accounts, in universal Persianate histories, such as the *Rawzat al-Safa*, as Faraydun's division of the world.[75] In the *Atashkadih* this story appears as history, not myth.[76] The genealogy of these lands, once united and then ruled by brothers, however bitterly they may have fought, depicts related regions springing from one origin. The ensuing conflict between the brothers is caused by envy of Iraj's lot, because the throne of Iran is the coveted choice portion. As the original seat of rule, Iran is connected to, but hierarchically above, neighboring lands. The resulting envy-fueled aggression of Iraj's brothers and their descendants renders them, and thus their lands, as ethically lower than Iran.[77] Though sharing common origins with Iran, the relationship is conflictual. Iran has higher moral status because of its ruler's more virtuous behavior.[78] In this most primordial of stories, a land's moral status, bestowed through rulership, distinguishes its geography.

As empirical ground, land was made malleable by these other forms of landscaping, as shown in Azar's description of Balkh, which he lists among the domains of Turan. This attribution contrasts with older commemorations of place, as in the *Shahnama*, which locates the Oxus river as the border between Turan and Iran.[79] The region of Balkh lies to the south of the Oxus, and its prosperity is identified with Kaykavus, whose lineage reaches back to the earliest pre-Islamic Persian sovereign, Kayumars. This shifting border, however, reflects political realities of the more recent past. Azar notes that "in former times, it was a great province of Iran. It was counted as one of the cities of Khurasan, and now it has been years since it has been under the occupation (*tassaruf*) of the dynasties (*salātīn*) of Turan."[80] Azar evokes older history to underscore the illegitimacy of Uzbeg rule of this erstwhile Khurasani city. Regardless of legitimacy, rule by successive Turan-based dynasties had shifted the geographical location of this domain from Iran to Turan.[81]

Conflict, enmity, and competition characterized the hierarchical relationships that constituted Persianate lands. By the eighteenth century, the inclusion of Hind in the tripartite division of the Persianate world, even in the reproduction of only some manuscripts of the *Atashkadih*, reflected the intelligibility of Timurid Hindustan as Persian. This occasional inclusion updated fifteenth-century geocultural mapping of *Rawzat al-Safa*,[82] but it is precarious and unevenly reflected in the *Atashkadih*—not in descriptions of the larger land of Hindustan but in descriptions of smaller domains and cities. Significantly, though, the text does list Hind, and not Rum, in its tripartite division of the Persianate world. Nevertheless, for Azar, Hindustan is outside pre-Islamic Qur'anic and Persian history, a place where "the customs and rules (*rusūm va qavā'id*) of that place are for the most part contrary (*khilāf*) to [those of] the inhabitants of Iran and even Turan."[83] The qualities of the land itself further underscore the opposition between the customs defining their two societies: "The strange fruits of that place cannot be found in this region [Iran]."[84] The Azar's Hindustan consists of Deccan, Delhi, Sirhind, Kabul, Lahore, and Kashmir, a jumble of cities and domains reflecting his loose grasp of its geography.

Yet individual descriptions of these smaller regions and cities are far more equivocal about their relation to Iran. Azar describes Delhi as a city exceptional because of its verdant gardens, delightful plains, and high-quality air and water. Immediately following is the history of Delhi, starting with its conquest by Muslim rulers in 1192 AD/588 AH (the Ghurid conquest of Delhi), after which it was a center of Muslim rule by "dynasties of great nobility." Skipping ahead to the latest of these dynasties, Azar focuses on the architectural contribution of Shahjahan, who filled the gaps in Delhi's structures, ensuring the city would flourish, and giving it the name Shahjahanabad. "At this time, which is the year 1179 [1765–66] successive events, caused by the arrival of Nadir Shah Afshar and Ahmad Shah Afghan [Durrani], have brought extreme disorder and ruin [to the city]."[85] For Azar, an author affiliated with the former Safavid capital of Isfahan, Iran was not the only land to have fallen to ruin. Hindustan had also been laid low by invaders and resulting chaos. By this time, many of Delhi's literati had migrated to other cities, mainly regional centers of Fayzabad, Hyderabad, and Murshidabad.[86] They generally agreed with Azar's assessment, although many also praised the concomitant flourishing of these regional centers.

The context of Azar's composition is the ruin of Iran, a perception that undergirds the *Atashkadih* and is essential to its rhetorical labor. Khurasan, "a province consisting of old and great cities, is the great cornerstone (*rukn*) of the region (*diyār*) of Iran. At this time, like the rest of Iran, it is ruined."[87] In describing places such as Kirman and Sabzavar, Azar elaborates that cities and their populations have been much reduced by "the vicissitudes of the times (*inqilāb-i zamānih*)."[88] Although they may differ on why, Azar, Hazin, Kashmiri, and others writing in the middle decades of the eighteenth century reiterate this perception of Iran and of Timurid rule.[89] Different views of events thus share an understanding of these lands and their meaning. Iran and Hindustan have contrasting relationships, moral valences, and cultural knowledge. The direction of an author's travel, together with the matrix of his origins and reasons for writing, also structures the meaning of these two lands and their affiliations. The next chapter explores these particularities and their articulation of inclusion or exclusion.

CHAPTER 2

Remembering, Lamenting

UNDERSTANDING WHAT IRAN AND HINDUSTAN meant in mid-eighteenth-century Persianate terms requires attention to the framing of their pasts. Remembering near and distant pasts was part of constituting both the character of a place and the morally justified hierarchy between places. Depending on their affiliations, Persians might differ on and contest the meaning of a place, but they nonetheless articulated the range of possible meanings in the same terms. To examine articulations of place and its meanings, this chapter turns to memories of the Safavids and the Timurids in the prose works of Hazin Lahiji and 'Abd al-Karim Kashmiri.

Unlike modern literary scholars, eighteenth- and nineteenth-century writers, especially in Timurid Hindustan, considered Hazin one of the foremost poets of the eighteenth century.[1] Modern historians, concerned principally with the reliability of the narrative, have largely mined his memoir for facts. Most of their works are political histories of the late Safavid period and of subsequent invasions, occupations, and the reign of Nadir Shah, all told as the story of great men and great events.[2] Other scholars have read Hazin's pronouncements denigrating India, together with its inhabitants and its rulers, as the apogee of "Iranian" cultural chauvinism. They equate origin in a political kingdom with cultural affiliation, applying a modern conceit that likens narrative self-representation in a commemorative text with the author's subjectivity.[3] However, even in post-romantic contexts, an autobiographical text cannot be read as the straightforward re-flection of the author as subject.[4]

Attention to the text's particular concerns allows new interpretations that can enhance understanding of how Persianate selves related to place.[5] Hazin was a specific type of exile, a refugee from catastrophic events that he perceived to have destroyed both his home and any future access to it. *Tazkirat al-Ahval* was written in Delhi (1742 AD/1154 AH), in the aftermath of Nadir Shah's invasion of Hindustan, just as Hazin had secured the means to set himself up as a man of substance in the city. The text functioned as a statement of self among Delhi's elites, even as Hazin sought to distinguish himself from them. In contrast, Kashmiri occupied a more modest position at court. He wrote as a pilgrim, traveling with the army that had sacked his imperial city and brought its ruler low. Despite continuing disorder and po-litical chaos, Kashmiri wrote the *Bayan* after returning home. In the midst of different writing contexts, both use historical narrative to idealize the past and lament the present.

Hazin states that his text is meant as a warning (*'ibrat*), to preserve mem-ory (*yādgārī*) and alleviate the pain of exile.[6] He remembers Iran under Safavid rule, and its meaning, together with the fall and irretrievable destruction of Sa-favid domains, defines him as a poetic persona, as "Hazin" (grieving, sad). This exaltation of Safavid-ruled Isfahan contrasts with his location in Timurid-ruled Delhi. Similarly, Kashmiri, a resident of the Timurid imperial capital, defines himself according to the exalted realm that city represents, in contrast with the victorious, yet base and illegitimate, ruler of Iran, Nadir Shah. Hazin's view of history and politics is thus as much Isfahan-privileged and Safavid-centered as Kashmiri's is Delhi-privileged and Timurid-centered.

For both Kashmiri and Hazin, a ruler's character was a metonym for the character of a realm, just as an imperial city was a metonym for a whole king-dom. Monarchs were the jewels of these imperial seats and gave character to their cities. Regnal self-representation, in turn, gave features to a place, as a monarch's acts of rule emanated outward, pervading the empire. For those from capital cities, homeland was embedded in a sense of loyalty to the mon-arch and, through him, to the realm.[7] Hazin and Kashmiri each affiliated with an imperial city, its ruler, and his dynasty, as the perfected representation of the character of an entire realm.

Hazin: Land, Inhabitants, and Rulers

The rough trajectory of Hazin's closely intertwined account of his life and of larger historical circumstances contains three phases. The first outlines his youth, situating his family and early life through social connections and education. He describes places at length through the men of learning who inhabit them, presenting a symbiotic relationship between the moral state and physical appearance of a place. Beyond obvious physical features, such as built environment, he makes moral character manifest in the ethical intercourse of a place's inhabitants.[8] This connection was not limited to cities. Hazin narrates the province of Gilan as a land of substantive purity and manifest beauty that mirrors the learned state and noble manner of its inhabitants.[9] Noble manners are a sign of learning (*fazl*), a term for virtue itself. The link between manners and virtue stems from a notion of learning in which disciplined upbringing and/or formal education trains moral perception and thus ethical conduct.

Upon reaching adulthood, Hazin travels through the province of Fars to continue his studies, and he describes places through his acquisition of friends and education.[10] He thus characterizes home by the presence of the learned and upright, whose virtuous conduct makes possible the intimacies of friendship. When he returns from Fars to Isfahan at the behest of his father, Hazin spends time with his family and friends. He calls these interactions, "among the precious blessings of life (*ni'mat-hā-yi girānmāyih*)."[11] This dual acquisition of friendship and knowledge in his early travels is punctuated by the experience of carnal love, subsequent musing on it, and his ultimate rejection of it, as well as the rejection of marriage (an endeavor separate from love).[12] The celibacy he chooses is a necessary element of his morally upright quest for knowledge and telling of the ways in which "noble-mannered" and "learned" signify in relation to each other for Hazin.

The second phase of his trajectory begins with the Afghan invasion of Iran, leading to the siege of Isfahan and the hardships and mayhem that followed. Hazin lost his whole family and most of his friends in the Afghan conquest of Isfahan and the upheavals of the following years. From this point, the larger political landscape is closely interwoven with his personal trajectory, indicating its effect on his life. In each section Hazin alternates between the movement of armies and their battles and his own movements and actions. During this period, his account is most like an elegy lamenting the Safavids and all they represented culturally and morally, layered into a lament for all his dead friends and family, narrated as the cream of late-Safavid society. The self is thus interwoven with historical accounts of the larger world, reflecting the connection of moral virtue with its worldly manifestations of order and harmony, as well as a heightened sense of past glory indivisible from present grief over death and disorder.

After years of upheaval all over the country—with instability reflected in Hazin's own constant motion—the Afghans are repelled, largely through the military abilities of Tahmasp Quli Khan (1698–1747), later Nadir Shah Afshar, who brings the rest of former Safavid domains under his control by also expelling the Russians and Ottomans.[13] Instead of the restoration of the Safavid government, and thus the moral restoration of the land of Iran, however, Nadir Shah's rapacious governors set upon the already ravaged people. Hazin presents his occasional involvement in politics as an act of self-sacrifice, necessary to achieve the greater virtue of improving the populace's welfare. He moves from place to place, lamenting the sad state of the country, and cannot bring himself to settle down. His account of the people of Lar's oppression at the hands of Nadir's governor is indicative of this woeful state.[14] The events that lead to the governor's assassination are narrated as a violation of ethical behavior, not just of a governor in relation to the common people but also to the local elites.[15] Hazin's suspected involvement in this assassination (which he vehemently denies) makes his presence in Nadir Shah's Iran untenable. After unsuccessfully attempting to live incognito in Kerman and finding the roads to the Iraqi shrine cities blocked by Nadir's wars, Hazin ignores the urging of an English captain to go to Europe and sets out for Hindustan.

The third phase of his trajectory is marked by his flight to the subcontinent. From the time he arrives in the region of Sindh, the pitch of Hazin's laments grows more fevered. We are given only a skeletal account of his movements, devoid of interactions with people. During his stay in upper Sindh, he states that "seeing this domain (*mamlakat*) [even] this much is extremely abhorrent (*makrūh*)" and that he does not have the patience to write of the happenings of his time in this region (*diyār*).[16] In fact, he goes so far as to declare, "I do not count the time of my residence in this domain (*mamlakat*) as part of my life."[17] Instead, Hazin offers a historical account of the treacherous, base behavior of Timurid rulers toward the Safavids. This story of dynastic relations serves to manifest Hindustan's degraded moral nature, representative of the substance and conduct of its people, presented as derived from the land.

The near past distinguishes places and offers a portrait in contrasts. Hazin begins by outlining the way Babur (1483–1530, Kabul r. 1504–30, Hindustan r. 1526–30), the first Timurid ruler of Hindustan, benefited all of his life from the continual support and aid (*tamassuk va tavassul*) of Shah Isma'il (r. 1501–24), the first Safavid king, whom Hazin likens to Solomon.[18] Only with his aid was Babur able to gain the throne of Hindustan, since by his time the constant bickering of Timurid princes and the tyranny they practiced had reduced their domains (Khurasan and Turan) to a pitiable state. Babur, in appropriate acts of friendship, duly acknowledged the centrality of Safavid aid to his fortunes, establishing a relationship with implied obligations. In times of helplessness and need, Babur's children and grandchildren also sought aid (which was, of course, granted) from the Safavids, but these subsequent generations always neglected to properly reciprocate. This betrayal of the relationship established by their forefather was a serious breach of the ethics that demonstrated the base character of Timurid kings as self-serving friends. Likewise, it demonstrated the superiority of Safavid kings as selfless friends, continuing to provide aid despite the lack of appropriate response.[19] Here, a person's comportment in a relationship manifested their character. As Hazin elaborates, when times were troubled in Iran but tranquil in Hindustan, the Timurids' friendly

> manner changed to one of abundant haughtiness and pride, they barred the path of familiarity (*āshnā'ī*), and this custom (*'ādat*) has been established in the nature of Babur's line. Apparently, the prevalence of this manner is from the effects of Hindustan's water and climate, since it is apparent that the people of this region do not seek friendship without selfish intentions.[20]

The Hindustani kings' betrayal of the obligations of friendship renders Hindustan less moral than Iran, a quality that permeates the very air and water and pollutes the land's inhabitants, including its Timurid rulers. Hazin thus links duplicitous and self-interested behavior, a sign of ignoble virtues, to the land.

Proof of this character also lies in the far past. Ignoble behavior on the part of Hind's rulers (*rā'īān*) toward Persian (*'ajam*) kings predates Islam. Whenever Persian kings, defined as rulers of *Īrān zamīn* (here a reference to the pre-Islamic land of Iran), approached Hindustan with an army, the rulers of Hind recognized their inability to prevail and became humble and submissive tributaries.[21] Soon after the Persians returned to Iran, those of "turbid judgment/dark princes (*tīrih rā'ī*)" were seduced by the promise of worldly prestige and wealth.[22] Overtaken by inappropriate pride, they forgot their promises and falsely boasted of their power across the land.[23] Specific dynastic relations between the Safavids and Timurids are presented here as the latest instance of a relational paradigm between the rulers of Iran and Hindustan, repeatedly enacted since pre-Islamic times, affirming the inherent character of the respective lands themselves.[24] This paradigm is brought to bear on Hazin's present, when the lack of a proper ruler has left Iran in a state of disarray, in contrast with Hindustan, where the qualities of the land preclude a noble ruler. This painstaking attempt to set Iran and Hindustan in opposition to one another is written against a general acceptance of these two realms as socially and culturally affiliated, mirrored in the long history of their kings as both friends and competitors.[25]

Hazin recoups the fall of the Safavids as a result not of weakness, but of betrayal and a general discordance of fate, which has caused reversals in the natural (virtuous) order of things. Here the fall of the Safavids and Hazin's forced exile in Hind are narrated as extensions of the calamity of betrayed friendship. Hazin narrates Iran as the ever-selfless friend, true to the obligations of aid, exchange, and support, while Hindustan is the selfish friend, exhibiting only fair-weather loyalty, inconstant and heedless of obligations. With the Afghan invasion, when "all that tumult spread in the provinces of Iran, as was the manner of the king of Hind, the custom of inquiry [after the Safavid Shah's well-being] (*rasm-i pursishī*) never crossed his mind, rather he observed the way of friendship and amity (*vadād*) with Mir Vays [d. 1715] the Afghan."[26]

The Safavids' failure to hold the throne was thus due to the Timurids' betrayal of the obligations of friendship, part of the wider breakdown of ethical order. Such a causal formulation allowed Hazin to recoup the Safavids as paragons of "chivalric manhood (*javānmardī*) and loyalty, guardians of virtuous manliness (*murūvat*) and justice."[27] Furthermore, Nadir Shah's invasion was brought on by the treachery of the Timurids-as-representative-of-Hindustan, and even Nadir Shah acted with nobility and friendship.[28] These representations are a stark contrast to Hazin's general disapproval of Nadir Shah as a brutal, base usurper, because in this context (and context is everything), Nadir represented the realm of Iran. Hazin's rhetorical exertions can be partly attributed to the general perception that a dynasty that failed to hold its throne had suffered from the moral weakness of unjust rulership.[29] Yet Hazin attempts to shift the source of moral deficiency from the Safavids to the Timurids and so justifies the brutal sack of Delhi by Nadir Shah, now ruler of Iran, in whose aftermath he writes.

An intense nostalgia for an Iran now maimed and disfigured, to which Hazin can no longer return, and a profound expression of estrangement from his surroundings are context for the polarization of Hindustan and Iran. Representations of Iran's glory and perfection are a product of its loss, and demonstrations of the present, including Hindustan, are set in opposition to this perfect past. This context informs statements equating the end of his life with his arrival in Hindustan. Hazin renders himself according to the figure of the stranger, defined by the moral high ground of suffering in a time when learned men, ethical friendships, and any form of comfort are impossible in a place so temporally and geographically removed from home. While certainly a product of the immense losses and hardships he suffered, not least the death and dispersal of his entire family and social world, his language of ethics, moral states, and noble manners demonstrated in the faithful fulfillment of oaths and obligations—or their lack—mirrors Iran's fate with his own.

Significantly, it is not just Hindustan that is devoid of virtue; so is the entirety of the present. Hazin continually states his rage, sorrow, and frustration at the oppression suffered by the people and the destruction wreaked upon the cities of Iran. Returning to Isfahan after the expulsion of the Afghans, he notes, "in spite of the presence of the king [Shah Tahmasp II, r. 1722–32], the city seemed extremely ruined and desolate (*kharāb*) to me and hardly anyone remained of all those people and friends."[30] He then goes to Shiraz, where he finds the situation much the same. Because of the sad state of his deceased friends' families and the hardships of the people, he finds it difficult to remain there.[31]

Finding a similar situation in Lar, Hazin comments, "the laws and regulations have fallen to pieces and there was need for a king possessing power and ability" to tend to the condition of each town and village and restore the country (*mulk*) to a sound state. Yet Hazin notes, "in this short time [since the expulsion of the Afghans] none of this had happened," and he comments, "in all the places on the face of the earth there is no ruler that has the virtue (*salāhiyat*) of rulership," except for "some of the rulers of the kingdoms of Europe (*farang*), who are constant (*ustuvār*) in their laws, ways of livelihood and administration of their affairs."[32] In the spirit of indirect criticism (Nadir Shah was still alive at the time of writing), Hazin has excluded not only the Shah of Hindustan but also the current ruler of Iran, Nadir Shah, from the category of virtuous rulers. These descriptions need to be kept in mind when considering his denigration of Hindustan, which relies on a contrast not with a contemporary Iran but with the eulogized, perfect Iran of yesterday. Here, temporality, the catastrophic severing of the past from the present, creates the moral distinctions that inhere in place.

By the end of Hazin's memoir, which concludes with the death of Shah Tahmasp II (1740) at the hands of Nadir Shah's son, a number of well-known states coalesce around the poles of past and present. The present is Hindustan, where he is estranged in exile (*ghurbat*), as opposed to being at home. Exile is characterized by loneliness (*tanhā'ī*) because he is a stranger (*bīgānih*), as opposed to home, where one has the intimacy of friends.[33] Frequent illnesses, a physical manifestation of estrangement, begin with the Afghan invasion and grow more acute after Hazin's migration to Hindustan, when geospatial loss compounds temporal loss of home.[34] This solitude is not literal, but instead indicates the absence of ethical society. Hazin states that since his arrival in Hindustan, "the difficult sorrow of loneliness and forlornness (*bī kasī*)" has been the constant companion (*musāhib*) of his time. The lengthy visits of various worldly people (*ansāf-i khalq-i rūzgār*) leave him drained in body and soul (*tan va jān gudākhtih*).[35] As an ethical choice, solitude is preferable to social entanglements with those unworthy of friendship. For Hazin, these are people without moral integrity, caught up in worldly wealth and position.

Perpetual loneliness and poor physical health reflect the threat of the land's own disasters (such as floods), painting a picture of discord. These details draw on well-known ideas relating the humorial theory of health to a justly ruled realm, which shared a notion of individual and collective bodies in harmony with their environment. The elements of a land, like its air and water, could affect the humors of a porous body. Both individual and collective bodies needed the help of a physician (or ruler) to keep them balanced and thus healthy, especially in a challenging environment.[36] Hazin calls into question the possibility of balance in such an environment, but lack of proper governance to counteract the effect of the land has precluded the possibility of ethical behavior in both Iran and Hindustan. In this lament of the present, the possibility of proper self-governance remains, however, and Hazin claims an ethical imperative to seek solitude, free of social bonds, as conduct proper to this discordant time and place.

Adab is central here. Through it, we can see that origin as either land or lineage was not destiny. The moral opposition between people in Iran and Hindustan was mutable, as the decline of Babur's house shows. Though air and water carried the characteristics of land to people's bodies, ethical comportment, not origin, was a necessary manifestation of moral substance that preserved individuals from a land's base qualities. Indeed, Hazin's invectives target those from Iran who came to Hindustan and dispensed with the virtuous suffering of the stranger.

> That person who has a place of residence (*maqām-i iqāmatī*) like the domains (*mamālik*) of Iran, which, delightful in essence and noble in presentation, are the most beneficent and perfect habitation in the known world, can never choose to reside in Hindustan. The disposition [of such a person] is formed by nature such that other than from the condition of necessity, they would never consent to stay in this land (*sar zamīn*). This understanding (*ma'nī*) is shared by kings, commoners, and soldiers. Such is the condition of all those of sound faculties, who have been reared in a different air and climate, especially in the domains of Iran or Rūm [Ottoman domains], unless they have come ignorant and uninformed to this region and do not have the power of return. Or, if, on account of difficulties and accidents, they no longer have the opportunity of residing in a place [in another region] and have passed the preceding days with complete difficulty and wretchedness, arrive at the contemptible (*bī i'tibār*) wealth and

position [of Hindustan] and, being of extremely weak sensibility (*iḥsās*) and base manner (*siflih nihād*), become attached (*dil bi-ān bandad*) to that [wealth and position] and gradually becoming accepting of customs (*ʿādat*), grow familiar and complacent (*uns va ārām*).[37]

For Hazin, no one who has lived in other places, especially in lands like Iran and Rum, could possibly choose to live in Hindustan. Some physical calamity or moral deficiency would have to force such a person to stay. Moral deficiency diminishes a person's ability to see the truth of the place and to succumb to its corruption, but even those who recognize the true state of things can bring moral degradation on themselves. The base ethics Hazin identifies with Hindustan are thus defined by behavior, which can extend to Iranis who accept positions at the Timurid court. Criticizing other Iranis in Hindustan, Hazin makes his own sufferings an expression of ethical virtue and his continuing presence in Hindustan a result of physical calamity. For him, home is not his contemporary Iran or people from Iran; rather, it is the social world of his youth, a place characterized by just government and ethical society, now gone. With it, the possibility of home is also dead.

In Arabic poetry, the state of *ghurbat*, the exilic longing and nostalgia for a homeland, is often also a longing for the past and a powerful metaphor and rhetorical means for establishing a poetic persona.[38] In Persian poetry and prose as well, such metaphors remember a lost homeland. The act of commemorating *ghurbat* creates a nostalgic idealization that depends on a present depicted without redeeming features. Such powerful metaphors matter, for understandings of both place and of self, but they cannot be taken as empirical indicators. In a later example, Mir ʿAbd al-Latif Shushtari (1759–1806), a migrant from Zand-era Iran, describes his desolation and loneliness as a stranger in Calcutta, which made socializing difficult. This state is relieved by the arrival of his paternal cousin, Mir ʿAlam, whom he describes as a brother.[39] The presence of people thus changes the experience of place. When his cousin leaves, Shushtari describes his resumed loneliness (*bī kas va tanhā*), though in the pages that follow, he admiringly describes all his prominent friends whose company he enjoyed.[40] Here, as in the case of Hazin, to take these representations of the self uncritically, as documentary evidence of a life, is problematic. Hazin also participated in the social and cultural life of Delhi and Benares, where he made both friends and enemies; taught students from Iran and Hindustan, both Hindus and Muslims; and lived more than comfortably off the financial generosity of the Timurid emperor.[41]

One danger of reading this rhetorical strategy literally as subjectivity is that the individual can far too easily be made to represent a (usually protonational) collective subjectivity. For instance, Alam and Subrahmanyam note that "[t]he account of Hazin is an important marker of the fact that some two and a half centuries into Mughal rule in northern India, many Iranian travelers or intellectuals still could not look to those lands—which had been chosen by a substantial number of their own compatriots over Iran—with any attitude other than condescension and contempt."[42] That Hazin's view is that of an unequivocal stranger, not an Iranian, is underscored by an earlier migratory relationship.

In the mid-sixteenth century, Husayn al-'Amili was one of the Shi'a scholars who migrated to Iran from what is now southern Lebanon, fleeing persecution and discrimination in an Ottoman-ruled Sunni environment.[43] Scholars such as 'Amili saw Iran—a Shi'a-ruled domain with a state policy that promoted proselytizing—as the land of patronage and opportunity. Al-'Amili could have stayed in the holy shrine cities of Iraq, where he would have faced persecution and limited opportunities.[44] He justifies leaving the holy shrine cities because he cannot pursue knowledge in Iraq as he can in Iran. This justification anticipates accusations that he migrated out of desire for worldly wealth.[45] Here is the same moral danger, and its textual articulation, the need to ethically cast an action that could be interpreted as lust for worldly wealth and position.

For Hazin, moral meaning inheres in place. His view of the ethics of land and its effect on inhabitants is extreme, but it was based on a wider perception, shared by many eighteenth-century Irani and Hindustani Persians, that Iran was central to Islamic heartlands and an originary and authoritative site of Persianate culture. But this idea was contextually specific to Persianate culture between Iran and Hindustan in the post-Safavid eighteenth century. For al-'Amili, a Shi'i Arab moving eastward in the early Safavid period, valuations of land and people were reversed. Al-'Amili's approval of Safavid sovereignty (*dawlat*) does not extend to the people of Safavid domains. They are Persians (*a'ajim*), a derogatory term in Arabic akin to barbarian, marked by their "ignorance, lack of training in the religious sciences, base character traits and questionable morals."[46] Al-'Amili goes so far as to compare Iranian judges and religious officials to dogs but notes that this comparison is unfair to dogs, who, unlike religious officials, are blameless. His censure of religious officials is particularly harsh because he holds them responsible for the locals' corrupt morals. Far from unique, this prejudice against Persians, as al-'Amili defines the kingdom of the Safavids and "other such regions," is shared by his teacher. The perception of ignorance and corruption echoes the disdain of some learned Persians from Iranian lands, Hazin among them, expressed toward Persians in Hindustan, as well as toward Shi'a and their 'ulama in Hindustan.[47] In such expressions, knowledge is a signifier of virtue that characterizes a place through its inhabitants. As with Irani Persians in Hindustan two hundred years later, al-'Amili was not immune to this corruption; he laments the detrimental effects of exile on knowledge and morals.

These echoing contrasts demonstrate that while ethical criteria were a lens of valuation, the way in which a land was given meaning was deeply contextual. For both al-'Amili and Hazin, 'ajam was a geocultural line separating the two Iraqs, despite their shared Shi'ism, according to language traditions. In the Persianate east, Hazin sought to deny Hindustan the moral certitude he gave Iran by attempting to undermine its claim to 'ajam (rather than making recourse to its lack of Shi'ism). He sought to discredit the Timurids' obvious claim to 'ajam by linking Hindustan's pre-Islamic past to its near past.[48] Significantly, behavior and precedent in the past, not sectarian persuasion, were the grounds for making moral claims.[49] Morality gained meaning (and was contested) according to an economy of circulation between inhabitants, rulers, and the disposition of the land itself.

Kashmiri: Differences in Common

By contrast, Kashmiri shores up Hindustan's inclusion in 'ajam, but draws on this same linkage between the character of the land and its rulers' ethics. This linkage was grounded in a broader Islamicate humorial conception of the human body and its relation to just rule shared across the linguistically defined border of 'arab and 'ajam. However, the specific part to which Kashmiri laid claim, 'ajam, and the particular articulation of those claims, in terms of universal Persian historical narratives, made them Persianate. In the sixteenth century Arabic context, al-'Amili calls Iran "the realm of believers" (*dawlat al-mu'minīn*), comparing his move there to the Prophet Muhammad's flight from Mecca to Medina, since he saw the Safavids as rulers of the truth faith (Shiʻism).[50] The words for realm, *saltanat* and *dawlat*, could also mean the rule of a sovereign. The semantic range of these words show how a ruler or ruling house could stand in for the character of its domain. These linkages between king and domain operated similarly in the eighteenth century Persianate. For Hazin the meaning of Iran was bound to his understanding of the Safavids, even as Kashmiri's Hindustan was tied to his representation of the Timurids.

Kashmiri also references the relationship to the Safavids in his evocation of the Timurids. As an affiliate of the Timurid imperial capital, however, Kashmiri differs from Hazin in his view of this relationship, downplaying the Safavid role in Timurid rule of Hindustan and recasting relations between the two dynasties. The *Bayan* introduces the Timurids as "the sons (*awlād*) of his majesty the Lord of the Auspicious Conjunction, the conqueror of the world, Amir Timur Gurgan" (1336–1405) to whom came "the rule (*saltanat*) of Hindustan" when "Zahir al-Din Muhammad Babur Padshah killed Sultan Ibrahim Lodi, the king of Delhi, and took possession of Hindustan" (1526).[51] This assertion foregrounds Babur as the heir to the charismatic and awe-inspiring Amir Timur, whose descendants are Persianate royalty of the highest order, reflecting centuries of efforts to redeem Timurid sovereignty after its symbolic submission to the Safavids.[52]

Kashmiri then turns to Humayun (r. 1530–40, and 1555–56), Babur's successor, who "conquered and administered Hindustan, from Badakhshan to the edge of Bengal and from Gujarat to the mountain of Kuma'un by the force of his sword."[53] In the midst of this prosperity, Humayun suffered betrayal and then military defeat at the hands of one of his lords, Shir Shah Sur Afghan, and then his own brothers. After much hardship he fled to "Iran and 'Iraq"[54] to the presence of Shah Tahmasp Safavid (r. 1524–76), and "they became brothers to each other and he [Humayun] returned [to Hindustan] with the help of the Shah."[55] Humayun fulfilled his oath to Tahmasp to take Qandahar from his hypocritical (*munāfiq*) brothers, after which he gave the Safavid army leave to return to Iran and alone wrested Kabul from his brother Kamran Mirza.[56] This victory in Kabul, where he regained the

mantle of kingship at the site of his father's seat of power, together with
the subsequent reconquest of the climes (*iqlīm*) of Hindustan, establish Humayun as king by his own might. The Safavid army helped him conquer
Qandahar, an important staging point but not as integral to his rule as Kabul.
The emphasis on Humayun's recovery of his kingdom with the help, but not
the instrumentality, of the Safavid king was critical to upholding his status
as Tahmasp's brother and equal. Such a view corresponds to Timurid narrative and pictorial commemorations of Humayun and Tahmasp as equals,
in contrast to Hazin's Safavid-centric depiction of the Timurids as derelict
vassals.[57]

The *Bayan*'s account quickly glosses over the reigns of Akbar (r. 1556–1605)
and Jahangir (r. 1605–27), setting the stage for the more significant rulers of
this line, Shahjahan (r. 1627–58) and 'Alamgir (r. 1658–1707).[58] Shahjahan is
titled "the second Lord of the Auspicious Conjunction," indicating that, like
his illustrious ancestor, Amir Timur, he was a world conqueror and a *ghāzī*
(Muslim warrior).[59] "During the just reign of that king, the equitable exercise
of government in all matters [caused] the splendor, cultivation, and prosperity of the realm of Hindustan to arrive at such a place that it became heaven
on earth (*bihisht rū-yi zamīn*) and no opposition remained in this country,"
except in remote border areas.[60] Kashmiri describes the signs of heaven on
earth as a flourishing environment (agriculture and gardens) and urban structures (mosques, baths, bazaars). Together they are physical manifestations of
harmony for all and political unity brought about by the (Muslim) Timurids'
just rule. The *Bayan* then outlines Shahjahan's specific exploits, such as his
territorial acquisitions in the east and the south, especially the kingdoms of
Bijapur and Golconda (which he calls Hyderabad) in the Deccan.

Toward the end of Shahjahan's reign (citing seventeenth-century chronicles completed in 'Alamgir's reign), the ignorance and foolishness (*nādānī
va kam 'aqlī*) of the Crown Prince Dara Shikoh, forced Awrangzib 'Alamgir
ghāzī to rise up against and vanquish his three brothers while his father still
lived and held power.[61] Kashmiri justifies this dubious act of rebelling against
one's father as necessary to rectify the Crown Prince's behavior and further
notes the "many victorious battles [won] with the aid of the lords of the land"
that followed, which "increased the splendor of the throne." Political unity
under the strong leadership of 'Alamgir led to a state of affairs positioned

as the apex of Timurid rule in Hindustan. "During the 50 years of his rule the springtime rose garden of Hindustan increasingly became the envy of all paradisiacal gardens" because

> matters of religion (*dīn*), Islam, the ordinances of divine justice (*iḥkām-i shar'*), and the traditions of the best of men [the Prophet Muhammad], blessings and peace be upon him, had accrued all the defects of erroneous practices because of Akbar Padshah's deviations at the instigation (*ighvā'ī*) of idolaters. Though this matter had been ameliorated (*ābī bi-rū-yi ān umūr āmadih*) somewhat compared to previous [times] during the time of Shah-jahan, it was in the reign of 'Alamgir *ghāzī* that as much should and could [be done was, and] the splendor of these ordinances and regard for the bounds of divine law and Islam advanced higher than the highest degree.[62]

The might to defend and expand the realm, and to keep it unified according to "correct" institutes (enacting the morality of Islamic principles in forms proper to the context) is a notion of just rule widely shared in early modern Persianate culture.[63] Contrary to modern narratives that exalt Akbar and denigrate 'Alamgir, the *Bayan* idealizes the latter's stricter adherence to what was seen as true Islam, as part of the specifically Persianate paradisiacal quality he claims for Timurid Hindustan. Here justice is presented as government and administration according to Islamic principles, legal institutes, and exemplary practices, bringing happiness and prosperity to all. At first compromised through the deviations arising from unduly influential non-Muslims, 'Alamgir corrected these deviations, thereby legitimizing Timurid rule of Hindustan. Kashmiri could thus figure those who did not submit to the Muslim rule of the Timurids as internal enemies of justice, and the low-born usurper to the Iranian throne, Nadir Shah, who sacked Delhi and humiliated its glorious dynasty, as the external enemy of justice. The universal Persianate idea of justice is thus aligned with the specifically Timurid rule of Hindustan, most perfectly manifested by 'Alamgir, in contradiction to both regional rebels and the ruler of Iran. In this narration, the disambiguation of Iran and the Persianate is total.

Though his assessment of dynastic history differs greatly from Hazin's, Kashmiri similarly finds a dearth of wise men and a lack of ethical conduct in Hindustan.[64] Kashmiri also evinces a feeling of living in a period of decline from previous, more illustrious times. His account of events in Bengal begins with the explanation that "in these days, because of the weakness of the rule (*za'f-i saltanat*)" of Muhammad Shah "and the absence of unanimity (*ittifāq*) of his lords (*umarā*) with one another" the Marathas had taken over Bengal, including Hugli, the port to which Kashmiri returns from hajj in 1743.[65] The calamities of his time were due to the mayhem that broke out among 'Alamgir's sons and grandsons after his death, abetted by the selfishly divisive acts of unethical nobles, which weakened Hindustan.[66] This theme is oft repeated in the text: the weakness of Timurid government due to factional conflicts between officials, opening the realm to depredations.[67] Its significance is underlined by the verses, "All good-fortune arises from unanimity (*ittifāq*)"/ "Misfortune arises from discord/hypocrisy (*nifāq*)."[68] This infighting leads to the betrayal of Gurgani (their dynastic name) kings, causing the noble line of Timur to be dishonored.

The narrative reaches a fevered pitch by the end of the text, so that the *Bayan*'s assessment and method of describing the state of matters in Hindustan is, in the end, not so different from Hazin's. Like Hazin, Kashmiri transfers blame from the ruler to those who failed to fulfill their reciprocal obligations. In descriptions of various seditions during the reign of Shah 'Alamgir II, Kashmiri states that the nobles have caused the rule (*saltanat*) of Hindustan to be ruined (*vīrān*) and that "the 400 year [old] honor (*nāmūs*) of the Timurid family has been lost (*bar bād raftih*)."[69] Through infighting and selfish power grabs from the rightful sovereign, the lords of the realm have allowed the ruler's honor to be violated, thus showing themselves to be thoroughly dishonorable. The moral bases of these historical narrations are not accidental. Islamicate histories, both Arabic and Persian, were read in part as examples of ethical conduct, since the lessons of history were moral.[70] What made some of these histories Persianate was their particular cast, script, and narrative meanings.

The *Bayan*'s description of Mirza Hashim Shirazi—titled 'Alavi Khan, the doctor with whom Kashmiri goes on hajj and who treats Nadir Shah during the journey from Delhi to Qazvin—provides a picture of both another kind of migrant and another type of imperial servant. 'Alavi Khan was born in Shiraz, where he received his education. In 1699, he migrated to Hindustan and received honor and position from 'Alamgir, continuing to serve subsequent Timurid emperors. In 1741, Kashmiri and 'Alavi Khan parted ways from Nadir's army in Qazvin to travel to the *'Atabat* (Shi'i shrine cities in *'Iraq-i 'arab*) and then to the Hijaz on pilgrimage. After hajj, they returned to Delhi, where 'Alavi Khan rejoined the service of Muhammad Shah as head physician (*hakīm bāshī*).[71] He appears often in the *Bayan* as one of the few whose skill and sage advice curbed Nadir Shah's cruelty and who was greatly honored by all the rulers he encountered in the course of his journeys with Kashmiri.[72] The extensive description of 'Alavi Khan as a learned, refined, ethical man, excellent in his craft and devoted in his service, contrasts with the depictions of other Timurid nobles as selfish and unethical.[73]

The figure 'Alavi Khan cuts in the *Bayan*, one among many other migrants in the *tazkirih*s of the time, reveals that Hazin was hardly iconic of migrant attitudes toward Hindustan among his Delhi contemporaries. Rather, through denigration of Hindustan and service to its rulers, Hazin sought to distinguish himself from other Iranis. The representation of 'Alavi Khan exemplifies a life worth emulating, underlining the *Bayan*'s theme of betrayal and decline. As a voluntary migrant from Iran who served both Muhammad Shah and Nadir Shah, 'Alavi Khan fell firmly outside Hazin's designation of those in possession of ethical discernment. But read against contemporaneous texts, Hazin's memoir contests the more widely accepted possibilities of finding home in Hindustan. Notably, no Timurid-affiliated Persian accounts of 'Alavi Khan found anything odd about his pilgrimage-facilitating service to Nadir Shah. To remain a loyal Timurid servant and a transregionally recognizable ethical Persian, he had no need to repudiate his origins or even shun the service of other rulers.

As men of the old imperial orders, Kashmiri and Hazin both experienced the invasion of their respective kingdoms and cities. They make many of the same evaluations: disdain for Nadir Shah, admiration for Europeans, and decline and ruin in their respective kingdoms and in surrounding lands. At times, different dynastic affiliations gave them contrasting relationships to the meaning of events. Yet a shared repository of Persian culture made possible a set of textual borrowings that expressed differing, sometimes conflicting, valuations and historical meanings. Disagreements occurred often between Persians, whether or not they originated from the same kingdom, but authors viewed these differences of opinion not as cultural divisions but as differences over meaning within a common culture.

Terms of Relations

Hazin's and Kashmiri's evocations of the long-standing relationship between the ruling houses of Iran and Hindustan were part of broader efforts to make sense of eighteenth-century presents. The fall of the Safavids was significant for the Timurids, given that Qandahar, the site of the Afghan uprising, was central to their northwest border security. In 1709, Mir Vays (d. 1715), the Ghilza'i chief, deposed the Safavid governor of Qandahar and took the city over which the Safavids and Timurids had often fought. This overthrow came in the wake of 'Alamgir's death, at a time of increasing instability in the Timurid center and growing weakness of its border administration. When Mahmud, Mir Vays's son, led the Ghilza'i Afghans across southeast Iran and successfully conquered the Safavid capital, there was some talk at the Timurid court of sending aid to Shah Tahmasp II. Instead, the resulting policy was to "establish friendly relations with Mahmud by an exchange of letters."[74]

In early 1730, the Safavid Shah Tahmasp II sent an envoy to Muhammad Shah's court with a letter announcing that Nadir Shah intended to march on Qandahar and asking the Timurids to close the border to Afghans once the march began. The letter cited the common interests of the two empires and evoked the old friendship between the dynasties. Muhammad Shah promised to comply, claiming that he had issued orders to the governors of Sindh and Kabul. In 1732, Nadir wrote on behalf of the infant Shah Abbas III and echoed the earlier letter, which received a similar response. In 1737, as he advanced against Qandahar, Nadir once again sent envoys reiterating these requests. These letters were reproduced in late eighteenth-century Timurid chronicles.[75] The last letter also claimed a Timurid obligation to pay an annuity to the Safavid throne for its assistance to Humayun almost two hundred years earlier, indicating the salience of Tahmasp and Humayun's historical encounter in the political rhetoric of the time.[76]

Over the eighteenth century, other Persians continued to commemorate this encounter as a way to give meaning to their respective presents. Writing in Iran in the 1760s, Lutf 'Ali "Azar" Baygdili included an entry on Humayun alongside a number of other Timurid and Safavid princes in his *tazkirih* of

Persian poets. There he narrates Humayun's flight to Iran and calls the aid and succor that Humayun (b. 1508) received from Tahmasp (b. 1514) "fatherly care (*navāzish-i pidarānih*)," even though Tahmasp was the younger of the two.[77] Here, as with Hazin and Kashmiri, the familial figuring of the transregionally potent relation between kings and their realms reflects claims to power and hierarchy.

By the turn of the nineteenth century, the Timurids and their historical relationship to the Safavids were commemorated with some important differences, from a present in which Iran was politically unified under the Qajars while Hindustan had fragmented into regional kingdoms. Writing in Hyderabad (1801), 'Abd al-Latif Shushtari wrote of his travels the previous decade around the eastern regions of Hindustan, past Shir Shah Sur's mausoleum in Shahsara'i (near Azimabad Patna). This account prompts a detailed commemoration of Humayun's defeat at the hands of his Afghan commander, Shir Shah Sur, and his subsequent flight to Safavid Iran. Shushtari narrates a weak and helpless Humayun in Kabul writing a supplicating letter to Shah Tahmasp seeking refuge. After a verse encapsulating the letter and its response, Shushtari regales his reader with details of the generosity and respect with which Humayun was greeted, received, and escorted all the way from Qandahar to Tahmasp's capital at Qazvin. Safavid official actions are framed as service to Tahmasp's station through the appropriate treatment of a fellow sovereign. Shushtari explicitly cites the *farmān* (royal order) Tahmasp issued in preparation for Humayun's arrival as documentary proof of his account, as "copies of that *farmān* are recorded in the books of the chroniclers of Iran and Hindustan."[78] These appropriate displays of respect toward Humayun, who was met by a welcoming party while still on the road and attended in cities by royal princes, demonstrate the manner and royal luster of Tahmasp as a "king of good morals (*nīkū akhlāq)*," whom Shushtari maintains is well known among Persians through transregional commemoration.[79]

This past is made to explain the present. Shushtari describes current Timurid rule by noting the ruined (*kharāb va vīrān*) remnants of grand Gurgani-sponsored buildings in Shahsara'i.[80] He uses the same adjectives to describe the formerly grand and prosperous capital of Shahjahanabad (Delhi). Just as Persians described Iran in the mid-eighteenth century, at the

turn of the nineteenth century, Shushtari notes that Delhi is inhabited by
"wild beasts." He does not mention the Marathas, who had control of the
city at that time. Rather, these references to Timurid domains falling to savagery and ruin after conquest and non-Muslim rule are about Europeans,
whom he claims kept ritually unclean animals in the Taj Mahal's mosque in
Akbarabad (Agra). Unlike the spectacular fall of the Safavids, Timurid rule
waned gradually, until, as Shushtari notes, an emperor named Shah ʿAlam
was on the throne in Delhi, though "but for his name, nothing remains of
him [as a shah]."[81] The weakness of Timurid rule had allowed all manner of
base acts and sociopolitical disorder to prevail, making perseverance difficult
even for men of ethical conduct. This shadow of former glory contrasts with
what immediately followed, Shushtari's detailed account of the near reunification of former Safavid domains by Aqa Khan Muhammad Qajar (1742–97),
an act Shushtari frames as restoring the glory and superiority of Iran.[82]

Shushtari's narrative of Hindustan's present echoes Hazin's, told as a paradigmatic history in relation to Iran stretching back to pre-Islamic times and
demonstrating a character that circulated from the land to its inhabitants and
rulers through its air and water. Proper conduct was vital, even if it could do
only so much in the midst of general disorder. Significantly, Shushtari situates
this narrative within a description of his family's political troubles, including
a scandal, and he wrote much of the *Tuhfat* while under house arrest. The
young woman at the center of the scandal, Khayr al-Nissa, was Shushtari's
paternal cousin, and her illicit marriage to the East India Company Resident
of Hyderabad led to the family's political downfall.[83] Using Hazin's paradigmatic formulation of the historical difference between Hindustan and Iran,
Shushtari identifies himself with the ethics imparted by knowledge of Iran
and attributes his migration to Hindustan to his ignorance of its character. In
Persianate terms he thus shifts blame for the family scandal onto Hindustan,
as a place where proper form can no longer prevail.[84]

Though kingdoms and their respective dynasties could at times play a
significant role in commemoration, these dynastic terms and its scale of place
were embedded among other elements that defy a nationalist story. The past
told the present with smaller and larger scales of places as well. Even at the
turn of the nineteenth century, the *Tuhfat*'s story of home focused on the

city and immediate surroundings of Shushtar, not on the kingdom of Iran. Furthermore, moral meanings manifested in recognizable forms, in word and deed and in cultivation with people and the environment, were the most significant terms of meaning. It is to these other forms of place-making and their definitive effects on the relative meaning and relations of place that we now turn.

CHAPTER 3

Place-Making and Proximity

PREMODERN CONCEPTIONS of place made lands familiar without sole reliance on "objective" proximity. Sacred sites could be linked, and the clime system yoked lands together under a rubric of geographic coherence. Most important, commemorative representations of place, disseminated throughout the Persianate world by wondrous stories and features, bestowed a sense of proximity or distance. Descriptions of physical features and social structures, often read as generic, formulaic, and unreliable (in a positivist sense), conveyed moral characteristics that manifested indelible meanings of places. Universal Persianate knowledge included a range of place-making features connecting past and present. Among these were the storied traditions of the Persianate past discussed in Chapter 1 and the more immediate past evoked in Chapter 2. To this kaleidoscope, the current chapter adds ornaments of place in representational stories, images, and descriptive accounts that we might call topographic and ethnographic, or else mythical and fantastic.

Places were commonly represented through two types of features. The first drew on notions of *madaniyat* or *tamaddun*, which meant something akin to sociopolitical order and proper urbane conduct. This type could include descriptions of rulers or learned men and idealized relations between them. The second drew on the built environment (*ma'mūr*) or its "built-ness" (*'imārat*), which included gardens.[1] Both types of representation worked together. Learned men animated the built environment, itself an indicator of order and just rule. Ideally, a Persianate place would have all the crucial ornaments.

In addition to (and sometimes as part of) Persianate universal histories, generically described features such as rulers, wonders, evidence of knowledge (signaling virtue), and built environment (articulating just rule) could make places legible and therefore familiar to Persianate audiences. These place-making practices are crucial to understanding the way in which particular places—cities, kingdoms, and smaller and larger domains—fit together in the Persianate. Ornaments of place also appear in narratives of lands beyond the Persianate (but still in the Islamic world) and in certain places beyond the Islamic and Persian-speaking world.[2] Differences conveyed by these features thus created an aporetic gradient, not a firm line, of familiarity.[3]

Making Proximity

When authors of commemorative texts represented places, they incorporated local texts and accounts into more universal narratives. These representations of place could then circulate, and their local images become integrated into universal Persianate knowledge. Persians thus came to know and gain a sense of proximity to other Persianate locales to which they might never travel. This circulation and integration evinces a technique whereby the generic was used to bring the particular into the ambit of the familiar. In this way, the Deccan was rendered familiar by the end of the High Persianate period. Two transregionally circulated texts—*Haft Iqlim* by Amin ibn Ahmad Razi (d. 1619) and Zuhuri Turshizi's *Saqinama*—produced the Deccan for Persianate audiences.

Haft Iqlim was a widely cited work that scholars more often read for its biographical entries than its narrative mapping of the world.[4] The text maps Persian poetry and prose, but poetry is not found in all the world's places. Nor are poets its only subjects. The text is divided into the seven climes, listing major places according to their great men, who include scholars, mystics, nobles, and kings. The outer climes have no great men (that register as such), and *Haft Iqlim* describes these regions only geographically, thereby distinguishing this text from the primary concern of *tazkirih*s as biographical commemorations. Razi variously introduces the known world, sometimes through descriptions of wonders that made a place strange, sometimes through men of learning that made a place familiar, and sometimes through the strangeness of such wonders that created familiarity.

Haft Iqlim presents a hierarchical world, but its hierarchical distinctions are not absolute. Razi lauds the third and fourth climes above all others and places the land of Iran (*mamlakat-i Īrānzāmīn*) in this central zone.[5] Most, but not all, cities of Iran lie in these climes, but the same climes include cities of other regions. In his description of the third clime, Razi calls the domains of the two Iraqs the heart of Iran and gives pride of place to *Iraq-i 'arab*, the half defined by its primarily Arabic-speaking population.[6] Similarly, Khurasan receives pride of place in the fourth clime, which "induces the increasing jealousy of paradise (*ghayrat afzā-yi jannat ast*)." The fourth clime's superiority stems from its form and substance, listed in pairs, literally as form (*sūrat*) and virtue (*afzal*). This beautiful, refined disposition (*husn-i khulq va lutf-i tab'*) is "manifested in various virtues and skills (*mazhar-i ansāf-i fazl va hunar*)," making this domain "the habitation of the nobility (*ashraf*) of the sons of Adam."[7] Some manifestations of these ideals, however, appear in other places and connect the most virtuous lands in the center with surrounding climes, which do not map neatly onto regions or kingdoms.

At the frontier of the Persianate world, the Deccan lies in the second clime. The Deccan takes shape as a site of forts and gardens, both characterized as vast and towering. Razi tells us that the Deccan is a place where "all needs can be easily met from within its domain (*mamlakat*)" and that "its air opens the bud of the heart's hope." The verse that follows extols the paradisiacal garden-esque nature of its water and air (meaning land and climate), before moving on to its hundreds (360, to be precise) of impenetrable, skyscraping forts.[8] This vision of firm, deft construction described in wondrous terms also characterizes descriptions of Ahmadnagar, though in the context of topoi specific to the city. Razi begins,

> Of all the cities of the Deccan, it [Ahmadnagar] is exceptional on account of [its] water and air, and the particularities of its hills and plains. On the outskirts of the city there are several continuously flowing subterranean canals (*qanāt*), which have not been produced in India until now. One

among the gardens within those pleasing (*dil-nishīn*) borders is the garden
of Farah Bakhsh, which is incomparable.[9]

Famous gardens, especially the Farah Bakhsh garden, an iconic feature
of Ahmadnagar, imprint the Deccan with the image of paradise. Razi makes
the Farah Bakhsh garden analogous to the Garden of Iram, the legendary
earthly garden as beautiful as heaven, with a pond containing a wondrous
structure defying engineering knowledge: "In grace and light [it is] heaven, in
elegance and beauty [it is] Iram / In grandeur and power [it is] the heavens,
in length and breadth [it is] the earth."[10] Immediately following this verse
is a description of an impenetrable fort on one side of the city, which "kings
have given up all hope of taking … and the hand of calamity has fallen short
of its skirt."[11] For a Persianate audience, this repeated attention to strength,
skill, and dimensions of the built environment signified a settled, prosperous
kingdom under idealized rule. Indeed, the term that later came to be used
for civilization, *madaniyat*, is largely absent.[12] What we often see is the term
ma'mūr, or built, evoking the grandeur or eminence of rulers through detailed
descriptions of buildings and gardens, their open-air counterparts.[13]

In poetry, ornaments also conveyed meaning about place. *Sāqīnāma*s
(songs of the cup bearer) painted vivid images of urban topographies and
were a popular poetic genre through the seventeenth and eighteenth centuries.[14] The most transregionally celebrated of these was by "Zuhuri" Turshizi
(d. 1619 AD/1025 AH), a migrant from Khurasan to Ahmadnagar and
then to Bijapur.[15] Commemorations linked the figure of Zuhuri indelibly
to the Deccan. The north-Indian-based Fakhr al-Zamani Qazvini wrote in
the early seventeenth-century *Tazkirih-yi Maykhanih* that Zuhuri "achieved
fame in the Deccan, and that he was the contemporary of Malik Qummi,"
adding, "between Malik and Zuhuri there was perfect love and concord, and
a great deal of sincerity and trust."[16]

These two friends are almost always mentioned in the same breath. They
were linked by Zuhuri's marriage to Malik's daughter, and they moved together from Ahmadnagar to Bijapur. Most importantly, they collaborated
on a number of literary projects at the 'Adil Shahi court. This relationship
is almost always part of Zuhuri's story in the Deccan; the idealized form

of Persianate friendship (evoked by the terms of love, intimacy, and trust—
muhabbat, ittihād, ikhlās, and *i'tiqād*) that he enjoyed with Malik connects
the context's specificity to the universality of aestheticized ethics in life and
literature. The perfect union with the beloved friend speaks of an elevated
moral state, manifested in their eloquent verse and prose, a generic sequence
enacted on the specific stage of the Deccan, bestowing upon it the highest
ornament of place.

Zuhuri's *Saqinama* contains vignettes of courtly life and settings, after
which the audience is taken on a tour of the public spaces of the city, called
"the new city (*shahr-i naw*)." Between the garden and the bazaar, the predominance of verdant images depicts Ahmadnagar as an urban place of flourishing
prosperity.[17] This lush imagery of a thriving city conveys virtuous rulership
that has successfully maintained harmony and order.[18] Sharma has noted
several important features of Zuhuri's poem, such as its heavy reliance on garden imagery and cityscapes, which together with its dedication to Burhan
Nizamshah II (r. 1591–95) identify the city.[19] The poem conveys the images
most often associated with Ahmadnagar—elegant structures, thriving marketplaces, and beautiful, impressive gardens—but in generic language.[20] This
ambiguity between the specific and the generic allowed places that shared
the universal features of Persianate cities (with certain features emphasized in
reference to a locality) to be inducted into Persianate geocultural space.

Through such generic features, poets could draw equivalences as they
likened different places or even exchanged one for another. Zuhuri himself
uses lines from his *Saqinama* that describe gardens in Ahmadnagar to praise
the gardens of the Bijapuri city of Nauraspur.[21] The late seventeenth-century
Safavid *munshi* Muhammad Rabi' similarly uses verses from Zuhuri's *Saqinama* to describe the gardenlike land of Aceh in the *Safinih-yi Sulaymani,*
a travel text written to explain a disastrous Safavid diplomatic mission to
Thailand.[22] In his *tazkirih* (c. 1672) Tahir Nasrabadi narrates Salim Tehrani
writing a *masnavī* about Lahijan (in Gilan) and then renaming it for Kashmir after going to Hindustan.[23] Both author and *tazkirih* writer casually
acknowledge that one lush, verdant place can be described as another.

These generic features have caused such poems to be dismissed by historians looking for verisimilitude and finding poetic conventions.[24] But these
are not pertinent terms by which to understand the labor such descriptions

performed. Rather, the extension of generic descriptions to new places was a practice of inclusion, whereby similarity was extended to a place and this description then circulated across a larger Persianate map. Through similar, highly mobile representations, poetic verses could render places coterminous. Images of Kashmir (as in the *Saqinama* of Fani Kashmiri [d. 1670–71 AD/1081 AH]), were often recited, excerpted, memorized, and anthologized, and they circulated far beyond *dīvān*s or *tazkirih*s.[25] Homologies with other places, as in the case of Kashmir with Mazandaran or Badakhshan, could also be made and circulated.[26] These and other ornaments were among the ways in which Persianate places were connected to one other and to the world beyond.

Association with Islam need not ornament place. Amin Razi describes Chin's (China's) idolatry but then discusses its well-known excellence in painting, a reference to the Alexander legends articulated in Nizami Ganjavi's *Iskandarnama*, in which Alexander debates and competes with renowned Chinese painters. Next is mention of the false prophet Mani, who managed to seduce even the Chinese with his beautiful pictures.[27] Chin is not under Muslim rule, nor does it possess any great men of Persianate learning, but Amin Razi is able to make it familiar through reference to tales of storied figures from the Persianate past. They have a king, he explains, as well as political practices such as royal audiences open once a year to both high and low. To be sure, these are strange ceremonies involving axes and wood, but they nevertheless are recognizable as kingship practices.[28]

Descriptions of China use wonders, amazing stories, and information about places that read to us like facts. But these modes of knowing the world are distinct from the positivistic claims of Orientalism. Rather, this Persianate practice draws from a textual tradition whose authority derives partly from reiteration and its own widespread textual travel (such as the second volume of the late Ilkhanid *Jami' al-Tavarikh* about the Yuan dynasty). Its iterative authority accommodates the accounts of a geographical text such as the thirteenth-century Hamdullah Mustavvafi's *Nuzhat al-Qulub*, with its wondrous, legendary, and attested stories.[29] For Persians, all these tales— from the wondrous to the historical—are testaments that require selective representation and homage because, in their own ways, they are all part of the truth, which in the end, only God knows perfectly.

Persianate modes of inclusion could sometimes be extended to places beyond the familiar geocultural grid. Such extension had little to do with actual proximity in a modern geographic sense and more to do with recognized features of place that acted as means of legibility and affinity. In this beyond, places could still be partially connected to a central Persianate world through the storied Persianate past, through wondrous features that associated them with Islam, or through features of the built environment or other signs of human construction that bestowed a place with system, order, and some modicum of good rulership, however strange and different. Without these ornaments, places were only legible as unfamiliar. Regardless, Persians evinced a shared hermeneutics of legibility across a number of texts.[30] These practices of place-making continued through the eighteenth century, beyond the formal collapse and unraveling of empires.

By the opening decades of the nineteenth century, perceptions of a ruined Iran had receded, and celebrations of Qajar rule over reunified former Safavid domains were still narrated according to the conventions of Persianate place. The centrality of city as homeland persisted even in a text written from Hindustan by an author commemorating a newly unified Iran under Fath 'Ali Shah Qajar (1797–1834).[31] Mirza 'Ali Maftun was born in Delhi and later moved to Azimabad (Patna). In November 1825, he undertook hajj, traveling to the Hijaz by way of Calcutta and the Indian Ocean. After performing hajj, he arrived in the port of Bushihr in November 1826, traveling through Shiraz, Isfahan, and Tehran on his way to the tomb of the eighth Shi'a Imam in Mashhad, and from there he returned overland to Hindustan. The minutiae about each stage of the journey (*manzil*), such as the state of the roads, caravanserais, nearby villages, and available food and water in marketplaces, suggest that he wrote the text as a practical manual for future pilgrims and travelers. As a travel and specifically of Shi'a pilgrimage text, the rhetorical labor of Maftun's narrative can be read as a forum where he displays his learning and virtue for his audience at home, confirmed by the luminaries of the Hijaz and Iran.

In the context in which Iran was a kingdom ruled by a strong Shi'a monarch, and the erstwhile Hindustan of the Timurids was a fragmented realm increasingly under the heel of the British, Maftun's travel text differs from its eighteenth-century predecessors. Previous travelers to Iran from Hindustan,

like Kashmiri, could proudly boast of the accomplishments of Timurid monarchs in turning Hindustan into a paradisiacal land prospering because of
just Islamic government and able administration. In contrast, Maftun's descriptions of rulers and their accomplishments in Iran, evident in cities and
across the land, hint at a comparison with such places as British-ruled Bihar
and Bengal. Written after Maftun had returned to Patna, the text does not
seem to have circulated beyond its locale.

For Maftun, even the tumultuous decades of late-eighteenth-century
Iran become linked to more stable times of security and good governance
under Karim Khan Zand. As Maftun notes, Karim Khan was known as *Vakīl*
(deputy or regent) because "he sincerely believed that he was not worthy
of taking the throne. Inspired by great belief in the Lord of the Age [the
Hidden Imam] he considered himself a deputy (*vakīl*) . . . entrusted with
the custody and guardianship of Shia populace and lords."[32] This image of
a properly functioning Shi'a realm extended to the Qajars. In the section on
Tehran, where he outlines the ongoing events of the second Perso-Russian
war, Maftun reports that in 1826, Sayyid Muhammad Tabataba'i, the foremost *mujtahid* of the Iraqi shrine cities, forced Fath 'Ali Shah to declare war
on the basis of reports of Muslim persecution under the Russians. Tabataba'i
issued a fatwa tarring as a *kāfir* (unbeliever) anyone who failed to do their
utmost against Russian dominion over the Shi'a subjects of former Iranian
domains. Maftun approvingly describes Tabataba'i's concern and initially
gentle attempts to convince the Shah, finally going so far as to travel from
Karbala to Tehran to rally support.[33] It is not that Maftun disapproves of
Fath 'Ali Shah, on whom he lavishes praise and titles such as "the second
Lord of the Auspicious Conjunction" and "celebrated amongst the Persians
(*jashn-i 'ajam*)."[34] For Maftun, the clergy is rightfully protecting the people
and obliging the Shah to do the same. This concept of the proper relationship between 'ulama and ruler is not specific to place of origin, but the ability
to realize this ideal relationship is specific to Iran in Maftun's time.

Maftun describes both the structures common to every Muslim urban
center and those that define Iran within the Persianate world, and he provides
painstaking details of the designs and inscriptions of *imāmzādihs* (shrine
tombs of the children of the Imams), together with poets and eminent political figures.[35] He carefully identifies a structure's location, builder, history, and

features. Previous travel texts certainly mention significant urban structures, but not in such minute, realistic detail, down to the type of stone, its color, and any inscriptions. In fact, Maftun maps every major city through which he travels, from end to end, beginning with each gate. He charts the city's major thoroughfares and sectors, offering three-dimensional detail of the structures he pinpoints and so presenting a new kind of imaginative map.

Maftun's detailed architectural descriptions convey meanings of place, in ways both familiar and new. Art historians have noted that textual and pictorial representations of architecture in Timurid manuscripts were a way to lend character to a place and commemorate the achievements of rulers.[36] Later paintings produced across the northern subcontinent presented architectural monuments as the sole subjects in more technical and clearly articulated detail, reminiscent of architectural plans drawn for functional purposes.[37] These new types of paintings, inserted in Timurid manuscripts recommissioned in the late eighteenth and early nineteenth centuries, emphasized architecture as an integral sign of certain rulers' achievements.[38] Maftun's descriptions of architecture and its ruler-patrons as central to the city's history echo this connection. After mapping the gates of Shiraz, Maftun notes that "in the direction of the western gate there are grand structures, exalted palaces without blemish, and gardens pleasing to the heart and without compare and the like, which are the constructions of Muhammad Karim Khan Zand, known as *Vakīl*, who at one time was the ruler (*farmānfarmā'ī*) of the domains of Iran."[39] He then goes on to detail these constructions at length. For instance, after pages of prose and poetic descriptions of Karim Khan's mosque and baths in Shiraz, Maftun continues,

> To the east of the mosque is the market square (*chār sū*) of the *Vakīl*, which without exaggeration has no equal in all the provinces of the seven climes. It is approximately just over 1500 paces length wise, and the same in width. In the center is a perfectly laid out, well-cut octagonal fountain/pool (*hawz*). In all four directions are sturdily built shops, possessing high, full ceilings, singular in height and width, and each property is in such an appointed condition which is not to be found elsewhere.

He goes on to identify which areas of the market square contain which wares.[40] These descriptions go on for over twenty pages in Shiraz, Isfahan,

Tehran, and Mashhad, cities presented as sites of power, prestige, and proper devotion.

Shiraz had been the seat of Karim Khan's rule. Contemplation of that rule included a careful cataloging of his architectural achievements, together with Maftun's wholehearted approval. Maftun describes Karim Khan as "protective of peasants, attending to the comforts of soldiers, the spreader of justice, a guide for manliness/virtue (*murūvat*), lord of the sword, politically astute." As if to underscore these qualities, Maftun notes that "his mind inclined greatly to building." What follows is a detailed description of these structures mapped onto the city of Shiraz.[41] Such connections between rulers and their structures are not limited to Karim Khan, as Maftun limns Isfahan with structures built by the Safavids, Tehran as built by Fath 'Ali Shah, and Mashhad as built by centuries of rulers, particularly the Afshars. Architectural structures mapped onto urban space as a sign of political order are the means by which Maftun narrates the city as a place, as an accumulation of its history.

In texts by and for Irani audiences, architectural patronage as a manifestation of the history of governance was also a means to articulate the character of a place. Azar Baygdili challenges the legitimacy of Ottoman rule over *'Iraq-i 'arab*, not formally part of Safavid domains since Shah Abbas' reign, including it in the larger region of Iran (as Amin Razi did). Azar notes that Baghdad was founded in the year 763 AD/146 AH, close to a garden built at the time of the Persian kings, near the palace of Ctesiphon. The seat of the Abbasid Caliphate is thus mapped onto a site defined by the power of pre-Islamic Persian kings. The next mention of architectural contribution is by the Ilkhanids (not the 'Abbasids) and then by Shah Abbas Safavid, "who built new fortifications around the city after conquering it."[42] This last patron serves to undergird the region's link to Iran by noting the role of its kings in the very physical structure of the city.

Making Connections

Generic ornaments and universal narratives, within which specificities could be embedded, connected Persianate places through criteria that had little to do with empirical geography. Lines of separation did distinguish linked places from each other, but even then, separation was not absolute, as other means (such as the clime system) provided connection. But not all forms of connection held the same importance or created the same degree of connection.

For example, though distinct from Iran geographically, Turan was nevertheless part of the Persianate world through its shared pre-Islamic Persian history (see Chapter 1) and its ornaments of place. *Mavara' al-nahr*, the land beyond the Oxus river, was one of Turan's three regions (along with Balkh and Khvarazm). In the *Atashkadih*, Azar, firmly located in *Iraq-i 'ajam*, describes Farghana as the farthest region of *Mavara' al-nahr*, "at the corner of the civilized world (*dar kinār-i ma'mūrih-yi 'ālam*)."[43] Elsewhere, Azar mentions other lands, such as Europe (*farangistān*), China (*khitā*), and Syria (*shām*), demonstrating that the term *ma'mūr* refers not to the known world but to the built civilization of the Persianate world. This Persianate specificity includes the possibility of civilization in other places, such as the Hijaz, which possesses the sacralized history of Islamic refinement. But though the holiest site of Islam, for Azar it does not possess the refinement of a long tradition of Persianate poetic culture, with its center in Iran, a history particularly significant at a time when Azar was self-conscious of a less exalted eighteenth century present.

Chapter 1 discussed the *Atashkadih*'s negative description of the larger domain of Hindustan. There, I also argued that smaller domains and cities were the crucial building blocks of these larger domains. Unlike the difference drawn between Hindustan and the domains of Iran and Turan, however, the *Atashkadih* celebrates both the people and the smaller places of Hindustan. These more positive portrayals read in tandem with the negative description exemplify the aporia of meaning in forms of Persianate place-making. Here connections at one level can exist simultaneously with separations at another. Ultimately, given the centrality of smaller domains and cities, these linkages were far more significant for creating a sense of proximity.

The example of Kashmir is instructive. Azar's description of the place is unequivocally glowing and so disrupts arguments that the *Atashkadih* glorifies the land of Iran in contrast to Timurid domains:

> From the abundance of gardens, trees, the multitude of rivers and streams, the whole city is a portion of the verdancy of heaven (*tamām-i shahr*

qit'ih'ī ast az marghzār-i jannat).[44] They say that its soil imparts great joy (*farahnāk*) and its air elicits delight (*'ishrat angīz*). During the reign of Sultan Sikandar the religion of Islam came to prevail. The weaving of shawls is the specialty of that region that they take to all parts of the world. That region yields a great deal of saffron.[45]

The physical character of the land is vaunted as heavenly, with the very earth and climate inducing joy and delight. This description reiterates Timurid representations of Kashmir. In the following section on Kashmir's poets, Azar refers to Binish as "from that paradisiacal region (*diyār-i khuld āsār*)."[46] Calling a land paradisiacal could be a form of demonstrating affiliation, a way of declaring home, but here it echoes an evocation of Kashmir as paradise-like, a claim that was part of the project of Timurid imperial possession of this province.[47] Azar had no affiliation with the Timurids or Hindustan, but this Timurid-specific image of Kashmir had been inducted into universal Persianate knowledge of places. By contrast, 'Abd al-Karim Kashmiri sings Kashmir's praises as a paradise-resembling place (*jannat nazīr*)[48] and describes Hindustan similarly (*bihisht rū-yi zamīn*).[49]

For someone like Kashmiri whose affiliation is clearly with Kashmir and Timurid-ruled Hindustan more broadly, the specificity of Kashmir's paradise-like qualities can exist in other places. Such similitude was part of a broader universal idiom of Persianate imperial power that marked certain places through homology. One such parallel, between Kashmir and Mazandaran, allows us to ponder what "the center" might have been in an early modern Persianate context, when Safavids and Timurids simultaneously claimed millennial sovereignty.[50] Some migrants from Iran in Hindustan certainly claimed authority over those with lineages of learning more local to the subcontinent. Transregional lineages, however, also belonged to the locally born, and posturing for authority points to the contestable and enacted nature of such claims.

'Abd al-Karim was born in Kashmir, and he identifies the region as his homeland (*vatan*), appending the usual modifying descriptors of allegiance celebrating its paradise-like qualities—*jannat nazīr, bihisht nishān,* and so on.[51] He sifts through local knowledge, sometimes incorporating it and sometimes rejecting it according to more transregionally recognized knowledge about Mazandaran. He begins by stating,

It has been heard from credible people that in the past, because of the great
number of trees and abundant undergrowth, the way to Mazandaran [from
Astarabad] was extremely inaccessible and oppressive (*sa'b va zabūn*) and
travelers had complete difficulty coming and going. Because the Safavid dynasty, especially Shah Abbas, was nobly filled with a desire to regularly visit
Mazandaran (*shawq-i sayr-i Mazandaran pīshnihād-i khatir-i 'ātir būd*), [they]
therefore uprooted the trees along the way and built twelve halting stations on
a road made of stone and plaster (*sang va gach*). At every halting station they
built a structure so that it would not be necessary for a tent, because of the fact
that rainfall becomes quite heavy there, as is the case in Bengal.[52]

This is local knowledge: the previous state of the passage between Astarabad
and Mazandaran, the changes wrought by the erstwhile Safavids, and information about the climate, which he likens for his audience to Bengal, a
region many of his immediate readers in Delhi would not have visited but
would know as a place of heavy rainfall.

This local knowledge is articulated in a way familiar to his Hindustani
audience. Kashmiri transfers the script according to which the Timurids had
asserted their authority over a territory to explain the Safavid's relationship to
their own paradisiacal land.[53] He marks Mazandaran's similarity with Kashmir
by noting that, just as the emperors Jahangir and Shahjahan would often go
with their entourages to Kashmir, likewise Shah Abbas I would go to Mazandaran "with some of his intimates and attendants for feasting and enjoyment."[54]
The two places are framed not just as sites of similar beauty but also as paradise-
like destinations for the contemporaneous kings of two Persianate dynasties,
both of whom held them in special regard as places to pass certain seasons.
This is universal knowledge: a host of people who had never been near Kashmir, including Persians writing in Iran, referred to it as a paradise-like place
of temperate weather and heavenly gardens. That a Timurid functionary could
recognize and articulate this kind of imperial place-making among Safavids also
speaks to shared political practices that were transregionally legible.

Describing Mazandaran's cultivated places (literally *ma'mūrih-hā, or*
"built environments"), Kashmiri waxes lyrical about Ashraf, a site of Shah
Abbas's gardens, "where at night the song of crashing waves and the uproar
of the sea are heard and are the accustomed sound for the inhabitants."[55]

However noteworthy Ashraf may be, Kashmiri nevertheless relates that the locals (*mardum-i ān mulk*) refer to the Caspian as Qulzum and that this was wrong (*ghalat*), citing textual sources in support of his authority. He says,

> Qulzum is in the environs of Mt. Sinai, and His excellence Musa Kalimullah (PBUH) was on the shores of the Qulzum Sea. Qulzum is connected to the Surrounding Sea (*daryā-yi muhīt*) [the ocean thought to encircle the earth]. This sea of Mazandaran, which the books of predecessors/ancestors (*salaf*) call Absukūn or Abgūn and is written as the Khazar Sea, is not connected to the Surrounding Ocean when the seven seas are taken into account. Moreover, all four sides are surrounded by dry, flourishing land.[56]

Kashmiri's Persian education, and its shared traditions of knowledge, acquired however far away, corrects local knowledge. Qulzum was one of the names used in Arabic for the Red Sea, and it was disseminated more broadly in famous geographical, travel, and nautical texts as the name of this body of water, along with other names that constituted universal knowledge.[57] Alexis Wick notes, "this toponomic multiplicity and polysemy should not come as a surprise, as it was a common feature of geographical knowledge until recently," but that

> this makes a significant difference ... in the political-ideological field ... from the central imperial perspective, these maritime areas were viewed through the intercession of local intermediaries. Their definition and classification were produced, not as a limpid representation inscribed into abstract space from the desk of an imperial bureaucrat in Istanbul [he speaks of the Ottoman Empire], but rather as connected to and dependent on another locus of knowledge and authority ... this is emphatically *not* a matter of greater or lesser empirical correctness.[58]

While Kashmiri charges local usage with error, he claims no empirical "truth," where one meaning cancels another according to a categorical distinction of mutual exclusivity. Following a commemorative tradition of including multiple historical narratives of relative verifiability about the past and its meaning, he still includes this local knowledge as part of what Mazandaran is, in addition to the more universally recognized ("correct") information he provides alongside it.[59] Both types of knowledge are worthy of commemoration.

Kashmiri's view of Mazandaran's people is also quite sympathetic. After listing the foods that they eat, including their wondrously sweet bread, he claims that

> the people of Iran tell strange tales with regard to the inhabitants of Mazandaran ... about their simple-ness (*sādagī*). More likely they [the strange tales] are [in spite of the Mazandaranis'] elegantly adorned characters and in truth have no basis, or else because, since they call Mazandaran paradise-like (*bihisht nishan*) it will be for this very reason, that the people of heaven are simpletons (*bulh*). It is an amazing coincidence (*turfih ittifāqī*) that in Hindustan they write Kashmir as *jannat nazīr* and in Iran Mazandaran as *bihisht nishān* and that the people of both domains because of these paradise-like-nesses (*dar haqq-i īn bihishtī-hā*) subject the poor [Kashmiris and Mazandaranis] to much abuse (*sarzanish*).[60]

Kashmir and Mazandaran are not the same, but their domains are synonymously paradise-like, as *bihisht* and *jannat*. Accordingly, the relationship of their inhabitants to the rest of their respective empires is homologous, as is their domains' significance for their imperial rulers.

Sympathy is not a determinant of Orientalism, as Said has shown with respect to Louis Massignon's love of his subject matter.[61] Significant here is not Kashmiri's sympathy toward his subject but the parallel he draws between his Kashmiri homeland and the envied, abused people of Mazandaran. The parallel articulates an intimate similitude based on geographical and political homology, for all that the Mazandaranis lack proper geographical knowledge. His privileging of universal knowledge inscribes hierarchical valuation. But including local knowledge alongside and within a framework of homology avoids Orientalism's production of alterity that made what was conflictual threatening. Significantly, Kashmiri's universalizing amendments to local knowledge were enacted by a Hindustani Persian writing about a Safavid locality, thereby disrupting anachronistic associations of Iran as the authoritative center of Persianate ways of knowing. In the midst of this correction, our universal Persian is simultaneously also a Hindi speaker and a local Kashmiri empathizing with Mazandaranis' plight in Iran. Kashmiri treats Timurid Hindustan as his Persianate center, and his audience is clearly Timurid Hindustan. For instance, he provides the names of local flora and fauna in Iran and then their local "Hindi" equivalents.[62] But this implied reader also has a locality, which he addresses by translating Iran's local knowledge into an imperial Hindustani vernacular (Kashmir as paradisiacal). Both scales of local knowledge—the smaller domain and the imperial realm—lie easily alongside transregional universal Persianate knowledge.

According to Persianate geoculture, certain places, like Kashmir, were understood as paradisiacal regardless of whether an author had been there or the place was within a domain to which that author was affiliated. Writing seventy years after Kashmiri, Maftun also used the same image of Kashmir's beauty to familiarize his readers with the highlands of Fars. When extolling the natural beauty of Shiraz and its environs, Maftun comments that "its green plains and verdant city are the cause of shame and the hyacinth and narcissus filled hills are the envy of the agreeable hills of Kashmir."[63] Maftun was born in Delhi and a resident of Patna. Nothing in his biography, little known as it is, indicates that he traveled to Kashmir, nor did he have reason to assume his readers would have seen the region. Rather, Maftun and his readers were familiar with the commemorated image of Kashmir as a paradisiacal land. The extension of similar generic descriptions to other places created linkages, and these descriptions then circulated across a larger map of imagined Persianate places. Unlike 'Abd al-Karim Kashmiri, writing in the mid-eighteenth century, who links the beauty of Kashmir with Mazandaran in a much more equitable way, Maftun in the early nineteenth century extols the beauty of the Shirazi countryside above Kashmir, perhaps reflecting a more favorable ethical perception of Iran relative to the Hindustan of his time.

In the early nineteenth century, Abu Talib Khan translated Persianate geocultural knowledge into British terms while maintaining practices of imbuing place with meaning through history. Describing his seaborne arrival to Istanbul, he wrote, "It must be known that this Marmūrih [Marmara] sea is the divider between the land of *farang* and *'ajam*, which the English call *'Yurup'* and *'Āsiyā'*. To the west and north of this sea's mouth is a connection (*ta'alluq*) to *farang*. To the east and south are the *'grīk'* cities."[64] Here, "Greek cities" are both within the Ottoman Empire and outside Europe, lying to the southeast of the border, along the coast of Anatolia. Only lands northwest of the mouth of the Marmara Sea connect to Europe.

Immediately following this description, Abu Talib provides an account of the famous figures involved in the ongoing conflict over this border between Europe/*farang* and Asia/*'ajam*. He begins with Alexander and Lohrasb, the military deputy (satrap) of Ruham ibn Gudarz, and continues with accounts of the Roman Caesars and the Ashkanians and Sassanians up through the advent of Islam. By way of metacontext Abu Talib notes, "the explanation of these events is not thoroughly recorded in Muslim books due to the [general] loss of [historical knowledge of] events (*fiqdān-i vaqāyi'*) before Islam, so much so that Firdawsi says: I have heard nothing about the Ashkanians/nor have I seen anything in the Book of Khusravān."[65] Significantly, even with the influx of European knowledge, Firdowsi's *Shahnama* is still cited as a historical source.[66] Given this paucity of knowledge, not of pre-Islamic history but of the conflict between the Romans and the Ashkanians and then the Sassanians, Firdowsi has particularly little to say about the former. By contrast, "the books of the Greeks written two thousand years ago, which have been translated into English and which I have seen, record in detail the wars and transactions between the Caesars and the Persian kings (*salatīn-i 'ajam*)."[67] Here the historical relationship between Persian rulers and Greek, then Roman rulers imbues the geographical division between *farang* and *'ajam*. A border thus gains meaning as a line of conflict between adjacent imperial domains. To limn a geocultural landscape through history, Abu Talib draws on the other side's more thorough accounts. In the process, he figures the English as translators and possessors of the old Greek histories and their heirs in *farang*/Europe.

In contrast with the far past's separations, these lands were connected in the near past through political rule. "Because of the Ottoman sultan's rule (*hukmrānī*) over these two lands (*bar īn du zamīn*), meaning 'Yurup' and 'Āsiyā,' and these two seas (*bar īn du bahr*), meaning the Ūnān (Aegean) Sea and the Aswad (Black) Sea, he is called '*sultān al-barīn*' (*King* of the two shores/high king) and '*khāqān al-bahrayn*' (*Lord* of the two seas/generous lord)."[68] Europe and *'ajam*/Asia are geographically separate, and at the same time united as part of the Ottoman domain. The connection is aporetic; the same term—dominion—that separated domains also offers unity at the scale of political domain. Separation and connection simultaneously exist as part of the same story.[69] Layers of history can thus lie alongside each other without

the modern need for reconciliation, creating the potential for aporetic meaning of places. It was not an aporia embraced by the European side.[70]

Alternative Geographies

Like historical narratives, varieties of place-making coexisted, ultimately constituting place in palimpsestic layers. Empirical geography as we know it lay
alongside other forms of geographical knowledge, including the clime system
and its humorial understanding of the relationship between land, climate, and
people. As we have seen, alternative modes of geographical knowledge, crucial
to the meanings of place, undermined modern empirical geography's singularity and fixity. Azar describes Lahore as "a famous city of Hindustan. Even
though it is in an area with a warm climate they say that in the summer snow
and ice come to hand and it has good fruits. Its people are shrewd (*zīrak*)."[71]
Lahore was seen as part of Hindustan, yet related to neighboring lands. For
instance, Abhishek Kaicker notes that in a mid-seventeenth century text authored by a Hindustani Persian Qadiri disciple, Lahore was "visualized as a
sort of inland port connecting India to the lands of Īrān and Tūrān."[72] In addition, Lahore's past was part of the Ghaznavid Empire (along with Khurasan
and parts of Turan), in contrast with other great cities or domains of Hindustan. Its sense of proximity to Khurasani and Turani lands stemmed not
only from circulations inaugurated by past rulership, but also from continuing
flows of people engaged in trade, devotion, learning, flight, and patronage,
enabled in no small part by shared Persianate forms.

Geography gained meaning according to climes, where regions accrued
character in a symbiotic relationship between the inhabitants, rule, land, and
climate. The work of humors facilitated these relationships. Together, climes
and humors

> provided medieval Muslims with a way of dividing the world into civilized
> and uncivilized zones. An excess of either heat or cold was thought to cor-
> rupt a person's humors, and this had a number of corollary, and unfavor-
> able, effects on appearance, behavior, habits and ability to think rationally;
> while conversely, temperate regions were thought to have a beneficial influ-
> ence on a person's appearance and faculties.[73]

Climate worked on the humors of inhabitants' bodies to affect both form (appearance) and substance (faculties). Yet the ornaments of place, according to which Persians attributed civilization and which could be found outside their own lands and climes, were the product of learning as much as potential realized (or squandered). Even in the medieval Arabic context, the possible moral benefits of city dwelling outweighed strict notions of humoral theory, in which rural life was best for the human body.[74]

Even at a broader geographical level, things were more complicated and differentiated. Aside from differences in attributing civilization to places within the same clime, hierarchy existed within the central climes, though not in the way we might imagine, as we saw in the case of Kashmir. For the purposes of geographical schemata, Persianate regions are intertwined within the clime system, without correspondence between climes and larger regions. The middle of the seven climes, the fourth and the most temperate, extends from Iran to regions of Turan and Hindustan, such as Balkh and Kashmir.[75] Some of the smaller, constituent domains of Turan are partly in the colder fifth clime, along with parts of Iran.[76] Smaller portions of larger domains could thus lie in different climes, alongside domains of other larger regions. For instance, the warmer third clime contains many cities of Iran, such as parts of Khurasan, 'Iraq-i 'arab, Fars, and parts of 'Iraq-i 'ajam, along with cities such as Delhi.[77] Azar describes Fars as having been "the seat of most of Pīshdādī and Kiyān kings [from pre-Islamic Persian dynasties]. They say that Persepolis (*Istakhr*) is the first of cities of Iran to have been built in the inhabited world (*rub'-i maskūn*)."[78] Despite its venerable age and pre-Islamic Persianate history, this integral part of Iran is in the third clime, along with important cities of Hindustan. Clime-based geography is thus another way in which differences between domains and their larger regions are overlaid with connection and similarity. The land of Iran lies across multiple climes, connected with portions of other lands. While in the *Atashkadih* Iran is made central and vaunted above other regions, these alternative schemas of place problematize reading this hierarchy according to categorical distinctions of modern nationalism. Sometimes historically linked, sometimes geographically similar, such partial connections challenge narratives of radical difference or unique singularity of definitive historical homelands or self-evident units of study.

The land's depiction, what this meant about the moral constitution of the inhabitants (and vice versa), and how meaning was assigned to a place indicate a humorial understanding of connections among land, people, and polity. Much as the body was understood to be porous in relation to a land, so too was a society in relation to its rulership.[79] As we have seen, political rule—that is, justice or its lack—and the ethical conduct of its inhabitants, from king to beggar, characterized a kingdom. For Hazin, the imperial city of Isfahan, now ruined, with its illustrious families dispersed, "is still the best of the inhabited places of the world," despite the fall of the Safavids and the subsequent oppressive rulers.[80] Isfahan still had "so many learned/virtuous and able/worthy men (*afāzil va mustaʿiddān*) that a full account of their names would take too long to finish. Truly, such a collection [of learned and worthy men] in a large city cannot be found in the cultivated places of the world (*maʿmūrih-yi ʿālam*)."[81]

Hazin admits that Isfahan is not as great as it could be but notes that other ornaments of place, like learned men, the product of earlier Safavid rule, remain. He claims that if the fires of oppression were diminished only briefly, Isfahan could regain its glory.[82] The power of place, constituted by its bygone and recent social and political ordering (what we would call its history), lives in a symbiotic relationship with the character of its inhabitants. People can be transformed through learning or the guidance of the learned. For Hazin, Shiʿi Islam informs this hierarchical valuation, but it is written in the language of Persianate *adab*, without explicit qualifications. Virtuous men of learning can exist in the cities of Iran, though they are not Shiʿi or even Muslim.

This potential for inclusion is borne out in the text. Of all the worthy, learned men (*afāzil va mustaʿiddān*) in Yazd, the one man Hazin describes at length is a Zoroastrian (*majūsī*) named Rustam, an astrologer-astronomer (*munajjim*). After outlining his breadth of knowledge, Hazin tells us he has spent considerable time with Rustam and so links social familiarity with Rustam's admirable qualities, such as learning and ethical behavior.[83] Even for Hazin, preoccupied with recouping a Shiʿa, Safavid-ruled Iran, this land's qualities can extend to its non-Shiʿa and non-Muslim men of learning, who evidence shared admirable characteristics. In the absence of just rule, Hazin emphasizes the link between a virtuous land and virtuous people.

Because land and climate give character to the inhabitants of a region, character was mutable with mobility or with the arrival of ornaments. Azar notes that the shoemaker poet Aqa ʿAbdullah "Shaʿif" was "from Qum but he had an extremely pleasant disposition," a statement that points to common views of the disposition of Qumis.[84] Their essence, however, could be altered. The poet "Dami" was the son of a Hamadani, "but he himself was born in Isfahan and the temperate water and air of that paradisiacal region nourished the sapling of his body/form (*qāmat*), he knows himself as an Isfahani."[85] Circulating features of the land, such as water and air, could interact with a person's body and transform his nature. Though less mutable than people, land also gained character from its inhabitants, especially its rulers, under whose stewardship the sociopolitical order took shape. By the eighteenth century, Iran had been under the Safavids for over two centuries, and, as we've seen, their rule provided character to the realm's inhabitants. This imperial character was layered in with other sorts, such as those deriving from the regions and cities with which people also simultaneously associated. In contexts pertaining to kingdoms rather than the more usual smaller places, this character floated to the top. Significantly, however, the meaning that place gave selves and groups was never singular, as we see in the next chapter.

By the early nineteenth century, with former Safavid domains newly restored by the Qajars, guarding the virtue of home in the absence of just rule was no longer at stake, as it was for Hazin. Persians were aware of increasingly fragmented Hindustan. Yet the same understanding of place, its moral valences, and relations to people animated these new concerns. Aqa Ahmad Bihbahani was a juris-consult (*mujtahid*) who traveled Hindustan from 1805 to 1810 in search of position and patronage. For Bihbahani, ethical behavior and collective harmony could bestow characteristics to place. He notes, "unlike the residents of the island of Mumbai, where everyone is a blood-thirsty enemy (*dushman-i khūnkhvār*) and seeks to ruin each other's business," all of the merchants from Iran in Masulipatnam "appeared in unanimity (*muttāfiq*) with each other." Because of the "beauty of unity and morals (*husn-i ittifāq va akhlāq*) [of the merchants of Masulipatnam] that port has come to resemble (*nimūnih-yi*) Iran."[86] Here it is not the presence of Iranis alone but their ongoing enactment of morality through *adab* that gives a place moral meaning. Unlike Hazin, Bihbahani seeks an Iran that can exist in Hindustan. Yet Hazin's invectives against the Iranis in Hindustan who had degraded themselves by adapting to local customs rest on the same hermeneutical ground.

PART II

Origin

"Did we not agree to speak here of the language called
maternal, about birth as it relates to soil, birth as it
relates to blood, and birth as it relates to language,
which means something entirely other? And about the
relationship between birth, language, culture, nationality
and citizenship?"[1]

LET US BE MODERN for a moment, for comparison. Jacques Derrida
questions language as a natural possession. He uses his own "Franco-
Maghrebian" origin and its relation to the French language.[2] He asserts, "I
have only one language; it is not mine."[3] This articulation of origin vexes
dominant scripts aligning language to a (national) cultural identity that tells
a necessarily singular truth about itself. A preoccupation with cultural truths
inhering in and expressing intertwined "modes of belonging"—culture, nationality, and citizenship—is fundamentally modern.[4] But the title of Derrida's work prompts us to ask whether origin was always prosthesis. How was
origin understood before modern discourses welded soil, blood, language,
and culture according to a strict binary of a Mono-logical self and Other(s)?[5]
Can we conceive of origin as something more gradient than a prosthesis, an
artificial appendage opposed to a natural possession?

Origin has come to mean place, but it is a cipher for much more. For the
Persianate, origin was valuable but unintelligible according to the logic of
modernity. Place appears in the narration of origin but functions differently,
inflecting the lineages that constitute Persianate origin. A person's origin encompassed inherited status, trajectory, station, and relative position, yet not

every element present at birth was memorable, evoked, or narrated. Much had
to be accrued, earned even. Origin was a story, a presentation, whose shape was
guided by Persianate *adab*. It answered the question "Who are you?" and provided meaning for the answer to "Where did you come from before you arrived
here?" Origin was a shifting truth, not a self-evident "natural" fact. Answers
depended on changing spatial and temporal moments of articulation. To translate Persianate origin requires that we move past modern, mutually exclusive
binaries of natural and artificial. We must reconsider origin aporetically.

In response to colonial narratives, which split hairs creating categories to
determine who was native or foreign, postcolonial scholarship on India has
concerned itself with making Muslims native.[6] Seeking something unique to
India, which transregional cultural complexes associated with Muslim rule
could not provide, anticolonial nationalists accepted these categories. Thus
what was Indian, or "Indic" as it is now called in scholarship, became what
was proper to the subcontinent, such as Sanskrit and its associated traditions (Hindu, Buddhist, and Jain).[7] According to this nativist logic, Hindu
is something "Indic" because it originated in the place we now call India and
symbiotically defined it, embedding racialist notions of descent in a territory.[8]
In these mutually exclusionist regimes of origin, place, and selfhood, Muslims
are foreign, having arrived from elsewhere, often violently, and Persians are
essentially and naturally Iranian.[9] The nativist binary operates so pervasively
that scholars contesting the attribution of Persian as a communally Muslim
language must make the uneasy admixture called Indo-Persian, a "secular"
language, to allow for both non-Muslim Persian adepts and the seemingly
unreligious uses to which it was put.[10] The more multicultural narrative has
India "absorbing" these foreign groups and domesticating their culture, resulting in hybrid Islamicate culture (Indo-Islamic).[11] Such hyphenated, hybrid
notions, however, apply modern epistemologies and occlude the historical
logics with which people have thought of themselves.

Scholarship has answered some of these problems by relying on notions
of "ethnicity," in which "common descent" shares biological presumptions
with modern notions of race.[12] In his classic work on early eighteenth-
century history, Chandra notes that opportunities for political patronage in
the *jāgīr* system declined at the end of the seventeenth century. With these
positions increasingly inherited, the central government's ability to provide

patronage to migrants from Iran and Turan decreased dramatically. "One benefit of this was the closer identification with or absorption of the existing Iranis and Turanis into the Indian social order."[13] Chandra labels the different factions at the Timurid court "ethnic and regional groups," though Iranis clearly fit under the former (as non-Indian ethnicities), while the latter refers to groups such as Rajputs (ethnically Indian but differentiated by regional affiliation). He observes that "mixed contingents" were the norm among nobles, dominated by "Mughals", a word "loosely used to denote those who had recently come to the country from Iran and Turan."[14] Here these migrants possessed a different ethnic identity, which set them apart from native Indians.[15] Yet Chandra protests the "doubtful validity" of modern scholarship, which follows colonial historical narratives by lumping Mughals with foreigners, in contrast with indigenous Indians. He justifies this challenge by asserting that "once they joined the emperor's service, they made India their home, and hardly kept any contact with the land of their birth."[16] In other words, extended stay and severed links with birthplaces produced a simulacrum, however uneasy, of the natural(ized) Indian (proto) citizen.

Chandra's critique, however, retains the epistemology of native-foreigner and thus reinforces its logic. Its premise is that origin is singular and dependent on homeland, so much so that homeland ties were mutually exclusive and assuming one required relinquishing another. Applying such modern binaries as native-foreign has also resulted in narratives of miscegenation that render categories of people, such as Mughals, foreign "adventurers" or, in the case of their sons, tainted by foreign origin, which may (or may not) be mitigated by their birth in the subcontinent.[17] But, as we saw in Chapter 1, homelands were small places, towns, or cities. Furthermore, they could be successively accrued and were not always synonymous with birthplace. Homelands were but one element of origin and not always dominant.

Something called ethnicity is even more problematic. The term often connotes tension between mutable cultural features and immutable notions of descent, which might be vested in land. In many studies, ethnic identity is considered far more enduring and fundamental to nation building. Origin stories are made to embody ethnic identity.[18] Scholars of different times and places, such as ancient Greece, use ethnicity as an "objectivistic" category, even as they show that a group's history is contingent or socially constructed.[19]

Origin becomes related to "common ancestry"[20] so that our notion of "natural" is reified in the genealogy of origin, since "sharing an ancestor implies biological links, if not the modern idea of race itself."[21] Even self-consciously critical work distinguishes ethnicity from other social collectivities as "putative subscription to a myth of common descent and kinship, an association with a specific territory and a sense of shared history."[22] In this identification of Greek genealogies as "mythical" or "fictive" is a particular notion of "real" descent. Anidjar has argued that this understanding of kinship, rooted in a blood-based biology specific to a Western European Christian past, has now universalized itself as modern.[23] This definition of ethnicity simply does not work in earlier Persianate contexts. As the following three chapters show, people from different homelands subscribed to overlapping lineages of origin and could thus be understood as related to one another.

Furthermore, modern notions of kinship were not the organizing principle of descent. Origin was narrated as a multiplicity of lineages, envisioned as chains as well as trees, connecting people in different forms of kinship. Lineages could include kin we now define as biological but were then defined according to birth, wombs, and the legal relationships that created patrilineal descent (*nasab*). Origin was thus significantly different from a discourse of shared blood. Lineage exceeded legally recognized relationships, and the shared language of kinship made other relationships part of genealogical descent. *Adab*, the proper form according to which relations between people became intelligible, gave meaning to both relationships regulated by law and those governed by social expectations alone. It governed how origins were conceived and narrated, situated people (in positions they had to assume according to its proper form) and related them to one another. To understand the meaning of origin and its constitutive lineages, we must dispense with a supposedly objective, biological explanation or a sole reliance on legal relationships and view kinship through the lens of *adab*.

Explanations of assimilation based on ethnicity, like Chandra's, narrow the interpretive possibilities for understanding how centuries of migrants came to the subcontinent and quickly became integral to South Asian politics, society, and culture. Notions of ethnicity reduce such mobility to a celebration of Indian multicultural magnanimity.[24] But, I argue, a set of ideals circulated within the Persianate world as resources that could then be articulated in particular regions and political regimes. Articulations were mutually intelligible across regions, so that individuals moving from Safavid to Timurid domains were newcomers but nonetheless possessed familiarity with the ideas they encountered. Lineages were not only transregionally intelligible but shared, since ancestry included mobile fathers, teachers, masters, patrons, and other kin.[25]

As a category of persons, Mughals embodied the aporetic status of transregionally mobile Persians, simultaneously strangers to the particular and intimates of the universal.[26] They could be either migrants or their descendants born in the subcontinent, often for several generations. The category Mughal was specific to the subcontinent because such people existed nowhere else.[27] To become Mughals, migrants from Iran and Turan had to come to Timurid-ruled domains of Hindustan and stay. According to a similar logic, travelers from Safavid domains became Iranis only after leaving the kingdom, though in other places, they were often defined according to more important distinctions. They were called 'ajam when distinguished from non-Persian speakers, or Qizilbash, first to distinguish the military forces of the ruler of Iran (versus another political kingdom) and later to distinguish Shi'a Persians from former Safavid domains from other Persian speakers. Qizilbash, like Mughal, was a particular term for Persians, who could also be called by the universal term Fārsī gūyān," as those defined by their knowledge of Persian.[28] Mughals participated in intellectual efforts to synthesize Sanskrit traditions, activities that those from Safavid domains had also undertaken in Iran, following a tradition outlined under the Ilkhanids.[29]

Persianate universalism was not specific to Hindustan. This assessment does not preclude the search for regional specificities, merely demands that it be undertaken from a ground more justified than modern (proto-nationalist) assumptions. Asking how eighteenth-century Persians understood origin and named affiliation and difference is a starting point, both for setting aside these assumptions and for thinking about what was shared transregionally. These commonalities are thus the basis for a reconsideration of regional specificities. They allow for reconceptualizing the link between origin and belonging, and, perhaps, reappraising reified boundaries that produce hybridity.[30]

The following chapters explore the adab of telling a person's origins. They explain how origins are articulated and signified, and how their narratives are sedimented in names. The shifting truth of origins provided the meaning of people's present, both in self and biographical representations. Articulations of origins, captured in moments of commemoration, were perspectival, varying over time and social location and governed by a common lexicon and principles of meaning. Origin as *asl* was the portion inherited. My definition of origin, however, goes further. It includes the place from which a person came before arriving here (at the time of writing) and what the story of that before meant. Origins were multiple, and their organizing principle, contingent on commemorative concerns, was produced through negotiations with *adab*. The attributes of origin included not only characteristics present at birth, including legacies of various ancestors, but also those acquired throughout life, which could be transmitted to descendants. Furthermore, lineages often crossed the line from something we would call biological to something mythical or fictive. Before the triumph of modern positivism, lineages were proudly presented in their entirety, with little indication of where such a line might be for their audiences. Distinctions existed, but they were not the same as ours. Some things were true and some false, but in a world where certainty belonged to God alone, most things were, to varying degrees, likely and thus mentioned together.[31]

Persianate lineages were understood according to various formal relationships across a spectrum of kinship inherited, acquired, accrued, and transmitted. Some relationships were designated in law, while some depended on social regulation alone. All could create kinship. All were formally encompassed by the social ethics of *adab*, linking family, teachers, patrons, and other intimates in similar ways. Fathers and teachers could be equally important aspects of origin, reflecting an inclusivity obscured by overemphasis on biological relation or legal definition. Critical work on milk kinship is instructive here. Commenting on recent arguments that the model of fluid exchange governing milk kinship was the same as the presumed blood descent of *nasab*, Parkes inverts biological determination of legal structure and social belief. He argues that laws regulating marriage according to birth, marriage, and milk relations (*nasab*, *musahara*, and *rida'a*) "actually appear to be consistent deductions from a set of explicitly stipulated axioms, which ultimately concern moral proprieties of appropriate conduct among equivalent (natal and adoptive) jural kin."[32]

Lineages thus connected people through both legally defined forms of kinship and those that depended on social recognition alone. The latter were usually based on the transmission of knowledge (to students) and/or fulfillment of services (for patrons or clients). The language and practices that suspended or granted privileges and obligations of legal kin also marked relationships of service, tutelage, patronage, discipleship, and learning. This spectrum of kinship provided various genealogies, whose meaning was in the composition of their accumulation. Androcentric descent could locate a person within the family or household of a prominent person or in a larger social collectivity. It could signal more distant but no less significant descent, such as from the Prophet Muhammad, a prominent Shaykh, or various dynastic lineages.[33] Geoculturally significant lineages were not limited to Muslims; Persianate history could provide others with genealogical prestige.[34] Aside from legally regulated relationships, the transmission of knowledge—poetic, esoteric, mathematical, rhetorical, administrative, legal, or medical—or the exchange of services—protection, military service, revenue collection, labor, or skill sets (from crafts to poetry) created lineages. On the basis of relations that gained form from the ethics of *adab*, they mitigated the limits of parentage (*nasab*). Not mutually exclusive, various kinds of lineages might intertwine, as when students married the daughters of their teachers.

The multiplicity I emphasize destabilizes the role of mono-logical origin in determining affiliations. Different places of origin were distinctive but not the sole organizing principle of who a person was and what that meant. Belonging to the same place did not preclude a sense of commonality among people based on other shared attributes. When foregrounded in commemoration, places marked an itinerary ultimately legible within the story of a person's substance, social station, or occupational position. Origins of place were a list constituted by birthplaces, ancestral or adopted homelands, sites of pilgrimage, or catalogs of migration in pursuit of study, trade, service, or rule. Places were the descriptors of broader genealogies, far more determinative of origins and the possibilities of affiliations.

CHAPTER 4

Lineages and Their Places

REPRESENTATIONS OF ORIGIN framed the narration of a person's life in a variety of commemorative texts. They told the truths of a person, and in these truths lay the potential for affiliations that gave contour to various collectives. This chapter explores the significance of place in representations of origins. It argues that individual selves and collectives were given meaning through origins, articulated as a wide range of lineages, including those of place. Although place was part of origin, it did not by itself structure origin's meaning. Even in lineages of place, a person's birthplace and subsequent homes constituted a list, along with other types of places, such as ancestral homelands, site of study, destinations marking passages, or locations of professional or devotional apogee.

First, let me anticipate a question: What do the narrative representations of commemoration have to do with lived experience? Language is not merely the articulation of something that exists independently, something "real." Such a formulation "presupposes a potential adequation between the 'I' that confronts its world, including its language, as an object, and the 'I' that finds itself as an object in that world. But the subject/object dichotomy, which here belongs to the tradition of Western epistemology, conditions the very problematic of identity that it seeks to solve."[1] The assumption is that what we do is real, whereas what we write is not, significant on a page but disconnected from reality. Yet we understand our actions in a particular manner and our ability to access that understanding depends on the *adab* (proper form) of its telling. We must suspend hard distinctions between action and narration. What is articulated on the page tells us much about experience and about the stakes of engaging with the world.

Adab gave intelligibility to Persianate being through its modes of speech, comportment, and distinctions. *Adab* as a manner of narrative was no less integral. The Persianate was a space where words were real, where they were reiterated and circulated, giving truth to lives by manifesting and signifying those lives.[2] Attention to the relation between language and life must attend to "the enabling conditions for the assertion of 'I'" that are "provided by the structure of signification, the rules that regulate the legitimate and illegitimate invocation of that pronoun, the practices that establish the terms of intelligibility by which that pronoun can circulate. Language is not an *exterior medium or instrument* into which I pour a self and from which I glean a reflection of that self."[3] Language and the experience of self are aporetic. To understand the possibilities of social being, we turn to this process of accrual and sedimentation and its variations in representation.

Learning and service were among the important lineages that commemorated origin. In the preface to the *tazkirih Gul-i Ra'na* (1768–69 AD/1182 AH), its author refers to himself (in the third person) as "this slave, Lachmi Nara'in, pennamed Shafiq, Aurangabadi, who from the beginning of eternity (*rūz-i azal*) has his excellency Azad Bilgrami's brand of bondage (*dāgh-i ghulāmī*) on his forehead."[4] Writing in Aurangabad, he identifies himself as Aurangabadi, which, when uttered in that place, seems to indicate an immutable and autonomously native identification. Yet Shafiq is speaking to an audience broader than his own locale. He calls himself Aurangabadi, speaking to Persians from elsewhere or in another locale. In anticipation of the text's travels, he introduces himself with a proper name (*ism*), a pen name (*takhallus*), and a place moniker (*nisbat*), before distinguishing himself as literally marked by his teacher.[5] Sayyid Ghulam 'Ali Azad Bilgrami was the noted poet, scholar (of Persian and Arabic), and participant of the prominent Nakhshbandi center (*takiyyih*) of Aurangabad.[6] Shafiq's relationship with his teacher is a lineage of knowledge, part of his origin.

Later, in his biography, before any mention of his own birth, he narrates this story:

Shafiq pennamed, Lachmi Nara'in Mathur, the author of these pages, is
of the Kathri Kapur people (*qawm*). His grandfather, Bhavani Das, accompanied 'Alamgir's camp from Lahore to the Deccan. He laid the colors
of settlement in Aurangabad and entered into the relationship of service
(*sīghih-yi nawkarī*). He achieved great honor [in this work] and came to be
possessed of children. His middle son, Ra'i Nisa Ram, who is father of the
author, was ten years old when Bhavani Das gathered his things for his last
journey [died]. The father [Ra'i Nisa Ram] was educated in the shadow of
Lala Jasvant Ra'i's affection, [a man] who was both a grandfather (*jaddī*)
and qualified in science and learning (*'ilm va fazl*). In the time of Navvab
Asaf Jah, he [Ra'i Nisa Ram] was appointed to deputyship of the administration (*pīshkārī-yi sidārat*) of the 6 districts (*sūbih*) of the Deccan and until
the time of writing he continues in this work, for what is now forty years.
The deceased Navvab Samsam al-Dawlih Bahadur Aurangabadi, who was
unmatched in his day in sociability and beneficence (*ādam-shināsī va fayz-
risānī*), in the days of his deputyship, granted him [Ra'i Nisa Ram] a *man-
sab* [rank] at the request of his excellence Azad Bilgrami. Favored with the
deputyship of the paymastership (*bakhshī al-mamālik*) of the Deccan, he
incorporated service to the dervishes (*fuqarā*) with service to the nobles
(*umarā*). He always observed the manner of conferring the kindness of fa-
vors, and my father accomplished both forms of dignified service according
to all the necessary customs (*ā'īn*).[7]

Shafiq's origins are in terms of what we would call his *jātī* (not a term he
uses) and paternal ancestry, alongside and intertwined with lineages of teachers and patrons. His origins and their names, Khatri Kapuri (and its subcaste
designation, Mathur), Lahori and Aurangabadi, imperial and paternal, come
together to make him a Hindu, a Timurid administrator, and a Persian man
of letters. Prominent in this story is his father's mastery of the *adab* (as ethics)
appropriate to his social location in imperial administrative service, a product of many other relationships. Ra'i Nisa Ram's perfect enactment of the
expected customs of conduct toward all kinds of people—from the masters
of the hidden world (dervishes) to those of the manifest world (nobles)—indicate the basis of Shafiq's own learned potential as a master of *adab*. Shafiq's
account of his origins is typical in its primary emphasis on genealogies and

in the specifics of his occupation. In the midst of these origins, place appears but does not alone constitute origin. Rather, place was almost always bound up in other kinds of lineages and almost never singularly given.

Locating the Self in Lineages

Commemorative texts began with the *hamd*, or praises to God, the Prophet, and whomever else the author's proclivities exalted. The author then introduced himself.[8] As the *hamd* situated the author in a broader community, this introduction located the author in paternal genealogies, a list of men generally linked to one or more places, emphasizing certain ancestors and places that underscored the author's rhetorical labor as preformed in the text. The language of lineage was a powerful means of expression. Not only did biographical and autobiographical representation, which always began with origin, pervade commemorative texts, but lineages narratively conveyed interpretation.

Recall another administrative man of letters, Khvajih 'Abd al-Karim Kashmiri (d. 1784), author of *Bayan-i Vaqi'*, discussed in earlier chapters. In accordance with his approbation of Timurid Persianate universalism, he praises God, the Prophet, his descendants, and his companions.[9] Next he identifies his homeland as "fixed (*tavattun*) within the borders of paradisiacal Kashmir," which he had to leave just as Adam was forced out of paradise. Then he names himself "'Abd al-Karim son of Khvajih 'Aqibat Mahmud son of Khvajih Muhammad Balaqi son of Khvajih Muhammad Riza."[10] This list of forefathers articulates a sense of order whose perversion is manifest in the tyrannical and uncouth behavior of Nadir Afshar as ruler of Iran and Hindustan. This overarching theme of the *Bayan* becomes more prominent in the first section after the *hamd*, which contains reasons for writing, and the author's self-introduction, called "mention of the character and lineage (*hasab va nasab*) of Nadir Quli Bayg Afshar, and his attainment of the position of iron-fisted (*jabbār*) kings." Assuring the reader that he reports only information given by "credible people who are his companions of old" Kashmiri tells us that Nadir "is the son of Imam Quli Bayg of the indigent men (*sā'ir al-nās*) of the town of Abivard who lived his days in states of need and privation."[11] Nadir could not name any ancestors beyond his father, and his lack of lineage articulated his lowly origins. Nadir's general baseness, the disaster of his rise to power for Iran, and his subsequent invasion of Hindustan resulted from such a man attaining an unbefitting position over the nobly descended Safavids and especially the Timurids. Here lack of lineage explains his uncultivated brutishness. It indexes his station, a manifestation of the truth of his character. Amid these rhetorical labors, the specificity of his place of origin is but a detail.

The calamities stemming from Nadir's lack of lineage do not end there. Kashmiri notes that Nadir's two sons with the daughter of the Abivard Afshari chief (Baba 'Ali Bayg) each married the daughter of a Shah.[12] The first, Riza Quli, married the daughter of Shah Sultan Husayn Safavid, "the ruler (*vali*) of the dominions of Iran." The second, Nasrullah, even more inappropriately married the daughter of Muhammad Shah, from "the family of the Lord of the Auspicious Conjunction, meaning Amir Timur Gurgani."[13] These reminders of status underline the inappropriate marriages between the exalted lineages of Iran and Hindustan and the sons of a base-born father. Gender is relevant in this kind of kin-making—accepting a daughter in marriage was a great honor for the daughter's family. The woman cemented a bond; she was a gift that acknowledged the social superiority of the recipient and whose acceptance acknowledged a protective alliance.[14] Narrating that Safavid and Timurid daughters were given to Nadir's sons under terms of political prostration was a powerful way for Kashmiri to cast a dubious light on Nadir's rapid rise to power and dazzling military victories. For an audience that would have known of the slaughter of Timurid troops, the bloodletting of Delhi's inhabitants, and the plundering of its wealth, the narrative depicted Nadir as an ignoble tyrant. The lack of names to make any kind of lineage provides Kashmiri with the resources to put forth this interpretation, and to attribute causality for current political disasters to a perverted social order.

Kashmiri's lineage overshadows Nadir's. The subtext here is that even a modest functionary (*mutasaddi*) is descended from three generations of learned men, in contrast with the man who usurped the throne of Iran and took Timurid daughters into his house. Given that Kashmiri attained his father's station, as evidenced by their identical titles (*khvajih*), a lineage of learning shadows his paternal lineage. Fathers were likely also teachers. Kashmiri's self-representation within the thematic context of the *Bayan* is as a Kashmiri in Delhi, a man educated in the administrative arts and in

Timurid service, which distinguish and locate him within a community of *adab* that excludes Nadir Shah, but not others from Iranian lands.

When places were prominent, they formed an itinerary that accrued to lineage. Another kind of learned man, Shaykh Muhammad 'Ali Hazin Lahiji (1692–1766), establishes his origin with a venerable list of sixteen ancestors woven through a geographical landscape, intermeshing the temporal movement of genealogy with the spatial movement of itinerary. Chapter 2 showed the centrality of Safavid Iran for Hazin's self-representation. Hazin's genealogy requires veneration of the dynasty; the Safavids traced their lineage of learning and discipleship to Hazin's paternal ancestor. The progenitor of his illustrious patrilineage is Shaykh Zahid Gilani, the esoteric guide of Shaykh Safi al-Din, the founder of the Safavid Sufi order (later the Safavid dynasty). This overlay of paternal and learned genealogical chains (*silsilih*) links them in the story of Hazin's life, and his narrative ends with the death of the Safavids, though he would later figure in his students' genealogies.

All these men are titled as shaykhs, marking their learning. Hazin's eighth removed ancestor, Shaykh Shahab al-Din 'Ali, moved to Lahijan, "and from that time onwards, Lahijan became the homeland of [my] forefathers (*mawtin-i ajdād*)." Next, Hazin skips to his great-grandfather, who was a poet and scholar, and then his grandfather, an ascetic, both of whom foreshadow Hazin himself.[15] The generative power of origin grows with Hazin's father and uncles, who are scholar-poet-ascetics. Hazin's father traveled to Isfahan to make the acquaintance of the learned men of *'Iraq-i 'ajam*.[16] These noted ancestors are all located in a place, but most prominent are their lineages of learning. Shaykh Zahid links Hazin's line to the Safavid Shaykhs and Shahs (in Ardabil), and Hazin's grandfather is an intimate of Shaykh Baha' al-Din 'Amili (in the then Safavid capital of Qazvin). Place is of overarching importance only for Shaykh Shahab al-Din, who establishes the family homeland in Lahijan. Writing in Delhi, after his flight from Iran, Hazin's immediate homeland is the city of his birth, Isfahan. Lineages of origin often entwine with places, but as with Hazin, paternal and learned lineages structure self-representation of origin. In the lineaments of lineage, Ardabil, Lahijan, Qazvin, and Isfahan gain meaning.

Lineage works the same way for Joseph Emin (1726–1809), showing us that the Persianate could exceed not only the *umma* but also the Persian language itself. Emin, an Armenian from Hamadan, fled the turmoil of Nadir Shah's Iran to Calcutta, then to London for almost a decade, before attempting to travel through West Asia, ostensibly to liberate his ancestral homeland, a place he had never seen. Following the death of Karim Khan Zand, Emin left Isfahan, where he had married and settled for several years, and made a final migration to Calcutta, where in the 1780s he wrote his memoir.[17] Though written in English, Emin's text evinces aesthetic forms and even knowledge of Persian by proudly citing Hafiz's verses at the appropriate occasion.[18] Emin's text begins with praises, a dedication to God, and then an account of his patrilineal descent as would any Persianate author introduce himself in the context of his family. Again, the origin narrative is selective and strategically designed to position the author. He begins with Emin the first, the ancestor who established the family's origin in Armenia, and then Emin's grandson Theodorus, who marks the family's forced relocation to Hamadan. Next, two immediate ancestors represent the ethical warrior Emin presents as his inheritance. Emin the second, born the year the family moved to Hamadan, is a great warrior in Shah Abbas's army, while Michael, the author's grandfather and teacher, is distinguished by his upstanding piety.[19] These two ancestors establish Emin, too, as a *javānmard*, an ethical warrior. As Arly Loewen expounds, "such a person possessed the aggregate of all positive virtues of manhood—courage, honesty, hospitality and generosity." *Javānmard* literally meant young man, whose perfect appearance and ethical behavior signaled an idealized masculinity.[20] Origin, including place, is integral to Emin's self-representation, but even for this explicitly Armenian patriot, places are an itinerary subordinated to patrilineal descent. Places mark a narrative of origin in which he answers the question of who he is, a *javānmard*.

Into the nineteenth century, place is similarly subordinate to lineage in autobiographical and biographical descriptions. This era's authors are one or two generations removed from the fall of the Safavids or the dissolution of Timurid central power, and their itineraries reflect the changed times. In Hindustan, migrants and travelers went to regional centers (Bombay, Hyderabad, Lucknow, Calcutta) instead of Delhi. In Iran, centers of learning had dispersed from Isfahan and Shiraz to smaller towns and into Ottoman-ruled *Iraq-i 'arab*. Place still appeared as accrued itinerary, in tandem with other signifiers of origin and commemoration. In their well-known early nineteenth-century texts, Mir 'Abd al-Latif Shushtari (1759–1806), a migrant from Shushtar (Iran) to Hyderabad (Deccan), and Mirza Abu Talib Khan Isfahani, the son of an Isfahani migrant to Lucknow living in Calcutta, describe each other.

In the 1790s, Shushtari spent time in Calcutta, where he acted as envoy to the East India Company for his paternal first cousin, Mir 'Alam, a powerful figure at the Asaf Jahi court at Hyderabad. He marks this time in *Tuhfat al-'Alam* by describing individuals with whom he kept company, giving prominence to Tafazzul Husyan Khan, an older learned friend and teacher.[21] Born into one of the great families of Lahore, Tafazzul Khan now served in Calcutta, however reluctantly (as befitted a man without worldly ambitions), as the representative of Asaf al-Dawlih, the Navvab of Awadh.[22] His official position, but not his age and stature, makes him Shushtari's peer. Most of Shushtari's description frames this scholar, whose accomplishments, comportment, learned lineage, and worthiness as a teacher make him ideal for diplomatic statesmanship. Part of this lineage is Tafazzul Khan's own teacher, Shaykh Hazin Lahiji, under whom Tafazzul Khan "reached a high degree of attainment (*martabih-yi buland*)" in religious sciences.[23] Shushtari's emphasis on his teacher Tafazzul Khan's lineage of learning adds to both their standings. Significantly, Shushtari fully expects this lineage to be intelligible to his readers, placing a man born in Lahore in a chain of intellectual descent with men born in Isfahan and Shushtar. Establishing such lineages was possible not because of birthplace but because of overlapping itineraries. Places are important because of what they produce, here a lineage of learning that easily contains ancestors of varied transregional natal descent.

Shushtari also met "Mirza Abu Talib Khan, son of Hajji Bayg Khan Tabrizi Isfahani." This title of address defines Abu Talib as educated, a Mirza, and as the son of a Hajji and a Khan from Isfahan with an earlier origin in Tabriz.[24] Hajji Bayg Khan came to Hind from Isfahan during Nadir Shah's reign and settled in Lucknow. Shushtari then describes Abu Talib's laudable qualities, providing biographical information to explain them. Abu Talib has a "quick and witty intellect (*zihnī rasā*)," having been educated by "the great intellectuals of the time and wise ones from among the Qizilbash," a term referring to Persian Shi'a migrants from former Safavid domains. This lineage of learning, narrated in the name *Qizilbash*, explains his poetic verses, described as unparalleled in rhyme and meter, as an inheritance. This lineage parallels Abu Talib's lineages of place, but Abu Talib comes into relief though his genealogy of learning, rather than homelands. Such descriptions of companionship with the virtuous were among Calcutta's ornaments of place in this late eighteenth-century account. But they are examples of how places accrued the moral meaning that defined them as much as material features more broadly in commemorative texts.[25]

When discussing his origins in *Tuhfat al-'Alam*, Shushtari intertwines the history of his sayyid family with a history of Shushtar. His account of the town's history predates his family's mid-seventeenth-century arrival from Jazayir. The prominence of this homeland is explained in his introduction, in which Shushtari provides "a summary of the conditions (*awzā*) of Shushtar, with brief mention of the good works and attainments of [our] virtue spreading grandfathers, uncles and sons of uncles who had fixed their residence in that city."[26] This "brief mention" of his family is in fact slightly longer than the full historical, geographical, and architectural account of Shushtar. Together, they are important to his origins, shared with his cousin and patron Mir 'Alam, who has never traveled outside Hindustan. As the current homeland of the far-flung sayyid clan, Shushtar functions as a setting for the structuring feature of origin, the more extensive description of their Nuriyyih sayyid lineage, which originates in Jazayir and in the Prophet.[27] Homelands, unlike birthplaces, could be acquired and accrued.

Patrilineal descent and learned lineage could infuse each other. Abu Talib's commemoration of Shushtari also focuses on his lineages, with its attendant itinerary. The origin (*asl*) of "the Nuriyyih sayyids of Shushtar" is from Jazayir, an arid plateau amid the rugged Sinjar hills north of the alluvial plains between the Tigris and Euphrates. Virtue, piety, learning, and intellect distinguish these sayyids, who have held the position of Shaykh al-Islam of Shushtar for a long span of years. Abu Talib details how in the mid-seventeenth century, Shushtari's forefather, Sayyid Ni'matullah ibn 'Abdullah, traveled to Shiraz and Isfahan and studied with distinguished 'ulama, such as Aqa Husayn Khvansari (d. 1687) and Mulla Muhammad Baqir Majlisi (d. 1699), before arriving in Shushtar.[28] The inhabitants of Shushtar, honored by his arrival, begged him to stay and gave him spiritual and worldly authority over them.[29] Shushtar is a setting for the specifics of Shushtari's lineage, the central feature of his origin. Furthermore, Shushtar is a recent homeland joining Jazayir and intervening locations and thereby disrupting place as an exclusive basis of origin.

Solidarities and Factions

The importance of place was the work it did within lineages. Place distinguished a person from others. Immediate homelands could enable other relationships, such as service and learning, which were described as intimacies. Abu Talib's father, Muhammad Bayg Khan, "became the companion (*rafīq*)" of Safdar Jang, the second Navvab of Awadh, whose service he entered. Through this patronage, Muhammad Bayg married the daughter of a migrant from Nishapur. Abu Talib's maternal grandfather, an old friend (*az dūstān-i qadīm-i vay*) from the same hometown (*hamshahrī*) as the first Navvab of Awadh, Burhan al-Mulk, had followed Burhan al-Mulk to Hindustan after the fall of the Safavids and had entered his service.[30]

These connections may seem to reinforce scholarly contentions that "ethnic" identities, Irani and Turani, were affiliations similar to nationalist alignments of language, culture, and place (with Irani as Persian from Persia and Turani as Turani Turk, although most migrants from Safavid Iran spoke some form of Turkic as a first language). But as I argue, ethnic identity does not apply to the Persianate. Social affiliations that bound political alliances could be explained by shared homelands *or* by the lineages that crisscrossed them. They could be established by marriage, which presumed the same sectarian affiliations, or by extralegal adoption or pledged service, which did not. Once a person was geographically transplanted, their immediate place of origin could become the ground for social or political solidarity. Beyond homeland, shared origin from the same political entity could (but need not) make kingdom intelligible as a referent. Thus Muhammad Bayg, an Isfahani Turk originally from Tabriz, came to ally himself with a Nishapuri transplant, and this act of alliance undertaken in Hindustan seems to have wiped away local specificities, crystallizing a proto-pan-Iranian identity that became the basis for loyalty.

This interpretation, however, ignores another reading, which ultimately undoes it. Muhammad Bayg is identified as a Turk, allied with the

putative head of an "Irani" faction that scholars say opposed a Turani faction distinguished by its Turkic-ness. Muhammad Bayg Isfahani's origin is
his Turkic-ness, distinguished by his birth in Abbasabad of Isfahan. With
the vaunted place of spoken Turkish at the Safavid court and capital, the
large number of Turkic speakers in Iran, as well as the prevalence of Persian
as a language of education throughout Iran, Hindustan, and Turan, these
alignments of language with place, together with the very concept of native
language, are tenuous at best. They ignore the storied lineages foundational
to social grouping. For individuals whose lineages tied them to the broader
social collectivity of "Turk," sub-Turkic lineages constituted origin (see the
next chapter).

Lineage (or language), therefore, did not inhere in place, nor did it
preclude loyalties between people from different places, whether specific
homelands or larger regions. Sayyid Riza Shushtari ('Abd al-Latif's uncle),
and subsequently his family, arriving from Iranian domains, attached themselves to the Nizams of Hyderabad, a family considered leaders of the Turani
faction.[31] Muhammad Bayg's identification as a Turk of Isfahan did not preclude "native" proficiency in Persian, nor did this Turkic lineage link him
to those from Turan who lacked "Turkic" lineages. Organizing principles
of origin could include language, collective lineages (sublineages of Turk,
Kurd, Arab, and so on), androcentric descent, and homelands temporally and
geographically far and near. Existing in tandem, aspects of origin grew in
prominence according to loyalties of social and political contexts.

If we read place as itinerary, structured genealogically, place becomes
the origin of ancestors; the birthplace of individuals; the site of upbringing (*nashv va numā*), study, and service; and the destination of travel. These
events could happen in the same place, and for more modest people, they
usually did. But even without travel, most people knew travelers, whose logic
of origin would have been widely intelligible. Without lineages, places could
suffice, but unless a slave, the humble remembered their fathers, their social
collectives, ties, and homelands. Place was multiple.

In his *tazkirih*, 'Abd al-Hakim "Hakim" Lahori describes the origin (*asl*)
of Mir Muhammad 'Ali "Afsah" as the Razavi sayyids (descended from the
eighth Shi'a Imam Riza) of Mashhad. In Timur's time, Afsah's forefathers
took up residence in the Shahrisabz in Turan. In 'Alamgir's time, his father

arrived in Hindustan, where he married the daughter of Sarbuland Khan Mir Bakhshi (paymaster general).[32] Afsah's origin is his sayyid lineage. Mashhad distinguishes these Razavi sayyids. This origin then accumulates an itinerary, with the lineage's journey to Turan and then Hindustan. Though nearly three hundred years in Turan pass between the family's origin in Mashhad and arrival in Hindustan, they are not Turani sayyids. Afsah is also maternally descended from a high official in 'Alamgir's court. This less extensive maternal (though ultimately androcentric) lineage meshes his paternal line with descendants of a prominent Timurid official. Here too, descent, rank, and service structure the story of lineages, further distinguished by their itineraries.

Individuals such as 'Abd al-Karim, Hazin, and Emin narrate lineages that bestow prestige in various ways, denoting links to other prestigious lineages or articulating transmission of ancestral characteristics like virtue, learning, and ethical comportment. These lineages covered places and accrued the histories of those places to a person's origins. This was also how collective lineages, such as those of sayyids and "Turks," accumulated meaning, but because these lineages had their own corporate histories, they were less subject to the locations of their descendants. Places, both larger regions and individual cities, had their own characters, accrued through their histories, as we saw in the last section. Regions were named for eponymous ancestors, such as Sham (Syria), Rum (roughly, Asia Minor), Khurasan, and Azarbayjan, all grandsons of Shem, son of Noah.[33] That they were people first, ancestors of glorious groups that spread over a place, gave them names, and laid the ground for later accumulation of histories, underscores the primacy of lineage even to place.

Those Who Cannot Be Placed: Princes, Nobility, and Women

The sections on princes and nobles and on women in Lutf 'Ali "Azar" Baygdili's *Atashkadih* are instructive of how lineage can outstrip place's importance. Azar's effort to map poets onto Persianate places (and render former Safavid domains central) was part of a larger project of creating poetic lineage based in 'Iraq-i 'ajam for his aesthetic community. This text is exceptional in organizing the central section on past poets according to birthplace, a counterexample attesting to the difficulty of reducing origin to birthplace. Collective lineage, as well as lineages of rule and service, define these princes (of dynastic and/or sayyid lineages), nobles (often from Turkic lineages), and women (who form their own collectivity because they can only hold or transmit androcentric lineage).

The title of the first section admits that certain people, such as princes and nobles, literally cannot be products of a city or region. It is called, "kings and princes of every land (*har diyār*) and commanders of great power of every dominion (*mamlakat*), including Turks and others that in truth are not connected to a [particular] land (*mansūb bi-vilāyatī nīstand*)."[34] For some groups, patrilineal and collective lineages, social station, gender, and service—rather than place—define the origins of individuals. The kings and princes range from descendants of Sultan Mahmad Ghaznavid, to Seljuks, Safavids, and Timurids of Iran, Turan, and Hindustan.[35] Most attention is given to progenitors of a given line, such as the lengthy description of Shah Ismaʿil Safavid's genealogy of androcentric descent. This shah is most important for instituting Safavid dominion, rather than his poetry, which was mostly written in Turkish.[36] Azar also provides sizeable entries, more historical than poetical, for a number of his sons and descendants.[37] Pre-Safavid rulers also dot the pages of this section, among them Sultan Yaʿqub, who is "the son of Hasan Padshah Turkoman. [Judging by] that which has been gleaned from histories, there had never been such a king among the Turks (*atrāk*)."[38] This social collectivity refers here to a specific dynasty, the Aqquyunlu, who ruled from Tabriz in the fifteenth century. "Turk" in the context of Iran and lands eastward refers to a broader Turco-Mongol group from which Azar hails. "Turk" also includes the descendants of Amir Timur Gurgan, including the rulers of Hindustan.[39] These rulers were foremost defined as originating from the Timurid royal line. At different times, its princes ruled various domains in Iran, Turan, and Hindustan. Here, too, lineage defines them, as no single place can.

Descriptions of nobles (*umarāʾ*) focus less on forefathers and more on broader lineages of social collectivity (named with a variety of words—*tāʾifih, uymāq, ulūs*—usually translated as tribe or ethnicity), which are further defined by ethically valorized service to kings of Turan, Iran, or Hindustan. Azar describes the origin of poet Bikhvudi as a collective lineage, the Rumlu (*aslash az tāʾifih-yi Rūmlū*), noting that he grew up in Farah.[40] The poet Salim is identified as "from the Shamlu *uymāq* and a resident (*sākin*) of Tehran and Qazvin."[41] For men from these Turco-Mongol *uymāq*s, collectively known as the Qizilbash, this lineage was their origin but place did less work to explain their belonging. They were residents of cities, sometimes more than one, but place merely functions to distinguish them individually.

Other Turks had a similar relationship to place. The poet Juzvi's origin is "the Chaghatai people (*ulūs-i Jaghatā'i*)," and he grew up in Isfahan.[42] Terms such as *ulūs* applied to more than high nobles. When 'Abd al-Karim narrates Nadir Shah's origins, detailing first the marriage of his widowed stepmother to the head of the Abivard Afsharid chief and then Nadir's own marriage to the chief's daughter, he notes that after Baba 'Ali Bayg's death, "people of the tribe (*mardum-i ulūs*), who were close to forty households, willingly accepted him as the head of the tribe and became obedient and submissive to him."[43] This subgroup (the Afshar *ulūs* in Abivard) was not large, and its leadership was local. *Ulūs* defined collective lineage that could, but need not be, overlaid by birth. It could imbue a place (and could be imbued by sojourn in a place) but remained a mobile social collective constituted by common history and shared loyalty. The Afshar, for example, also resided in other regions and towns.

Other figures belong to multiple lands because of political loyalties. Bayram Khan Baharlu was "of the *uymāq* of Baygdili Baharlu'i Turcomans. From the beginning of Humayun Shah's reign he renounced service to the Safavids and went from Qandahar to Hindustan."[44] In Azar's narrative, Bayram Khan's move occurs in tandem with his switching loyalties from one ruler to another, not a praiseworthy act. But his immutable origin is this Turcoman Baygdili Baharlu collective lineage, inflected by his service to various rulers. This collective, originally from Turan, partly overlaps with Azar's own Baygdili lineage, though his ancestors remained with the Safavids. Bayram Khan's son, 'Abd al-Rahim Khan-i Khanan "Rahim," is described in gentler terms, as a "worthy" youth and a generous patron of many accomplished migrants from Iran to Hindustan.[45] He keeps to his father's loyalties in service but also honors his forefathers by including the migrants from Safavid domains in his patronage, itself an ethical activity for a military noble. For both Bayram Khan and Rahim, belonging to a land stems from service to its rulers, appropriate for their social location as military nobles (*umarā*). A Turcoman Baharlu with an itinerary through Iran also belongs to Hindustan through ties of loyalty to its Timurid kings. His son, in the same service, creates a celebrated haven of generous patronage for accomplished migrants from his family's previous place of residence. These narratives thus align with multiple lands, as lineage and patronage hark back to Iran, even when Rahim is in service only to the ruler of Hindustan.

Writing at the end of the eighteenth century, 'Ali Ibrahim Khan "Khalil" Banarasi (d. 1793–94) parses lineage and place similarly for sayyids who were also nobles. Burhan al-Mulk, the autonomous governor of Awadh, is "from (az) the most honored sayyids of that place [Nishapur] and the high-ranking military nobles (umarā) of Hindustan."[46] He is a sayyid, more narrowly distinguished, relative to his subsequent migration to the Timurid capital, by a location in Nishapur. He is also "from" or "among"—the term az can mean either and is structurally applied to both parts of the sentence—the military nobles of Timurid-ruled Hindustan. Here, a lineage (modified by place) and a social station of service constitute origin's matrix.

Women were different because of their sex, which trumped all other aspects of origin. For women, lack of fixity to a land at first seems related to the mutability of familial affiliation as a daughter, wife, or mother whose male relatives are more geographically fixed.[47] The only information Azar provides for Nur Jahan Baygum is that she was "the wife (haram) of Jahangir, the king of Hindustan." Her two verses are prefaced with vignettes about improvisation in her interaction with Jahangir.[48] Nur Jahan is defined by her husband, a king, not her father, who was less prominent. In addition, she composed her known poetry at court, a contextual affiliation likely mentioned for a male poet as well. Sons, like daughters, were defined by affiliations with prominent men, though only women's spouses are mentioned. Other details, such as place of origin and social station, are included in their biographies when available. Mahsati's entry is the longest provided for a woman and fairly substantial in the *Atashkadih* regardless of sex. The only male mentioned is the ruler at whose court she enjoyed prominence and patronage. Sultan Sanjar's presence serves to historicize and specify her position, much as it would for a man. Azar's description of Mahsati as a noble from Ganja is a marker easily given to any male poet,[49] but she is not listed under Azarbayjan's poets. Instead of a poet of Ganja, Mahsati is a woman poet, who happens to be from Ganjah. Her womanhood, not her location, is defining of her origins.

Women poets were apart from the general category of poets, presumed to be male. This difference is indicated with a gendered language of morality.

Women's difference was transmitted to Azar in the form of the loss of and lack of preservation of women's work, as well as scanty biographical information. Azar reproduces this particularity in the structure of the *Atashkadih:* the poet 'A'isha "is from the people of Samarqand (*az ahl-i Samarqand*)." This is the only biographical specific Azar can include, except for what he extrapolates from her poetry, "that her words are sweeter than sugar." The verses he provides consist of what remains, as he remarks, "[no] verses besides these two *rubā'ī* have reached my consideration, it can be comprehended that she had a pleasant (*khawsh*) disposition." Not only has her work failed to circulate, but also "copies of her thoughts have disappeared."[50] Even the work of the more famous Mahsati "was lost over time, especially in 'Abdullah Khan Uzbeg's conquest of Herat."[51] Paucity of poetry and biographical source material haunts the *Atashkadih* as a whole, but overwhelmingly here, on the margins of the Persianate community of *adab*.[52]

Even if geographical origins of some women are known, their womanhood trumps location as a definitive attribute. Azar titles their section "an account of the circumstances [of the lives] and poetry of virtuous women linked to every land who lived in different times and whose words robbed all [others] of eloquence."[53] That this eloquence refers only to other women poets is clear when Azar comments that Mahsati "of all the types (*asnāf*) of women no one with such an incisive (*diqqat*) disposition has been seen."[54] Women are compared to each other, cordoned off from male poets irrespective of different stations, affiliations, or geographical and genealogical origins. Women's placement at the end of the *Atashkadih* indicates their relative value. The gendered language of morality mirrors and engenders this separation—masculinity is morality; femininity is its lack. The exception is the single feminine virtue of chastity (*'iffat*).[55] By contrast, the word for manhood (*mardānigī*) is a moral ideal, and its traits—courage, strength, and wisdom—are explicitly masculine.[56]

Moral valuation is reproduced in the structure of the text. Princes and nobles, distinguished from other poets by their station, come first, followed by the main (male) historical poets mapped onto a hierarchical geography— first Iran, then Turan and Hindustan. Women are last, before the author's autobiography.[57] An autobiography, however, had to serve a greater purpose, and even the use of "I" was eschewed in favor of self-deprecation, lest the author's moral integrity be compromised by vanity or arrogance. Women, therefore, precede only an abject author speaking of himself.[58]

Womanhood's lesser value is also evident in the language and detail of the biographical entries. Azar remarks that Lalih Khatun "ruled the region of Kirman in a manly/capable way (*mardānih dar rāh-i jahāndārī*) for a time."[59] No specific male accords her biography distinction, but the gendering of capable, just, and strong leadership equates her with masculinity, both literally and figuratively. To praise her, Azar evokes an abstract male, in contrast with its contemptible opposite, to which she becomes an exception.[60] Texts and their representations, however, are sites of negotiation and struggle, and those relegated to the margins might not quietly concede ground. Women could contest the dominant view, in the selfsame language of morals to claim access to its ideals.

In her poetry, Lalih Khatun uses the expectations of ideal womanhood to underscore her capability as ruler.

> I am that woman whose every act is a good deed
> > so much is the sovereignty beneath my veil
> Travelers of the Zephyr have difficulty passing
> > inside [this] curtain of chastity (*'ismat*) that is my dwelling place
> I withhold my shadow's beauty
> > from the sun since it wanders the city and bazaar
> Not every woman with a veil of two yards is mistress of a house
> > not every head with a hat is worthy of leadership.[61]

The speaker declares herself a woman who has mastered the morality of womanhood. Drawing on the ideals of a sex-segregated, homosocial regime by which women must protect their chastity by making any view of their persons inviolate to all marriageable men, the speaker makes mastery of these expectations a source of strength. For Lalih Khatun, mastery of womanhood's morality makes her capable of all (manly) morality. If she can defend the inviolate space beneath her hijab, she can protect a city as sovereign. She can even prevent the sun from casting her shadow in the public spaces. Though not every woman in a veil can be the capable mistress of a house (*kadbānū*), neither can every man with a ruler's hat lead a collective. She detaches excellent rule from manhood and makes it transferable to the womanhood she proudly proclaims. The city is as the house, and she can rule both. Mastering the norms of good womanhood is one road to worthy rulership; a broadening of the dominant association, enacted through its own terms. These verses reconcile the violation of gender norms caused by a female ruler by collapsing the separation of women from the virtues of a sovereign.[62]

To laud her, Lalih Khatun's biographers liken her to a man, even as she renders honorary manhood unnecessary. Nevertheless, the disconnect between biographical representation and self-representation is evident, reinscribing a male poetic community in which Lalih Khatun remains, inescapably, a woman. To overcome this limitation, she binds herself more tightly to her gender identity, with hierarchical implications.[63]

Paucity of preserved work and biographical information, absence of proper names (leaving largely pen names), and gendered behavioral norms flatten geographic, temporal, and social distinctions of origin. Set apart from men distinguished by their place of birth, rank, or temporal proximity to Azar, women become lesser poets, whose sex becomes their most important characteristic. Their marginality indicates one limit of the Persianate. Women are linked with its (male) center, but not diffusely (though they try to instill aporia in its norms). They remain separate, a bottom bracket that closes the social hierarchy opened by the kings and high nobles at the start of Azar's text. Between the brackets are the poets of the three Persianate lands, inscribed with their own hierarchies of place and style. But as the language of contestation shows, the margins remain internal. Whether by social location or place of birth, the origin of all these poets was the Persianate.

Lack of centrality for place is the defining feature of origin in sections on kings, princes, high nobles, and women, in which the intermeshed social, political, and cultural landscape of a larger Persianate exceeds the Irano-centric concerns of the *Atashkadih*. By the same token, Iranian domains are the site of many lineages, which together do not map on to a singular "ethnicity," family, or even language, though all belong to the Persianate. More broadly, when included in the story of origins, place is multiple and accumulated in a narrative determined by lineages of descent, learning, patronage, service, and rule rather than by locations.

CHAPTER 5

Kinship Without Ethnicity

PREMODERN SOCIAL COLLECTIVITIES of affiliated individuals have all too often been translated as tribes or ethnicities. But the affiliations, articulated as lineal connections that defined social collectivities, do not map neatly onto what we understand as ethnicity, or even kinship. This chapter argues that those who shared lineal connections, beyond those created by birth alone, shared what we understand as kinship. Kinship in the form of lineages was the basis of affiliation and constituted social collectives. In the Persianate, meaningful social bonds that we might call kinship were articulated not as blood but as connections spanning legally defined family and beyond, articulated with the same rhetoric of lineage. I have thus eschewed the term "ethnicity" in favor of social collective or collective lineage. Scholars have most commonly understood collective lineages as the basis of ethnicity (in a "real" sense as "blood ties" or a "mythical" sense through eponymous ancestors), along with history, customs, language, and land. But as we have seen, these bases—lineage, history, affiliations to places or homelands, and language—do not necessarily map onto each other in Persianate contexts. Instead, they shift and intersect with other persons or groups.

Here we must pause on lineage and the ways in which it has been made to constitute modern ideas of kinship. This distinction between real and mythic indicates a conceptual ground. In eighteenth-century Persianate contexts, social collectives and their constitutive lineages cannot be understood as ethnicity without obscuring their historical meanings. Imposing our categories on historical contexts forecloses access to resources with which we might imagine a way beyond an analytic of ethnicity rooted in the universality of a blood-based descent that has generated biological racism. Transhistorical application of this resolutely modern concept disfigures previous notions of origins, lineages, and the understandings of kinship that informed possibilities of affiliation and collective belonging.

Studies of ethnicity in ancient and modern times generally agree that ethnicity is constituted by a common story, usually presented as shared natal ancestry. Lineage articulates this descent, and in any version, scholars connect generations through blood. In West, Central, and South Asian studies, ethnicity is often made interchangeable with tribal belonging, with descent biological and blood-based.[1] Deemed primordial, physiological descent is assumed to be the basis of a natural allegiance.[2] But "from reproduction to lineage and heredity, and blood as the common substance shared by kin and nation, the line is far from obvious or necessary and its connection to ancient Greek physiology more than tenuous."[3] Here I question whether the emphasis on birth, certainly part of lineage, is the same as sharing blood, and further ask what descent as birth but not blood might mean. What might lineages and their possible forms of kinship mean for origin and belonging if the link "between blood and community" were "unsettled and de-sedimented"?[4]

Anachronisms of Ethnicity

Ethnicity, we are told, is based on objective cultural traits and common descent. Even in critical analyses, ethnic groups are equated with ancient societies, but the meaning of descent is left unquestioned.[5] Substance uniformly bestowed by blood, whether "real" or imagined, is transposed onto a primordial social, itself a notion based on a distinction between nature and culture. Race then lingers, unnamed, in the assumption that "real" descent is biological.[6] It requires us to ask how this distinction is the product of *our* moment of human consciousness. How are the unexamined terms we use to analyze historical concepts imbued with a specificity that at least warrants interrogation?[7]

Even scholars seeking to apply a transhistorical ethnicity in, say, ancient Greece, from where the ancestor of the modern term derives, are unable to argue that Greeks themselves had ethnicity. These studies acknowledge that Greek identity was not fixed and that different groups could lay claim to it on bases ranging from origins (of territory, ancestry, historical participation) to behavior (language, customs, religious rites).[8] Why then is being Greek (or Hellene) an ethnicity and not something else? Classicists making this argument admit "no single term that might equate to our word 'ethnicity.'" *Ethnos* "simply designates a class of beings (humans or animals) who share a common identification."[9] "Attributing social solidarity of *ethnos*" to birth and kinship was "about as close as they could come to our concept of ethnicity."[10] Nevertheless, some scholars press on with ethnicity's story because it makes sense to *us*.[11] But at what cost?

Across the Persianate, origins were the basis of cohesion and explanation for a person's or group's characteristics. Narrated as the story of lineages, origins accrued up to the present. Origins were thus about where one originated, but according to who they were and what that meant about the work of representation at its present moment. To equate a group's origin with an ethnicity, however, is as misleading as equating an individual's origin only with their natal lineage understood as "real" (biological) family. To make descent a matter of biology is to reduce kinship to blood and, simultaneously, to take a particular interpretation of a physical fact as "natural."[12] For medieval Europe, blood was a vehicle for characteristics; later, as race fell into disgrace, anthropologists (for instance) still "saw kinship as constituting the political structure and providing the basis for social continuity in stateless societies."[13] Even if, in theory, we reject the universal applicability of "the logic of the purity of blood" as an ostensibly objective basis for understanding kinship, it remains as a particular notion of natural which transmits by way of biology.[14] Thus discussions of "real" descent almost always make recourse to biology and blood. As English-speaking heirs of these concepts, we must scrutinize this universalizing tendency in our analytic language and assumptions to avoid reproducing it. That "the language of kinship serves here to construct the social order" is not in doubt. But if "the very act of generation, defined in terms of consubstantiality contained in the blood . . . at least from Christian times has been the major symbol of our [European] kinship system," what symbols apply to Persianate kinship?[15]

Biology as timeless truth has been well historicized. Gender studies has "defamiliarized the natural," demonstrating that gender creates sex as natural in order to justify itself.[16] Following that insight, we must distinguish birth, biology, and descent as "naturally" coeval. Birth as biological truth depends on an older history whereby "a conception of kinship based on consanguinity" came to predominate.[17] Anidjar has argued that Christianity (from the twelfth century onward) "simultaneously invented the community of substance as the community of blood."[18] It is here that "real" kinship took shape, so that "the distribution of blood between realms and spheres, including the distinction between literal (or 'real') blood and figurative (or 'symbolic') blood, is an essential mechanism for the distribution and operations of blood in Christianity."[19] Formulated together, "along with life, blood became sacred through a series of rituals whose aim was precisely to separate blood into different kinds. Thus, some bloods are more sacred than others, as are some lives," and "whatever blood is, it cannot be understood as a biological substance."[20] No fact of birth can account for blood's meaning, though blood naturalizes its effects, hiding its labors, behind the fact of birth. According to a liberal (liberating) narrative, blood is presumably part of the past (of Europe). Yet "the very notion of a collective us—whether familial, tribal, national, or racial—lingers with blood still."[21] So if our analytic categories are stiff with the figuring power of blood, does the blood of Christian Europe feature in every past?[22] What might refraining from these "universal" categories of origin show us about the Persianate?[23]

Ethnicity might be vested in genealogies deemed "mythical" because we define them as other than actual ancestors. This structuring absence as myth informs our "objective" idea of ethnicity, analytically and historically, especially when in tension with historically "subjective" conceptions of ethnicity (in part produced by our search for ethnicity). Thus studies of early Islam presume a unified group of people, "Iranians," defined as inhabitants of "a territory centered on a plateau, and in recognition of shared linguistic and cultural patterns that do have antique origins . . . encompassing a variety of groups." In contrast, "the major identity that cut across regions was a 'Persian' one," denoted by widespread use of the term *al-Furs*. The meaning of this Persian identity was "in different ways at different times" something "intersubjective and contextual."[24] But the logic of these designations quickly comes into tension with the notion of Persians as "a particular ethnic group,"[25] defined as "recognition of shared customs, language, homeland, history and descent."[26] What began as "an identity" that "cut across regions" becomes an ethnicity focused on a shared descent and homeland (envisioned as?). Perhaps it is only that modern notions of identity are not epistemologically equipped to contain certain historical logics.

Nothing I argue contradicts Savant's assertion that "for groups, as for individuals, loyalty and a sense of belonging depend on how they make sense of the past, including their origins, their ancestry, and the achievements of previous generations." But only the implicit assumption that shared blood, real or imagined, constitutes origins and transmits ancestry and past achievements leads to ethnicity.[27] Despite a wealth of evidence that even patrilineal descent is not constituted by biological truth, the bloody logic of our present obscures understanding. This is the challenge: descent, lineage, genealogy, and ancestry exceeded those legally defined as kin, and even those forms of lineage were not structured by biology or blood, though it included relationships defined by birth. Savant's otherwise illuminating work is typical of treatments of identity and ethnicity in medieval history. We lack critical work on later periods, when questions about who is Arab or who is Persian have been subsumed by both becoming Muslim.[28] Lineages that defined Arabs in an earlier period are referenced only vaguely (if at all), while Turkic or Turco-Mongol lineages are more often detailed.

Turco-Mongol Lineages, Affiliations, and Social Collectives

By the eighteenth century, Persian was not an ethnicity in terms of real or imagined biological descent, nor did Persianate universal histories, significantly developed since early Abbasid times, belong to the inhabitants of Iranian lands. Origin stories of collective lineages often proudly announced their attachment both to a homeland and to previous locations, often non-Iranian. Indeed, by the eighteenth century, Turco-Mongol lineages had joined Persianate universal histories through Genghisid charismatic authority and the imperial glory of the Timurids.[29]

Azar Baygdili's account of his own origins gives us a window through which to view "Turks." He is ostensibly a Shamlu and thus of the Qizilbash, but we must account for the fact that he does not identify himself as such. Bashir outlines the changing nature of this term and its relationship to the Turcomen *uymāq*s who brought the Safavids to power and acted as their military elite during the first hundred years of their empire, noting that "the symbolic weight ascribed to the term Qizilbash seems to have increased in tandem with a decline in the actual political power wielded by those who have been referred to as the Qizilbash."[30] Defined collectively as "devotee-soldiers committed to the Safavid dynasty," each group had its own history and intertwined lineage, which overlaid and encompassed relationships of birth.[31] Turco-Mongol descent, with lineages of discipleship and service to key rulers such as Timur and the Safavids, defined Azar. Timurid lineages share features of other Turco-Mongol lineages, even of service to Genghis Khan's line, though Timurids are primarily distinguished by rulership. This is why I discuss the poet Azar's lineage, defined by nobility and service, alongside the Timurid emperor Akbar's. Rather than "ethnic" Turkish tribes, Turco-Mongol lineages, like those for a time known as Qizilbash, were distinct social collectives, connected to the history of Persianate kingship across multiple lands.[32]

Such meanings are present in Azar's self-representation:

> The origin (*asl*) of this traveler on the pathways of concord (*sālik-i masālik-i yak-dilī*) is the praised house (*dūdih*) of Baygdili. The reason for this group's (*tā'ifih*) naming is that this illustrious group's entire patrilineage (*nasab*) reaches to Baygdil Khan, the third of the four sons of Idguz [Yulduz] Khan, the third of the six sons of Ughuz Khan. Ughuz Khan is several generations (*vāsitih*) descended (*mukhallaf*) from Turk ibn Yapeth ibn Nuh [Japheth son of Noah]. In light of his [Ughuz Khan's] essential nature (*fitrat-i aslī*), which was formed in his youth through [his] making of the structures of dominion and world governance, his name is remembered with those of just kings. Due to this utmost grandeur he is known as Jamshid of the Turks. The patrilineage (*nisbat-i nasab*) of the most Turkic groups' kings, puissant as Jam and magnificent as Faridun, reaches back to that mighty king [Ughuz Khan]. Such that, at the order of [the Ilkhanid] Sultan Muhammad Olja'itu, Khwajih Rashid al-Din Tabib Hamadani has written a book recording the lineages of the Turkic groups (*tavā'if-i Turk*), which is known as *Jami'-yi Rashidi*. The origin and lineage of the groups (*uymāqāt*) is clearly delineated there, and, as it should be, they are distinguished from one another.

In short, this poor one's fathers and grandfathers were continuously in Turkistan as rulers (*farmānfarmā*) and commanders of their sub-group (*riyasat-i qabīlih*). They lived in obedience to the passing of times until, in the era of Sultan Mahmud Ghaznavi or during the Gengisid tumult, they came to Iran with a number of [other] groups/tribes (*tavā'if*) of Turkistan. Some [of the groups] became residents (*sākin*) of this domain (*mamlakat*) and some immediately continued on to the region of Syria (*Shām*) in the service of my fathers. They arrayed the furnishings of residence (*rahl-i iqāmat*) in that place until, in the era of Timur's reign, when that world-seizing commander undertook the conquest of that region and he recognized the patrilineage (*nasab*) of that group (*gurūh*). In consideration of their worthiness and shared language (*ahlīyat va ham-zabānī*), with the utmost kindness he decamped those groups (*tavā'if*) in their entirety from Syria and brought them to Iran with the intention of resettling them in Turkistan, which was their homeland (*mawtin*). After arriving in Ardabil and attaining the honor of service (*khidmat*) to Sultan 'Ali Siyahpush Safavi, the leaders of that people (*qawm*) made that most majestic one their intercessor (*shafī'*). With the intercession of that king of the world of [hidden] meaning (*sultan-i 'ālam-i ma'nī*), they sought leave from the companionship of Timur's camp and permission to delay in that region [Ardabil]. [Then,] directing the hand of their will to that province's prince (*vālī-yi diyār*), they lived as an order of disciples firm in their belief, until the sun of the Safavid's fortune rose from the horizon of rule. From the beginning of Shah Isma'il Safavi's reign until Shah Tahmasp II's time, which is approximately 250 years, they were the bulwark of those heavenly ranked kings at the imperial court/threshold (*āstān-i khilāfat*) as high-ranking officials and military nobles possessing virtuous well-being (*umarā-yi sa'ādatmand*).[33] Due to offenses against them they became dissatisfied in the customs/obligations of service (*marāsim-i khidmatguzārī*) and self-sacrifice. A summary of the state of some of them has been recorded in Iskandar Bayg's *Tarikh-i 'Alamara*. In short, those from among this group (*tā'ifih*) who migrated from the domain of Syria are called Baygdili Shamlu and those who remained in Turkistan or Iran and did not go to Syria [are called] Baygdili and not Shamlu. The essence of Baygdili is amongst (*miyān*) the Baygdili, and Shamlu is both general and specific in the sense that some Baygdili are Shamlu and some Shamlu are Baygdili.[34]

This passage leads us from lineage and place to the question of lineage and kinship. The assertion that the Baygdili lineage is an origin unto itself ("the essence of Baygdili is amongst the Baygdili"), with place a distinguishing marker for its subgroups, also explains the absence of Shamlu in Azar's original statement ("the origin (*asl*) of this traveler . . . is the praised house (*dūdih*) of Baygdili"). That he is specifically a Baygdili Shamlu is stated toward the end, a particularizing feature his origin's core. Shamlu is a place name moniker, shared with other lineages, which functions both to distinguish the itinerary of a subset of the Baygdili collective and to mark a particular (Shamlu) collective, distinguished by its arrival from Syria to Iran and its service to the Safavids.[35] Nowhere does he use the term *Qizilbash*. By the eighteenth century, the term *Qizilbash* had taken on new meaning, with its mark of service and affiliation extended to others (see Chapter 6).

Azar's origin story is about three main collectives: his family line and the larger Baygdili and Shamlu groups. His family lineage accrues meaning not just from its early ancestors (Baygdil Khan, Ughuz Khan, Turk), who populate Persianate universal histories, but also from its role in a wider story of transregional Persianate ruling authorities of Shaykh and Shah.[36] As the narrative's subject shifts, different singular and plural words refer to a group of people, some irreducible to the English word *tribe*.[37] First, Azar uses the word for group (*tā'ifih* and its manuscript alternative, *tabagih*) for both his direct line and the Baygdili collective. *Tā'ifih* can refer to any social grouping, such as an occupational group or a school of thought. For the family line, he uses *tā'ifih* interchangeably with *dudih* (house or family), *nasab* (lineage), and *gurūh* (group). For the Baygdili collective, over which his family holds leadership and to whom it gives its name, he uses *tā'ifih* interchangeably with *qabīlih* (most often translated as tribe). In contrast, the Shamlu collective comes into being through their residence in Sham, and, crucially, their departure, not through descent from or rule by a particular family. When Timur conquers Syria and meets Azar's forefathers, whose lineage (and language) he recognizes, the Turkic groups there are referenced in the plural as *tavā'if*, used interchangeably with another plural term specific to Turco-Mongol groups, *uymāqāt*. By the time these Turkic groups arrive in Ardabil with Timur and their leaders (including Azar's ancestor) pledge service to the Safavid Shaykh, they have become a singular people (*qawm*), the Shamlu.

Family line and social collective are distinct but not completely. A common synonym for Turco-Mongol groups missing here is *ulūs*, which can also mean a family and its following.[38] Indeed, in the Qur'an, the words for family can mean both common natal lineage and those who share a household.[39] The last statement ("some Baygdili are Shamlu and some Shamlu are Baygdili") speaks the logic of aporetic categorization; each is a collective that contains members of the other group. Even after the coherence of the Shamlu has been established in the narrative, the Baygdili remain a coherent group within other collectives ("those from among this group (*tā'ifih*) who migrated from the domain of Syria are called Baygdili Shamlu.") This simultaneous belonging, neither an accident nor a contradiction, is yet another distinction from modern notions of ethnicity. It applies even to Baygdil Khan's direct paternal line, after whom the social collective is named; the ruling lineage names the collective, yet they remain a distinct family. Kinship here derives from relations of rule. Azar may share legally defined kinship with individuals in other groups and not with members of his own collective(s).

Azar locates his forefathers' lineage in larger collective lineages. The former is based on paternity, requiring legal recognition to tie a child to the father. The latter coheres around service and itinerary.[40] The Baygdili collective was formed in Turkistan, already distinct when it followed Azar's forefathers out of that land. "They [his forefathers] came to Iran with a number of the groups of Turkistan." Those who stayed in Iran continued to be called Baygdili; those who, in service, accompanied Azar's forefathers (*dar khidmat-i ābā-yi faqīr*) to Syria became Baygdili Shamlu. This latter group had links with other Shamlu Turks and other Baygdilis.

This great migration out of Turkistan took place either during the reign of Sultan Mahmud of Ghazna (d. 1030) or the conquests of Genghis Khan (early 1200s). The next event is the arrival of Timur in Syria, where he "recognizes the lineage of that group," presumably the Baygdili Shamlu. In response, given the "worthiness and shared language (*ahlīyat va hamzabānī*)" of the Syrian-based Turks, he relocated "those groups" to Iran, intending to return them to Turkistan. The Baygdili are one subset among the Shamlu, who become defined as such in Ardabil, distinguished from the Baygdilis who remained in Iran. The Shamlu cohere around a return that never happens, in effect a departure, and become a singular group by acquiring an origin narrated through lineages of discipleship and service to the Safavids.

The layers of meaning that the terms *tā'ifih*, *gurūh*, and *qawm* can hold become clear in Timur's recognition of the Shamlu in Syria, on the basis of their linguistic commonality and their substantive merit. Thus far social collectives are constituted by lineages of natal descent, rule, and service, distinguished sometimes by their itineraries, language, and manner of living.[41] But are Turks as a whole a meaningful lineage, constituting an ethnicity? "Genealogy provides the historical validation of kinship and all that it involves"[42] at the individual level of worth and potential, as well as "one of the most important organizing principles in Muslim societies," by claiming to reflect "natural" order.[43] As a system of knowledge, genealogy is a socially constituted practice of verification through testimony and text, companionship, and recognition.[44] Some lineages are widely accepted; others are contested, not successfully laid claim to. Their shape and articulation tell a story with significance different from "truth" (in their times and our own). Even the well-known lineage of descent of Turks and their Ughuz rulers, which Azar indexes, builds upon and reflects broader sensibilities of lineage in High Persianate times.[45] The Baygdili lineage first gains distinction from an eponymous ancestor, located in a Qur'anic line as Turk son of Japheth, one of Noah's three sons.[46] But throughout the rest of the passage, the term Turk refers to a more specific group than its Qur'anic line, which includes Tatars, Uyghurs, and Qarluqs. Ughuz Khan is the crucial ancestor between Turk and Baygdil Khan who bestows social specificity, nobility, and the genesis of rule that defines his descendants' potential. According to our truth, Ughuz "is probably a term denoting some kind of tribal confederation," and "the various tribal groupings bearing the Oğuz name in one form or another were all part of the Eastern Türk khaganate (552–630, 687–741 [AD]) centered in Mongolia" and migrated to Turan in early Islamic times.[47]

The relationship between Ughuz Turks and other Turkic groups is more explicitly articulated in other well-known genealogical accounts. Abu'l-Fazl's transregionally circulated *Akbarnama* discusses Ughuz Khan in its commemoration of Timurid genealogy, a more illustrious Ughuz lineage than the Baygdilis. Here, Ughuz Khan has significance parallel to Jamshid among the Persians (*'ajam*): both worshipped God and ordered world rule.[48] After

announcing that all those whom he calls Turks, specifically Ughuz, are descended from the twenty-four branches into which his grandchildren split
(one of which is Azar's eponymous ancestor, Baygdil Khan), Abu'l-Fazl
explains,

> The word Turcoman did not exist in olden times. When their sons (*awlād*)
> entered Iran and successive generations were born and begot in that land
> (*tavallud va tanāsul dar ān sarzamīn*), gradually their faces became like
> those of the Persians (*Tājīk*). Because they were not like the Persians, the
> Persians called them Turk-mān, meaning Turk-like (*Turk mānand*). Some
> believe that the Turcomans are a separate people (*qawm*) and do not have a
> near relation (*nisbat-i qarābat*) to the Turks.[49]

Turks and Turcoman have an unsettled relationship. They could be descendants of the Ughuz collective lineage or of a more distant ancestor, like
Turk himself, who is only two generations removed from the ancestor of
humankind.[50] Historically, the term *Turcoman* dates from the tenth century,
distinguishing Ughuz Turks that had become Muslim, and then in Seljuq-
era texts to distinguish those who followed the Seljuqs into Turan, Iran, and
Anatolia in the eleventh century. But Ughuz Khan's story took definitive
shape in the Turcoman-Mongol encounter of the thirteenth century and
finds its full articulation in Ilkhanid texts (such as Rashid al-Din's), which
exerted a tremendous influence on later accounts.[51]

As ancestor of Genghis and Timur, Ughuz Khan was the progenitor of
the most important Turco-Mongol lineages of High Persianate times.[52] For
Abu'l-Fazl (and Azar), the category Turk means Ughuz, subsequently used
interchangeably with Mongol. Other descendants of Turk son of Japheth are
Tatars and Uyghurs, described in conflict with Ughuz descendants and in
partnership with the invader of Turkistan, Tur, the brother and enemy of Iraj,
ruler of Iran. Similar to the reconciliation of Qur'anic and pre-Islamic Persian history in earlier periods, Turco-Mongol lineages became embedded in
and reconciled with this universal history. In these High Persianate narratives,
Turco-Mongol lineages are allied with Iran's ruler. The Ughuz descendant El
Khan fought this confederation of Tur and Sevinch Khan (leader of the Tatars
and Uyghurs), with "the best of the Mongols" with whom he was on "good
terms," an alliance heralding the later confluence of these two lineages.[53]

Abu'l-Fazl presents the descendants of another of Ughuz Khan's grandsons as losing Turan to the invading Tur, sojourning in a secluded valley (*Argunih-qun*) in Mongolia for two thousand years, and generating new collectives (*qabā'il*) before returning to reconquer "their kingdom (*mulk-i khud*)" from the Tatars and others toward the end of the Sassanian king Anushiravan's reign (531–79 AD). The leader of the reconquering Ughuz collectives was Yulduz Khan, who Abu'l-Fazl tells us was the only fit ruler of the Mongol people (using *ulūs* and *qawm* interchangeably). After sojourns in Mongolian lands, these collectives grew, transformed, and became Mongols (*ulūs-i Mughul*).[54] Yulduz Khan, their leader at the time of return to their homeland, is also the grandfather of Alanqoa, the female ancestor, likened to Mary (Jesus's mother) and impregnated by a ray of light, who distinguishes Genghisid and Timurid lineages from other Ughuz lineages.[55] Whatever we may think of these narratives, they are neither forgeries nor myths, not for Abu'l-Fazl, Azar, or their contemporaries, who understood false claims, fabrications, or distinctions in forms of kinship. Reading these narratives as myth depends on modern assumptions that one form of lineage is true, biologically (and thus empirically) verifiable, and constituted by blood ties.[56]

Another salient aspect of Abu'l-Fazl's Turcoman story is the word *nisbat*, which means both relationship and trait or attribute. As the description earlier shows, a collective lineage's attributes were malleable, with mutable physical traits, unlike biological notions of race. Discussion here is not about blood but of moving and settling in a land where, through successive generations of birth, Turks come physically to resemble its Persian (*Tājīk*) inhabitants. But looking like Persians does not make them Persians. The groups are distinguished by Turkish vernacular, dress, manner of living, and lineages.[57] This aporetic kind of difference is underscored by shared knowledge of the Persian language and growing prestige of Turkish under the Safavids. Azar narrates that Timur identified the Shamlu in Syria by their common tongue and their worthiness. Vernacular tongue and enduring merit, then, are the basis of kinship, while shifts in geography engender changes in physical appearance. For Abu'l-Fazl, the Turcomen look different from Turks and have uncertain origins. But familiar attributes, such as language, make them Turk-like. Origin holds the truth of a person or group, but lineage is a story that accrues ancestors and places, whose form manifests the virtues of forefathers and their deeds. The substantive of their virtues are recognizable through narratives of social ties (*adab*) that realized, acknowledged, and potentially transmitted the truths of origins to subsequent generations.

Azar's origins are constituted by crucial service lineages. Its first figure is Amir Timur, who recognized the descent of Azar's forefathers and gathers the Shamlu in service on the basis of their common language and merit. This is no casual relationship; when the Shamlu leaders arrive in Ardabil and, as is custom, attend upon the Safavid Sufi order's head, Sultan ʿAli Siyahpush, they are moved to accept him as their guide. But to have him as their intercessor with God, he must also intercede with their earthly ruler, Timur, to release them from the formal companionship (*rifāqat*) of Timur's camp, the proper ethical action that preserves the moral integrity of their lineage. They are then free to devote themselves as disciples to "the king of hidden meaning" until decades later, when the Safavids attain earthly power as well and the Shamlu become a bulwark of the Safavid state, as commanding nobles possessed of virtuous well-being through devoted discipleship and loyal service. They grow dissatisfied with fulfilling their obligation and engaging in self-sacrifice, due to "offenses," for which details Azar refers the reader to the seventeenth-century chronicle, *Tarikh-i ʿAlamara-yi ʿAbbasi*.

Through their service lineages, the Baygdili and the Shamlu are distinguished from the many other Turkic and Ughuz groups. Patrilineal descent from Baygdil Khan gives Azar one aspect of his origin, while equally important relationships and itineraries of service to Timur and the Safavids define the Shamlu aspect. Service similarly defines Lachmi Naraʾin Shafiq, whom we met earlier. But rather than an administrator's service, Azar's service lineage is specific to his station, as a commander of men, one of the *umarā*. As we shall see later, lineages of men occupying different stations connect them to corresponding figures, with relationships structured by fixed obligations and privileges, granting particular inheritances.

Birth, Law, and Beyond

Legally defined lineages, then, form but one kind of kinship, specified by birth, contract (as with marriage), and milk. They are distinct, but only aporetically so. Natal kinship figures through women, whose legal bonds to men create paternity.[58] Bellies (*batn*) and their wombs, not blood-linked generations, form a *nasab* lineage. The *Akbarnama* narrates the significance of the Mongol ancestor Qiyan, whose line of sons (*farzandān*) "ruled over the tribes in *Arguna-qun*," the secluded valley, where they sheltered after the fateful invasion of Turkistan and Transoxiana (*Mavara' al-nahr*) by Tur, son of Faridun, and his Tatar and Uyghur allies. Qiyan's descendants ruled "generation after generation (*batn^{an} b'ad batn^{un}*)" for two thousand years, until, in the time of Anushiravan, Yulduz Khan led the tribes to retake their kingdom (*mulk*). Therefore, "among the Mongol people (*qawm*) that person who is of the proper lineage (*durust nasab*) and suitable for leadership is he who can trace their paternal descent (*nasab*) to Yulduz Khan."[59] This forefather's achievements transmit fitness to rule to his descendants, and the generations are linked from belly to belly.

Birth creates the coherence of *nasab* kinship, as underscored in 'Abd al-Karim Kashmiri's discussion of Nadir Shah's two oldest sons, born from his successive marriages to two daughters of Abivard Afshar chief Baba 'Ali Bayg. Nadir's second wife is the mother of Nasrullah, who "came into being from her belly (*az batn-i ū ba-vujūd āmad*)."[60] Furthermore, these marriages cemented his leadership over the Abivard Afshars, above the claims of the former chief's sons. Originally, the tie was through Nadir's step-mother (*mādarandar*), who had become Baba 'Ali Bayg's second wife after Nadir's father's death. Here marriage made a son, allowing a legally recognized kinship bond to form a succession and be the means to skip sons of the paternal line. Paternal descent requires a legal bond connecting men to the women who bring forth generations. Marriage creates natal kinship for men. Paternity bestows *nasab* but is gendered, based not on positivist truth but on agreed-upon forms of knowledge, evidenced by the role of testimony in verifying uncertain genealogy.[61] The story of androcentric lineage is also subject to other social needs, as women can sometimes bring their paternal lineage to the story of origin.

In Islamic discussions of procreation, blood lies alongside bone and semen, and given the definition of paternity, is not the basis of familial descent.[62] Both men and women were thought to produce semen, a substance derived from nourishment that "comes from all parts of the body of each parent, and goes to all parts of the body of the child."[63] Musallam notes that extrapolations of procreation in Qur'an and hadith corresponded with Galenic and Hippocratic notions that both parents shaped the form and matter of the child, even as semen performed gendered labor.[64] In the hadith referenced in philosophical, legal, and theological writings, man's semen "forms the bones and tendons," while women's semen "forms the flesh and blood."[65] This gendered parsing separates blood from patrilineal descent and inheritance.

A child's blood also comes from the mother through the womb, and it is the womb itself and the birth that it signifies which are central to the concept of descent, but only after a legal tie connects the mother to a man.[66] As a general principle, "the Sharīʿa stretched the limits of conception and pregnancy with a view of ascribing children, as much as possible, to the 'marriage bed' [the *firāsh* principle]." Here "the basic and primary legal assumption," of laws around paternity, operated "in the interest of preserving social harmony and the integrity of the family."[67] The institution of marriage offered moral regulation and stability, not biology. *Nasab* was about birth but not as a physical fact because relation through procreation is insufficient for establishing *nasab* in Islamic law. *Nasab* accrues to those (theoretically) conceived within marriage. All children born to a married woman—after a minimum period from the marriage contract and before a maximum period following its dissolution through death or divorce—are children of her husband.[68] A "uterine sibling" was sometimes distinguished from one that shared only a father, but their legal status was the same. Even if we attempt to impose an Islamic blood matrix, only uterine siblings shared blood, which determined neither sibling status nor kinship more broadly. Generally, blood is mentioned only in conjunction with moral depravity or excess, signaling violence, bloodshed, or hostile relations that undermine social harmony.[69]

Though distinguished from natal kinship, adoption, fosterage, clientage, and alliance created kinship and types of "relatives (*aqārib*)," with blurred distinctions rather than a clear contrast with an ostensibly natural truth.[70] Milk kinship, for example, carries prohibitions for marriage almost identical to natal kinship.[71] "Breast milk is believed to derive from the woman's blood" and so shares with natal kinship a connection between mother and child.[72] Milk kinship extends legally like paternity, so that the nurse's partner is a milk father only if he is married to the mother at the time of nursing.[73] Natal and nursing bonds with the mother then extend legally outward somewhat differently, stipulating, for instance, that unlike birth children, milk children were not heirs to property.

Nasab is thus a legally recognized relation, dependent on marriage. It lies alongside other legally recognized forms of kinship constituted by marriage ties and milk bonds that define and regulate privileges, obligations, and prohibitions, some ensconced in law and others recognized only socially.[74] In early Islamic times, non-Muslims or converts could become adoptive clients (*mawālī*), entering into forms of kinship with (usually Arab) Muslims and creating social bonds of obligations and privilege that often became the framework for cementing other kinds of kinship, such as fosterage, milk-kinship, or marriage.[75] These "adopted familial connections to other Muslims," as well as "other forms of kinship, such as tribal lineages, or descent from Sufi saints, conferred similar forms of belonging, prestige, and benefits."[76] Acknowledging kinship's variegated bases should open new vistas of inquiry uncircumscribed by assumptions about "blood ties."[77] Family and kinship, though intertwined, need not be based on birth, and the language of legal kinship often applied to other types of lineage as well.

Kinship as Spectrum

Asad notes that no Qur'anic term corresponds precisely to the English "kinship." There are gendered words for near relatives, spouses, and members of larger social collectives ("tribes" and "subtribes"), marriages affines, and a host of others that refer both to formally recognized relatives and to friends. The polysemy of these terms underlines intimacy as the basis for words that can mean wife, brother, relative *or* companion, friend, close friend.[78] Not all of these words are common in Persian, but the same polysemy appears among terms that refer both to legally regulated relationships and to those dependent on social recognition alone.[79] Regardless, "neither in the matter of moral exhortation and prohibition, nor in that of defining succession to property rights, are the people concerned necessarily connected by 'biological links'." For Asad, the simultaneity of meanings linking family bonds to other intimate social bonds "raises the question of how so-called primary meanings are to be determined." In other words, why must we assume that one is necessarily derivative of the other, rather than co-constitutive?[80]

Lineages constituted by social, political, or intellectual formations are far from unique to the Persianate or to Islam. South Asian studies have shown that family does not "have a single, clear and fixed meaning. Instead, meanings in this domain were multiple, shifting, and contextually variable."[81] In practice, therefore, within a "semantic scope," meanings could be manipulated.[82] Struggles over meaning were part of larger power struggles.[83] Language was the ground of these struggles, with family as a political entity of shifting boundaries and obligations. Sreenivasan notes that the narration of family in early modern Rajasthan was according to "the importance of the kinship network as it entered into relationships with the state, rather than the accurate recording of an entire lineage for its own sake."[84] These studies remind us that kin relations were historically constituted by sociopolitical struggles within particular hermeneutical contexts. Relationships outside those legally recognized as family were just as "real" for social order and lived experience. Chatterjee notes that Buddhist lineages in northeastern India were "formed by a mode of ritual initiation" that was "adequate to constitute a relation of power and affection, and had material and political effects. To accept initiation was equivalent to submission to a legal-moral and disciplinary practice that was identified with particular teachers." Here monastic governance linked individuals across families that could cross parochial lines between Hindu and Buddhist.[85] These modes of connection, grounded in social practices of companionship, resonate with Sufi orders, in which esoteric learned lineages bound individuals from different families or even parochial communities, significantly though not legally.[86]

Progenitors of Sufi orders were seen as heirs of the Prophet Muhammad, a lineage based on transmission of esoteric qualities, much as the Qur'an figures Muhammad as the kin of previous monotheistic prophets. Indeed, "in one Hadith, Muhammad is quoted as saying that the prophets are sons of one father by different mothers," referring "to them as brothers."[87] Nothing here is biological, yet these connections are the most meaningful kinship. Familial language connotes common proximity to God, manifest in prophecy and enacted perfection. In the context of the Naqshbandi, an important Sufi order in the Persianate Islamic east, each "disciple has a *nisba* (Persian *nisbat*) [relationship/connection] with the Prophet, derived from the formal spiritual connection to his or her spiritual mentor; the mentor has the same type of connection with his spiritual guide." The resulting genealogical chain (*silsilih*) transmits the knowledge of "divine grace or auspiciousness (*fayz*, *barakat*) from God."[88] Significantly, "this Sufi *nisba* overrides all other *nisba*s such as place of birth or blood ties."[89] Familial meaning in these relationships offered lineage outside legally delineated relationships.

Extralegal kinship was thus socially recognized, part of a spectrum that included legally sanctioned relationships. Service constituted one type of relation, often discussed in contractual terms used for marriage, as *sīghih*, meaning form, shape, or mold. Legally it denoted the proper way to offer a contract.[90] Later it came to be used as the Persian term for *mut'ah*, a limited-term marriage, distinct from *nikāh*.[91] The language and forms of legal kinship were invoked for extralegal kinships, bringing the idealized intimacy of one to the other, overlaying such relationships with the familial that could then be realized by adoption or marriage.[92] These forms of kinship, legal and beyond, created meaningful connections, which could be brought to bear on the story of origin. Kinship must be understood as a variety of forms—alliance, companionship, intimacy, connection—that entailed socially recognized privileges and obligations and could transmit meaning. In the Persianate, they were bounded by *adab*. The law defined for us our milk siblings and proscribed inheritance and marriage relations, but *adab* signified what a sibling relationship should be, one based on intimacy, trust, protection, and generosity, especially when relations to natal siblings precluded such ideals.[93]

When Aqa Ahmad Bihbahani traveled through Hindustan in the early nineteenth century, he encountered the practice of adoption and fosterage. In a section on the "well-known customs and habits of Hindustan (*rusūm va 'ādāt-i ma'rūfih*),"[94] he notes that in India "they rear the children of others and adopt them as their own children, and consider them the same as their true children (*awlād-i dīgarān rā parvarish mī-kunand va ba-farzandī-yi khud bar mī-dārand va misl-i farzandān-i haqīqī-yi khud mī-dānand*)." Specifically, when a child is adopted, the family "does not observe the rules of hijab with them and they are given a share of inheritance (*mirās*)." In addition, the adoptive family "considers it forbidden (*harām*) to marry them [adopted children]," elaborating that "if a man takes a girl as his daughter and then marries her (*nikāh*), then they will rebuke (*tawbīkh*) him."[95] This practice has no place in Islamic law, yet the forms of legal kinship structure the socially recognized practice of kin-making that go into adopting a child. Social censure resulted from its violation. That Bihbahani himself adopts a son in Fayzabad attests to his lack of opposition to such a practice.[96] These aporetic forms of kin-making were embedded in broader modes of social affiliation, such as service and learning, which also used familial language.

Learning often led to overlapping lineages of origin. Teachers, especially early teachers, were sometimes relatives—grandfathers, fathers, uncles, or cousins. After studying with learned family members, a student might study with those prominent in a field of knowledge or with whom one's family had a connection. As in Sufi lineages, these teachers might become fathers-in-law, thereby merging two types of lineage. For example, Mirza Muhammad Hashim Mu'tamid al-Muluk 'Alavi Khan (d. 1749) was a migrant from Shiraz in Delhi. He was included in most mid-eighteenth-century poetic *tazkirih*s, though he was primarily known as a physician and lacked a pen name (*takhallus*). Beginning with 'Alavi Khan's birth date (January or February 1670 AD/Ramazan 1080 AH) and place of birth (Shiraz), Valih Daghistani's extensive biography launches into the line of his teachers and the itinerary of this education and career. The first and most prominent is 'Alavi Khan's well-known father, Mirza Hadi Shirazi, known as *Qalandar* (mendicant), under whom he "reached the highest stage of scientific learning," before studying with other luminaries of late seventeenth-century Shiraz, from whom he gained his medical, as well as religious, ethical, and poetic instruction.[97] 'Alavi Khan's learning becomes clearer in Mirza Hadi's own entry.

Given that Valih's commemoration of 'Alavi Khan focuses on his excellence as a physician as well as his moral rectitude, Mirza Hadi not only provides paternal lineage but also, along with his other teachers, shows 'Alavi Khan's genealogy of knowledge.[98] 'Alavi Khan's moral state and ethical behavior are situated within his patrilineal and learned descent. The connection is explicit between Mirza Hadi's "plentiful portion of the reservoir of mysticism (*tasavvuf*)," together with his ability "to enact Christ-like cures to illness" and 'Alavi Khan as "the Hippocrates and Galen of the age, who is his true successor/son (*khalaf al-sidq*)."[99] The dual meaning of *khalaf*, as son or successor (or both) underscores that a knowledge ancestor need not share a *nasab* tie to figure significantly in a person's origin. Learned descent was thus co-constituted by words connoting legally defined kinship and recognized as genealogy.

In poetic *tazkirih*s, narratives foreground poetic lineages. Just as places of origin and patrilineal descent situate a person, poetic lineage ascribes social and aesthetic locations in poetic circles and styles. One of the most transregionally prominent poetic ancestors was Sa'ib Tabrizi, a notewor-thy lineage that could offer the basis for a poet's inclusion in a *tazkirih*. For Azad Bilgrami, who never met Mulla Muhammad Nasir "Fa'iz" Abhari, the most important feature is his poetic lineage as "the senior student of Mirza Sa'ib," from whom he received his pen name.[100] Fa'iz's students gain prestige through this learned lineage.[101] For students such as Qizilbash Khan "Umid" (d. 1746), the multiple *tazkirih*s that remember him focus entirely on this po-etic lineage.[102] The near total omission of Umid's natal lineage is significant, especially given the respect he was accorded in social rank and commemora-tive intimacy. Perhaps his natal lineage was unremarkable, so that his learned lineage was more significant and, in the *adab* of telling, could alone bear the burden of genealogical origin.

The Work of Lineages

Together, various kinds of lineages performed important labor, demon-strated in the range of ways in which they could be evoked. Azad Bilgrami's narration of Murshid Quli Khan "Makhmur" shows poetic authorization be-stowed through a longer chain of descent and the way learned lineage fits the overall story of origin:

> His original name is Mirza Lutfullah. His father, Hajji Shukrullah Ta-brizi, entered Hindustan from the land (*diyār*) of Iran and established his residence at the port of Surat. Murshid Quli Khan was born in Surat in the year AH 1095/AD 1684. . . . After he had arrived at the age of cognition (*tamyiz*) he was at the service (*khidmat*) of Aqa Habibullah Isfahani, one of the established men of learning resident in Surat, who was one of the senior students (*shāgird-i rashīd*) of [the prominent Safavid scholar] Aqa Husayn Khvansari.[103]

Born in Surat, Murshid Quli Khan had links elsewhere. He was a Safavid migrant's son in Surat and educated by another migrant, distinguished by his relationship to one of the most illustrious late Safavid 'ulama. The ben-efits of this kind of service, as a pupil, included location in a learned lineage. The other half of the entry, the description of his life, mirrors these exalted origins, with details of illustrious patrons and high positions in Bengal and Hyderabad.[104] Here late Safavid learned lineages, far more prominent than

natal lineage, adorn Persianate courts of the subcontinent, connecting them
to Iranian domains.

Lineages of origin loomed large in other kinds of commemorative texts.
In 1809, after almost five years traveling through Hindustan and just before
traveling to Calcutta to board a ship for Iran, Aqa Ahmad Bihbahani wrote
Mir'at al-Ahval-i Jahan numa.[105] Kinship informs the work as a whole. The
first four volumes (out of five) function as his narrative of origins, containing
substantial biographical accounts about the life and work of his patrilineal
and learned forbearers. Volume one focuses on Mulla Muhammad Taqi
Majlisi (d. 1659), the Shaykh al-Islam of Safavid Isfahan, Bihbahani's ancestor five generations removed, all the way down to his grandfather and father,
Vahid and Muhammad 'Ali Bihbahani. The accounts revolve around a list
of their major works, accomplishments, and kinship connections, including
teachers, in-laws, and children. These links show Ahmad's relation to almost
all the major scholarly families in *Iraq-i 'arab*, Iran, and Bengal. In his case,
learned descent between teacher and student had been reinforced by marriage ties, intertwining two types of lineage. In cases where lineage remained
extralegal, the family members of teachers are still described as kin, with
reference to their common ancestor, which for one may be a father and for
Bihbahani a teacher.[106] That Bihbahani opens his "travelogue" with such a
lengthy origins narrative as prelude to his autobiography is no coincidence.
Unsuccessful in securing patronage in Hindustan, in conflict with the Shi'a
'ulama and rulers in Lucknow, this extended account of his illustrious genealogies of family and learning functions to assert his worth as an ethical
juris-consult (*mujtahid*).

In these first four volumes, Bihbahani is a product of his lineages of descent. Mottahedeh notes that "Muslim scholars visualized the transmission
of most learning in genealogical terms, with chains of transmitters stretching
back across the generations."[107] Within the institutional structure of Shi'i
learning in the shrine cities, student-teacher relationships were based on
patronage. While the reciprocal relations that Litvak describes were not as
prominent in Bihbahani's time as later in the nineteenth century, a teacher
was revered by his students, who shared an intellectual commonality from
sitting in the same study circle.[108] Bihbahani, whose forbears numbered
among the most famed religious scholars of the seventeenth and eighteenth

centuries, shared a sense of kinship through affiliation with the men whose descent overlapped with his.[109]

After years of study under his father, at the age of twenty, Bihbahani gained his father's permission to journey to the shrine cities to study. Upon reaching Najaf in March 1796, he entered into service as a pupil of (*dar khidmat-i*) Muhammad Ismail Yazdi, a senior student of Sayyid Muhammad Mahdi Tabataba'i (often simply called Bahr al-'Ulum, after his most famous written work).[110] Here he narrates attending on a teacher to study with words also used for service (*khidmat*). Bahr al-'Ulum was among the foremost scholars of his time, proponent of the Usuli method of legal judgment reintroduced into Shi'ism by Aqa Ahmad's grandfather, Vahid Bihbahani.[111] Aqa Ahmad later attended Bahr al-'Ulum's classes directly with the latter's son, Muhammad Riza. According to Bihbahani, Bahr al-'Ulum treated him with "fatherly kindness (*shafaqat*)" and used to take Ahmad with him to Karbala on ceremonial occasions.[112] In addition to this learned tie, there were marriage ties—Bahr al-'Ulum's paternal aunt had married Aqa Ahmad's grandfather, Vahid Bihbahani, and Bahr al-'Ulum's son eventually married Aqa Ahmad's first cousin. Bahr al-'Ulum was thus connected to Ahmad through learned kinship, marriage ties, and shared descent from Muhammad Taqi Majlisi.[113] These forms of kinships intertwine and reinforce each other, playing a significant role for Ahmad's self-narrative as a juris-consult.

To understand social collectivity, we must dispense with modern alignments of language, family, homeland, and lineage that together function as mutually exclusive bases of connection. Even in a text commemorating Persian language and mastery of its norms, shared connections could bridge simultaneous belonging to another language. In the *Atashkadih*'s deterritorialized section on contemporaries, Azar Baygdili identifies Mirza Ashraf "Mashrab" as "an Arab noble (*a'rāb-i āmīrī*)." During Nadir Shah's reign Mashrab served as the *dīvān* of part of Fars. Afterward, he lost an eye, took up the robes of a dervish, and eventually died in Shiraz.[114] Azar also discusses Shaykh Nasir, "who was from the people of Najaf." Arabic was his first language, as notably "after the death of his father in his childhood, he came to Isfahan. In view of his innate poetic meter, his tongue became acquainted with Persian verse and he used to recite his thought-up verses for me."[115] Nasir, distinguished as an Arabic speaker from '*Iraq-i 'arab*, is a part of Azar's circle of Persian poets in

Isfahan. Similarly, Khan Arzu described his friend and fellow teacher of Persian poetry in Delhi, Shaykh 'Abd al-Riza "Matin," as an Arab (*az 'arab*).[116] While shared genealogical origins play a "powerful role . . . in holding groups together," a shared *adab* of legibility recognized diversity and allowed for coherence of and incorporation across differences. These "paradigms of connectivity" circulated to people with simpler origins.[117]

Lineages were polyglot, multiple, aporetic, and contextually determined. In commemorating Persian poetic community, a subject's most appropriately distinguishing details identified origin. These could be places as sites of acquired lineage, through birth, study, marriage, pilgrimage, adoption, or service. Names announced people's lineages, as with *nisbat*, a term that identified "a person's affiliations such as to a lineage, a group, a place or a profession."[118] Names were the condensed narratives of origin. People could be named for their teachers, a persona to which they aspired (such as expressed by a *takhallus*), acquired titles, eponymous ancestors of a social collective, or other distinguishing features, such as their renowned written works. To evoke differences of first language, places of origin, or collective lineages that could inhere in the designations of Arab or Turk was to make a generalized reference to belonging that distinguished an individual within a Persianate community. Such designations carried hierarchical implications, but just as references to lineages might paint one man loftier than another, perception of loftiness was specific to its context. Only through a nationalist lens does being a Turk or an Arab negate belonging to the Persianate.

Like collective lineages, those of individuals narrating origin in different religious communities distinguished, rather than excluded, a person from Persianate community. When recounting Muhammad 'Ali Bayg's genealogy, Azar explain that "he was the son of Abdal Bayg Naqqashbashi. His grandfather was 'Ali Quli Bayg Farangi, who in the art of painting was the second Mani and who during the reign of the Safavid dynasty found the nobility of Islam."[119] Descent from a grandfather who was a European convert to Islam distinguishes his genealogy. Azar goes on to note that this grandfather worked in service to the Safavids as a painter, and Muhammad 'Ali Bayg, following in his father and grandfather, was painter to Shah Tahmasp II and Nadir Shah. Born and raised in Isfahan and dying in Mazandaran in 1758–59 AD/1172 AH, Muhammad 'Ali Bayg was Azar's intimate, unparalleled in painting. Azar includes him in his *tazkirih* because of their friendship, commenting that "he understood the idea behind poetry well, attended well to its subtleties and sometimes (*gāhī*) composed verses." Not primarily or even prolifically a poet, Muhammad ʿAli Bayg was refined enough to understand and write as much poetry as any educated man, but not enough to have a pen name. Nevertheless, the number of verses Azar includes is greater than for many prolific, well-known poets, like Hazin, whom he had not met. Relationships largely dictated representation in *tazkirih*s and should caution us against reading these texts as modern scholarly works on poetic style disconnected from social and political entanglements. Azar's positive description and declared friendship with Muhammad ʿAli Bayg demonstrate that his descent from a European convert grandfather does not bar him from embrace within Azar's aesthetic, moral, and social community.

Even with historical figures, parochial genealogical differences are not criteria for exclusion from a poetic community. Valih describes Kayfi-yi Naw Musalman as "a Jewish youth. He went to Sabzvar from Sistan and became ennobled by the nobility of Islam. At the end he came to Hindustan in the reign of Jahangir Padshah. He has extremely good verses."[120] His Jewish origins do not interfere with Valih's positive reception of his verses and his inclusion in the *Riyaz*. Indeed, Valih provides less biography and fewer verses for many poets with Muslim lineages. Conversion to Islam might here bridge difference, but Kayfi's moniker (*laqab*) as New Muslim indicates origins that set him apart. Though we cannot know from Valih's entry, this less-than-exalted lineage suggests at least the possibility that inclusion need not mean equality.

Turks, women, Arabs, and those from other parochial communities were distinguished within the Persianate. But because it was premised on varying degrees of mastery of *adab*, these differences alone did not constitute the boundaries of Persianate inclusion. Though by the early modern period its ideal figure was male, Muslim, and of Middle Eastern origin, the Persianate included modes of intelligibility that could encompass, connect, and contain broader social collectivities of language, descent, gender, or religion. Evoking differences of origin thus referenced broader social belonging, distinguishing, rather than excluding, individuals within a community of Persianate *adab*.

CHAPTER 6

ℕaming and Its ℂAffiliations

NAMES WERE INDICATORS of the origins inherited at birth and further accrued in the course of a life. Proper names, forefathers' names, *nisbat*s, titles, and various kinds of monikers (for instance, pen names or *laqab*s) could mark affiliations and differences.[1] In commemorating lives, names evoked people and collectives; they played a role in telling, linking people to places, to each other, and to collectives, or else distinguishing them from one another. The form of their telling was transregionally intelligible across levels of education, in written and oral contexts. The vast scope of what it meant to be Persian is attendant in the range of names and naming practices. Even names that localized individuals and collectives were constituted against and often by the broader transregional nature of mobility in the Persianate. Names, how they evoke people and their connections to each other, tell us a great deal about what was historically possible with respect to conceptions of difference. In turn, these possibilities and conceptions underwrote the meaning of practices of affiliation. Attending to the historical forms of telling a person or a group's origin through the miasma of *our* present requires not only translating the cultural hermeneutics of origins but also considering the stakes of use as we refer to and thus evoke them. The *adab* of naming is thus the font from which we can consider a lexicon beyond the proto-nationalism of our current analytic language.

The significances of particular names were historically specific. Scholarship on early Islam has discussed ways in which *nisbat*s of place distinguished Arabs from non-Arabs (usually Persians),[2] but by the later High Persianate period this was no longer the case. But *nisbat*s also connected individuals to larger social collectivities. "Although quite different from genealogy, another term from the same root, *nisba*, pl. *nisab* [*q.v.*], the naming after an ancestor or tribe but also after a locality or profession, was seen as the same thing."[3] The word literally meant relationship or connection. As we saw in the last chapter, Baygdili Shamlu, for example, was Azar's *nisbat*.

But names, even of places or ancestors, were more complicated because, as I have argued, lineage was not limited to patrilineal descent (*nasab*). Names were condensed narratives of origins and thus a means of disseminating their lineages, situating individuals in the world according to their relationships, inherited and accrued, and communicating affiliations and differences. In addition to showing the ways in which individuals could be named, this chapter focuses on how Persians were named. In contrast with modern terms of identity, names for Persians were contextually determined, specific to the time and place. Sometimes these terms—Mughal, Qizilbash, '*ajam*, Tajik—reflected regions of origin, regions of arrival or utterance, natal lineages, or languages spoken, written, affiliated with. Context thus determined usage, and in the subcontinent, nomenclature distinguished between regions of origin, rather than language. This articulation contrasts markedly with a modern term like Iranian, which denotes an objective and autonomous national identity mutually exclusive from others. One is Iranian everywhere, whereas one was Mughal only in Hindustan, only when one had arrived from Irani or Turani domains, and stayed, or was born to such a father or forefather.

Qizilbash

The seemingly familiar term Qizilbash meant a number of different things through the early modern period. By the eighteenth century it meant something broader than the particular Turco-Mongol lineages that formed the backbone of Safavid power in the sixteenth century, though it retained its association with Safavid rule. In Hindustan, Qizilbash became one way to

identify a Persian from Safavid Iran. For example, Valih Daghistani says the
following about Qizilbash Khan "Umid":

> [H]is name (*ism*) is Muhammad Riza and his birthplace is Hamadan. He
> was raised and educated in paradise-like Isfahan. He received his penname
> from Navvab Mirza Tahir Vahid. He was a companion (*mu'āshir*) of Mir
> Najat, Fa'iz Abhari, and other poets there [in Isfahan]. At the start of Ba-
> hadur Shah's reign he arrived to Hindustan and through the mediation
> (*vasātat*) of Zulfiqar Khan he found distinction with the *mansab* of 1000
> and title (*khitāb*) of Qizilbash Khan.[4]

The list of his companions, offices, and migrations continues, but these first
lines give us an origin, told as the story of his names. He inherits little but a
proper name and a birthplace, though he accrues two more names. For this
refined man of letters, the first name beyond his proper name is his pen name
(Umid, meaning hope, trust, desire) bestowed by his poetic ancestor and his
circle of poetic elders, one of whom, Fa'iz Abhari, was the student of the
great seventeenth-century poet Sa'ib Tabrizi. This name is later joined by a
title granted by the Mughal emperor, making him an office-holding Khan.
Although Muhammad Riza has no stated natal lineage, his learned lineage is
sufficient; its story grants him distinguishing names, one of which is a *nisbat*
made title, that reflect his connections to social circles and their aesthetic
communities in Isfahan and Delhi (though more appear in the story of his
life that follows). Why, however, would an individual with no known link to
the Turkic *uymāq*s that served the Safavids be called Qizilbash Khan?

Forms of naming contain multiple meanings, which accrue over time.
Qizilbash expanded in meaning from a term used for the Turkic *uymāq*s sup-
porting the Safavids to indicating specificity to Safavid Iran. Tempting as it
is to oppose it to Mughal, a term evoking Timurid-ruled Hindustan, they
are far more aporetically imbued. The term Qizilbash originally referred to
the thirteen Turco-Mongol collectives (such as the Shamlu) whose red caps
marked them as the devotees of the Safavid Sufi Shaykhs and later as soldiers
who helped bring the order's hereditary leader to power as Shah.[5] At first
this name "applied only to those Turcomen tribes inhabiting eastern Anatolia, northern Syria, and the Armenian highlands, which were converted
by the Safavid *da'va*, or propaganda, and became disciples of the Safavid

Shaykh. Eventually, however, the term came to be applied loosely to certain
non-Turcomen supporters of the Safavids."[6] In eighteenth-century sources,
one use of this term meant something like Iranian, though not in the modern nationalist sense and only in some contexts. Its older meaning remained
alongside newer meanings. For instance, Arzu calls Ibrahim Bayg one of the
Qizilbash people (*mardum-i Qizilbāsh*), who came to Hindustan with Yadgar
'Ali Sultan, envoy of Shah Abbas (d. 1629), and stayed.[7] This is the original
sense of the term, indicating that Ibrahim Bayg was a descendent of one
of the Qizilbash collectives and also attached to the Safavid Shah's envoy.
Similarly, Valih used the term's original meaning when writing about Babur's
interaction with Shah Isma'il in the early sixteenth century, referring to the
Safavid army, which then consisted of Qizilbash. He calls them "Qizilbash
soldiers (*sipāh*)" and "Qizilbash commanders (*umarā*)."[8] This usage continued, however, even when these positions were no longer filled with those of
actual Qizilbash lineages.

Qizilbash later became a generic term referring to anyone associated with
the Safavid state, whether militarily, diplomatically, or administratively.[9] In
eighteenth-century sources written outside Safavid domains, the term Qizilbash came to be a floating signifier linked to the Safavid dynasty, detached
from the lineages of the *uymāq*s, and eventually extended to certain inhabitants of its domains. It may seem to approximate Iranian, but, significantly,
Persians made a choice to use Qizilbash, not Irani, in this capacity. Qizilbash
articulated an imperial association with the Safavids first and foremost. Their
domains, rather than an autonomously coherent idea of Iran as a land, were
the point of reference. In relation to something external or threatening to
this dominion—for example, Hindustan or local rebellions against central
authority—Qizilbash also referred to the military commanded by the Safavid
throne (eventually emptied of its Safavid ruler). When Hazin describes contemporary events, Qizilbash refers to the armed forces of Nadir Shah Afshar,
though these were mostly composed of Lurs, Kurds, Afghans, and various
Sunni Turkic tribes.[10] Though the term continued to characterize the Safavid
military, Qizilbash no longer dominated its leadership.

By the mid-eighteenth century, the term could be used to title a migrant recently arrived from Isfahan at the Mughal court. Qizilbash Khan
would have made no sense in a Safavid context, just as a place name moniker

distinguished people only *after* they had left a place.[11] Qizilbash came to
identify from the outside, even after the demise of the Safavid state, distinguishing a kind of Persian. Hazin, writing in Delhi about events in Isfahan,
notes that some former Safavid officials taught the Afghans "the laws of
rulership and dominion and ways and customs of livelihood and economy
(*qavānīn-i saltanat u jahāndārī va rāh u rusūm-i ma'īshat u dunyādārī*)." As a
result, the Afghans "began to imitate the manner (*tarīq-i taqlīd*) of the Qizilbash."[12] Hazin here uses the term to refer to Safavid imperial rule, not the
specific collectives that brought the dynasty to power. Beyond the military,
the term could be used for any other functions associated with Safavid institutions and practices. Many modes of rule, administration, and comportment
were transferable to Timurid domains—as the dense circulation of administrative elites between Iran and Hindustan attests—indicating that Qizilbash
identified practices recognized as Persianate governance.[13] In Hazin's usage
the term distinguishes Persianate forms in Safavid Iran from those of peripatetic Pashto speakers, whose social organization and customs differed.
Qizilbash inhered in no particular lineage, however, and could be assumed
with imitation, the first step to mastery.

Throughout the eighteenth century, Iran came to be specified by its Safavid past, especially after the dynasty fell. This link was writ large in the usage
of the term Qizilbash. Writing at the turn of the nineteenth century in Hyderabad, 'Abd al-Latif Shushtari, who came of age in Zand-ruled Shushtar,
recounts Aqa Muhammad Khan Qajar's attempts to force the Georgians to
renew fealty to the Shahs of Iran and so complete his restoration of Safavid domains. Shushtari calls the armed forces of Iran "Qizilbash warriors
[against non-Muslims] (*ghāzīyān-i Qizilbāsh*)" pairing such a description
with "the bold ones of Iran (*dilīrān-i Īrān*)," making Qizilbash a term for a
person who belongs to Iran as a realm. In recounting the battle, he calls them
"the leonine Qizilbash men (*shīr mardān-i Qizilbāsh*)."[14] After describing the
bloody sack of Tbilisi in 1794, described as redress for the Georgians' betrayal
of their loyalty oaths to the Safavids, Shushtari refers to the way in which
"the Qizilbash gave [them, the Georgians] morally-correct and manly justice
(*dād-i mardī va mardānigī*)." By this point, the main meaning of Qizilbash
had shifted from dynastic throne to its specific domains. Qizilbash referred to
the king of Iran's soldiers, and former Safavid domains were what was proper

to Iran. Like Hazin's earlier descriptions of Nadir Shah, Shushtari represents Aqa Muhammad Khan's exploits as restoration of Safavid Iran. Shushtari goes on to comment that if the "king of the Qizilbash (*pādshāh-i Qizilbāsh*)" can bring order to that piece of land, "he will be superior to all the kings of the world," and his status will be as paramount as it was in Kayanid times. The rule of the Kayanids is figured as a golden age, when "all the kings [of the world] partook from the beneficence of their table (*mā'idih*), and [were] obedient tributaries" of Iran's ruler. Shushtari further clarifies the meaning of "king of the Qizilbash," noting that a wise Russian told him that whoever secured rule over "the kingdom (*saltanat*) of Iran" was worthy of ruling the whole world.[15] This is an articulation of cyclical Persianate millenarianism: restoration of proper rule in Iran, inaugurating a return to a pre-Islamic political past as a worldly ideal.[16] Here restoration brings the triumph of good, triggering a paradigm in which Iran's ruler becomes the Shahanshah (king of kings).[17] This past future draws on concepts intelligible in the present, with Iran defined according to its Safavid domains. By this logic, Qizilbash were people with origins in Iran, and the king of the Qizilbash was the king of Iran. This king was Muhammad Khan Qajar and later Fath 'Ali Shah, demonstrating that, in the office of ruler, Safavid-specific meanings survived the Safavid dynasty and anchored early Qajar rule.

The early nineteenth-century use of the term Qizilbash, as a name for Shi'a originating in Iranian domains, underlines the significance of Safavid-specific markers, even as Fath 'Ali Shah had begun to craft a Qajar dynastic identity from the pre-Islamic past.[18] Both 'Abd al-Latif Shushtari and Aqa Ahmad Bihbahani name Shi'a migrants from Iran (and their descendants) as Qizilbash, in the context of other Persian speakers in Hindustan. Such a term of distinction was intelligible to Persians in both Iran and Hindustan, since Bihbihani circulated his text in both lands.[19] Describing how he passed his time in Calcutta, Shushtari notes the "comings and goings of the Qizilbash and their sons (*Qizilbāshiyyih va awlād-i īshān*)," in contrast with "some of the people of Hindustan (*mardum-i Hindūstān*) and other places."[20] Similarly, Shushtari mentions that "a large group of Qizilbash are resident" in Murshidabad. That this term does not refer to the twelve *uymāq*s of early Safavid fame is clear when Shushtari elaborates that "from that group was Sayyid Muhammad Khan, titled Shir Jang, from the Sayyids

of Kirmanshah. Because of Nadir Shah's revolution (*inqilāb*) and the Ottoman invasion of those boundaries (*ḥudūd*) he happened [to come] to Hind,
entered Murshidabad, and joined the ranks of the government."[21] The term's
Shi'a-specific definition is apparent as Shushtari eschews it when referring
to non-Shi'a from Iran, such as "wealthy Julfan Armenians" resident in Calcutta. Though Shushtari enjoys "a perfect friendship" with Khvajih Sarkis
and his son Khvajih Avanus, whom he identifies as "priest-born (*kishīsh
zādih*) and from the nobles (*nujabā'ī*) of Julfa Isfahan," these Khvajihs are
not Qizilbash.[22]

Terms like Qizilbash were intelligible across the Persianate, even as
they specified a locale to and in another place. Between his engagement in
trade with his Basra-based family and his political service to his family in
Hyderabad, Shushtari interacted frequently with travelers throughout the
subcontinent, Persian Gulf ports, and various cities inside Iran. His text was
broadly addressed beyond his locale, and it circulated in Iran.[23] Aqa Ahmad
Bihbahani references *Tuhfat al-'Alam* in an extensive description of Shushtari
and also uses the term Qizilbash to refer to migrants and their descendants,
whom he identifies with Iranian place monikers.[24] Indeed, Bihbahani identifies Shushtari as one of the Qizilbash, though Shushtari has no Qizilbash
natal lineage. In Hindustan, the term refers only to Shi'a Persians from
former Safavid domains, what was known then as Iran. In contrast, in the
Persian Gulf port of Bandar Abbas, Bihbahani describes the large number of
pilgrims and merchants as *'ajam* rather than Qizilbash, distinguishing them
from Arabic speakers.[25] Context thus determined usage, and in the subcontinent, nomenclature distinguished between domains of origin, rather than
language. This articulation contrasts markedly with the modern term Iranian,
which denotes an autonomous national affiliation, mutually exclusive from
others, where one is Iranian everywhere. In the Gulf, the basis of distinction was language, as many Arabs were also Shi'i and circulated through the
Iranian-ruled side of the Gulf. Bihbahani's text was written in Patna, just
before he journeyed to the Bengali coast to sail back to Iran. Though he left
five copies in Patna, the text is also written for an Iranian audience and dedicated to the Qajar Prince, Muhammad 'Ali Mirza Dawlatshah.[26] Bihbahani
could adopt the term Qizilbash without explanation because designations
were mutually intelligible to Persianate audiences.

Names, Places, and Possibilities of Affiliation

Too often scholars have misread place monikers as indicators of origin. For instance, Jean Calmard states, "As may be deduced from their names and origins, the scholars of Timurid-Mughal India who wrote on Safavid Persia were of Persian descent."[27] Like many others, Calmard uses the term Persian to refer to people from Safavid domains, equating land with language. As we have seen, however, place constituted origin through lineage, and Iranian place monikers might indicate birthplaces of fathers or grandfathers, sites of pilgrimage, or simply residence before a recent migration. Valih Daghistani's description of Mirza Majid Shushtari explains that he was born in Dizful, "one of the dependencies of Shushtar, in the year 1677–78/1088," but that "because he lived some of the time in Shushtar, he is known as Shushtari."[28] These multifarious meanings are even more obvious in the case of Darvish Haydar Yazdi, whom Valih notes "is that same Mawlana Haydar Khurasani, known as Tabrizi." Valih further clarifies that "he was the student of Mulla Lisani and spent time in companionship (*suhbat-hā dāsht*) with Mawlana Vahshi Yazdi, and so was for a time in Yazd. For that reason he has been known as Yazdi."[29] Darvish Haydar was known according to the multiple place monikers accrued in his peregrinations. He would have arrived in Yazd with a different place moniker and been known as Yazdi only after leaving Yazd for his next destination. The name then might have been replaced, augmented, or retained. Different people might have known him by various combinations of names. A person accrued names as they became part of his past, and these names joined together with origin to tell the truth of his present.

Names were used strategically. Moving between cultural zones, Joseph Emin changed the presentation of his name, easily shifting among Joseph, Housep, Emin, and Ameen. Joseph, his father's Christian baptismal name, is what he gives as his own first name to Europeans. In contrast, for the Georgian Prince Heraclius he is Emin, son of Joseph.[30] He also is careful to call himself Joseph or Yusef in Ottoman domains, "for the word Emin is an Arabic name, and he feared lest the deluded Turks should be troublesome to him."[31] As a traveler seeking aid (from the English and Georgians) or at least seeking to remain unmolested (by the Ottomans), Emin's naming strategies further his needs as a stranger (see Part I: Place).

Litvak's study of nineteenth-century 'ulama in Iraqi shrine cities contains even more explicit assumptions of place monikers as indicators of origin. He notes that in the shrine cities, "the gathering of individuals from diverse places sharpened the sense of otherness, and enhanced ethnic and regional consciousness, as was reflected even in the addition of place of origin to the name."[32] Place-name *nisbat*s certainly indicated connections to that place. However, they need not indicate a birthplace or ancestral homeland, and even then, that did not translate as proto-nationalist loyalty to larger regions. Rather than indicators of homelands, they are better understood as monikers. Less straightforward than birthplaces, they were often records of mobility, lineage, and achievement. Calling them monikers allows us to account for their relational nature, and the range of possible identifications through the course of a life.

Place monikers denoted the more capacious conception of origin than a singular ancestral home shown in previous chapters. Aqa Ahmad Bihbahani never set foot in Bihbahan. Rather, his place moniker indicated descent from his grandfather, the famous Muhammad Baqir (or Vahid), who was called Bihbahani after he moved to Karbala from Bihbahan. Aqa Ahmad's father took this name with him when he moved from Karbala to Kirmanshah, where Aqa Ahmad was born. But Vahid Bihbahani was not born in Bihbahan. Descended through his mother from the famous Majlisi family, he was born in Isfahan and lived there until his twenties before moving to Karbala at the time of the Afghan invasion. Finding the scholarly environment hostile to his Usuli ideas, Vahid then moved to Bihbahan, which had attracted a number of 'ulama because it was deemed safer than larger cities in the upheavals of the mid-eighteenth century. He stayed for about twenty-five years before returning to Karbala, where he began developing Usuli thought, gathering students, and garnering fame. Vahid's place moniker, passed on to his descendants, adhered to his name because he arrived in Karbala the second time from Bihbahan, where he became well known by the epithet "Vahid" (incomparable). He was likely known as Isfahani the first time he arrived in Karbala and perhaps even during his time in Bihbahan. Used in conjunction, Vahid Bihbahani's place monikers, together with his moniker of achievement, read like an itinerary.[33] He was born in Isfahan, where his parents lived, but he married into a family in Bihbahan, where he lived for two and a half decades.[34] Irreducible to birthplaces, place monikers are even less indicators of modern ethnicity.

Names gained permanence when the modern state demanded it or, more appropriate to Aqa Ahmad's time, when the name secured status by proclaiming descent from a famous forbear.[35] As he traveled through Hindustan seeking patronage as a jurist, Aqa Ahmad's self-designation, as descended from Vahid Bihbahani, offered a basis upon which to build a reputation as a Shi'i juridical scholar. Temporary or permanent, names evoked affiliations as "a political strategy, a highly mobile signifier of power relations."[36] Familial monikers gained meaning in a wider context of negotiating status and position. As the nineteenth century progressed, the British colonial state began to impose permanence on names. The colonial state sought to know its subjects as singular and fixed, causing place monikers to become surnames, made to represent origin and identity (and remaking these concepts in the process). Yet relational names and subject positions that overlap across communities still persisted, as subjects pushed back, seeking more expansive possibilities for affiliation and difference where strategically beneficial.[37]

Mughals and the Question of Loyalty

If fixed names were only partially realized in the nineteenth century, they make little sense projected further back. In discussions of eighteenth-century Hindustani courts, historians have read political factions in place monikers as indicators of origins and thus of "natural" loyalties. For example, Axworthy notes, "[t]he divisions at the Moghul court between factions among the nobles had weakened the Moghul state, making Nader [Shah]'s task easier. Many of the great Moghul nobles were adventurers who had come to India from lands to the north; another factor that had limited their loyalty to the Moghul dynasty."[38] Yet the head of the so-called Turani faction, Nizam al-Mulk Asaf Jah of Hyderabad, patronized migrants from Iranian domains and their descendants, such as Qizilbash Khan Umid and Sayyid Riza Shushtari. Men with more distant lineages, Shi'a whose families had migrated to Hindustan in the seventeenth century, also chose service to the Nizam.[39] These affiliations blur facile dichotomies between Irani and Turani factions, to which modern scholars further assign Shi'a and Sunni affiliation and Persian and Turkish ethnicity.[40] Assuming that affiliation with Irani and Turani factions precluded "real" loyalty to a presumably Indian Timurid imperial polity, historians contrast "true" Hindustanis, whose loyalties are presumably natural.

Yet Timurid emperors represented their origins similarly to adherents of the supposedly "foreign" Irani and Turani factions. Colonial Orientalism first articulated the narrow binary of native versus foreign, and its Hindu fundamentalist heirs have since taken up its refrain.[41] Its power partly derives from claimed historical bases, concealing past meanings, which have since been forced to fit a modern, mutually exclusive mode of belonging. So how do we understand the Timurids and the broader category of Mughals aporetically, in terms of the Persianate?

Timurid political legitimacy was both local and universal. In a study of Jahangir's memoirs, Balabanlilar notes that "although he had never set foot in the Central Asia he considered his patrimony, Jahangir insistently defined and maintained his imperial identity in constant reference to the Turco-Mongol Timurid legacy of his [paternal] ancestors." This elite lineage originated in Central Asia, but from the fifteenth century, its prestige was widely acknowledged across the Persianate world.[42] By Akbar's reign the Timurids had established the lineage in Hindustan, using the transregionally recognizable Persianate idioms of power to engage with regional ideas, practices, and paradigms.[43] Though they sought to set themselves above the Timurids, as we saw in Chapter 2, the Safavids acknowledged Timurid prestige and legitimacy and shared Perso-Islamic concepts and Turco-Mongol political culture.[44] Recognizing "the power of a prestigious genealogy in the establishment of dynastic political rights," the Safavids created genealogical ties to the Shi'a Imams, as well as political lineages from Timur.[45] Increasingly sophisticated understandings of Safavid and Timurid political cultures—linked and mutually intelligible through an earlier shared Timurid heritage and constant exchange of people, texts, and ideas—make protonationalist assumptions unsustainable. Scholarly assessments and terms, therefore, need revision. Among them are analyses of the political maneuvering of Sa'adat Khan, the eighteenth-century Navvab of Lucknow, as the fifth-column machinations of an Iranian "émigré" from Nishapur whose loyalty to Timurid overlords was ostensibly questionable.[46] Instead, his overtures to Nadir Shah in times of upheaval and political shifts must be read through the lens of *adab*.

Migrants from Irani and Turani domains, their descendants, and the Timurids were all Mughals. The imperial family located their lineages of origin in Khurasan and Samarqand.[47] Though the Timurids in Hindustan were called Mughals in English, continued scholarly use of this term as an imperial surname obfuscates both its broader meaning and Persianate perceptions of the imperial family, which did not use Mughal. Nor was it a surname in transregional parlance. Rather, it was used locally in Deccani courts, from where it likely entered European parlance.[48] Up until the early nineteenth century, when some Persians began to adopt the British designations, the imperial family was Gurgani (or Gurkani), after Timur's own title; otherwise it was the house of Timur. Gurgan was a Turkicized version of the Mongol word meaning son-in-law, indicating Timur's self-conscious aspiration to Mongol charismatic rule and his marriage to a Chagatai (Ghenghisid) princess.[49] What came to be the Timurid realm in the fifteenth century straddled eastern Irani and Turani domains and was populated by Turco-Mongol tribesmen, Persianized Turkomens, and Tajiks, the Turan-specific term for Persians.[50] Later, reflecting the melding of these collectives, the Safavids and the Uzbegs distinguished between Turks and Tajiks, categories indicating language groups, patrilineage, and places of origin. But these distinctions existed aporetically. In both Iran and Turan, Turkic and Persian lineage, language, and practices coexisted, sometimes in the same person.[51]

At the turn of the nineteenth century, some Persians, like Shushtari, began to call the family Baburid.[52] This name reassigned the family's origin to Hindustan and a progenitor less exalted than Timur. The name thus shed its previous places, making the lineage more sedentary, singular, and local. Chapter 2 noted how Hazin acknowledged the family's Timurid ancestry but had negative things to say about those who came after Babur. To level his criticism, he had to distance them from Timur, and he used the formation of the new Hindustani imperium to mark the break. This demotion, disseminated in naming, became increasingly intelligible according to broader perceptions of later eighteenth century Timurid rulers' debasement, but did not occur in Persian texts authored in Iran over the nineteenth century.[53]

Through the present day, Persian-language scholarship produced in Iran has retained the term Gurgani as the dynastic name for what English-language scholarship calls Mughal. But its meaning has become something closer to the

term Mughal. For instance, under the listing "the Gurkanis of Hind," Tawfiq
Subhani tells us that "the founder of this dynasty is Zahir al-din Muhammad
Babur." We are told that he is son of 'Umar Shaykh and grandson of Sultan
Abu Sa'id, but Subhani never makes the explicit linkage to Timur. Lineage's
significance is merely that "from his father's side 'Umar Shaykh [inherited]
the rulership of the small district (*nāhiyih*) of Farghana."[54] Writing at the end
of the eighteenth century, Persians began to demote the rulers of Hindustan
from Timurids to Baburids. In not so stark a contrast, modern Iranian scholars
have retained the term Gurgan, but its meaning has changed to something
like Baburid. Then and now, the change is enacted by severing Babur from
his lineages and replacing them with his new locale, making a singular place
bear an anachronistic burden. Modern meanings of the terms Gurkani and
Mughal obscure older ones that do not resonate with them; they need to be
reapportioned their historical significance. Such is the project of epistemological translation across the transforming divide of a modern logic.

Persians, Universally Local

Historically, Mughal meant something like what Qizilbash and Tajik de-
noted, a specific kind of Persian. The early eighteenth-century chronicler
Khafi Khan notes that from Akbar's reign "the term 'Mughal' became common for Turks and Tajiks of 'Ajam and even for the Sayyids of Iran and
Turan."[55] The Timurid emperor 'Alamgir (d. 1707) noted that Mughals could
be born in Iran or in Hindustan.[56] At the end of the eighteenth century,
Khalil Banarasi describes the origin of the poet Bidil (d. 1720) as "the Irlāt
Mughals of Turan," referencing the Turco-Mongol collective's location before Bidel's lineage arrived in Hindustan. Mughal as Turco-Mongol social
collectives had a longer history and broader meaning in Persianate parlance,
coexisting with more regional usages, like the Hindustani-specific term indicating Turani or Irani lineage. Mughal encompassed the Timurids, along
with many others. For example, Arzu describes 'Abd al-Hakim "Hakim" Lahori's origin as "from the Mughal people (*az mardum-i mughuliyyih*)." He
means

> His noble father was titled Shadman Khan. From the side of his grand-
> mother (*jaddih*) he is a sayyid, from among the sons of Qazi Mir Yusuf, one

of the esteemed sayyids of Herat. From his father's side he is [descended] from the *Awrāgh Dūrman* Uzbegs, who are among the nobles of the Uzbeg people (*qawm*). In the time of 'Alamgir, Shadman Khan came from Balkh to Hind.[57]

Hakim was a Hindustani-born Mughal, with lineages of place that included Balkh and Herat and with natal lineages from the Prophet—transmitted through a grandmother—and Uzbeg nobles.[58] For Arzu, Shadman Khan's move from Balkh to Hindustan and his immediate entry into high-ranking Mughal service raised no question of suspect loyalties. His son, Hakim, was Arzu's student, whose origins one generation removed from Balkh distinguished him among Arzu's learned descendants with various natal lineages and itineraries from across the Persian world. Hakim was a Lahori Mughal whose learned lineage also included Shah Afarin Lahori, a well-known Sufi adept and poet. Without migrants there were no Mughals, and for Arzu, a Hindustani-centric commemorator of Persian community, the Mughal-born were Hindustani.

The same principle applies for the Khatri Persian, Lachmi Nara'in Shafiq Aurangabadi, whose self-commemoration appeared in Chapter 4. His *taz-kirih*, *Gul-i Ra'na*, limits itself to the poets of Hindustan, subdivided into sections on Muslims and Hindus. The poets of Hindustan are "versifiers born and raised in Hindustan," meaning "nightingales for whom the flowers they sing among are in *this* garden." (The implication being that there were other possible gardens.) Among those Shafiq commemorates are large numbers of Mughals whose fathers, grandfathers, or other ancestors migrated to Hindustan from Iran and Turan.[59] Origin, or *asl*, from a place other than Hindustan coexists easily with being a poet of Hindustan and, in turn, with being Persian.

The Timurid court contained identifiable Irani and Turani factions, but they were both subsets of Mughal. Irani, Turani, Mughal, or even Persian fail to map onto *jins*, most often translated as ethnicity according to the blood logic of descent. Its meaning was simply type or kind. A wider consideration of the term demonstrates that a whole spectrum of lineages could form the basis for similarity of type (*jinsiyat*).[60] One could share similarity of poetic discourse (*jinsiyat-i sukhan*)[61] or could be of the same kind, 'ajam in Istanbul, through dress or language, as Abu Talib Isfahani was in 1801. He did not socialize with choice people (*a'izzih*) other than government officials because "my clothes were *'ajamī* and the Turks did not like [that]. The hostility of that group (*jamā'at*) toward Iranis at the level of the state and community (*mulk va millat*) is to such a degree that seeing their very faces is abhorrent (*makrūh*) and [shedding] their blood is considered permissible (*ḥallāl*)." In lieu of social interaction with the Ottoman residents of Istanbul, he had many visits with "Irani and Hindi strangers (*gharībān*) [to Istanbul], particularly Afghans of Peshawar and Qandahar and people of Punjab, who were resident in Istanbul for travel or study (*siyāhat yā tālib-i 'ilm*)."[62] Recall that Abu Talib's father was a Tabrizi Isfahani "from the Turkic groups (*az jamā'at-i atrāk*).[63] Here, a Turkic collective lineage was not a marker of sameness, as Abu Talib was dressed in *'ajamī* fashion (as Mughals in Hindustan were wont to do) and counted among the *millat* connected to the Irani state (as former Safavid domains). It is tempting to ascribe to this community a Shi'i basis. Yet people from Iran include Sunni Muslims with Afghan lineages, from the border region of former Safavid domains (Qandahar) and from a city in Hindustani domains (Peshawar). Sunni Afghans could be from Iran, and shared lineages could link people inside and outside those domains.

'Ajam could also refer to a language group, people who knew Persian, though almost always in a multilingual context. On his way to Baghdad, Abu Talib notices that in Mardin (in southeastern Anatolia), "the language of the common people (*'awvām*) is Arabic and Kurdish and for the elite (*khavāss*) in addition to these two is Turkish and Persian." He notes that from Diyarbakir (northwest of Mardin) "the knowledge of Persian begins. From Mardin to Baghdad all four languages are spoken."[64] In a village outside Nusaybin, Abu Talib meets Kurds who "know the Persian language (*zabān-i Farsī*). They knew me as Irani and of the same kind (*ham-jins*) and they were extremely solicitous and kind to us."[65] Exchanges of social *adab* occur on the basis of language, with *jins*, or kind, shared across differences of place, lineage, and sectarian affiliation. *'Ajam* could be a place, as much as dress or language and its proper forms. In Istanbul, he compares the practices of women with those of *'ajam* and Hind.[66] Though the referent for *'ajam* is unclear, this diminutive definition of the term refers at least to Iranian domains (and perhaps also

Turan). In contrast, he uses its more expansive definition elsewhere, translating it as Asia, with its border at the Bosphorus straits (Chapter 5).[67]

Irani and Turani political factions at the Timurid court date from the late sixteenth-century wave of migration when, to counter the power of the Chagatai elite, Akbar offered positions to migrants who had accompanied Humayun from Iran.[68] Rather than Iranians, Akbar was recruiting Persians without Chagatai lineages, to avoid rivals from lineages close to his own. When identifying nobles whose ancestry was from Turan, 'Abd al-Karim Kashmiri calls them Turani Mughals (*Mughuliyyih-yi Tūrānī*), distinguishing them from Mughals originating in Iran.[69] Besides places, Mughals possessed other lineages of origin. All Mughals were Muslims, educated, and thus Persianate. Some had lineages reaching back to Turco-Mongol, Kurdish, or Arab collectives, to the Prophet, to lineages of knowledge incorporated into Persianate universal histories or the storied figures of its widely circulated narratives. Yet not all Persians were Mughals, neither the Muslims with more local natal lineages nor Persians of other traditions, be they Hindus from the subcontinent or Armenians from Iran.[70] Mughal was a sociocultural identifier for Muslim in Hindustan with an itinerary of origin through 'ajam's other lands (Iran or Turan).

To call a corporate body Mughal was to categorize it according to its leader.[71] Kashmiri refers to Safdar Jang, the second Navvab of Awadh, as the leader of Irani troops (*sāhib-i fawj-i Īrān*) and the rival of the [faction of] people belonging to Turan (*ahl-i Tūrān*).[72] These designations could be read as evidence of place as the basis of affiliation, but they reflect leadership stemming from Safdar Jang's position as head of the Irani faction at the Mughal court, not because the army was "ethnically" Iranian, from former Safavid domains, or affiliated with its throne. The nobles around these two factions were sometimes migrants from Iran or Turan, but many were born in Timurid domains, like the head of the Turani faction, Nizam al-Mulk Asaf Jah. Naming according to these large domains of origin had distinction and prestige specifically in Timurid Hindustan. Like other ways of identifying Persians, these contextually defined names reflected a relational truth different from modern epistemologies claiming universal objectivity. The meaning of Irani or Turani Mughal, or even just Mughal was specific to Persianate Hindustan. Thackston notes that in the cities of Turan, the term Mughal denoted wild, uncivilized Turco-Mongol nomads with only a thin, dubious layer of Islam.[73] In Hindustan, Mughal indicated sedimentation of lineages and itineraries of prestigious origin. It could be the basis of affiliation, but not an indicator of national identity or loyalty. Such affiliations did not preclude friendships, alliances, or even marriages outside this basis. All of these connections were commemorated, they drew together overlapping collectives, through which they produced a range of possible Persianate selves.

CHAPTER 7

Commemorating Persianate Collectives, Selves

زاهد ظاهرپرست از حال ما آگاه نیست

در حق ما هر چه گوید جای هیچ اکراه نیست

در طریقت هر چه پیش سالک آید خیر اوست

در صراط مستقیم ای دل کسی گمراه نیست [1]

Absorbed with the superficial, the ascetic is not aware of our state

    There is no force to what he says of us

On the road, whatever comes to the traveler is to his good

    No one on the straight path, oh heart, is lost

THROUGHOUT THIS BOOK I have drawn heavily on Persian poetic *tazkirih*s, alongside other texts more commonly read as memoirs, histories, or travelogues. These texts share modes of biographical and autobiographical representation and are together concerned with commemoration of people and their lives. These accounts, I have argued, offer a range of possibilities for imagining place and origin. What I call "commemoration," Zaman calls "auto/biography." Both terms point "to the overlap between writing one's life, composing a history of one's times (which often includes biographical accounts of eminent men of letters) and locating one's authorial self within social, political, familial, and literary circles."[2] This chapter turns toward memory, both the act of remembering and what resulting commemorations tell us about this vast Persianate corpus and its possibilities for Persianate collectives and selfhood. These are not identities, but shared and mutually comprehensible modes of identification, enacted through *adab*.

The very act of remembering (re-membering) brings together memories in particular ways. Moreover, commemoration is an act of memory undertaken together. The commemorative texts that are the sources in this book recollect various assortments of figures, inviting readers to join their authors in acts of remembering. Narration also brings the author into being as a figure, with and through the assembly he remembers, both for himself and for his audience. In these textual acts of remembering, we modern readers can see the range of Persianate collectives that could be imagined and the Persianate selves that could be produced. As the preceding chapters have shown, these imagined selves relied on transregionally recognizable origins and modes of place-making.

Commemoration had a moral stake. Memory served to maintain mindful awareness, a deliberate action that made it "the guarantor of morality," which required discernment and judgment.[3] To act correctly in a given situation, one had to be able to remember previous knowledge and experience. In turn, cultivating moral integrity guarded against memory's loss. *Adab*—proper ethical and aesthetic form—manifested a self's moral integrity through proper behavior and collective moral integrity through proper order or governance.[4] As we saw in Chapter 3, *adab* could protect both selves and collectives from imbalanced humors resulting from extreme climates, intemperate social conditions, or chaotic turns of fate. Similarly, proper ethical and aesthetic forms—as actions in the world and as re-membered narrative assemblages—protected people, individually and together (they were indelibly connected), from descent into immorality caused by forgetfulness.

Memory was both instructive and collective. Commemorative texts were populated with others' voices and lives. They told "stories owned by many voices, and housed in many texts."[5] Auto/biographies brought their authorial selves, as moral subjects, into being as figures by recollecting (and connecting) lives of those worth remembering. To remember a collective was to make a claim about a selection of worthy lives.[6] As we have seen, narrated lives traced origins through lineages beyond the natal, including not only other kin but also peers and others with whom one affiliated or was affiliated (individual agency was not always determinative). A person was situated within a group, and its moral contours gave shape to an author's life. This author was usually, and ideally, a man, yet the memories and voices of women also run through commemorative texts. Women also commemorated, though in texts less often preserved or circulated. Because morality was male, women had to labor more to evoke stock moral figures—the wise elder, the strong protector, the devoted esoteric, the pious chivalric pilgrim—to overlay their own.[7]

One exemplary form of commemorative text, *tazkirih*s, blossomed in late fifteenth-century Timurid Herat. Either standing alone or contained in court chronicles, *tazkirih*s vaunted the learned figures that adorned the courts of Persianate empires. *Tazkirih*s "appeared in clusters, where unstable times led to the need to record lives" worthy of remembrance.[8] These lives and the collectives they commemorated were communities of *adab* that manifested moral order. In times of upheaval or transition, when moral lives were more difficult and an ethical subject's connections more challenging to maintain, *tazkirih*s preserved moral possibilities for better times. Perhaps unsurprisingly, as imperial structures began to unravel in the late seventeenth century, these texts proliferated, and, through the eighteenth century, this quickening happened largely outside formal court patronage.[9]

Commemoration's moral significances point to its political stakes. *Tazkirih*s provided collective moral possibilities, and in their very multiplicity, each moral collective was more than itself. Its figures could and often did belong to other collectives—a poet was also a statesman or a Sufi, a poet of Isfahan and of Delhi. Hindus and women were hierarchically differentiated from, but nevertheless placed separately or together with, Muslims and men. This supple and expansive plurality engendered by aporias of being and belonging allowed collectives to reassert themselves when the political structures that sustained societies failed. Commemorative collectives could also be the basis out of which new political structures asserted themselves. As moral practice, commemoration created continuity and shored up collectives, functioning as political anchor in the absence of stable government.

*Tazkirih*s brought together collectives under different rubrics. All represented aesthetic and social communities (intertwined but not always coeval) through the selection and narration of members, which was a means of affiliation allowing the author to utter "I." Even when limited to a locale or kingdom, most *tazkirih*s included Persians from a variety of origins, narrated according to "literary codes" that remained broadly meaningful far beyond that limited sphere.[10] Layered, overlapping, and multiple, the varied principles of organization do not allow any one of their distinctions, both within and between texts, primacy as an overarching category. Persians were not determined by any distinctions save one, *adab*. This heterogeneity of origin, social location, and sometimes gender and religion were the product of interregional mobility. Shared Persianate forms gave it texture, but its *adab* also encompassed vernaculars, such as Urdu. *Tazkirih*s could travel, bringing the collectives and localities of one place to another. Overlaps and shared forms eased arrivals and absorptions.

The poetic *tazkirih* was just one type. *Tazkirih*s memorialized other collectives, not mutually exclusive with poets, among them mystics, scholars, and statesmen at court.[11] Authors of poetic *tazkirih*s represented certain past and contemporary poets as part of a collective of ancestors and peers, within which their lineages and social relationships were nested. Knowledge of poetry and ability to compose linked a wide variety of occupational classes and social positions. Unlike *tazkirih*s centered on mystics or scholars, which focused on types of Islamicate communities (across languages),[12] or *tazkirih*s fixed on courts, which focused on geographically defined political communities, poetic *tazkirih*s explicitly attended to an aesthetically and socially constituted collective of Persianate *adab*. Their very scope and delimiting logic staged the diverse ways that collectives of *adab* could be imagined and the forms of Persianate selves these collectives could authorize.

The Role of Mobility

Mobility—imagined, received, undertaken, and observed—undergirded commemoration. Circulations of texts and their representations spread common rhetorical modes and forms of place and origin across the Persianate, creating familiarities and connections that made affiliations possible. These rhetorical representations of place and origin could condition experience and give places and people a legibility to Persianate audiences that might not have physically encountered them. Identifying the articulation and circulation of familiarity allows us to appreciate what imprints eighteenth-century specificities may have had on these imaginings.[13] My concern is with the perception of circulation or its lack, which authors narrate according to their ability to travel, to correspond, and to give and receive texts and visitors, through which they maintain a sense of connection to people and places across the Persianate. These connections reveal changes to the continuing circulation of texts and the possibilities for imagined communities. Concomitantly, altered connections changed the possible terms of self, which were always articulated relationally through the collective.[14]

Historically, the relationship between circulation and community did not rely on mutually existing distinctions. Commemoration need not replace history, understood as occurrences verifiable as fact and presumed to have always constituted the (transhistorically existing) "historical record." Recall the kaleidoscope as metaphor, discussed in Part I, through which we can see empirical forms alongside others, according to the aporias of Persianate *adab*. We must approach empirical history and structure its meaning by considering circulation through the lens of commemoration, a mode of recording and remembering the past less anachronistically restrictive for eighteenth-century Persianate contexts. The commemorative texts that I argue carried the potential for reinforcing and extending premodern imagined communities depended on existing networks of circulation. These networks enabled the creation of texts, as authors depended on both correspondence and travel for the acquisition of information and knowledge.

As Binbaş has shown, networks and their social practices formed the scaffolding of community. He reminds us that in the fifteenth century,

> distinct Sufi communities, which previously had been organized around influential Sufi figures, began to acquire an institutional character distinguished by several features, including: the principles of the master-disciple relationship, spiritual lineage (*silsilih*) connecting disciples to a leading [usually dead] Sufi Shaykh, the veneration of tombs, distinct rituals that provided an identity marker for members of the Sufi community, and a substantial amount of Sufi literature that served to reinforce all of the above.[15]

Here we have a collective with particular features: relationships connecting members to the living and the dead, lineages of origin (with the *silsilih* as a Sufi answer to the question "Where do you come from?"), a set of practices defining one's relationship with the hidden and manifest worlds, and commemorative writings whose circulation undergirded it all. Commemoration thus imagined the world according to particular stakes. It allowed individuals to lay claim to the collective and to answer its call, thus articulating themselves. With the two pillars of this formulation of prenationalist community—the *adab* of relationships with the living and dead and the *adab* of commemorating such relationships—we can read in commemorative forms the possibilities of Persianate collectives and embedded selves.

Lachmi Nara'in "Shafiq" Aurangabadi's commemorative project exemplifies the expansive potentials of community. *Gul-i Ra'na* (1767–68 AD/1181 AH), written from Aurangabad, offers a vision of the way geographically located collectives fit together in a broader Persianate space.[16] Shafiq describes his *tazkirih* as concerned with "versifiers born and raised (*mawzūnānī kih mawlid va mansha*) in Hindustan," meaning "those nightingales for whom the flowers they sing among are in this garden (*'andalīb īnkih gulzamīn-i ījād-i īshān īn būstān [ast]*)."[17] Among those he commemorates are Mughals whose fathers or other ancestors migrated to Hindustan from Iran and Turan. The text is divided into two sections, the first on Muslims and the second on Hindus, and he includes an entry on himself in the second section. This commemorative focus may at first seem to reinforce the idea that Hindustanis are, by definition, born in Hindustan. To understand the place of these "versifiers of Hindustan," however, we need to consider his larger commemorative project, of which this was the middle installment.[18]

Shafiq was also the author of two other *tazkirih*s, *Chamanistan-i Shu'ara* (1761–62 AD/1175 AH),[19] on *Rīkhta*/Urdu poets, and *Sham-i Ghariban* (1782–83 AD/1197 AH), concerned with "people who came to Hindustan from elsewhere (*az vilāyat-i dīgar*)." He notes in the introduction to the latter that after writing the *Gul-i Ra'na* (on the poets of Hindustan, "the sweetly singing [birds] of this garden"), he realized he needed to write another *tazkirih*, "another fresh sapling added to the path of discourse opposite the first sapling" about this "particular group (*guruh-i khās*)," meaning poets who came to Hindustan.[20] Different kinds of collectives adorn the space of Persian discourse, Hindus and Muslims, poets born here and those who came from other Persianate regions. Place or lineage was not determinative; only multiplicity was overarching.

From near or far, the distinction is not necessarily hierarchical. "The first of the high ones who entered paradise-like Hindustan" is Adam, whom he calls the father of mankind and a poet. His original residence was heaven

(*asl-i muskin-i ū bihisht*), and though there is debate about where he alighted
to earth, Shafiq cites the Qur'an's account as authoritative and provides an
interpretation of the relevant verses to mean that he alighted on "Sarandib
Hind," or the Ceylon of Hind, "and from then he lived here until the end
of his life."[21] This is a common story, repeated in Persian texts since at least
the sixteenth century.[22] But with Shafiq's ability to verify it according to the
Qur'an, its traditions of interpretation, and Arabic philology in general, a
mode of narration is connected with his own origins, particularly with his
teacher, noted Arabic and hadith scholar Azad Bilgrami.[23]

Gul-i Ra'na presents a collective organized by birth in Hindustan, even
if subdivided into those who are "poets defined by Islam (*mawzūnān-i
Islamiyān*)" and those who are "the versifiers defined by idols (*nuktih
pardāzān-i asnāmiyān*)."[24] Persian has other words for idol, but Shafiq
uses the word used for beloveds in poetry, connoting that they are as beautiful and worthy of devotion as *asnām*, or idols. Besides the sophistication
of writing in rhymed prose, this articulation offers a parallel: *mawzūnān*
literally means those who harmonize (as in writing in metered verse), and
nuktih pardāzān literally means those who make subtle distinctions. Both
qualities are integral to composing verse and are often used as synonyms
for poet. Together they are the two aporetic halves necessary for verse,
its substantive subtle points and its formal harmonious arrangement.
Their adjectival counterparts, Hindus and Muslims, articulate the verse
of Hindustan, distinctly but together, according to the epistemology of
Persianate *adab*.[25]

Shafiq can represent these two groups in a single *tazkirih* called *Gul-i
Ra'na* (fresh flowers) and envision it as a beautiful new shoot placed on one
side of a garden path, facing another sapling, the counterpart *tazkirih* of
poets who came to Hindustan from other lands. Both plantings are in addition to Shafiq's first *tazkirih*, of *Rīkhta* poets (called *Chamanistan*, or verdant
meadow, also written in Persian), as a miniplot ensconced within this larger
garden of discourse (*sukhan*).[26] The garden space is Persianate Hindustan,
though its path wends through other gardens as well. In its soil grows Persian
and *Rīkhta* poets, born here and born elsewhere, distinguished by their idols
(elsewhere he calls them *hunūd*) or their Islam. Not all lived out their lives in
Hindustan.[27] Such rigid exclusivities were unnecessary.

As we saw in Chapter 6, Mughal was not the ruling Timurid dynasty's family name—that was a European innovation—but a name for a people that no longer exists. Mughals are split between Shafiq's two *tazkirih*s of Persian poets. All are Muslims, and though some were born in Hindustan and some elsewhere, both groups—Mughal and Hindustani Muslims (along with Hindus)—are included in his *tazkirih* of *Rīkhta* poets. Shafiq's *tazkirih*s show us collectives, connected by separations that seeped into one another. Their shared space, Persianate Hindustan, is imagined as a garden, made up of multiple faiths and birthplaces. Mughals grew from both beds along the garden pathways. Included is the great Sa'ib Tabrizi, who returned to Iran after only seven years in Timurid domains and became indelibly associated with the Safavid Shahs. Because of his patronage and social ties to Timurid men of power he is also commemorated as part of Hindustan.[28]

Shafiq occupies a different section of this garden. He was not a contemporary but commemorates himself as part of the same larger space of *adab* in Hindustan, even as the garden contains those of Iran. *Tazkirih*s remember, but not in our historical sense. They remembered those who could write poetry according to the stakes of their present times, of a collective and its selves. A man named Lachmi Nara'in remembered a space that was simultaneously distinct from itself, as Shafiq (his pen name) in Persian and Sahib in *Rīkhta*. Shafiq was well aware of other poets, many of whom he did not commemorate. Who, then, was chosen for commemoration, and why?

The Social Labor of Commemorative Texts

The common (mis) translations of *tazkirih*s as biographical dictionaries has limited scholarly engagement with these texts by ensuring that they are read largely as reference texts. *Tazkirih* authors drew on both oral and written sources, as well as their own experiences, to write biographies they considered factual but with narrative features subject to the overarching theme of the text as a whole. The process of selecting both subjects and details of their lives memorialized something that was often explicitly outlined in the preface and underlined by the text's structure. In contrast, in modern encounters with these texts, the main concern becomes whether the information of its entries is "reliable" in a positivist sense. By default, such a reading renders aspects that do not fit into this epistemology "personal," "private," or "biased" and thus extraneous. For instance, E. G. Browne noted that, in general, "when discussing contemporaries the author is very apt to make mention of his personal friends, and to ignore those whom he dislikes or of whom he disapproves."[29] These elements are thus marked as "subjective" in contradistinction to the presumed "objective" expectation of the text. These subjective elements, usually autobiographical interludes, historical narratives, or anecdotal character sketches can cause a text to be viewed as unreliable.

This position is still largely shared by historians.[30] Some literary scholars, such as Paul Losensky and Sunil Sharma, have read *tazkirih*s to understand literary reception or the mapping of a literary culture.[31] More recently, Schwartz has mapped the circulation and continued prestige of Persianate literary culture into the nineteenth century, while Pellò has explored socioreligious heterogeneities of eighteenth-century Persian cultural identifications.[32] Here I examine *tazkirih*s for the various ways in which the *adab* of commemoration could be used to draw (and draw on) a space that authors might properly inhabit, thus becoming someone in its terms. This self was not an individual, single and separate, but was instead "a networked self-in-conduct."[33] Authors selected and emphasized details about their collectives in the service of particular representational preoccupations, including the manifesting of proper form for a moral subject. To focus solely on the "objective" truth, absent the author's "prejudices," erases the very practices of commemoration that tell us the most about historicized cultural meanings.

The epistemology of commemoration viewed what we call "objective" and "subjective" information as part of a continuum of legitimate and necessary ways to re-member the past. Clinging to the transhistorical truth of this distinction, most scholars understand texts translated as chronicles (*tārīkh*) as proper historical materials, as opposed to *tazkirih*s, or "literary" works.[34] Both, however, are commemorative texts, and their sources and approaches are similar, even if their content and emphases may vary.[35] Both use oral and written sources, which could include information that was both "reason-based," or *'aqlī*, and "transmission-based," or *naqlī*, as Khan has usefully distinguished. *Naqlī* accounts were those told and transmitted widely; they were an integral part of the written or oral tradition, and as we saw in Chapter 1, related alongside more verifiable accounts. They were possible truths, perhaps unverifiable or defying human reason, but they could still ultimately be true because, in the end, perfect knowledge and certainty rested with God alone.[36] Transmission and repetition functioned as their own authority. The form authors chose to transmit articulated their position and had the potential, dialogically, to transform that tradition.[37]

Hermansen and Lawrence have proposed thinking of Indo-Persian *tazkirih*s as "memorative communications."[38] Their memorative aspect functioned vertically by linking previous figures to the present, making previous times an integral part of the present and authorizing it. This tradition was thus self-consciously cumulative. *Tazkirih*s also functioned horizontally, placing contemporaries (and their authorizing predecessors) in communication with each another. This view acknowledges these texts as both "cultural artifacts and cultural reconstructions."[39] If *tazkirih*s are "literary texts that both remember and communicate," then analysis of what and how they remember can reveal meanings that guided their constructions and the overarching concerns they were made to address. If we regard *tazkirih*s as self-commemorations, the figure of the author comes into relief with the evoked assemblage of other biographical subjects. Previous poets provided aesthetic origins for the self; contemporary figures created the social world into which the self could be articulated. Through the selective process of including ancestors and peers, the author created community, which in turn produced a figured self, relational to and ingrained within the collective.

These contentions about selfhood are not entirely new, but they depart from previous scholarship that relied on already constituted categories. For instance, writing on self and autobiography, Malhotra and Lambert-Hurley assert that "it would be wrong to assume that social and cultural norms always act as constraints that stifle individual expression." To do so is to accept the notion of a sovereign, autonomous self, mythical even in Euro-American contexts, where it began as an ideal. Thus "the sharp distinction between self and society needs to be qualified." Drawing on a host of scholarship, they contend that "all selves are relational," not just South Asian selves. The terms by which they can understand this soft distinction, however, are that, in the seventeenth century, "society was tolerant of and gave space to individual preference, agency, and autonomy" and that individuals could articulate "disagreements and resistances against social and familial values and expectations."[40] They thus assume that preexisting individuals, with their own agency, were separate from society, which was nevertheless tolerant of them.

To historicize, however, requires that we avoid assumptions of autonomous individuals as the form of the self and allow space to understand the relation of the self to the collective, which may constitute these categories. To begin with individual agency is to accept an already constituted self with a given relation to collectives outside itself, which may be resisted or not. Such assumptions build on modern Euro-centric conceptions of a valorized freedom made transhistorical. In contrast, the Persianate selfhood I read in these texts is one whose life story does not end with narrations of an author's own life but extends to those surrounding it, through which it is articulated and self-articulates. Writing about others was a way of writing about the self, a fact underscored by the third person used to speak about oneself. Authors made narrative choices, but proper forms gave meaning to positions, relations, and valuations that one took up as best one could, before choices could be made in the service of social or cultural interventions.

Contemporaneous understandings of *tazkirih*s support this understanding, that the text realized something about the moral and intellectual substance of its author. In the early nineteenth century, 'Abd al-Latif Shushtari, when expounding on his friend Abu Talib Isfahani's literary talents, mentions that he has written a "commemoration of poets (*tazkirih al-shu'arā*), from which the amount of his learning and taste is evident (*miqdār-i fahm va salīqih-ash az ān huvaydā ast*)."[41] Abu Talib's learning is evident in his ability to provide poetry and biographical information, but his refinement of taste is also expressed by his choice of poets and selections of their poetry. For Shushtari, the text demonstrated something about Abu Talib. The perception of *tazkirih*s as texts of the self in their rendering of the collective thus partly defined their consumption. Underpinning this articulation of self was the possession of learning shared by others in a larger Persianate cultural community.

*Tazkirih*s could evoke collectives that overlapped to different degrees while remaining part of a broader Persianate *adab*. Authors were the product of "a process of moral and intellectual education designed to produce an *adib*, a gentleman-scholar," and as books of ancestors and peers, *tazkirih*s were "intimately connected with the formation of both intellect and character."[42] Though writing a *tazkirih* was a work of *adab* that partly manifested the author's substance, not all reached the same level of accomplishment. Hierarchy was accepted, necessary even, and accommodated through relative valuation. In creating horizontal connections, *tazkirih*s imagined collectives that transcended friendship, acquaintance, political loyalties, collective lineages, and formal social ties (such as those between teacher and student). These collectives constituted a community of *adab*, of the learned and those who aspired to be known as learned. Though knowledge and ability to compose poetry was an essential feature of this collective, many were better versed in other areas or even best known for other endeavors, such as medicine, accounting, religious sciences, political administration, military leadership, and even commerce. Reading *tazkirih*s as memorative communications can illuminate their authors' cultural and social contexts, apart from the factual content of the entries. Here context means less authorial biography and historical events than the function of commemoration in the world.

These selves were Persians, but "Persian" was not an attained truth for an individual or even for a collective. It was a self that required continual understandable and communicable identification. Memorializing the self created a figure related to the author but not as a straightforward representation. Paul de Man argues that the autobiographical subject is a constructed figure whose relationship to the author is mediated by genre and context.[43] Derrida goes further, posing the mode of saying "I" as instrumental:

> [A]utobiographical anamnesis presupposes *identification*. And precisely not identity. No, an identity is never given, received, or attained; only the interminable and indefinitely phantasmatic process of identification endures. . . . [I]n whatever manner one invents the story of a construction of the *self*, the *autos*, or the *ipse*, it is always *imagined* that the one who writes should know how to say I. At any rate, the *identificatory modality* must already or henceforth be assured: assured of language and in its language . . . the I of *I recall* is produced and uttered in different ways depending on the language in question. It never precedes them; therefore it is never independent of language in general.[44]

Instead of Persian as an identity, we can consider *adab* as the mode by which Persians identify. Narrated according to the *adab* of being in the world, *tazkirih*s, and their enactment of the third person as self, were the way Persians said "I," though not ever alone.

Whereas modes of uttering "I" must be particular to language and its meanings, commemoration made community through a broader process of establishing and sustaining identification. As Engseng Ho explains, "Persons separated from each other by generations and centuries think of themselves as members of the same community only if they share collective representations which allow them to identify with each other."[45] *Tazkirih*s commonly included contemporaries the author had never met, but most substantive entries are about people with whom the author had interacted or about bygone figures with whom he identified strongly. These interactions and identifications emphasize the author's social affiliations, political ties, and poetic commitments. These textual assemblies then circulated to others, for whom they were intelligible, but who might identify only partly or somewhat differently with those subjects.[46]

Social interactions in the world constituted and articulated textual authority. Greatest authority was given to personal experience, followed by first-hand accounts of social intimates. Written information was similarly evaluated, so that the account of an author who knew his subject was deemed more reliable than an author who relied on second-hand reports.[47] These stricter criteria characterized *'aqlī* accounts, and they lay alongside *naqlī* accounts, both in the service of affiliation.[48]

Consider the example of 'Ali Quli Khan "Valih" Daghistani, who figures in Azad Bilgrami's *Khizanih* as both an oral and a textual source (Azad citing Valih's *Riyaz*), in addition to being a commemorative subject. In his entry on the late Safavid poet Muhammad Nasir "Fa'iz" Abhari, Azad notes that Valih had met Fa'iz in Isfahan before he died during the Afghan siege (1721–22). Azad includes one of Fa'iz's *rubā'ī*, which he says, "Valih Daghistani recited in front of me on the road [between] Lahore and Delhi."[49] Through his time spent with Valih, newly arrived and accompanying him to the Timurid capital, Azad has access to source material on a contemporary poet he has never met. Fa'iz never set foot in Hindustan but is prominent for Azad because he was a student of the great seventeenth-century poetic exemplar Sa'ib Tabrizi.[50] Valih, in turn, had access to such verse through its circulation in Isfahan's social circles before arriving in Hindustan in 1732. Such relationships contributed to a sense of connection with *adab* circles in Iran that made the events surrounding the fall of the Safavids seem significant enough for Azad to have included an account.

In the midst of his entry on Fa'iz, Azad offers "an abbreviated account of the events of the siege of Isfahan and other history," from the ascension of Shah Sultan Husayn and the rebellion of Mir Vays in Qandahar up through Shahrukh Mirza Afshar's blinding, "since mention of the siege of Isfahan has occurred in the biographical notice (*tarjamih*) of Fa'iz."[51] Azad's commemoration of Fa'iz has few details beyond his teacher and his death in the siege of Isfahan, but prompts an *'aqlī* account of the siege as relatedly significant. The "biographical" and "historical" are both Azad's account and interpretation of Fa'iz's life, whose end was entwined with larger historical events that would also come to shake Hindustan. By using the term *tarjamih* to define his entries, Azad explicitly invokes the Arabic tradition, in which biography was written according to the science of history.[52] The section on the events leading to Nadir Shah's death are extremely specific and cite Nadir's murderers as source, making the entry on Fa'iz an explicit example of biography as history.[53] The predominance of this historical account in the entry signals Azad's interpretation of his subject, representing Fa'iz as part of the last generation of Safavid poets. He is also an elder in Azad's own world, through his student Qizilbash Khan Umid, with whom this chapter closes.

Aporias, Social and Textual, Self and Collective

If the collective engendered the self, the expanses and boundaries of the collective tell us about possible textures of selfhood in Persianate societies. Variations sometimes mapped onto modern categories of difference, but because the overarching criterion of inclusion was social and aesthetic form, selves could possess differences and still be Persian. Aporia created hierarchies understood as gradations that related to each other symbiotically. Differences of gender, religion, and lineages of origin were recognized in *tazkirih*s, but authors included subjects according to varying degrees of affiliation. Other sorts of differences, such as of aesthetics or social *adab*, could be far more decisive.[54] Hermansen and Lawrence argue that *tazkirih*s "make Muslim space," an argument easier to sustain in the context of Sufi *tazkirih*s.[55] At the very least, Muslim space accommodated non-Muslims, who were even expected to share it. Such inclusivity is more obvious in other *tazkirih*s, in which imperial service or knowledge of Persian need not be limited to Muslims.

Inclusion appeared as well at the level of idiom, as non-Muslims were often well versed in the esotericism that by then was universal.[56] Pellò has noted that many Hindu Persian poets were munshis, "often Kayastha or Khatri . . . whose intellectual education was indistinguishable from that of a Persianate Muslim intellectual of the same period, and whose textual and contextual referents he shared."[57] That non-Muslims, women, and people from diverse natal lineages could be included, despite their less-than-ideal differences, also tells us that other lineages of origin and identifications could create similarities and so render difference aporetic rather than absolute. Differences were recognized but permeated enough with similarities to make possible affiliations. Similarities did not create equality, but hierarchy was part of an ideal Persianate ethical order.

In biographical or historical commemorations, self-representation may not at first seem the project of either *tazkirih*s or other commemorative texts produced for a patron.[58] Yet the author remains relationally present with the subject matter—perhaps as a servant, a loyal court historian, or a beneficiary of the monarch—and is, by definition, part of the court or regime.[59] Late seventeenth- and eighteenth-century *tazkirih*s, however, bear the marks of social and political change. Because of the "shrinkage of employment opportunities consequent to the loss of large portions of the empire by conquest or by a process of open or concealed defiance of imperial authority by the provincial governors," rivalries at court for remaining positions and patronage heightened. In response to "the growing paralysis of central authority, each noble sought to create a band of devoted followers by a careful distribution of patronage."[60]

Most *tazkirih*s written in Hindustan at this time were produced by authors counted among these followers, and mostly outside the purview of imperial court patronage.[61] Correspondingly, contemporaries received greater emphasis, and the figural presence of the author was more defined than in earlier texts. *Tazkirih* production itself proliferated.[62] Affiliations with lands, kingdoms, and monarchs were still palpable features of self-definition, but the language of place and origin was put to the service of new concerns. The self's palette of representational choices engaged with other themes and tropes, as well as local and interregional upheaval, disintegration, and reconstitution.

Regardless of eighteenth-century specificities, homelands, lineages of
origin, and identifications with political orders or social locations (as a
mystic, scholar, or imperial servant) guided commemorations of Persianate collectives and selves. In general, the information provided in *tazkirih*
entries was fairly standard: what was known of the subject's lineages of origins, social connections, intellectual accomplishments, selections of poetry
that manifested substance, and anecdotes, including interactions with the
author or the author's friends and *naqlī* accounts.[63] In spite of this seeming uniformity, *tazkirih*s as a whole and their individual entries varied in
telling ways. They could be organized according to geographical divisions,
occupational groups, or alphabetical order of names, and they could have
different temporal and geographical scopes. *Tazkirih* entries depended on
how the author was situated in relation to the subject and then took up
this relationship, as well as the author's access to information and the text's
broader narrative engagement with its context. The actual production of
these texts depended on the constant circulation and mobility of their contemporaneous community, as the substance and content of entries evoke,
but relationships with earlier poets were also crucial.[64] To write a *tazkirih*
was to transmit knowledge and thus indicated the knowledge and narrative
strategies available to the author.

The substance of *tazkirih*s relied on relationships acquired throughout
a lifetime of learning, travel, and service, which were also integral to narrating subjects. In *Sham-i Ghariban*, Shafiq includes a short entry on Valih
Daghistani, whom he has never met. The entry is an abridged version drawn
from his dominant textual and anecdotal source, Azad Bilgrami. Shafiq recounts 'Ali Quli Khan's various positions in Timurid service, noting that he
died in the reign of 'Alamgir II as commander of seven thousand (the highest
attainable rank). After listing his death date, the next detail Shafiq provides
is that Valih was enamored of his cousin Khadijih and agitated by thoughts
of her throughout his life in Hindustan.

Directly following is a vignette regarding Faqir Dihlavi's visit, providing source material and testimony of Valih's tale. Valih was the patron and
beloved friend of Faqir, who entered Aurangabad on May 28, 1767, years after
Valih's death, on his way to pilgrimage to the Iraqi shrine cities. "He related
(*naql*) to the author [Shafiq] that, Valih proposed that 'you [Faqir] must set

to verse the story of my love.' And so, at his request, the *masnavī* of Valih Sultan was set to verse."[65] This vignette provides a vivid picture of Faqir on his way to the sacred Muslim heartlands, a trip from which he would never return, sitting with Azad Bilgrami and his young devoted Hindu Persian student, remembering his own friend, Valih, a decade after his death. Faqir's visit enabled Shafiq to add an original anecdote to his account of Valih. This transmission of oral information from the elder to the younger poet, who preserved it textually and is authorized by it, demonstrates the way in which social relations are intimately bound with textual content.

The aporia of social and textual practices offers a more satisfying lens through which to consider the proliferation of *tazkirih* writing in the mid-eighteenth century than those offered thus far. Shifts in location and the diminished opportunity for poetic patronage in the wake of political instability and military conflicts certainly played a part in the desire to commemorate. But commemoration was never a positivist project. It was necessarily "subjective," though not divorced from truth. Authors laid claim to different selves and thus commemorated more or less different communities. Multiplicity was expected; mutual exclusivity was not. Furthermore, the creation and circulation of texts and the commemoration of overlapping affiliations enabled the continuation of shared transregional Persianate forms across the eighteenth century.

The most restrictive example was nonetheless widely cited as a source by later *tazkirih*s.[66] "Hazin" Lahiji's narrowly focused *Tazkirat al-Muʿasirin* was completed in 1751–52 AD/1165 AH, after he had relocated from Delhi to Benares. The text is limited to contemporaries, a flexible timespan, here defined by Hazin's biography. The text remembers one hundred poets who were alive between the year of his birth (January 1692 AD/Rabīʿ al-Sānī 1103 AH) and the year he migrated to Hindustan (1734). These are not contemporaries in an absolute sense but poets he had met or knew about through his social circles. Religious community and political geography further delimited the text's scope: "The contents of this imperial/august book will particularly make manifest the poets of the Twelver [Shiʿa] people."[67]

The word "imperial" (*humāyūn*) in tandem with a Twelver Shiʿi people (*millat-i isnāʾ ʿashar*) points to a community specific to Safavid imperial domains, and its poets are indeed specific to its cities. The text's organization highlights this people's Shi'i core. The first section is specifically scholar ('ālim) poets; the second consists of poets with other occupations. The Safavid Shi'a community may seem to be an absolute, objective category, but it is relative to Hazin's own life trajectory as most members were inhabitants of Isfahan and Shiraz or his father's homeland of Gilan. The rest he had met in his travels through Safavid domains, or else the poets or their work circulated through the imperial capital. His *tazkirih* is thus organized and delineated by his identifications and itineraries, particularly by Isfahan, the capital sanctified by the rule of these ostensible descendants of the Imams.

Hazin's choice of poets and their representation convey his vision of a lost world, a loss intimately connected to his self-figuring as desolate (*hazīn*). Writing in Hindustan, he elegized this loss by memorializing its community, which defined him in the present. No poets from Turani or Hindustani domains are mentioned, and all the poets within are dead or presumed so because of age or lack of contact. Just as Hazin states in his memoir that he considers his migration to Hindustan the end of his life, the poetic community he creates for himself in his *tazkirih* also ends at that time. The text's selection is determined according to geographical and temporal particularities that cannot be conflated with proto-nationalist partisanship.

Hazin's *tazkirih* produced the loss, even as the text memorialized it. No migrants from Safavid Iran living in Hindustan were included. The elegiac concerns of his commemoration cannot accommodate their mention, so they fall outside his sorrowful self-figuring. Hazin's *tazkirih* reflected the destruction of his Safavid poetic community and the loss of his library in Isfahan. He wrote his text entirely from memory; as a result, biographical and poetic selections are short, and some biographies are devoid of poetic selections. In choosing to eschew the work of other *tazkirih*s or even available *dīvān*s, Hazin cut himself off from the ongoing circulation of texts and chose instead to memorialize a community that was also an explicit testament to his ability to remember.[68]

Hazin's view of Safavid Iran as utterly, apocalyptically destroyed is echoed in other *tazkirih*s, even when it imbues (self-) representations differently. For instance, Valih Daghistani, Hazin's friend and fellow migrant, describes the Afghan invasion and occupation as "a tumult (*āshūb*) from which calamity of the last days (*qiyāmat*) arose and indications of the last judgment (*mahshar*) were evident."[69] Even Lutf 'Ali "Azar" Baygdili (1723–80), writing in the 1760s

when western Iranian domains were under Karim Khan Zand's relatively
stable rule, describes Iran and especially Isfahan as ruined (*vīrān* or *kharāb*).[70]
All these authors saw the physical ruin of Iran as a kind of cultural death,
though they dealt with it differently in their *tazkirih*s. Written in Hindustan,
Hazin's *Tazkirat al-Mu'asirin* was a defiant assertion of late Safavid Persian
poetic culture at a time of burgeoning writing of *tazkirih*s increasingly focused on Timurid domains.

Writing later, Azar recouped the present destruction of Iran by asserting the primacy of its earlier poetic lineage to reconstitute a present local
community.[71] Even Valih, who chose to write the most geographically encompassing *tazkirih*, viewed the social and political ruin of Iran as foreclosing
the possibility of *adab*. In his entry on Mirza Sharaf al-Din 'Ali "Vafa" Qumi,
a recent young migrant to Delhi, Valih praises Vafa's learning, temperament,
and refinement, expressing surprise that a person born after the Afghan invasion was so accomplished "because at this time, especially in Iran, which has
become full of wild animals (*bahā'im*), beasts of prey (*sibā'*) and cattle (*an'ām*),
the appearance of this manner of man is an unexpected blessing."[72] The fall
of Safavid Iran and its aftermath were commemorated far and wide across
Hindustan, providing a crucial context for the possibilities of collectives.

Subjectivity and Multiplicity in Persianate Inclusion

The way in which commemoration created collectives that also expressed self
is less obvious in the more expansive "general" *tazkirih*s, which seem purposefully to render an "objective" picture of Persianate poetic culture. Valih's
Riyaz al-Shu'ara (1749 AD/1162 AH), Siraj al-Din Khan "Arzu"'s *Majma' al-
Nafa'is* (1750–51 AD/1164 AH), and Azar Baygdili's *Atashkadih* (1760–61 AD/1174
AH) are among the widely circulated texts of their time and are cited to the
present day. And yet, an enduring methodological proto-nationalism has
guided scholarly readings of these texts, which mostly assert that birthplace
is the governing logic of a person's affiliations and commemorative concerns,
something Chapter 4 has argued against. As a result, Valih's *Riyaz* is virtually
ignored as a source and has become a kind of homeless text for *both* Iranian
and South Asian history.[73] This development is particularly ironic since Valih's vision of self and collective hews closely to High Persianate universalism.
In contrast, both Azar and Arzu were more concerned with recouping social

communities through restructured aesthetic hierarchies that parochially valorized endangered politically defined regions.

Produced within a couple of years of one another in Delhi, Valih's *Riyaz* and Arzu's *Majma* contain many overlapping biographical subjects. Among their differences are choices in recent subjects, narrative emphases, and aesthetic valuations. Unanswered is the question of why two extensive *tazkirih*s were written in the same time and place by people who frequented the same social circles. Thinking about *tazkirih*s as texts of self through collective, however, makes their simultaneous authorship less puzzling because, in a period of fracturing polities, dispersed or lost communities, and catastrophic conditions of mobility, Arzu and Valih had different lineages of origin and divergent collectives and selves to commemorate. Moreover, each laid claim to particular social locations. Arzu was the consummate man of letters,[74] while Valih was the aesthetically refined imperial office holder. Given that "biographical narratives are filtered through the subjectivity of an author recounting his own life, and the author's account of his own life can only take place in reference to those other lives," multiplicity was expected.[75] Through their narrative sources, omissions, and emphases, Arzu's and Valih's overlapping commemorative subjects performed different labor in the world.[76]

The *Riyaz* was the first general *tazkirih* to be written in the Persianate world in over a century. Like its author, it circulated widely in Iran and Hindustan.[77] Its wide array of poets is listed in alphabetical order. Arzu's *Majma* has a similar organization and includes many of the same poets before the mid-seventeenth century, after which the emphasis shifts to poets who were born in or migrated to Timurid domains. The centrality of Timurid imperium to Arzu's *Majma* is mirrored in his life trajectory, which was largely spent within the smaller domain of Hindustan. The *Majma*'s view of the Persianate world is from within the Timurid imperial capital and, by extension, foregrounds his affiliation. Non-Muslims are not only part of Arzu's community but also his openly declared friends. Among these was Anand "Ram" Mukhlis (d. 1751), who was a fellow student of Bidil.[78]

Unlike Azad in the *Khizanih*, Arzu did not bother with oral sources about Irani poets. He needed to acknowledge poets outside Hindustan but not to commemorate them extensively. His inclusion of Irani poets is thus largely limited to ancestors who authorized Timurid poetic culture, those

who migrated or traveled to Hindustan, and some brief, perfunctory notice of more recent poets. For example, Arzu's biographical information on
a contemporary poet in Iran, Mirza Ja'far "Rahib" Isfahani, is a scant few
lines, which include the curious fact that Rahib remained in Isfahan despite the disorder there. Also included are just under a dozen of his verses.[79]
More were unnecessary for a poet who, in spite of his quality, remained at
the fringe of the Persianate world, as Arzu saw it from Delhi. He may not
have had access to more information about Rahib, but other *tazkirih* writers
in Hindustan who did deem him important, such as Azad Bilgrami, were
able to gather additional information through anecdotes related orally and
through correspondence.[80]

In contrast, for Valih, who knew Rahib personally in Isfahan and was
friends with his younger brother in Hind, Rahib has a central place. In the
Riyaz, Rahib has a vivid, fairly detailed biographical sketch, with a significant selection of his poetry.[81] Valih describes him as one of the best poets
since Sa'ib and, at the time of writing, the best poet in Iran.[82] Such aesthetic
judgments highlight the constitutive role of social relationships in the transmission and production of knowledge and self-representation. All three of
the poets Valih identifies as the greatest poets of the age—deemed capable
of something new after Sa'ib—are those with whom he has shared social
intimacy in Delhi or Isfahan: Hazin, Rahib, and Faqir. Hazin and Faqir, his
most recent companions, have extensive entries. His centering of community
on figures such as Faqir Dihlavi and other Hindustani-born poets, past and
present, contributes to the expansiveness of the text and places Valih as the
servant of two imperial realms.

The scope of the *Majma'* reflects an idea of Persianate collective in which
Delhi and, by extension, Timurid-ruled Hindustan, are preeminent. Trac-
ing past Persian poets from the Ghaznavids to the Timurids, the shift to a
Hindustani-dominated view of Persian makes the Timurid realm a central
site of inheritance for its culture, culminating in the fall of the Safavids. The
Majma' is specifically a genealogy of Persian poetry written backward from
eighteenth-century Delhi, almost exclusively male and explicitly excluding
women.[83] Alam defines Arzu's position as advocating the "translocality of
Persian" as part of "the image of universality that the Mughal state had created for itself" when that state was fragmenting politically.[84] Nevertheless,

this articulation of universality was the political ideology of a specific kingdom.[85] Arzu's *tazkirih* addressed contemporaneous concerns: to create a regionally focused collective that authorized his own aesthetic commitments to new forms of poetic expression.

By contrast, the *Riyaz* draws on poets from both Timurid and Safavid domains, both men and women, past and present, in keeping with Valih's self-representation as an interregional translocal Persian, a figure also marked by the suffering of exile.[86] Articulating himself as someone far from home, Valih was nonetheless within the Persianate, as evinced by his intimate relationships with political patrons and men of letters. Many of his aesthetic assessments, particularly about the value of eighteenth-century Hindustani Persian local idiomatic forms, diverged significantly from those of Arzu. In Valih's rendering, after the fall of the Safavids, Hindustan was the center of patronage and culture, home to two of the three best contemporary poets (Hazin and Faqir). In its local aesthetic style, however, Hindustan was not necessarily where Persian shined the brightest. Valih's style followed Baba Fighani, whose style has been dubbed the realist school (*maktab-i vuqūʿ*), particularly popular in the Safavid capital.[87] By Valih's time, writing like Fighani meant writing in the style of the ancients. As Schwartz has argued, the Isfahani circle of poets, including Azar, built on this style, inspired by followers of Baba Fighani.

But for a few instances, Valih was generally disdainful of Persian idiom of Hindustan, though he deemed it better than what remained in a ruined Iran. His entry on Kamila Baygum, a female poet, notes,

> the Persian language (*lughat-i Fārsī*) has increased over the course of time in Hindustan and continues to increase; from what we [I] see its men do not know Persian and do not understand it, let alone its women. That which they call Persian in Hind, its separate words/pronunciation (*alfāz*) are Persian but after composing and conversing (*tarkīb va takallum*) the language (*lughat*) becomes something else (*dīgar mīshavad*), which only they themselves understand and is understood by anyone else with difficulty.[88]

The language Valih uses to describe female poetic talent is similar to Azar's (see Chapter 3). He sees women as less capable than men. His aside about Persian in Hindustan, however, appears in other entries and is not unique to women.[89] In spite of its spread in Timurid domains since Fayzi's time (d. 1595), formal knowledge of Persian did not comprise the ability to compose or speak in a way readily comprehensible to people in other domains. Yet the pages of the *Riyaz* are filled with Hindustani Persian poets, past and present, men and women, Hindus and Muslims, Shi'i and Sunni. Valih's collective was expansive, including the mediocre and the marvelous, the familiar and the strange, with the awareness that not all were alike in gender, origin, position, and poetic stature.

Later, Azar Baygdili's Isfahani circle placed greater emphasis on the style of the ancients and took a narrower, more exclusive approach than their predecessors, like Valih, by rejecting poets of the new style, like Sa'ib. In keeping with the older ethos of the Safavid period, Valih celebrated the perfect (his own style) and the less perfect, new (post-Sa'ib) style.[90] This inclusive view of Persian was a continuation of the expansive sense of *adab* that had characterized earlier, general Persian *tazkirih*s, which were increasingly contested by narrower visions of aesthetic community, including those of Arzu and Azar, which sought to localize their presents. Nevertheless, hierarchically valued styles could still be celebrated as part of a totality.

Though many of the biographical subjects of Arzu's *Majma'* and Valih's *Riyaz* overlap, these entries differ because they are narrated within particular refractions of self and collective. Their differing treatments of Rahib, discussed earlier, provide an example of a peer in their collectives. 'Abd al-Qadir "Bidil" (1644–1720), a celebrated poet of the early eighteenth century, serves as an example of a predecessor. Arzu's text has a detailed, lengthy, and unequivocal entry on the greatness of Bidil's poetry, a man he calls teacher.[91] Arzu's own stature as teacher and scholar rests on this poetic lineage's authorization, which he represents as first rate. In contrast, Valih's entry on Bidil is laudatory, though far shorter in detail and poetic selection than Arzu's. Valih demonstrates knowledge and admiration of Bidil, but not emphatically, because his aesthetics and poetic legacy do not figure as part of Valih's own aesthetic commitments.[92] For Valih, exalted treatment of poetic ancestry is reserved for Baba Fighani Shirazi.[93] Though these *tazkirih*s represent a Persianate world broader than specific kingdoms, and their authors reside in the same city and social circles, the texts narrate their subjects according to the respective labor they perform in the text's commemorative project.

The commemorative tie between collectives and selves is starkest in the narration of younger contemporaries, who, unlike poetic elders, stood apart from lineages of origins. For Arzu, specificity of origins beyond the general region of Iran was less important than accomplishments and ties after arrival in Hindustan. Arzu's vague description of "Vafa" Qumi, discussed earlier, is typical. He was "born of the grandees of Iran (*az buzurg zādihgān-i Īrān*)." Though the name (*nisbat*) alludes to a specific city of origin, Arzu provides only the names of two of Vafa's distant maternal and paternal forebears, both famous, noting that such descent has granted him nobility (*najābat va sharāfat*) and ability in poetic composition.[94] Next, Arzu skips to Vafa's arrival into Hindustan (1749 AD/1162 AH) and identifies his patron as Valih Daghistani and his teacher as Arzu himself.[95] By contrast, Azar Baygdili's entry on Vafa focuses on his life before migration to Hindustan, with only a note that he has news of Vafa traveling to the Hijaz to perform Hajj in 1766–67. Vafa's nearly thirty years in Hindustan are absent in this commemoration, which Azar eschews for expounding on his (Shi'i) origin "from one of the illustrious sayyid [families] of the Abode of Believers, Qum, who are the guardians of Massumah's tomb shrine."[96]

Both Arzu and Azar were personally acquainted with Vafa. Their differing choices in constituting Vafa's origins reflect their figural locations and those of their respective collectives. Arzu's focus is on Vafa's lineages, famous figures from a broader Perso-Islamicate past. Specificity of place beyond the larger region of Iran is irrelevant. In contrast, Azar is focused on mapping the poetic lineage of Persian onto former Safavid domains, and thus Vafa's sayyid connection to an important Shi'a shrine in Qum is central while his life in Hindustan is not. Finally, for Valih, whose *tazkirih* reflects a Persianate community more inclusive than either of these two, familial position, prominent lineage, and location in both lands are all part of Vafa's origins.[97]

These almost opposing images of Vafa reflect the narrative focus of Azar's and Arzu's *tazkirih*s more broadly. As we have seen, the *Atashkadih* narrates a glorious literary past against the background of a ruined present, seeking to recoup aesthetic community. To recenter Persian poetic culture in Iran (mostly *Iraq-i 'ajam*), the place of his own circle, Azar commemorates a lineage for this location by densely populating Iranian domains and cities with Persian poets for whom these are places of origin. By reducing origin to birthplace, Azar glosses over the significant aspects of their lives that do not contribute to this project. He cannot, however, efface Hindustan entirely, as certain places and people demand narration.

As we saw in Chapter 1, Azar largely excludes past poets born in Hindustan. His inclusion of a number of Hindustani-born sayyid contemporaries, however, raises the question of whether this exclusion is due to poetic style, paucity of information, or the generally Shiʻi nature of his community (valorizing sayyids), rather than a disdain of birth in Hindustan.[98] Like the poets of Iran whom he has not met, the Hindustani-born sayyids and migrants to Hindustan from Iran that he includes all have short entries. Length and connotation, however, have little to do with birthplace. Azar's entry on the Delhi-born Faqir is far more complimentary than his entry on the Isfahani-born Valih, whose poetry he calls "hackneyed."[99] The longer entries commemorate Azar's close friends, overwhelmingly those who originated or had at some point in their lives lived in Isfahan.[100]

Whereas "Indian" poets are few, Hindustani domains are a site of poetic culture, but not as an organizing feature of the text. For instance, among past poets of Kashan, Azar includes migrants and travelers to the Shiʻi Deccani Sultanates and Timurid domains. Baqir Khurdihfurush's "origin was Kashan, but he went to Hindustan and died there." The rest of the entry consists of an anecdote and related *rubāʼī*, which Azar describes as inspired by the competition with "Zuhuri" Khurasani (Turshizi) for recognition and patronage at Ibrahim ʻAdil Shah's court at Bijapur. Baqir's *qasīdih* in praise of the Shah went unrewarded, and when he heard that Zuhuri had been exalted and given an appropriate gift, the fire of jealousy was lit within his breast inspiring the *rubāʼī* comparing himself to the spurned Firdowsi.[101]

Though Baqir is listed under the poets of Kashan, this drama played out in the Deccan. Like Baqir, other sons of Kashan spent only their early lives in Kashan and then traveled to other cities, often living their poetic lives outside Iran.[102] The *Atashkadih*'s organization thus appropriates poets whose work was produced in the subcontinent rather than in Iranian domains. Representing his own location, where his circle sought to authorize its own style, as the center of proper poetic form required mapping poets according to birthplace instead of where they found patronage, produced their work, and lived out their lives. Rather than reflect a commonly held idea, therefore, the *Atashkadih* challenged the notion of Hindustan as the center of poetic patronage and production. Understood thusly, the text is no longer of Iran alone but obliquely of the social context of the larger Persianate world in which the sons of its cities circulated. For many, like Baqir and Zuhuri, these Persianate social worlds were in the subcontinent. By failing to see the poets of Hindustan in the cities of Iran, we have perhaps taken Azar too literally.

This reduced focus on sojourns in Hindustan contrasts with Arzu's *taz-kirih*, which emphasizes the sheer number of poets who, regardless of origin, traveled to Hindustan. To establish Hindustan's centrality, though, the story of Persians from elsewhere embedded Hindustan within a broader world. In his entry on Muhammad Sa'id "Ashraf" Mazandarani (d. 1707), Arzu begins with Ashraf's origin, noting his descent from noted religious scholars, like Muhammad Baqir Majlisi, *Shaykh al-Islam* of Isfahan. Arzu does not mention this imperial position, merely referring to Majlisi as "an established (*qarār dādih) mujtahid* of the Shi'ites." The entry's main focus is Ashraf's position in Timurid service, through which "he became distinguished." The rest of the entry expounds Ashraf's refined (*zarīf*) and jovial (*shūkh*) disposition, as well as his poetic accomplishments, through stories orally transmitted from Ashraf's students in Hindustan. Information about Ashraf's youth, such as his habit of attending cockfights (*khurūs bāzī*) instead of classes with Majlisi, demonstrate Arzu's access to Ashraf's learned descendants, who were able to provide information about a youth spent in Isfahan nearly a century before.[103] A relatively stationary Persian, Arzu was nevertheless connected to previous times and other places through social relationships with the mobile members of his collective.

In keeping with his self-figuring as a discerning scholar, Arzu also notes that though Ashraf's poetry was generally excellent, he sometimes made errors in meter. Arzu cites an exemplary verse, noting that the mistake is not specific to Ashraf but that naming others would be ill-mannered (*dūr az adab*).[104] Corrections and commentary on the poetry of his subjects pervade many of Arzu's entries, especially those of well-known poets, and he positions himself as a scholar who can judge even his reputable Persian predecessors as poetically fallible. Arzu was defined by his homeland, the imperial city of Delhi, by his patrons (a Mughal family of imperial servants) and other social ties, and by his learning and subsequent position in Delhi's poetic debates, all of which are written into the detail and narrative of his *tazkirih*. He became a Persianate self distinguished by how he wielded the *adab* of commemorating his collective.

The more inclusive self-figuring of Valih's *Riyaz* was an impression shared by his contemporaries. Arzu describes him as "the place of refuge for Iran and Hind," a reference to his patronage of both Hindustani Persians and Persians recently arrived from Iranian domains.[105] Valih went to the trouble of having his *tazkirih* sent to Isfahan, indicating that he explicitly intended an audience in both domains. This more expansive self-figuring underscores the continuing intelligibility of a transregional Persianate, in transition from imperial collapse and devolution but not gone. In commemorative texts that show us how lives were remembered, narrative concerns are related to authors' self-figuring, drawn from their lineages of origin and their present affiliations, and manifest in commemorative style. Proper aesthetic and ethical form was the point of departure for commemoration's necessary and expected varieties, which proliferated across the politically fracturing eighteenth century.

The ways in which the same practices and forms of commemoration evoke variant collectives and demonstrate particular possibilities of selves evokes the image of the kaleidoscope discussed in the introduction to Part I. As with the many ways of knowing place, only some of these selves resemble our modern national ones. We might imagine Arzu as a proto-Indian self, and his community as one of *adab*'s inclusiveness (except for women), but limited to the parameters of India (as the subcontinent). And yet, this possible proto-nationalist self is but one color in a kaleidoscope, embedded in and infused with others, whose meaning is transformed by its ultimately relational nature. That it lies on a continuum with other types of selves, with lineages in Hindustan (whether Indo-Gangetic, Timurid, or subcontinental) and beyond, and whose collectives traverse and bisect categories we moderns consider overarching, ultimately makes the seemingly protonationalist something else.

As we saw with Persianate lineages, these selves cannot be reduced to the bounds of empirical geography, political kingdoms, natal lineages, or sectarian bounds. Other lineages that mattered, of knowledge, service, aesthetics, and devotion, created forms of kinship that connected people across such lines and thus demand a reconsideration of the nature of those lines. Selves such as Arzu and Azar, who focus on politically defined domains (there were other ways to define regions), are still connected to and on a continuum of intelligibility with transregional selves, like Azad and Valih. Exclusions that did occur were according to a logic of affiliation based on *adab* and its aporias. At the end of the day the staunchly Sunni and Timurid Hindustan-centric Arzu proudly claimed a patronage affiliation with a Shi'i family from Iran. Likewise, an Iran-centric Azar understood his ultimate origin as a collective lineage originally from Turkistan.

Aporias of Selfhood

Reading commemorations as articulations of self *in situ* allows us to glean much about the multiple collectives to which a person could claim membership. As we saw with Lachmi Nara'in Shafiq at the start of this chapter, Urdu and Persian were intimately related, defined by aporetic distinctions. But was this multiple belonging solely the purview of "Indians"? The various commemorations of Muhammad Riza Qizilbash Khan "Umid," who appears in most major *tazkirih*s of the mid-to-late-eighteenth century, illustrates the perceived relation between supposedly "Indian" Urdu and Iranian Persian through the aporetic ideas of place and origin interrogated in this book.

Valih notes that Muhammad Riza was born in Hamadan but raised and educated (*tarbiyat yāftih*) in Isfahan. As an origin, Hamadan is less important than his location among a group of teachers and peers, who included Fa'iz Abhari, the great Sa'ib Tabrizi's student, and Mirza Tahir Vahid, who gave him the penname of "Umid." Valih's figure of Umid gains shape and meaning through the accrual of names, positions, and itinerary, beginning with his migration to Hindustan during the reign of Bahadur Shah (r. 1707–12). With the intercession of Zulfiqar Khan at the Timurid court, Umid was granted the rank of commander of one thousand and the title of Qizilbash Khan. Valih presents Umid's verses that show his dissatisfaction with this rank. Afterward, Qizilbash Khan traveled to the Deccan, where he entered the service of Nizam al-Mulk, gradually advancing in rank and responsibility, including charge of the diamond mines. In 1735–36, he returned to Delhi, where he remained after Nadir Shah's invasion and Nizam's return to the Deccan, and where he lived out the rest of his days. Valih mentions his most notable accomplishment, that "in the science of music (*'ilm-i mūsiqī*) he was such an expert that the masters of this skill (*fann*) considered his abilities authoritative (*musallam*)."[106] The rest of the entry describes his qualities as a friend and fellow participant in Delhi's social circles.

In contrast, Arzu narrates a Timurid-centric figure of Qizilbash Khan Umid, with whom he, like Valih, was personally acquainted. The entry's focus is Umid's position and prosperity in Hindustan. The details of his origin are unimportant; Arzu mentions Umid's birth in Hamadan but omits his life in Isfahan completely.[107] The rest of the entry is concerned with his patrons, positions, and peregrinations in Hindustan's various cities. Arzu mentions that Umid was first the companion (*rafīq*) of Zulfiqar Khan, after which he became a companion of Nizam al-Mulk in the Deccan, but is silent about his move from Delhi and any dissatisfaction with the rank granted by the Shah. Umid's character and abilities are measured according to his facility with the local, the Hindustani:

> Though it has been nearly 40 years that he has been in this land, his tongue does not cleave well to the pronunciation of Hindi (*zabānash bih lahjih-yi Hindi khūb nimīgardad*), but he understands the language of this land very well. Most of the Mughal-born of Hind do not grasp the subtleties (*nuktih-hā-yi*) of Hindi songs (*naghmat*) as he does. He is so equitable that he passes fair judgment on most things of Hindustan.[108]

Arzu focuses on Umid's relationship to regional traditions; Valih comments on Umid's musical excellence without specifying the Hindi aspect (likely the Braj poetry popularly sung in courtly circles).[109]

For Arzu, Umid's facility with the musical tradition and comprehension of the vernacular, despite his poor pronunciation, implies a migrant as local as the Hindustani born. Inherent in Arzu's compliment is a sense of difference but not the stark contrast inherent in the modern notion of a native. Because he was a Mughal, Umid is linked to those born in Hindustan. As we saw in the last chapter, the lineages of the sons of Hindustan, who spoke unaccented vernaculars, could be transregional. Umid's talent was extraordinary because it surpassed the Hindustani born, whose tongues presumably cleaved to the right tones. Like Valih's comments on Persian in Hindustan, these pre-occupations with language and idiom arose within the poetic disputes that raged in Delhi. Comments on idiomatic differences were made of poets from within the same kingdom and cannot be read as signs of nationalism. Given its idiomatic particularity everywhere (even within Iran), we might consider Persian simultaneously as a vernacular and a transregional language. Arzu's representation of Umid in terms of his uneven vernacular reflects the growing presence of a new poetic language, not entirely separate from Persianate poetic and social circles. Rather than Persian, other registers of *Rīkhta* (later Urdu) were the uneasy interlopers in Delhi's growing vernacular poetic culture.[110]

Qizilbash Khan's ability in Hindustani music, proficiency in the vernacular, and illustrious connection with poetic luminaries of Delhi also gained him a place in Mir Taqi "Mir"'s (1723–1810) *tazkirih*.[111] Written in Persian, *Nikat al-Shu'ara* is devoted entirely to *Rīkhta* poets, many of whom also composed Persian verse, as did Mir.[112] In the introduction Mir states, "Let it not be concealed that until now no book has been compiled on the states (*ahvāl*) of poets of this art of *Rīkhta*, which is the poetry in the manner (*bi-tawr-i*) of Persian poetry [but] in the language of the exalted camp (*urdū*) of Shahjahanabad Delhi . . . though there is *Rīkhta* in the Deccan, because there is not one poet from there who is not wanting, [I] have not begun with their names."[113]

Informed by disputes over proper usage in *Rīkhta*, Mir's *Nikat* champions the Delhi register over the Deccani and promotes this vernacular as poetic language by asserting Delhi's Persian tradition as its ancestor. The first two entries of the text are the famous poets, Amir Khusraw and Bidil. From there the entries are listed in alphabetical order, beginning with Khan Arzu, who wrote only in Persian, though he championed the highly Persianized Urdu poetry that Mir favored and was teacher to many Persian and *Rīkhta* poets. These three Persian ancestors form the lineages from which Mir sees himself and his peers descended. It is a particularly innovative style of Persian (exemplified by Bidil and regulated by Arzu), specific to Hindustan in its diminutive sense but not yet separate from the Persianate poetic tradition.[114]

Biographically more sparse than Persian poetic *tazkirih*s (to which *Rīkhta tazkirih*s often refer their readers), the *Nikat* nevertheless narrates Umid into his *Rīkhta* collective, countering the presumed constitution of difference, whereby (Muslim) "Indians" supposedly embraced a "native" Urdu poetry in preference to the "foreign" Persian.[115] There is little biographical information about Qizilbash Khan, just that "he was a distinguished Persian poet" and "a Mughal man (*mardī Mughulī būd*)." As we saw in Chapter 6, a Mughal could be born in Iran or have a lineage several generations removed from a migrant ancestor (such as Mir himself). Qizilbash Khan could thus simultaneously be born in Hamadan and be Mughal in Hindustan. The same lineages of origin that identified him within a Delhi-centered *Rīkhta* community also distinguished his place in the Persianate and were articulated according to its sensibilities. Indeed, Mir's depredations of Deccani Urdu poets were uttered in the language of dispositions and states. In contrast, Mir describes Umid as jovial and kind, with his sociability the grace of many gatherings where he was esteemed by the great.

Commemorating these gatherings rendered them part of the Persianate. Umid recited two verses of *Rīkhta* to Mir at a wedding celebration, prefacing them with the comment, "I too have recently composed two verses of *Rīkhta*."[116] Besides this occasion, there is no indication that Umid composed poetry in *Rīkhta*. More was unnecessary because the purpose of the entry, commemorated in Persian, was to show this well-known figure's participation in *Rīkhta*, which took place in Persianate social circles of the imperial capital. Mir's entry relied upon Qizilbash Khan's popularity in these social circles and renown in Persian *tazkirih*s. Its purpose is not to make Qizilbash Khan known to his audience but to commemorate his *Rīkhta* verses and to add the shared social context of their transmission to the shared imaginary of a Persianate *Rīkhta*. This addition thereby included Umid in Mir's aesthetic and social collective—a plot within the same garden that Shafiq composed, where Hindus and Muslims, some of them Mughals, from here and from elsewhere, circulated. They were all part of a circle of intimates, imagined and experienced, proximate and far, previous and present.

At the core of Persianate selves was a necessary and constitutive multiplicity, within and between their aporetic collectives. While not the only commemorative texts, the proliferation of *tazkirih*s in the eighteenth century, which saw imperial devolution and the dispersal and reconstitution of communities, is significant. Given their nature, *tazkirih*s defined Persianate collectives simultaneously seeking to establish polities with claims to moral standing that evoked hierarchical multiplicity, without exclusionary differentiation. The cacophony of commemoration, and the range of interpermeable collectives and selves it brought into being, shows the whole, the Persianate, in the eighteenth century. The *tazkirih*s written at this time were circulated, celebrated, reiterated, adapted, and drawn on to write still more. Commemoration linked the living and the dead, the near and the far, all as the perfect and less perfect masters of Persian *adab*. Commemoration was an ethical enactment of preserving moral communities and their selves by bringing them into being and passing their possibilities onto various audiences who remembered them.

Memories and Multiplicity
(Lost and Lingering)

"Khūsh āmadīd ba mamlakat-i Yazd." (Welcome to the
domain of Yazd.)

—An old man's greeting in the Yazd bazaar
upon hearing I had come from Tehran,
April 2008

THE QUESTION I WAS ASKED IN MY YOUTH, "Are you Persian or
Iranian?" had no adequate answer, and this was not the case just for me. One
need not dig far past the veneer of the Iranian national story to find the ves-
tiges of older Persianate forms, which belie the narrative of a timeless, stable
Persian identity as the basis of the Iranian nation. My maternal family's history of generations spent in Hindustan and Burma is but one example of
the enduring complexities of the Persianate. Once I knew the questions to
ask, it seemed as if every other Iranian Persian had some connection to other
West or South Asian lands. The modern story of Iranian national identity, I
realized, was meant to reshape this more expansively constituted Persian in
the image of Europe's imperial racism. It required suppression of multiplicity.

This national project was uneven and imperfect at the best of times,
and it remains unfinished to this day. In the mid-twentieth century, Mughals, whose place monikers (*nisbat*s) had hardened into surnames, poured
into Iran from British India and Burma. These migrants were asked to
change their names at the border. They included Shirazis and Shushtaris;
my maternal grandmother's family, surnamed Kabuli (but claiming origin in
Nishapur), had a more tenuous claim to being Iranian. Some people gained
permission to adopt surnames from relatives in Iran. Others had to choose

from a book of surnames provided by the government, and some had such poor Persian that bureaucratic officials gave them humorous names, such as *sabzpar* (green-winged).[1] They were thus scrubbed of their previous names, but memories of an older kind of Persian lingered, to be shared with grand-daughters like me over preparation of Indian and Burmese foods (which I thought were Iranian), in Persian and imperial English, with Urdu words thrown in for emphasis.

Colonial modernity and its nationalist articulations did not completely change the terrain of place and origin. New logics organized belonging, but old meanings and their multiple possibilities remained. The old man who welcomed me in the Yazd bazaar called Yazd a *mamlakat*, a relational use of the word for a domain, which sat easily alongside Iran, a *mamlakat* in a broader context. *Achchā* (Urdu: I understand), I wanted to tell him, in the language of my grandmother.

The history of older selves that this book has pursued raises questions about historicizing the possible styles of imagined communities.[2] If, as Anderson proposes, "nationalism has to be understood by aligning it, not with self-consciously held political ideologies, but with the large cultural systems that preceded it, out of which—as well as against which—it came into being," then a better understanding of what came before is important for modern histories of nationalism.[3]

Anderson's critics have accused him of a Eurocentric account of nationalism, with religious community and dynastic realm as the relevant cultural precedents.[4] In a famous rejoinder to Anderson's formulation, Chatterjee cites language as one of "the areas within the so-called spiritual domain that nationalism transforms in the course of its journey." For Chatterjee, in the context of Bengal, English and the written vernacular functioned "as the language of bureaucracy" and, in place of Persian, "the most powerful vehicle of intellectual influence on a new Bengali elite."[5] In this new contradistinction, Bengali emerged as the language of the people, a site of indigeneity and authenticity previously unnecessary in the Persianate context. We need to historicize the Persianate, a cultural system through which later forms of imagined belonging came into being.[6] There is also something to be learned from older times (not entirely past), in the possibilities overwritten by nationalism. We can better appreciate what colonial rule, with its changes in forms, including language, and its modern logics, including nationalism, meant for Iran, Hindustan, and the Persians in between by looking to earlier empires, which had their own forms and logics that underpinned, sustained, and ultimately outlived those empires.

The fall of the Safavids, together with its representation and interpretation, is central to understanding changing interactions between Persian migrants and travelers across eighteenth-century Iran and Hindustan. This event and its aftermath created a perception of Iran as a ruined land, a view widely shared among Persians in both Iran and Hindustan. The fall of the Safavids ultimately led to the devastation of northern Timurid domains under Nadir Shah and, coupled with the devolution of Timurid central power, a sense of waning imperial might in Hindustan. These momentous events marked the meaning of place in commemorative texts from the middle decades of the eighteenth century, in a context refigured from imperial heydays. Nevertheless, even in the aftermath of empire, Iran and Hindustan remained marked by both affiliation and rivalry between Timurid and Safavid dynasties, evident in the recurrent evocation of the sixteenth-century relationship between Tahmasp and Humayun.[7] Their relations, however, remained aporetic and their shared Persianate meanings irreducible to the singularity and radical difference of modern nationalism.

Dominant readings of Hazin's *Tazkirat al-Ahval* and Azar's *Atashkadih* as iconic of proto-national chauvinism stem from the preoccupations of modern readers, not from the texts themselves. In their own times, these texts did dispute existing meanings, but such challenges could be interpreted as proto-national only much later. Hazin sought to recoup the prestige and virtue of Iran after the Safavids. Iran as a unit of place, however, was produced in context, in a discussion of legitimate rulers, made in reference to his location and audience in Delhi, the imperial capital of Hindustan. Azar sought to situate a new poetic style in a present defined by Hindustani domination of poetic patronage and the political upheavals in Iran that followed the Safavids. Both texts intervened in their contexts, contesting the relative meaning of Iran within the Persianate world. We may consider them iconic of the Persianate hermeneutical ground upon which they waged their contests. Refiguring Iran required drawing on a shared universal Persianate history, which undergirded ethical valuations of the immediate past and the present. This history and its attendant ornaments of place signaled *adab*, as well as geographical systems (such as humors and climes) that imbued places with moral meaning. The stakes and substance of these contestations changed by the early nineteenth century, but *adab* remained central.

Despite differences of interpretation with their contemporaries, Hazin and Azar deploy the same meanings of place as those with whom they disagree. These disagreements took place within the Persianate; they do not signify alterity. When read alongside contemporaneous texts with other prerogatives, such as Kashmiri's *Bayan*, or later texts governed by different historical concerns, such as Maftun's *Zubdat*, conceptual similarities of place emerge. Among these are the meaning of home and its relation to kingdoms and other domains, small and large. Differences between lands and their inhabitants were recognized but not absolute. Rather, the value of lands and inhabitants was mutable, aporetic, and relative.

The lens of home reveals different ways of invoking the past across the eighteenth century and the multiple ways that place had meaning. These relationships to previous times, as not entirely past, differ significantly from our modern understanding of empirical, positivist history. Commemorative texts evoked figures and events from universal histories of the far and near past, as well as stories from epic literature. The definitive authority of these figures circulated and was reiterated through the common corpus of Persianate texts. Storied figures were invoked not for their facticity but for the meaning they could offer more recent occurrences and the imagination of place. In this sense, they were part of the present. They provided a nexus of meanings that defined events and places, constantly contested but in the same language, with similar reference and on the ground of common assumptions about home and place.

The language of place had an *adab*, a defining set of generic conventions that made certain places part of a Persianate universal, within which particularities could be accommodated. These conventions ornamented places with cultivated gardens, built (usually urban) structures, men of learning, and connections to the storied Persianate past that could evoke ideal polities and virtuous societies. In the symbiotic circulation of porous bodies and lands, people and their collective arrangements gave meaning to place, just as places altered people. Non-Islamic places and people could be aporetically tied to

Islam through the moral meaning of these ornaments, and universal Persianate knowledge could make sense of unfamiliar local notions, giving the strange a place in the Persianate.[8]

The importance of previous times in constituting present meanings points to the importance of origin. At the end of the High Persianate period, origins were multiple, and their elements narrated according to a person's station, as well as the imperatives of representation. Place was almost always part of origin, inflecting its more significant lineages of birth, collective, rule, learning, service, and discipleship. As an accrual that gained meaning in sedimentation, place appeared as itinerary in the midst of the structuring force of lineages (absent only when someone was represented as a brute—like Nadir Shah—and then place, along with all elements of origin, was impoverished).

Origins constituted the basis of possible affiliations (or their lack). Its lineages reflected moral substance and ethical realizations, both inherited and accrued. Many modes of identification were articulated as genealogies, laying the basis for kinships that brought people together in ways incongruent with modern parochial categories of family, nation, ethnicity, and even religion. Origins were relationally articulated and always situated. Their *adab* of telling and naming made them meaningful. There were many ways to be Persian, and one need not be Muslim or born in an Iranian city to be a master of its *adab* and all that it implied morally, though one had to inhabit its forms.

These arguments challenge the notion of ethnicity as an objective, transhistorical category. Scholarly use of ethnicity presumes that its distinguishing feature is common descent "originally" tied to a territory. Whether descent is considered fictive or real, the very distinction assumes a "true" lineage rooted in conceptions of a biological, blood-based kinship specific to European Christian history. However, to speak of collective categories like "Turks" (a word keyed to Orientalist meanings in European languages) requires us to ignore a multiplicity of complex relations.[9] Analysis of the Persianate, therefore, demands a fundamental rethinking of ethnicity as a universal category. Otherwise, the term's reductive strictures, projected onto the past, hobble our thinking.

In the Persianate, relationships constituted lineages, which formed, transformed, and transmitted moral substance and ethical behavior. *Adab* was both the social and the aesthetic form that manifested (even as it ontologically

realized) moral substance. Accordingly, kinship stemmed from the principle of lineages. *Adab* regulated an understanding of kinship distinct from
blood, situating Persians ontologically in a world of relationships. *Adab* was
the form of belonging. It outlined proper conduct, which encompassed the
"moral proprieties of kinship" crucial to a virtuous social order.[10] The ethical relations that manifest moral order depended on legal regulations, forms
of knowledge, and socially sanctioned hierarchies through which obligations
and privileges circulated. Whether through births, deaths, gifts, permissions,
companionships, or legal contracts, its hermeneutical scaffolding gave certain
relations formal meaning as kinship. These were commemorated as lineages.
All were encompassed by the logic of *adab*.

Relations we now recognize as biological were important, but they were
incorporated into lineages that challenge current analytic uses of ethnicity or
nationality as the means by which people understood themselves. Kin and
descent were spread across distinct but aporetic relations created by birth,
milk, marriage, learning, service, and patronage. These formed connective
chains that could be overlaid and combined. Persianate belonging was thus
multiple, based on a kinship that linked place, learning, family, service, and
social collective. Across parochial lines, these supple lineages were central to
the constitution of selves and of their relations to one another and their collectivities. People and collectives wore these relations in their names.

Broadly speaking, Persians named and distinguished one another in a
number of contingent ways. Shafiq and others could speak of Fārsī-gūyān,
'Ajamī, Tājīk, Qizilbash, and Mughal. These names no longer exist, but they
explain how a person could belong to one place, even as they had an origin
elsewhere, because these origins were all part of the Persianate. They included
internal distinctions, to be sure, but these became the basis of difference only
in particular contexts. Potentially, there was always a sense of similitude that
could generate affiliation, even if particular circumstances prevented it. These
distinctions, however, were voiced through common hermeneutics mutually
intelligible even in moments of contestation (indeed, they were required for
contestation). Attending to this language of belonging reminds us that "even
within the theories that maintain a highly qualified or situated subject, the
subject still encounters its discursively constituted environment in an oppositional epistemological frame. The culturally enmired subject [supposedly]

negotiates its constructions, even when those constructions are the very predicates of its own identity."[11]

In other words, an elision of epistemology appears even in modern contexts. When we turn from our own rootedness in that epistemology, we have a duty to account for the historical epistemology governing meaning in the spaces of our inquiry by acknowledging the specificities of meaning in our own language. Otherwise, we are left with a "horizontal trajectory of adjectives," often hyphenated—Indo-Persian, Perso-Islamic, subaltern, Indic, elite—which even by its own logic "invariably fail[s] to be complete." Butler tells us that "this failure is instructive," a sign of "the illimitable process of signification itself. It is a *supplément*, the excess that necessarily accompanies any effort to posit identity once and for all. The illimitable *et cetera*, however, offers itself as a new departure."[12] Here we can understand Persianate origins as ongoing sedimentation, which in its very contingent motion functioned as the truth of lives.

Terms like Iranian are not interchangeable with Persian. Iranian is a modern term, keyed to the impoverished mono-logic of nation-states that claims an autonomous meaning. Yet Iranian still functions differentially, against other national formations and territorially rooted ethnicities—Turks, Kurds, Arabs, Indians, and others. The Persianate provides the schema of another logic, with hierarchies and distinctions but with interpermeable truths and links structured by *adab*.

Form was also central to commemoration. Collectives and their selves memorialized in concert. There was competition, but it functioned constitutively, rather than exclusively. Claims to moral standing evoked hierarchy, and no one could stand at the apex of a hierarchy without a connected array of necessary multiplicity held together by the shared meaning of *adab*. Indeed, to articulate distinction, the aporetic logic of *adab* required commonality. Its logic persisted through the nineteenth century, even as new logics appeared. Early national selves still invoked older Persianate ideas.[13] These modern logics, of categorical difference and mutual exclusivity, could not entirely erode the space of aporia.

Persianate collectives comprised selves across time and space. Their lineages, social connections, and circulations between places crossed many of our modern boundaries of ethnic, religious, territorial, and even linguistic belonging. These collectives were bounded, but by our standards they sprawled, linking places, lineages, and overlapping aesthetic, political, social, familial, and devotional communities. Persianate selves developed heft and meaning through and with this sprawl, crossing what we now consider as national boundaries. To insist otherwise is to miss and dismiss the critical distance from which we might see anew and imagine new futures.

In the late eighteenth and early nineteenth centuries, *tazkirih*s written in South Asia evinced an awareness of one another, a companionable mutual referencing to assert themselves as regional polities. *Adab* continued to be central to self and to collective legitimation, whether of local men of power or East India Company officials. The idea that collectives brought forth selves, the lingering need for multiplicity, also appears in early articulations of national belonging. Though *tazkirih*s produced at the Qajar court increasingly looked to texts produced in their own lands,[14] Persians continued to reference one another. Iranians articulated themselves in relation to Indians; they remained connected through Persian, Islam, or shared Asian-ness.

Such logic goes a long way toward explaining why a Persian such as Mirza Fath ʻAli Akhundzadih, a resident of Russian-ruled Tiblisi who never traveled east of Tehran, would articulate his reformist vision of an Iranian in conversation with an Indian, a descendant of ʻAlamgir (d. 1707), the Timurid ruler of Hindustan, whom he calls Gurgani.[15] More examples abound, even as late as the 1890s, in the pages of the Calcutta-based newspaper *Habl al-Matin*, often credited as a central forum for modernist ideas and political change. There a long-running column in dialogue form staged a discussion between two Persian friends who shared a morally beneficial companionship, with all the trappings of proper conduct, in which an Indian schooled an Iranian on reformist ideas, from economics to education to civic engagement.[16] These lingering memories of older Persianate selves and collectives pose powerful questions to scholars of modernity and nationalism. What does social and cultural history look like through historicized eyes that do not assume relations among people, places, their meanings, and their names? Is the relevant history of the nation the territory of the state, always? Now, even?

Taking care to historicize discussions of the early modern Persianate—the creation, transmission, and reception of place in the material circulation of people, texts, and their ideas—can put valuable pressure on India as an assumed category of local or regional coherence, and on its cultural corollary, Indo-Persian. This discussion of broader circulations and connections need not imply that literary culture, textual production, and reading communities in the subcontinent lack specificities or are irrelevant to the study of Persian. Rather, a more self-reflective historical lens can show how Persianate societies and cultures in various South Asian locales were often as connected, or sometimes more so, to people and places outside, in West and Central Asia.[17] Conceptualizing the Persianate subcontinent—with its specificities and its extensions to other regions—as "Indo-Persian" indicates a resolute modernity that is singularly inadequate. Persian was Indian, Iranian, and more, so much as to call into question the meaning of those terms or to render them less relevant.

The arguments of this book are meant to provide impetus for asking what is obscured when we take one aspect of place—territorial political kingdom—as the definitive scope of culture, especially when a language, its forms, and its denizens circulated transregionally. What elements that we presume specific to Timurid Hindustan or Indo-Persian or Safavid Iran are shared? Beginning with what was shared can help us identify what was specific to those places. These are questions—about the local and the transregional, about belonging and difference—that I hope others will join me in considering. We can learn much by thinking through and with connective circulations between these lands, between people, texts, and ideas, and the larger Persianate of which they are a part. We can also gain valuable resources for our impoverished present.

Notes

Introduction: The Shadow of Nationalism

1. Hāfiz Shīrāzī, *Dīvān-i Hāfiz*, 271. Unless otherwise indicated, all translations are my own. I thank Farbod Mirfakhrai for helping me select these verses and for feedback on their translation.

2. Avery, "Foreword: Hāfiz of Shīrāz," xi. For an overview of his life and work, see Lewisohn, *Hafiz and the Religion of Love*, especially "Prolegomenon," 3–73.

3. I utilize Ahmed's definition of Islam as hermeneutical engagement with the Pre-Text, Text, and Context of Revelation. Here, Hafiz's Hidden World is engagement with the Pre-Text through a (Persian) poetics as Context, with frequent recourse to the Text (Ahmed, *What Is Islam?*, 32–38, 345–62, 405–24). Hafiz's poetry itself came to hold a significant place in the Context of Revelation.

4. On the Iranianization of the *Shahnama*, for instance, see Tavakoli-Targhi, *Refashioning Iran*, 96–104.

5. On nineteenth-century discourses of civilization across Europe and Asia, see the essays in Pernau et al., *Civilizing Emotions*, including Kia, "Moral Refinement and Manhood."

6. Burbank and Cooper, *Empires in World History*, 287–329.

7. Zia-Ebrahimi, *Emergence of Iranian Nationalism*, 1–7. Vejdani demonstrates that the Pahlavi state narrated Islam as a cause of decline only after the Second World War ("The Place of Islam"). Mozaffari details that an alternative Shi'i collective imagination has existed alongside the pre-Islamic in modern times (*Forming National Identity*).

8. For recent accounts of twentieth-century nationalism, see Kashani-Sabet, *Frontier Fictions*; Tavakoli-Targhi, *Refashioning Iran*; and Marashi, *Nationalizing Iran*.

9. Ahmed, *What Is Islam?*, 115–24, 176–82, 187–97.

10. Ibid., 405–8.

11. Zia-Ebrahimi's outlining of this process is nevertheless relentlessly Eurocentric and modernist in its analytic assumptions. He ignores early modern Iran's deep imbrication in the world, as well as Persianate and Islamic universalisms' nuanced relationship to religious difference. Rather, he posits a simplistic "traditional contempt for things 'infidel,'" a claim he makes courtesy of sources such as consummate Orientalist Bernard Lewis and infamous racist Arthur de Gobineau (*Emergence of Iranian Nationalism*, 22, quote from 25). This flattening of all things premodern into an impoverished caricature of "traditional" (or medieval) distorts not only an understanding of the early modern but also the substance and meaning of modernity's changes.

12. For an overview of Persian in South Asia, see Alam, "Culture and Politics of Persian."

13. Haneda, "Emigration of Iranian Elites," 130.

14. For an example of Persianate practices of power shorn of their linguistic sheath, see Wagoner, "'Sultan Among the Hindu Kings'." He calls these practices in Vijayanagara (in south India) "Islamic-inspired forms and practices" (852–53), though he refers to the same themes in later work as Persian; see Eaton and Wagoner, *Power, Memory, Architecture*, 3–38.

15. Recent scholarship has made the convincing case that a conception of Iranian nationalism in the sense of a modern nation-state existed only from the mid-nineteenth century and then only among a few elites and intellectuals. The process by which these ideas became dominant was long, uneven, and fitful (see note 8). For South Asian examples, see Chandra, *Parties and Politics*, xviii; Alam, *Crisis of Empire*; and Ray, *The Felt Community*. For a discussion of this tendency in historiography on Iran, see Kia "Imagining Iran," 89–90.

16. Kashani-Sabet, *Frontier Fictions*, 15–18. Similarly, see Amanat, *Pivot of the Universe*, 13.

17. See Amanat, *Pivot of the Universe*, 2–8, for a discussion of the Qajars' political conception of the land of Iran. It was in the Qajars' interest to set themselves up as protectors of the guarded domain of Iran, the latest link in a chain of dynasties to occupy the Iranian throne, abstracting Iran from the Safavids. This notion was especially helpful because Qajars had no charismatic lineage linking them either to the Safavids or to the Prophet (Amanat, "The Kayanid Crown," 28–29). These early Qajar rulers sought, therefore, to tap into the pre-Islamic millenarian ethos by crafting the imperial character of their rule with such accoutrements as the "Kayanid" crown, which in actual design was a simplified version of the Qizilbash cap. Amanat seems to think this resemblance is something of an accident, even while noting Aqa Muhammad Khan's post-coronation pilgrimage to Shaykh Safi al-Din's tomb in Ardabil (22–23).

18. Bayly, *Origins of Nationality*, 4.

19. Ibid., 11.

20. Ibid., 21. This emphasis on the local as the authentic site of "the people" is also an extremely modern notion, though Bayly also claims that "the bearer[s] of these emergent identities" were both literate Mughal nobles and other "literacy-aware" groups (20). At the very least the presence of multiple meanings (and languages) would complicate the picture.

21. For a valuable study that that relies on the contrast between physical space and interpretive space, see Antrim, *Routes and Realms*. By contrast, Green understands space as something made. Yet physical features, such as territory and the structures built on them, still stand in contrast to narratives, memory, and imagination (*Making Space*). Also see Mozaffari on place-making as a process, involving the investment of material sites with layers of meaning (*Forming National Identity*).

22. Alam, "Culture and Politics of Persian," 148. Tavakoli-Targhi, *Refashioning Iran*, 24. Casual references to such entities as "Indian scholars," meaning Persian-speaking literati of Hindustan, pervade this work. Tavakoli-Targhi also uses Persian interchangeably with Iranian in some places (27), though he clearly means Persian to refer to Persian speakers from either Iran or Hindustan (26). The aim here is not to denigrate Alam and Tavakoli-Targhi's foundational scholarship but to note that neither analysis utilizes a notion of place with historicized meanings of affiliation or culture.

23. For instance, an excellent general work focusing on political culture between 1200 and 1750 that seeks to present "India as a world region" where "there was constant movement into and out of the subcontinent," ultimately ends up drawing on modern nationalism's timeless geographical empiricism. We are told that "the word 'subcontinent' used to describe the South Asian landmass highlights the fact that it is a natural physical region separate from the rest of Eurasia." The authors draw this "natural" boundary to the north by invoking the Himalayas, "beyond which lies the arid and high Tibetan plateau," which "has largely sealed off access to the subcontinent from the north" (Asher and Talbot, *India Before Europe*, 5). Yet recent work has shown that this is a colonial vision, taken up by nationalists. Up to the early nineteenth century, northeastern India was intimately connected with Tibet socially, politically, and culturally (see Chatterjee, "Connected Histories"). Such scholarly interventions concede the very conceptual ground to nationalist visions, which limit their impact.

24. An important example of this mode of analysis is Antrim's book. She makes place, produced through a discourse about an actual physical territory, the primary basis of belonging (*Routes and Realms*, for instance 1–3, 5–7). Even by her own admission, however, place was not the only basis, thus raising questions of what belonging might look like if we consider land alongside other bases.

25. Tuan, *Space and Place*, 1–7.

26. The *farsakh* was a distance measured in a unit of time spent traveling (per hour, approximately six kilometers) (Hinz, "Farsakh"). For examples of variable *farsakh*

measurements according to faster train travel over the same stretch of land in the late nineteenth century, see Sohrabi, *Taken for Wonder*, 93–94.

27. A recent call to overcome the historical discipline's allergy to theory has noted the field's *"unquestioned allegiance to 'ontological realism.'* Central to this epistemology is a commitment to empirical data that serves as a false floor to hold up the assertion that past events are objectively available for discovery, description, and interpretation. Here the tautology is exposed: empiricist methodology enables the rule of this realism while this realism guarantees the success of empiricist methodology" (Kleinberg, Scott, and Wilder, *Theses on Theory and History*, I.4, emphasis in the original).

28. Mitchell, "Am I My Brother's Keeper"; Ateş, *Ottoman-Iranian Borderlands*; Zarinebaf, "Rebels and Renegades" and "From Istanbul to Tabriz"; and Vejdani, "Contesting Nations."

29. Recent work includes those mentioned in note 8, as well as Vejdani, *Making History*. For new work on the shared nature of Iranian and Indian modernity, see the articles by Grigor, "Persian Architectural Revivals"; Jabbari, "Making of Modernity"; and Vejdani, "Indo-Iranian."

30. Bonakdarian, *Britain and the Iranian Constitutional Revolution*; and Kia, "Indian Friends."

31. Partha Chatterjee has argued that this colonial narrative was incorporated into nationalist self-fashioning in the context of what he calls the spiritual domain ("Histories and Nations," in *Nation and Its Fragments*, 95–115). Scholarship on colonial history has explored the function of these narratives in colonial governance and their absorption into indigenous elite discourse. See Cohn, *Colonialism and Its Forms*; Mani, *Contentious Traditions*; Sen, *Distant Sovereignty*; and Travers, *Ideology and Empire*. For work dealing with these issues in the Iranian context, see Tavakoli-Targhi, *Refashioning Iran*; Dabashi, *Iran*, especially chapter 1; and Marashi, *Nationalizing Iran*, especially chapter 2. See also Zia-Ebrahimi, "Emissary of the Golden Age." Vejdani's recent work problematizes the dominance of this narrative across the Pahlavi period (*Making History*).

32. Vejdani, "The Place of Islam." Reformist narratives in the late nineteenth century were not anti-Islamic. See Kia, "Moral Refinement and Manhood."

33. Chatterjee, "The Nation and Its Pasts," chapter 4 in *Nation and Its Fragments*, 76–94.

34. This basic education is outlined in Alam, "Culture and Politics of Persian," 163 and 166. This education included books widely read across the Persian world, such as Sa'di's *Gulistan*, the most read Persian book of this time (see Kia, "*Adab* as Literary Form.")

35. The terms and degree of Sanskrit-Persian intellectual exchange have not received enough attention. Pollock cites social divisions between Brahmins who were Sanskrit scholars and those who learned Persian and entered Timurid service as indications that, apart from some narrow scientific forms of exchange, formal scholarly exchange was not

widespread between languages. This assertion, however, does not address the informal reading habits of learned, multilingual individuals who may have been writing in only one language but who were nevertheless engaging in transcultural exchange (Pollock, "Languages of Science," 35). More recently, Truschke gives an example of the exchange of knowledge through the oral medium of Hindi, which facilitated communication for the translation of Sanskrit literary texts into Persian at Akbar's court ("Cosmopolitan Encounters"). Similarly, Allison Busch has shown the ways in which Persians' cultivation of Braj literary and aesthetic culture, itself drawing on Sanskrit, actually blurs the distinction between cosmopolitan and vernacular poetic circulation (*Poetry of Kings*, 130–65).

36. Szuppe, "Glorious Past," 41. Her repeated emphasis on a shared culture specifically limited to the eastern part of Iran is belied by at least one of her authors originating in Asadabad (near Hamdan in '*Iraq-i 'ajam*) and others traveling to Shiraz and Isfahan for study.

37. *Adab* had specificities relational to context. For a discussion of the centrality of *adab* to Sufi orders, see Bashir, *Sufi Bodies*, 78–85.

38. This shared cultural framework seems to have been sustained by regular contacts among individuals, family groups, and social groups functioning within the political units of the post-Timurid space, who "traveled frequently between Central Asia, Iran and India, thus promoting cultural, literary, and spiritual exchanges through direct personal contacts, and generating an overall climate of profound interest in literary trends, accomplishments and production in all parts of the Persianate world" (Szuppe, "Glorious Past," 41).

39. Ahmed, *What Is Islam?*, 109, 335–36, 368–77, 397–404. The harmony of unity in seeming contradiction or paradox is elaborated by Melvin-Koushki, "Imperial Talismanic Love."

40. Ahmed, *What Is Islam?*, 377–82. He illustrates this concept of connectedness in his reading of the hierarchies of meaning in representations of wine drinking (417–24).

41. Derrida, *Aporias*, 20. Derrida presents three types of aporia, stating that "the partitioning among multiple figures of aporia does not oppose figures to each other, but instead installs the haunting of the ones in the other" (20). The classification of aporia proceeds according to the definition of the concept itself.

42. Derrida, *Aporias*, 64.

43. I borrow Hall's concept of culture as based on shared meanings produced and exchanged through the representational system of language ("Work of Representation," 15). Meaning in language tells us about much more than just language itself. Thus I use culture "in its broadest sense to denote those practices and ideas which help to make sense of the world" (Chatterjee, *Cultures of History*, 3).

44. Dabashi, *Iran*, 21.

45. *Mavara' al-nahr* (Transoxiana) is generally understood to be a part of Turan, along with other regions, such as Khwarazm (see Chapter 3). I use *Turan*, since it is

imbued with geocultural meanings specific to Persianate history and is the counterpart to Iran as a larger region.

46. Such plurivalence also characterized another part of the Persianate world that I speak of only in passing. *Rum* originally referred to Byzantium (or eastern Rome). Later, it sometimes referred to Ottoman heartlands centered on Anatolia and sometimes to the whole empire. By the eighteenth century, Rum was not often included in discussions about Persian-speaking contexts. For more on Persianate Rum, see Melville, "Early Persian Historiography of Anatolia." The move from Persian to Ottoman Turkish was not one of radical rupture; as Yildiz observes, the cultivation of Turkish literary culture was "based on Persian models *in place of* Persian" ("Ottoman Historical Writing," 438, emphasis in original).

47. This may be confusing for those used to treating the fifteenth-century Timurid rulers of Iran and Turan as a dynasty separate from the sixteenth-century rulers of Hindustan. This separation is unjustified, however, as Babur considered himself part of the same line (Timur's) and sovereignty was corporately shared by the family. The continuity is well documented in Balabanliar, *Imperial Identity*. The convenience of distinction provided by different names carries too high a cost of historical obfuscation.

48. Here I am inspired to Joan Scott's injunction to critique: "When any taken-for-granted idea or established fact is understood to be an interpretation of reality rather than reality itself, its history can be written by specifying its operations and resurrecting its forgotten alternatives. It is not, then, an inevitable consequence of the march of time, but a set of options that prevailed by ruling out others. The result of this kind of enquiry is an opening to reinterpretation" ("History-Writing as Critique," 28).

49. Hodgson defines "Islamicate" as "a *culture*, centered on a lettered tradition, which has been historically distinctive of Islamdom the *society*, and which has been naturally shared in by both Muslims and non-Muslims" (*Venture of Islam*, 1:58, emphasis in original). He further notes that "all lettered traditions of Islamdom have been grounded in the Arabic or the Persian or both" (1:59). Here Persian is "a major cultural vehicle," that constituted "a new overall cultural orientation within Islamdom." Futhermore, "most of the local languages of high culture that later emerged among Muslims likewise depended upon Persian wholly or in part for their prime literary inspiration. We may call all these cultural traditions, carried in Persian or reflecting Persian inspiration, 'Persianate' by extension" (2:293–311, quote from 293).

50. Alam's work on Indo-Islamic political thought is exemplary, though he does not use the term Persianate. Even his nuanced location of Islamic north India in the context of broader intellectual and historical trends of the Islamic world still reproduces empirical geography's modern assumptions, especially about language. His story is of the "Indianization" of "a Perso-Islamic polity," emphasizing the assimilation that Persianate Islam went through in a South Asian context, defined through contact with the Indic. What is good (tolerant) in Timurid imperial ideology becomes a product of

contact with the unique local, rather than a regional articulation of the broader Islamic universalism dominant at the time (*Languages of Political Islam*, quotes from pages 3 and 141, respectively. See the introduction and chapters 3 and 4 for these arguments). In fact, Alam marks these transregional circulations as "encouraging a kind of anti-tolerant worldview at elite levels," particularly because Persian was "an alien language" and thus "drove, in some ways, a wedge between the Mughals and their subjects," because it "was not an Indian language." The dominant Persian influence in Timurid Hindustan "went against the tradition of accommodation at northern Indian courts" and was sustained partly by "the continued flow into India of immigrant princes, noblemen, and men of learning from Iran and Central Asia." Alam contrasts the "rise of the Persian language and Iranian emigres," both of which are foreign (and whose presence creates intolerance), with the local north ("non-immigrant") Indians who know how to get along with, and ultimately share much with, their Indic others (quotes from 142–44).

51. Ahmed relies on Clifford Geertz's definition of culture, summarized as "a semiotic one where culture is conceptualized as a complex of meaning expressed in signs and symbols" (*What Is Islam?*, 246). I share Ahmed's objection that this does not always translate into a scholarly practice that historicizes understanding of "how particular communities read authoritatively their symbolic forms to produce culture/meaning/religion" (248).

52. Ahmed, *What Is Islam?*, 380–81, 492–94.

53. Ibid., 83–85.

54. Ibid., 524–27.

55. Ahmed simply describes instances when non-Muslims used Islamic terms with little explanation of how (*What Is Islam?*, 435–52). The invocation of 'Ali by Ahmed's Sikh wrestler (445–46) is best explained through the Persianate figure of the wrestler (Flatt, "Young Manliness," 159–61). For an example of professed hostility to Islam, though not always to Muslims, see Emin, *Life and Adventures*.

56. The rise and dominance of the occult sciences, particularly in Persianate contexts, provided the basis of a universal epistemology that facilitated encounters with other knowledge systems. On the rise of the occult, see Melvin-Koushki, "Powers of One." Also see Sheffield, "Language of Heaven." On modes of inclusion and coexistence of other traditions, see Bashir, "A Perso-Islamic Universal Chronicle," 219–21; and Kamola, "History and Legend," 557–58.

57. Kinra shows that the seventeenth-century Hindu munshi Chandra Bhan used a language of Sufi concepts to speak of moral substance and ethics ("Master and Munshī," 542–47).

58. Melvin-Koushki and Pickett use "High Persianate" as "a heuristic for mapping a discrete cultural formation, quite distinctive aesthetically, literarily, intellectually, religiously, socially, culturally and politically, that crystallized in Timurid Iran and persisted robustly as a framework for the Persian cosmopolis, from Anatolia and the Balkans to

Central Asia and India, for more than half a millennium." This periodization is better suited to the "multiple temporalities" of the Persianate than the "too uselessly and terminally Eurocentric" notion of a "rupturous" and "teleologizing" early modernity ("Mobilizing Magic," 233).

59. Alam, *Languages of Political Islam*, 128–33.

60. There were an estimated seven times more Persian speakers in India than in Iran (Cole, "Iranian Culture and South Asia," 15–18).

61. Meisami, *Persian Historiography*, 51.

62. Shafiq, *Gul-i Raʿnā*, f. 2a. On this early history, also see Alam, "Culture and Politics of Persian," 132–58. The narrative I give below, however, is one less invested in delineating a proto-nationalist "Indian Persian." Alam seeks to counter Iranian nationalist scholarly views of an "Indian style." But in taking this twentieth-century term to task, Alam creates a literary historical narrative territorialized in the subcontinent. His central argument is that "*Sabk-i Hindi* should not be understood as solely the articulation of Mughal India." But in place of a literary culture linked to a political dynasty, he gives us a nationalist genealogy, territorially rooted, with "roots in the early-medieval efflorescence under the Ghaznavids ... in Lahore with Masʿud Saʿd Salman during the eleventh century, reaching a first maturity at the time of Amir Khusrau Dihlavi in the late thirteenth and fourteenth centuries. It continued to evolve in the context of medieval Sufism before being redeployed in Mughal times after a possible detour through Herat" ("Culture and Politics of Persian," 131–32). In these pages, I hope to show that such a reduction of Persian in Hindustan to a stage solely limited to the subcontinent and "Indian origin" propagates what Indrani Chatterjee calls in another context, "a denial of connected pasts." Such narratives "circumscribe the horizons of scholarship, both literally and methodologically" (Chatterjee, "Connected Histories," 83). Instead of seeking to make Persians Indian, I hope to make Persians translocal, in Hindustan and elsewhere.

63. Shafiq, *Gul-i Raʿnā*, ff. 2a–2b.

64. For an excellent account of how migration from elsewhere could foster community in the early modern period, see Nile Green, *Making Space*, for example, 17–32, 116–27.

65. Meisami, *Persian Historiography*, 15–19.

66. On the impact of the Mongol invasions on historiography and political culture, see Bashir, "On Islamic Time," 534; and Alam, "Culture and Politics of Persian," 132–34, 152–54. On early political rule of Turco-Mongol rulers, see Jackson, *Studies on the Mongol Empire*. For the central role of this migration for the Delhi Sultanate, see Jackson, *Mongols and the Islamic World*, 396–97; and on the spread of Persian culture, see Eaton and Wagoner, *Power, Memory, Architecture*, 23 and 25.

67. On this circulation, see Gould, "Geographies of ʿAjam."

68. Thackston, "The Genghisid and Timurid Background," xliii.

69. Specifically, by the eve of Timurid rule in Hindustan, "as had occurred with Chingis Khan, Timur's own lineage became sacralized, infused with tangible political force and luster, imbuing his descendants with political authority and cultural prestige" (Balabanlilar, *Imperial Identity*, 38).

70. Bashir, "On Islamic Time," 533–37. On the importance of Timurid heritage, see Balabanlilar, *Imperial Identity*; and Moin, *Millennial Sovereign*, especially 23–55, who extends this significance to a form of early modern Persianate "sacred kingship" legible across West, Central and South Asia (21).

71. Eaton notes a shift in mid-fourteenth-century Bengal from an emphasis on Muslim symbols of rule to Persian forms of legitimacy: "[T]he political and cultural referents of these kings lay, not in Delhi or Central Asia, but much further to the west—in Mecca, Medina, Shiraz and ancient Ctesiphon [a former Sassanian capital]" (*Rise of Islam*, 49–50); also see Sardar, "The Bahmanis," 32; and Subrahmanyam, "Persianization and Mercantilism." For Shirazis in Bijapur, see Haidar and Sardar, *Sultans of Deccan India*, 102, 114, and 132.

72. For studies of circulation, largely about merchants and goods, see Dale, *Indian Merchants*; Levi, *Indian Diaspora*, Aslanian, *From the Indian Ocean*; Jabbari, *Trade and Commerce*; and Subramanyam, "Persians, Pilgrims and Portuguese." On other types of circulation, see Subrahmanyam, "Iranians Abroad;" and Foltz, *Mughal India and Central Asia*.

73. Richards, "Formulation of Imperial Authority," 128. On patronage of Persian, see Alam, "Culture and Politics of Persian." For a study of the imperial system, see Richards, *The Mughal Empire*.

74. For a statistical analysis of different groups, see Dadvar, *Iranians in Mughal Politics*. For travel accounts, see Alam and Subrahmanyam, *Indo-Persian Travels*. On Hindu munshis and their migrant patrons, see Kinra, "Master and Munshī."

75. Khan estimates that the royal and noble courts of Hindustan had quadruple the resources for patronage of the courts in seventeenth-century Iran (*Iranian Influence*, 5–9.)

76. For some of these events, see Babayan, *Mystics, Monarchs and Messiahs* and "The Safavid Synthesis"; Babaie, Babayan, and Baghdiantz-McCabe, *Slaves of the Shah*; and Mitchell, *Practice of Politics*, especially 145–97.

77. See Husain, *Nobility Under Akbar and Jahāngīr*; Ali, *Mughal Nobility*; Subrahmanyam, *"Un Grand Dérangement,"* 344–49; and Chandra, *Parties and Politics*, 29–39. This later migration has received far less attention, perhaps because fewer primary sources from this period have been translated into English.

78. Robinson, "Perso-Islamic Culture," 112–14.

79. Ibid., 113.

80. For instance, see Malik, "Muslim Culture and Reform."

81. Rahman, "Decline of Persian," 50.

82. Ibid., 52.

83. Robinson, "Perso-Islamic Culture," 113. Robinson further notes that there were "important areas of shared experience and significant systems of connection between the Middle East and South Asia. If this is true of the structural characteristics of the Ottoman, Safawid and Mughal empires, and if this is also true of their commercial organization and techniques of trade, it is no less true of the content of their systems of formal learning . . . and of the ways in which they were linked by the connective systems of learned and holy men." He notes that the itineraries of the learned were "the channels along which ideas came to be shared; the centers at which they congregated were the places from which ideas were broadcast" (Robinson, *'Ulama of Farangi Mahall*, 211). For more on Mirza Qatil, see Pellò, "A Linguistic Conversion."

84. The process by which one kind of Persian was replaced by another occurred gradually, through the very end of the nineteenth century. See Kia, "Indian Friends."

85. Kinra, "This Noble Science," 362–64.

86. For example, see Babayan, *Mystics, Monarchs and Messiahs*, 161–96.

87. Persian was not the first language of most inhabitants of Safavid domains. A spoken or literary Persian was usually a subsequent acquisition. Floor and Javadi provide examples, beyond the official language of the court, of Turkic sometimes used in official correspondence and literary composition ("Role of Azerbaijani Turkish"). On literary exchange, see Csirkés, "'Chaghatay Oration, Ottoman Eloquence'."

88. Perry, "Turkic-Iranian Contacts." Also see Floor and Javadi, "Role of Azerbaijani Turkish."

89. Perry, "Historical Role of Turkish," 195 and 199.

90. Pollock, *Language of Gods*, 319. A mother tongue draws on a European-specific idea of the vernacular as natural and naturally singular (318–19). Pollock argues against the existence of a mother tongue in the modern sense in South Asia, asserting that this expectation of "linguistic monism" is entirely "Western" (505–11, quote from 508).

91. For new approaches to regional specificity, see Khera, "Marginal, Mobile, Multilayered"; Sheikh, *Forging a Region*; and Sela, *Legendary Biographies*.

92. Pollock has argued that "we cannot know how colonialism changed South Asia if we do not know what there was to be changed." Though a "breathtakingly banal" point, it is nevertheless necessary, as studies of modernity presuppose knowledge of the preceding period, on which little work has been done (Pollock, introduction to *Forms of Knowledge*, 1).

93. Haneda also notices this designation in "Emigration of Iranian Elites," 130. This usage appears in texts written inside and outside Iran, by authors born in Iran and Hindustan, and thus is not linked to place of origin or political allegiance.

94. Historically, earlier conceptions of Iran were different, both territorially and linguistically. For instance, Mottahedeh notes that the Buyids, ruling Fars and *'Iraq-i 'ajam*, adopted Sassanian titles but "never showed any interest in New Persian" and

chose to patronize Arabic works, in contrast to contemporaneous rulers of Khurasan and Turan ("The Idea of Iran," 154).

95. Texts generally classified as histories, autobiographies, or travelogues, as well as *tazkirih*s often explicitly evoke the work of *tazkar*, or memorialization, as one of the purposes of writing. For instance, see Hazīn, *Tārīkh va Safarnāma*, 144–45.

96. Farid al-Din ʿAttar was the first author to use this term as a title for his biographical compendium of God's friends, quoting a Qurʾanic verse "to exhort believers to follow the path of mindful awareness" (Losensky, translator's introduction to *Memorial of God's Friends*, 1–2. The text enjoins readers to awareness of a particular kind of esoterically enlightened self, coalescing around a group of ancestors. He represented these ancestors according to the ideals he felt most important to his present, valorizing devotion to God above worldly power and wealth.

97. Reynolds et al., *Interpreting the Self*, 38–40.

98. Ibid., 47. There are important departures between the Arabic and Persian traditions, but this particular linkage remained. See Alam, "Culture and Politics of Persian," 150; Losensky, "Biographical Writing"; Melville, introduction to *Persian Historiography*, xxvii–xxviii, xliii–lv; and Daniel, "Rise and Development."

99. Losensky, *Welcoming Fighānī*, 56–57.

100. Chatterjee notes the ways in which early modern forms of history memorialized "events and processes of past times, together with their outcomes," causing them "to be a repository of cautionary tales and morals." Further, "if the term culture is taken in its broadest sense to denote those practices and ideas which help to make sense of the world," then "history constitutes an important medium" through which we can understand the culture of a particular present "in the context of its past" (*Cultures of History*, 3).

Part I: Place

An earlier and more extensive version of parts of this chapter was published as Kia, "Accounting for Difference."

1. Darwish, acceptance speech for the Prince Claus Award in Amsterdam.

2. Said, *Culture and Imperialism*, 3.

3. On the discourse of place as a means for articulating belonging and loyalty in medieval Arabic, see Antrim, *Routes and Realms*.

4. At the time, Benares was ruled by Raja Balwant Singh on behalf of the Nawabs of Awadh. Hazin was revered there as a friend of God by local people during his life and afterward. Khatak, *Shaikh Muhammad ʿAli Hazin*, 101–4 and 116–17. On Hazin's life and work, see Khatak, *Shaikh Muhammad ʿAli Hazin*; Shafīʿī Kadkanī, *Shāʿirī dar Hujūm-i Muntaqidān*; and ʿAlī Davvānī, Editor's introduction to *Tārīkh va Safarnāma*, 16–140.

5. Alam and Subrahmanyam, *Indo-Persian Travels*, 226–39. Their sole attention to this section is surprising since the authors initially state their opposition to taking the

texts apart "into bite-sized chunks" and propose instead "to follow our travelers and listen to them, and also take the manner in which they organised their materials seriously" (xiii).

6. Hazin did not give this text a title, nor did it circulate with one in the eighteenth century. The text circulated widely among the literati of Hindustan and eventually Iran, and nearly all the sources in this book mention it. For example, see Shūshtarī, *Tuhfat*, 413–19. Multiple manuscript copies exist in various collections in England, India, and Iran. For a partial list of these, see Davvānī, editor's introduction to *Tārīkh va Safarnāma*, 52–54. There are also five copies alone (HL 223, HL 268, HL 269, HL 275, and HL 1776) in the Khuda Bakhsh Library in Patna. The earliest Persian edition was published (London, 1831) as *Tārīkh-i Ahvāl: Bi-tazkirih-yi Hāl-i Mawlana Shaykh Muhammad ʿAli Hazin* (History of Conditions: Memoir of the Times of Mawlana Shaikh Mohammad ʿAli Hazin). An English translation had been published the previous year (*The Life of Sheikh Mohammed Ali Hazin*).

7. Little is known of Kashmiri's early life. With forty-five years between Nadir's invasion and Kashmiri's death, however, it is unlikely that he was older than his mid-thirties.

8. Alam and Subrahmanyam note that the section of the text beginning with the death of Mohammad Shah (1748) is likely written by Muhammad ʿUmar ibn Muhammad Bakhsh "Ashub," an early copyist and admirer of Kashmiri (*Indo-Persian Travels*, 289–90). I have treated the text as a single entity because that is the form in which the text circulated, and my analysis does not depend on unitary authorship. In the introduction, Kashmiri outlined a different ending, which was never provided. Instead, Ashub continued an ongoing chronicle of high Mughal politics. More than a dozen copies of this text are in manuscript collections all over the subcontinent and the United Kingdom. For a partial list, see K. B. Nasim, introduction to ʿAbd al-Karīm Kashmīrī, *Bayān-i Wāqiʿ*, xi–xvi. The published version I quote throughout ends in 1779 AD/1193 AH.

9. The text circulated widely in Persian- and English-language circles, as evinced by multiple Persian manuscript copies in India, Iran, and Britain, together with a translation into English soon after the text's completion. The shoddy English translation by Gladwin, *Memoirs of Khoja Abdulkurreem*, was published in Calcutta (1788 and 1812) and in London (1793). Gladwin excludes the first section on the fall of the Safavids, the rise of Nadir Shah, his invasion of Hindustan, and the events occurring after the death of Mohammad Shah. The sections pertaining to the politics of Hindustan after Kashmiri's return are also greatly abridged. The better translation is by Francis Pritchard, in manuscript form at the British Museum (Add. 30,782). For a detailed overview of the *Bayan*, see Alam and Subrahmanyam, *Indo-Persian Travels*, 247–90.

10. These include ʿAlavi Khan (Nadir's head physician) and Mirza ʿAli Akbar Shirazi (Nadir's chief minister) (Lockhart, *Nadir Shah*, 301).

11. Rosenthal, "The Stranger," 42. For positive and negative aspects, see 42–54. My thanks to Naghmeh Sohrabi for directing me to this article.

12. Some scholars point to the lack of patronage for poets caused by the devolution of central Mughal power, but lack of patronage is part of a broader set of events. The changing stakes of migration were also affected by contexts of origin. The fall of Safavid Iran explains the acute lamentations of home and exile resulting from a loss of home in the temporal, not just geographical, sense. See Alam and Subrahmanyam, *Indo-Persian Travels*; and Sharma, "Land of Darkness."

Chapter 1: Landscapes

Earlier and more extensive versions of parts of this chapter were published as Kia, "Accounting for Difference" and "Imagining Iran."

1. I had originally written "a person's relationship," but Philip Grant pointed out to me that a woman's relationship to home may be different. Men certainly understood their relationship to place as different from women's (see Chapter 4). Women's writings would have to be examined to see whether they contested the weaker relationship to place ascribed to them by men and articulated the same sensibilities of belonging. A published text to which one might make recourse is a *hajjnāma* written by an Isfahani widow in the late seventeenth century (*Safarnāma-yi Manzūm-i Hajj*). On this text see Babayan, "'In Spirit'"; and Alam and Subrahmanyam, *Indo-Persian Travels*, 24–44.

2. For a discussion of *vatan*, see Tavakoli-Targhi, *Refashioning Iran*, 114–16.

3. Ārzū, *Majma'*, 1:165.

4. Alam, "Culture and Politics," 134. Under the Samanids in Khurasan and Turan, Persian prose was patronized later than Persian poetry, mainly to mobilize political legitimacy autonomously from the Abbasids (Meisami, *Persian Historiography*, 15–46). For poetry in the Ghaznavid period, see Sharma, *Persian Poetry*.

5. A sense of regional literary style existed from the beginning. In the introduction to his divan, Amir Khusraw Dihlavi reviews the regional variations of Persian in Iran and Turan and claims that Persian spoken in Hindustan was sweetest because it was the closest to written Persian (*Dībāchih-yi Dīvān*, 28–29 and 63–64). For more on the Delhi Sultanate, see Auer, *Symbols of Authority*; and Kumar, *Emergence of the Delhi Sultanate*.

6. See Balabanlilar, "Lords of the Auspicious Conjunction" and *Imperial Identity*.

7. On Timurid rule of Iran and Turan, see Manz, *Power, Politics and Religion*.

8. In the mid-fifteenth century, the Aqquyunlu ruled western and central Iran (along with the Caucasus, northern Iraq, and Eastern Anatolia). See Woods, *The Aqquyunlu*. In the eighteenth century, Karim Khan Zand ruled much of western and northern Iran, while Shahrukh Mirza retained the rule of Khurasan as a tributary of Ahmad Shah 'Abdali. See Perry, *Karim Khan Zand*.

9. Kashmīrī, *Bayān*, 94–95.

10. Hazīn, *Tazkirat al-Muʿāsirīn*, 220. This is also an example of return migration before the Afghan invasion, when Jawzani, an accountant (*siyāq*), went to Hind, made his fortune, and returned to his home.

11. Hazīn, *Tazkirat al-Muʿāsirīn*, 207.

12. Hākim, *Mardum Dīdih*, 156.

13. Āzar, *Ātashkadih*, 4:525.

14. Kashmīrī, *Bayān*, 164.

15. Under Persianate, mostly Shiʿa rulers, the Deccan had long been a contact zone between the Timurids and the Safavids (Alam and Subrahmanyam, "The Deccan Frontier," 368–78).

16. Mīr, *Zikr-i Mīr*, 1928, 62.

17. Tavakoli-Targhi, *Refashioning Iran*, 114.

18. For instance, see Hazīn, *Tārīkh va Safarnāma*, 265.

19. Kashmīrī, *Bayān*, 45.

20. Hazīn, *Tārīkh va Safarnāma*, 268. Kashmiri uses almost the same language to describe Nadir's enthronement.

21. Kashmīrī, *Bayān*, 175.

22. Āzar, *Ātashkadih*, 1:99–100.

23. Hazīn, *Tārīkh va Safarnāma*, 265.

24. Kashmīrī, *Bayān*, 88.

25. Ibid., 172.

26. Ārzū, *Majmaʿ*, 1:186.

27. Āzād, *Khizānih*, 1871, 246.

28. On administrative variations in different Hindustani Timurid domains, left over from their lives as autonomous polities, see Alam and Subrahmanyam, introduction to *The Mughal State*, 1–71.

29. Kashmīrī, *Bayān*, 164–65.

30. Respectively known as *dār al-saltanat*, *Mashhad-i muqaddas*, and *dār al-ʿilm*.

31. Manz, *Power, Politics and Religion*, 280.

32. On Safavid centralizing measures, see Babayan, *Mystics, Monarchs and Messiahs*; and Mitchell, *Practice of Politics*. For the importance of local forces in the eighteenth century, see Perry, *Karim Khan Zand*.

33. Noted with respect to Kashmiri in Alam and Subrahmanyam, *Indo-Persian Travels*, 281–90.

34. For a view that privileges Yazd, see Mancini-Lander, "Memory on the Boundaries."

35. Hazīn, *Tārīkh va Safarnāma*, 267.

36. Ibid.

37. I have located this Caucasian border near modern-day Tiblisi because Kashmiri lists the cities of Azarbayjan as "Tabriz, Ganjah, Qarabagh, Shirvan, Shamakhi,

Nakhjavan, Yerevan, and Ardabil," a number of which are north of the current border at the Aras River (Kashmīrī, *Bayān*, 102).

38. This linkage of ruler, kingdom, and land was ingrained in medical notions of individual and collective health, as well as of moral philosophical notions of justice. The ruler acted on the collective body just as the physician acted on the porous individual body conditioned by its environment, to bring its humors into balance (see Chapter 3) (Alavi, *Islam and Healing*, 25, 27–28, 30–31.

39. Hazīn, *Tārīkh va Safarnāma*, 267. This association of a just ruler with the prosperity of the kingdom has been a common theme of Persian historiography since the beginning. See Meisami, *Persian Historiography*, 43.

40. On Persianate ideas of ethical governance, see Arjomand, "Salience of Political Ethic."

41. Pollock's discussion of Sanskrit's geocultural space is different in a number of respects, though he also notices multiplicity and mobility of the geographical imagination (*Language of the Gods*, 189–204, especially 193).

42. For example, Kashmiri quotes a couplet from the poet Saʿdi when discussing the extortion of supplies and wealth by Ahmad Shah Durrani's troops from the inhabitants of Lahore (*Bayān*, 193). On the use of Saʿdi's verses from the *Gulistan* as synecdoches for the meanings evoked by their exempla (*ḥikāyāt*), see Kia, "*Adab* as Literary Form."

43. Meisami discusses "set pieces" in *tārīkh* texts that express certain truisms, like the murder of viziers, as told through the well-known murder of Abu Muslim or the downfall of the Barmakid viziers ("History as Literature").

44. Babayan, *Mystics, Monarchs and Messiahs*, 29. Persian as a language of literary production, rather than consumption, had declined in Rum (Ottoman domains) by the eighteenth century.

45. Mitchell, *Practice of Politics*, 14.

46. Ibid., 14–15.

47. Kashmīrī, *Bayān*, 210.

48. Vālih, *Rīyāz*, 1:287.

49. Sharma, "Production of Mughal *Shāhnāma*s;" and Khan, "Marvellous Histories."

50. Vāʿiz Kāshifī, *Akhlāq-i Muhsinī*, 1913, 15–18. For the same selections in an abridged colonial-era English translation, see *Akhlāk-i Muhsinī*, 1850b, 9–13. This "literal" translation is from an abridged Persian edition (*Akhlāk-i Muhsinī*, 1850a). For more on this transregional staple of Persian education, see Subtelny, "A Late Medieval Persian *Summa*," especially 609–10 on the variety of figures in the text and 612 on its popularity.

51. Saʿdī, *Gulistan*, 76–77.

52. See Quinn, *Historical Writing*, 127–36. The early Timurids ruled Irani and Turani

domains up through the fifteenth century, whereas later Timurid rule was based in Hindustan from the early sixteenth century.

53. Tavakoli-Targhi, *Refashioning Iran*, 85. On the medieval development of this narrative, see Meisami, "The Past in the Service." For the text itself, see Mīr Khvānd, *Rawzat al-Safā*.

54. For the structure of the work, see Beveridge and Manz, "Mīrkhwānd." The second volume begins with the birth of the Prophet Muhammad, the advent of Islam, and the first four caliphs. The third and fourth volumes give the subsequent history of caliphs and imams until the Mongol invasion under Hulagu Khan, especially the rulers of eastern Islamic lands. The fifth volume covers the rule of Chingiz and his successors, particularly Ilkhanid rule in Iran and Mesopotamia. The sixth section covers Amir Timur and his descendants until the year 1426 AD/830 AH. The seventh volume, written by his grandson Khwandamir, deals with Sultan Husayn Bayqara and his sons through the early sixteenth century.

55. On Khwandamir's *Habib al-Siyar* and its narrative and conceptual components (including multiple temporalities), see Bashir, "A Perso-Islamic Universal Chronicle" and "On Islamic Time," especially 531–35. On the importance of *Rawzat al-Safa* and its role as a model for *Habib al-Siyar*, see Quinn, *Historical Writing*, 35–43; and Alam and Subrahmanyam, *Indo-Persian Travels*, 216. As late as the mid-nineteenth century, Riza Quli Hidayat, a poet and scholar in the Qajar court, updated *Rawzat al-Safa*, extending it to Nasir al-Din Shah Qajar's time, under the title *Rawzat al-Safa-yi Nasiri* (Rawzat al-Safā, vol. 12–14). In 1608–9 AD/1017 AH, a courtier at the court of Shah 'Ali 'Adilshah of Bijapur wrote *Tazkirat al-Muluk*, which was an abridged version of *Rawzat al-Safa* and *Habib al-Siyar* preceding a history of the kings of the Deccan. It began with the Bahmanis, continued through the 'Adilshahis, and included accounts of the sultans of Gujarat, Ahmednagar, and Golconda, together with the Timurids. The last section covers the reign of contemporaneous kings, including the Ottomans and the Safavids. The conclusion includes extracts from the *Shahnama* (Rehatsek, *Catalogue Raisonne*, 73–75).

56. Shahjahan's governor of Ghazni commissioned one such prose retelling ostensibly for Timurid officials who did not have time to read the full poem. The text, *Shahnama-yi Mukhtasar-i Shamshir Khani*, by Tavakkul Bayg, was commissioned in 1652–53 AD/1063 AH. Copies of this text were made well into the nineteenth century. The Bombay-based Mulla Firuz's manuscript copy is dated 1716–17 AD/1129 AH (Rehatsek, *Catalogue Raisonne*, 152). The Sikh ruler of the Punjab, Ranjit Singh, presented an 1835 copy to the French Lieutenant-General Comte de Rumigny. This copy at least interposes verses from the poem with prose abridgements ("Shamshir Khani: From Pen to Printing Press, Ten Centuries of Islamic Book Arts," Indiana University Collections, accessed June 30, 2011, http://www.iub.edu/iuam/online_modules/islamic _book_arts/explore/shamshir_khani/index.html). In the Walter's Art Museum collection is a nineteenth-century illustrated copy from northwest India, possibly Lahore,

titled "Abridgement of the Book of Kings (*Shahnama*)" (Walter's manuscript W.597, accessed September 13, 2012, http://art.thewalters.org/detail/35658/abridgment-of-the -book-of-kings-shahnama). For more on this text, see Khan, "Marvellous Histories"; and Sharma, "The Production of Mughal *Shāhnāma*s."

57. On this movement, see Kevin Schwartz, ""Bâzgasht-i adabî," 1–13 and 30–75. Azar's work on the text continued until his death in 1779 AD/1193 AH.

58. Tavakoli-Targhi, *Refashioning Iran*, 105. Though they take generic context and literary history more into account, most scholarly treatments of the *Atashkadih* assume this proto-nationalist impulse. Sharma, "Redrawing the Boundaries of 'Ajam," 52–54; and Alam, "Culture and Politics," 176 and 178.

59. Tavakoli-Targhi notes that in the wake of the *bāzgasht*, Persian in Qajar Iran was written in a new, simpler style. He frames this change as part of the genealogy of modern Iranian nationalism, but in the first half of the nineteenth century it was considered a style of writing, not a practice of national identity. Its practitioners, such as Yaghma Jandagi (d. 1859 AD/1271 AH), called it *fārsī-yi basīt* (basic Persian) or *sādih nivīsī* (simple prose) (*Refashioning Iran*, 107). For more on the problematics of Sabk-i Hindī, see Ahmadi, "Institution of Persian Literature"; and Kinra, "Make It Fresh."

60. Perry notes that none of the big literary names of the time lived in Afsharid-ruled Khurasan, which he claims stagnated culturally and economically after 1750 (*Karim Khan Zand*, 244).

61. Āzar, *Ātashkadih*, 1:101.

62. These domains, descriptively mapped out, are larger than their modern versions. For instance, Azarbayjan includes Mughan, Shirvan, Kurdistan, Armenia, and Georgia (Āzar, *Ātashkadih*, 1:101). Sistan is included as part of Khurasan (1:212). Tabaristan consists of Astarabad, Gurgan, Rasht, Lahijan (Gilan), and Mazandaran (2:777). Tabaristan has no description of its own, although each constituent region has its own description.

63. Āzar, *Ātashkadih*, 1:101.

64. Such stories fit within the larger historical context of the *Shahnama*, but in histories like the *Rawzat al-Safa* they are specifically narrated, animating the basic *Shahnama* chronology. Shapur was the son of Ardashir, the first Sasanian king. For an abridged prose translation that provides the basic plot structure, see Ferdowsi, *Shahnameh*, 574–76.

65. See the example in note 66 below.

66. Āzar, *Ātashkadih*, 2:865. Azar closely follows *Rawzat al-Safa*, including the reasoning at the end (Mīr Khvānd, *Rawzat al-Safā*, 2:641). This story fits chronologically into the wars of Iran and Turan during the end of the Pishdadiyan period, although the *Shahnama* and *Rawzat al-Safa* emplot it somewhat differently (Ferdowsi, *Shahnameh*, 110–41; and Mīr Khvānd, *History of the Early Kings of Persia*, 171–77, and *Rawzat al-Safā*, 2:638–42.).

67. Faruqi, "Unprivileged Power."

68. Hushang was the grandson of Gayomars and an early pre-Islamic king (Ferdowsi, *Shahnameh*, 1–4).

69. Maftūn, *Zubdat*, 110.

70. To elaborate on Genghis (Chingiz) Khan, Maftun cites Hamdullah Mustawfi Qazvini (1281–1350), who wrote epic poems, histories, and geographies in service to the last Ilkhan, Abu Sa'id (Maftūn, *Zubdat*, 110).

71. Pasha Mohammad Khan calls this transmissionist, or *naqlī*, history "the dominant form or subgenre for most of the history of the Islamicate *tarikh* genre" ("Marvellous Histories," 541–44, quote from 541).

72. Azar's inscription of pre-Islamic Persian history onto Turan extends to smaller regional and city descriptions. For Balkh, see Āzar, *Ātashkadih*, 4:241. For Badakhshan, see 4:348.

73. This is a lithographed copy of an Iranian manuscript (Āzar, *Ātashkadih*, 4:11).

74. Āzar, *Ātashkadih*, 4:239.

75. On Faraydun's sons, this division, and the leadup to war, see Mīr Khvānd, *Rawzat al-Safā*, 618–22.

76. See Ferdowsi, *Shahnameh*, 36–37. Pre-Islamic Persian narratives that do not fit our criteria of history are usually marked as "myths" or "mytho-history" (for example, see Marashi, *Nationalizing Iran*, 61 and 63; and Mitchell, *Practice of Politics*, 3, 4). While myth can mean "a usually traditional story of ostensibly historical events that serves to unfold part of the world view of a people," it also carries connotations of being imaginary, unverifiable, or even false (Merriam-Webster, https://www.merriam-webster.com/dictionary/myth, accessed February 26, 2019).

77. See Ferdowsi, *Shahnameh*, 37–41.

78. Āzar, *Ātashkadih*, 4:239.

79. See, for instance, Ferdowsi, *Shahnameh*, 139.

80. Āzar, *Ātashkadih*, 4:241.

81. This malleable understanding of geographical regions appeared earlier. Bosworth notes that the extent of *Mavara' al-nahr*, which in Arabic sources seems to refer to the larger region of Turan, tended to correspond to the extent of Arab military expansion. Here geography was similarly given contour by political control (Bosworth, "Mawara' al-Nahr").

82. As noted, Azar draws on and echoes the *Rawzat al-Safa*. The *Atashkadih* has a short entry on Mirkhwand, largely because of the *Rawzat*, since he did not have a *takhallus* and only occasionally wrote poetry (Āzar, *Ātashkadih*, 4:282.

83. Āzar, *Ātashkadih*, 4:417.

84. Ibid., 4:417.

85. Ibid., 4:423.

86. Alam and Subrahmanyam, "Of Princes and Poets"; and Faruqui, "At Empire's End."

87. Āzar, *Ātashkadih*, 1:212.

88. For Sabzivar, see Āzar, *Ātashkadih*, 1:397; for Kirman, see 2:611.

89. Valih also shares this perception. For example, see Vālih, *Riyāz*, 1:147.

Chapter 2: Remembering, Lamenting

An earlier and more extensive version of parts of this chapter was published as Kia, "Accounting for Difference."

1. Edward G. Browne's pronouncement in this regard is typical. Browne acknowledges Hazin as one of the two main poets of this time (along with Azar Baygdili) but dismisses his poetry in favor of his prose (*Literary History of Persia*, 277). Historically, migrants to Hindustan, such as 'Abd al-Latif Shushtari, held Hazin in high regard and quoted his poetry in their texts. See Shūshtarī, *Tuhfat*, 68; and 187–89.

2. For a discussion on Hazin's memoir, see Browne, *Literary History of Persia*, 277–81. On the high politics of the late-Safavid and Afsharid period, see Matthee, *Persia in Crisis*; Lockhart, *Nadir Shah*; Tucker, *Nadir Shah's Quest for Legitimacy*; and Axworthy, *Sword of Persia*.

3. See Alam and Subrahmanyam, *Indo-Persian Travels*, 174–242; Robinson, "Perso-Islamic Culture," 114; and Tavakoli-Targhi, *Refashioning Iran*, 181n12.

4. de Man, "Autobiography as De-facement," 920–21. Also see Najmabadi, *Women's Autobiographies*; and Fay, *Auto/biography*.

5. For an excellent study that demonstrates the rich interpretive possibilities arising from analysis of the rhetorical labors of a text, see Sohrabi, *Taken for Wonder*.

6. Hazīn, *Tārīkh va Safarnāma*, 144. Hazin also notes that he wrote his account in the space of two nights, when he was unable to sleep or concentrate on anything, and that the writing eased his "disturbed heart and mind" (262).

7. Local elites from other domains within the empire also participated in this ruling culture, but sometimes locally derived self-conceptions of place came into tension with these views from the center. For instance, see Mancini-Lander, "Memory on the Boundaries."

8. As Hazin travels in its circles of great and learned men in the course of his education, he describes Isfahan as the quintessential great city (Hazīn, *Tārīkh va Safarnāma*, 163–65).

9. Both of these attributes are accorded only to the upper strata, but the common people are also described as virtuous according to the noble manners appropriate to their station. Gilan was his father's birthplace, as well as the source of his family's income (*Tārīkh va Safarnāma*, 167–68).

10. For instance, see his description of Shiraz, *Tārīkh va Safarnāma*, 177–80. The age of majority, twenty years, was a common age for young men to set out on their own to further their educations through travel.

11. Hazīn, *Tārīkh va Safarnāma*, 191–92.

12. For a translation of the passage on carnal love, see Kia, "Muhammad 'Ali 'Hazin' Lahiji."

13. There is some disagreement about Nadir's birthdate. Some give it as early as 1688. Lockhart provides a persuasive reason for why the latter date is more likely (*Nadir Shah*, 291, n1).

14. Hazīn, *Tārīkh va Safarnāma*, 245–47.

15. Ibid., 248–51. For another version, see Vālih, *Rīyāz*, 1:633.

16. Hazīn, *Tārīkh va Safarnāma* 261.

17. Ibid., 260.

18. On the specifically Islamic significance of Solomon, see J. Walker and P. Fenton, "Sulaymān b. Dāwūd."

19. Though he acknowledges the Timurids' venerable and exalted descent from Amir Timur Gurkan, this prestige is dimmed by Hazin's elaboration on the injurious behavior of Timurid princes toward each other, which resulted in the oppression of people under their rule. This subsequent sordid dynastic history is meant to display a moral degeneration, one that predates their arrival in Hindustan. Hazin posits Sultan Husayn Mirza Bayqara, the ruler of Herat, as the exception to this rule (*Tārīkh va Safarnāma*, 270–71. For the important distinction between the selfish and selfless friend and their relative moral statures in two of the most widely read Persian moral philosophy texts through the early modern period in both Iran and India, see Tūsī, *Akhlāq-i Nāsirī*, 321–34; and Davvānī, *Akhlāq-i Jalālī*, 281–86.

20. Hazīn, *Tārīkh va Safarnāma*, 271–72.

21. This linkage of 'ajam (Persian) with a specifically pre-Islamic Iran puts forth a view of the origin of this culture in the land of Iran. By the early modern times, a wide variety of individuals and collectives identified with this pre-Islamic Persian past. It could be claimed by both Muslims in other lands (the Timurids), non-Muslims in Iranian lands (Jews or those of Christian Caucasian origin), or both (Vijayanagara Sultans or the Maratha Bhonsles). For more, see the next section.

22. This double meaning keys tropes of black Hindustanis and serves to highlight a contrast to the fairer countenance of Persians, as the outward manifestation of immoral or moral behavior.

23. Hazīn, *Tārīkh va Safarnāma*, 272.

24. He mentions incidents from the reigns of Manuchihr, Kayqubad, Iskandar, Ardishir, Babak, and Anushiravan (Hazīn, *Tārīkh va Safarnāma*, 272). He also refers to a story about Zahak and Hindustan in what he calls *Tarikh-i majūs* (History of the Magi) (273). This paradigm, both timeless and every time, is an example of what Babayan has called Persianate cyclical time. See *Mystics, Monarchs and Messiahs*, 9–45.

25. The longstanding understanding of these dynasties as friends, if with a competitive edge that belies their equal status, is exemplified by the famous paintings

commissioned by the emperor Jahangir. For more about these paintings, see Koch, "How the Mughal *Pādshāhs* Referenced Iran."

26. This is also corroborated by later Persian chronicles that serve as the source materials for modern histories. See, for instance, Chandra, *Parties and Politics*, 280.

27. Hazīn, *Tārīkh va Safarnāma*, 274.

28. Ibid., 275–78 and 280–81.

29. Arjomand, "The Conception of Revolution."

30. Hazīn, *Tārīkh va Safarnāma*, 237.

31. Ibid., 238–40.

32. Ibid., 240.

33. This idea is pervasive. See, for instance, *Tārīkh va Safarnāma*, 261–62 and 285–86. In his divan, see *Dīvān-i Hazīn-i Lāhījī*, 62–64 and 97–98.

34. In spite of his constant lamentations of ill health, Hazin managed to live until the age of seventy-eight.

35. Hazīn, *Tārīkh va Safarnāma*, 259–60.

36. The relationships between governance and the humors are outlined in Alavi, *Islam and Healing*, 27–28, 32–33. On the relationship of proper conduct and health, see 30–31. What she calls "the legacy of Greece and Rome," however, was understood by that point as part of the Islamic universalism of the time as articulated in the High Persianate tradition (32).

37. Hazīn, *Tārīkh va Safarnāma*, 272–73.

38. Meisami, "Places in the Past."

39. Shūshtarī, *Tuhfat*, 359.

40. Ibid., 363.

41. On Hazin's later life, see Khatak, *Shaikh Muhammad 'Ali Hazin*, 64–78, 103–17.

42. Alam and Subrahmanyan, *Indo-Persian Travels*, 239.

43. On the migration of Arab Shi'a 'ulama from Lebanon, Bahrain, and Iraq to Safavid domains, see Abisaab, *Converting Persia*.

44. See Stewart, "An Episode," 500–501.

45. Ibid., 501–2. He further finds legal justification for this move in the obligation for those who cannot practice the rituals of their religion and so seek out a place where they can.

46. Stewart, "An Episode," 503–4.

47. Ahmad Bihbahani was an example of the latter. A traveler from Iran to Hindustan in the early nineteenth century, he quarreled with the chief *mujtahid* of the city over proper celebration of Shi'a rituals. The fallout caused Bihbahani to claim that there were no true *mujtahid*s in Hindustan and to evoke Hazin's migrant experience to give moral meaning to his own (*Mir'āt al-Ahvāl*, 286–90). For the quarrel itself, see Bihbahānī, *Mir'āt al-Ahvāl*, 141–42; and Cole, *Roots of North Indian Shi'ism*, 136–37.

48. For the privileged position of the Timurids as purveyors of Persianate refinement through the early modern period, see Moin, *Millennial Sovereign*, chapter 3, especially pp. 56–57; and Balabanlilar, *Imperial Identity*, 11–17, 38–42. For the Hindustani context, see Alam, "Culture and Politics of Persian."

49. Several scholars have recently noted the inadequacy of sectarian categories for accounting for sensibilities, stakes, and practices, as well as broader hermeneutical distinctions. For instance, see Moin, *Millennial Sovereign*, 77–78 and 84; and Mitchell, "Am I My Brother's Keeper?"

50. Stewart, "An Episode," 501.

51. Kashmīrī, *Bayān*, 215. On Timur as Lord of the Auspicious Conjunction, see Moin, *Millennial Sovereign*, 23–55. Moin notes that Safavid kingship redeployed specifically Timurid rituals and practices (89–91).

52. Humayun's submission to Safavid authority conflicted with his son Akbar's claims to universal kingship, an issue Akbar's court historian, Abu al-Fazl finessed in his chronicle, the *Akbarnama* (Moin, *Millennial Sovereign*, chapters 4 and 5, particularly 125–27 and 137–38). Moin also notes that Babur submitted to the authority of Shah Isma'il, though he had not made claims to universal kingship, as Humayun would (58–59, 74, and 84–88).

53. Kashmīrī, *Bayān*, 215.

54. These terms refer to '*Iraq-i 'ajam* and Khurasan, where Humayun spent time on his way to Qazvin. Many Indo-Persian texts refer to Iran or Khurasan as *vilāyat*, a significant interchangeability. In 1780, "Shafiq" Aurangabadi describes Valih Daghistani's migration to Hindustan from Isfahan as "from vilāyat," this time, as from Iran (Shafiq, *Shām-i Gharībān*, 282). Calmard notes that the term generally referred to a distant homeland or a separately ruled domain ("Safavid Persia in Indo-Persian Sources," 383–84).

55. Kashmīrī, *Bayān*, 215.

56. Tahmasp lent aid to Humayun's endeavor partly in exchange for Safavid suzerainty over Qandahar. See Richards, *The Mughal Empire*, 6–12, and Ray, *Humayun in Persia*.

57. See, for example, the miniature of Tahmasp greeting the exiled Humayun illuminating an early seventeenth-century (1603–4, by Sanwla) copy of the *Akbarnama*, in which the latter is seated next to the former on his *masnad*, indicating equal status. This image is in the public domain (see https://commons.wikimedia.org/wiki/File:Shah_Tahmasp _and_Humayun.jpeg, accessed August 18, 2014), in the British Library, Or. 12988, f. 98, and also on the cover of this book. For the contrasting mid-seventeenth-century Safavid image among the frescoes of the Chihil Sutun pavilion in Isfahan, see Moin, *Millennial Sovereign*, 236. In the Safavid fresco, while both figures are seated on the same *masnad*, more subtle nuances, such as headgear, depict Tahmasp in greater kingly splendor. Moin comments that "Humayun's presence in these Chihil Sutūn murals was meant to remind

visitors—such as Prince Akbar when he arrived there in 1688—of the historical superiority of the Persian [Iranian] dynasty over the Indian Timurids" (235–37). For Zand-era
commemorations of Humayun and Tahmasp, see Vasilyeva and Yastrebova, "The Muraqqa' Album of the Zand Period," 363 and 365.

58. This summary account contrasts markedly with modern scholarship, which lingers over these two figures. The *Bayan* depicts Akbar's kingship as the result of the
efforts of his good servant, Bayram Khan. In the middle of his reign Akbar took over
full sovereignty and successfully subdued the rebelliousness of the "rajas" and Afghans.
During the reign of Jahangir, "the preliminaries of royal administration and manage-
ment (*muqaddamāt-i zabt va nasq-i pādshāhī*) increased daily, until it was time for the
prosperous kingship" of Shahjahan (Kashmīrī, *Bayān*, 216).

59. This was a common designation for someone who fought wars of conquest over
non-Muslim lands, as a way to legitimize aggression. As with Ottoman wars against
the Shi'a Safavids, sectarian differences could provide the basis for this designation
(Trausch, "Ghazā and Ghazā Terminology," especially 249).

60. Kashmīrī, *Bayān*, 216.

61. Kashmiri refers to *Pādshāhnāma-yi Shāhjahānī*, '*Ālamgīrnāma*, "and other histories" as works in which these ignorant and foolish deeds are detailed at length (*Bayān*,
217). Also see Kinra, "Infantalizing Bābā Dārā."

62. Kashmīrī, *Bayān*, 217.

63. For more on justice in Persian political thought, see Arjomand, "Salience of
Political Ethic." These ideals of a prospering realm and just polity were remarkably du-
rable, still defining the discussion of crisis in late nineteenth-century Iranian modernist
writing. See Kia, "Moral Refinement and Manhood."

64. On how these texts fit together, see Kia, "Accounting for Difference," 227–28.

65. Kashmīrī, *Bayān*, 161.

66. Ibid., 217–18.

67. For instance, see ibid., 169–70.

68. "*dawlat-i hamih zi ittifāq khīzad / bī-dawlatī az nifāq khīzad*" (Kashmīrī, *Bayān*,
162).

69. Kashmīrī, *Bayān*, 270.

70. Khalidi, *Arabic Historical Thought*, 91; and Meisami, *Persian Historiography*, 7.

71. For the description of his life, see Kashmīrī, *Bayān*, 248–53.

72. On Nadir's high regard for 'Alavi Khan and reluctance to release him from
service, see Kashmīrī, *Bayān*, 112–14. For 'Alavi Khan's attempts to temper Nadir Shah,
see 172.

73. The *Bayan* is not alone in its approbation of this celebrated figure. Most eighteenth-century poetic *tazkirih*s that focus on Delhi describe 'Alavi Khan similarly,
though he wrote only as much poetry as expected of an educated man. Primarily a physician, the figure of 'Alavi Khan as an ethical and accomplished man is the centerpiece

of these entries. For instance, see Ārzū, *Majma'*, 2:1507–8; and Khalīl, *Suhuf*, 186–87. He is also a figure in the witty tales (*latā'if*) appended to Mīr Muhammad Taqī Mīr's late eighteenth-century memoir (*Zikr-i Mīr*, 1999, 135–36).

74. Chandra, *Parties and Politics*, 278–81.

75. Chandra cites Muhammad Bakhsh Ashub's *Tarīkh-i Shahādat-i Farrukh Siyār va Julūs-i Muhammad Shāhī* (*Parties and Politics*, 283 n14 and 284 n18).

76. Chandra, *Parties and Politics*, 284, n19. For a sixteenth-century account of Humayun's flight and stay in Safavid Iran written by one of his retainers, see Jawhar Aftabachi's "Tazkirat al-Vaqi'āt," 118–29.

77. Āzar, *Ātashkadih*, 1:100.

78. Shūshtarī, *Tuhfat*, 409. For instance, it is preserved in its entirety in the *Akbarnama*. See Abu'l-Fazl, *The History of Akbar*, 2:51–71. Iranian copies of this *farmān* have also survived apart from chronicles. See Navā'ī, *Shāh Tahmāsb Safavī*, 53–61. For a manuscript copy, see Anonymous, *Majmū'ih*, manuscript, London, British Library, IO Islamic 379, ff. 95a–102b. Many sixteenth-century *majmū'ih*s contain this *farmān* (Colin Mitchell in personal correspondence, August 2012). On the *farmān* in the context of sixteenth-century Safavid-Ottoman politics, see Mitchell, "Am I My Brother's Keeper?"

79. For the account, see Shūshtarī, *Tuhfat*, 407–10.

80. Ibid., 407.

81. Ibid., 432–33.

82. Ibid., 339.

83. Dalrymple writes, "at the time he [Shushtari] was writing the affair led to the destruction of all his hopes—and those of much of his family—of wealth, success and power" (*White Mughals*, 138). For more on the scandal see 125–39.

84. For the sections that closely follow Hazin's narrative about Iran and Hindustan, see Shūshtarī, *Tuhfat*, 458–63.

Chapter 3: Place-Making and Proximity

Earlier and more extensive versions of parts of this chapter were published as Kia, "Limning the Land" and "Imagining Iran."

1. On the prominence of architecture in the panegyric court poetry of early modern Persian, see Losensky, "Square Like a Bubble." For a similar discussion of early Islamic Arabic sources, see Antrim, *Routes and Realms*, particularly chapters 3 and 4. She notes that "authors employed a set of textual strategies to make plots of land recognizable as cities and distinguish them from homes and regions," including "naming and locating the city, assembling a foundation or conquest narrative, and describing its built environment" (34).

2. Here, however, I examine their use and circulation within the Persianate world.

3. I have dealt more with the extension of these ornaments to places beyond the Persian-speaking and Muslim worlds in Kia, "Necessary Ornaments of Place."

4. On Razi and his text, see Memon, "Amīn Ahmad Rāzī"; Losensky, "Biographical Writing," 28–29; and Tāhirī, preface to *Tazkirih-yi Haft Iqlīm*. Tahiri uses three manuscripts from Iranian libraries (two in Tehran and one in Mashhad), but they were originally copied in India in the seventeenth century. Interestingly, two of the manuscripts were copied by the same scribe six years apart (1615 and 1621 AD/1024 and 1030 AH), indicating that perhaps scribes specialized in particular texts (davāzdah-chahārdah). Throughout the eighteenth century, *Haft Iqlim* was frequently mentioned in *tazkirih*s such as Azar Baygdili's *Atashkadih*, written in Qum, and Shahnavaz Khan's *Ma'asir al-Umara*, written in Aurangabad (see list of sources in 'Abd al-Hayy's preface to Maāthir-ul-umarā, 1:3). Manuscript copies that contain only the geographical accounts attest that these portions were at least as important to eighteenth-century readers (see, for instance, British Library, manuscript, IO Islamic 2409).

5. For descriptions of the third and fourth climes, see, respectively, Rāzī, *Tazkirih-yi Haft Iqlīm*, 1:83–84 and 2:517–18.

6. Rāzī, *Tazkirih-yi Haft Iqlīm*, 1:83–84.

7. Ibid., 2:517.

8. Ibid., 1:50.

9. Ibid., 1:68.

10. "*Bah lutf va nūr bihisht va bih husn va zīb iram/ bih farr va qadr sipihr va bih tūl va 'arz zamīn*" (Ibid.)

11. Rāzī, *Tazkirih-yi Haft Iqlīm*, 1:68.

12. The transformation of this term in the nineteenth century was part of a broader global conversation about civilization. See Kia, "Moral Refinement and Manhood."

13. Razi uses this term to describe "Telangana" (the name he uses for Golconda, its capital city), paired with *ābādān* (*Tazkirih-yi Haft Iqlīm*, 1:69). Azar also uses *ma'mūr*. See Kia, "Imagining Iran," 98. For an example in the context of travel writing, see Kia, "Limning the Land," 56–61.

14. Developed almost in tandem with the dominant (Fresh) style (*tāzih gū'ī*) in poetry, when South Asian courts were centers of Persian literary patronage, it is a poem in which the speaker repeatedly calls for the *sāqī* (*biyā sāqī*) and a singer (*mughānnī*) or musician (*mutrib*) to provide a song. Wine is a polyvalent image: "it could provide solace for the outcast, open the doors of mystical transcendence, or sanctify the communal festivities of the court" (Losensky, "Sāqi-nāma"). Earlier examples of this genre were also popular among non-Muslim poets in Iran, such as the fifteenthth-century Jewish poet Emrani (Yeroushalmi, "Emrani").

15. Most sources refer to his birthplace as Turshiz, but he locates his own birthplace in Ka'in. Born and educated in Khurasan, Zuhuri began his career at the provincial court of Yazd and then moved to Shiraz, before emigrating to India in 1580 AD/988 AH. He immediately settled in the Nizam Shahi court of Ahmadnagar but subsequently moved to Bijapur (c. 1596 AD/1004 AH), where he remained under the patronage of

Ibrahim 'Adil Shah II until his death. See Losensky "Zuhūrī Turshīzī"; and Gulchīn Ma'ānī, *Kāravān-i Hind*, 823–38.

16. Qazvīnī, *Tazkirih-yi Maykhānih*, 363–64. Quote from 363.

17. Sharma, "Nizamshahi Persianate Garden," 159–61.

18. Ibid., 163–64. Indeed, "a legible city in the discourse of place usually featured a description of monumental structure . . . such structures clearly commanded the visual imagination and were often explicitly associated with claims to political and religious authority" (Antrim, *Routes and Realms*, 62). By the early modern period good rulership took the form of divinely inspired and positioned kingship (Moin, *Millennial Sovereign*; and Melvin-Koushki, "Early Modern Islamicate Empire"). For evocation of paradisiacal beauty that functioned as political discourse for the Timurid consolidation of rule over Kashmir, see Maurya, "Of Tulips and Daffodils."

19. Sarkhvush also makes this connection, noting that Zuhuri's *Saqinama* was "written in the name of Burhan Nizam al-Mulk" (a common Timurid renaming of the Deccan rulers, demoting them from the title of Shah) (*Kalimāt*, 129–30). Interestingly, neither the city itself nor any of its sites are explicitly named in the poem; the connection is implied through the poem's dedication.

20. For a detailed analysis of these descriptions, see Sharma, "Nizamshahi Persianate Garden," 159–72.

21. Ibid., 168–69.

22. Muhammad Rabī', *Safīnih-yi Sulaymānī*, 173–74. Thanks to Thibaut d'Hubert for bringing this to my attention. See his "Living in Marvelous Lands."

23. Nasrābādī, *Tazkirih-yi Nasrābādī*, 338. Another migrant from Iran, Kalim, exposed the renaming. Shahjahan was not pleased, but this reaction, as Sharma points out, does not detract from Salim's familiarity with the image of Kashmir, which was enough to choose it as a substitute (*Mughal Arcadia*, 125).

24. Sharma, "Nizamshahi Persianate Garden," 170.

25. On Fani Kashmiri, see Sarkhvush, *Kalimāt*, 147; Ludī, *Mir'āt al-Khayāl*, 146–47; Ārzū, *Majma'*, 2:1273–79; and Vālih, *Riyāz*, 3:1674. Nasrabadi, like his contemporary Sarkhvush, has only a short entry on him (690) but a far more extensive entry on his famous student, Ghani Kashmiri, who also wrote poems about Kashmir (287–89). See also Gulchīn Ma'ānī, *Tazkirih-yi Paymanih*, 325–62.

26. On the composition and labor of topographical poems, see Sharma, *Mughal Arcadia*. Sharma's book was published after I had already written this one, and its discussions of Kashmir and place poems of the sixteenth and seventeenth centuries are in the service of a different argument. Still, many of its arguments enrich mine, so much so that I point to the work as a whole.

27. Rāzī, *Haft Iqlīm* (1960), 1:28.

28. Ibid., 1:28–29. For other Persian representations of China, see Hemmat, "Children of Cain."

29. As Derrida says, "It is as if the order of attestation itself testifies to the miraculous, to the unbelievable believable: to what must be believed all the same, whether believable or not. Such is the truth to which I am appealing. . . . Even in false testimony, this truth presupposes veracity—and not the reverse" (*Aporias*, 20–21).

30. For a more extensive discussion, see Kia, "Necessary Ornaments of Place."

31. For more on this text, see Kia, "Limning the Land."

32. Maftun cites the inscriptions on his coins as evidence of these claims (Maftūn, *Zubdat*, 9).

33. Maftūn, *Zubdat*, 117–18. The wars were over the Caucasian provinces of Armenia and Georgia, which the Shah eventually lost, along with the northern part of Azarbayjan. At the end of summer of 1827 AD/1242 AH, in the section on Tehran, the Qajar capital city, Maftun details the wars at length (Maftūn, *Zubdat*, 117–27).

34. Maftūn, *Zubdat*, 126.

35. For example, ibid., 24.

36. Chanchal Dadlani, "'Palais Indiens' Collection," 186–87.

37. Ibid., 188–89. The difference is that architectural plans served strictly functional purposes and were not drawn with aesthetic concerns. In contrast, the *Palais Indien* paintings were idealized representations drawn with color, flourishes, and materials reminiscent of works of art.

38. Dadlani, "'Palais Indiens' Collection," 191–92.

39. Maftūn, *Zubdat*, 9.

40. Ibid., 18.

41. Ibid., 10.

42. Āzar, *Ātashkadih*, 3:915.

43. Ibid., 4:411.

44. Referring to Kashmir as a city is not Azar's only geographical error. He calls the Deccan a *vilāyat*, though from the description, it is obvious that he is referring to the city of Hyderabad (or Golconda, as it was known until the late seventeenth century) (*Ātashkadih*, 4:419).

45. Āzar, *Ātashkadih*, 4:441. Sultan Sikander "*butshikan*" (idol smasher) was the second ruler of the Sayyid dynasty and ruled Kashmir from 1389 to 1413. For an overview of early Muslim rule in Kashmir, see Annemarie Schimmel, *Islam in the Indian Subcontinent*, 43–47.

46. Āzar, *Ātashkadih*, 4:441.

47. For instance, Valih calls Isfahan "*bihisht nishān*" (*Rīyāz*, 2:885). Azar calls Isfahan "*khuld nishān*" (*Ātashkadih*, 4:590). Both Azar and Valih were born in Isfahan and considered it their homeland. On the Timurid figuring of Kashmir, see Maurya, "Of Tulips and Daffodils," especially 39–43; and Sharma, *Mughal Arcadia*, 126–66.

48. Kashmīrī, *Bayān*, 1.

49. Ibid., 216.

50. Moin, *Millennial Sovereign*. Sharma has also noted this similarity, first made by seventeenth-century poets from Safavid domains at the Timurid court (*Mughal Arcadia*, 126–29).

51. For instance, see Kashmīrī, *Bayān*, 105.

52. Ibid., 104–5.

53. Maurya, "Of Tulips and Daffodils," 42.

54. Kashmīrī, *Bayān*, 105.

55. Mazandaran was the site of royal attention because it had been Khayr al-Nissa's (Shah Abbas's mother's) *vatan*. Her Marʿashi sayyid family (which also claimed descent from the Sassanians) had been the local rulers (Quinn, *Shah Abbas*, first page of chapter 2; Blow, *Shah Abbas*, 16–17).

56. Kashmīrī, *Bayān*, 105.

57. Power, *The Red Sea*, 148; Wick, *The Red Sea*, 30, 38, 84. It was also the name of a port, near Suez, as the sea was called by the ports on its shores.

58. Wick, *The Red Sea*, 84. Emphasis in original.

59. On the inclusion of multiple narratives in Persian historiography, see Bashir, "On Islamic Time," 533, 542–43; and "A Perso-Islamic Universal Chronicle," 223–24.

60. Kashmīrī, *Bayān*, 106.

61. Said, *Orientalism*, 264–72.

62. Kashmīrī, *Bayān*, 103. I put this name in quotation marks because it was used to reference a number of local vernaculars, not necessarily the modern Hindi language.

63. Maftūn, *Zubdat*, 8–9.

64. Abū Ṭālib Isfahānī, *Masīr-i Ṭālibī*, 349. Charles Stewart, an East India Company scholar of Persian who had worked first at Fort William College in Calcutta and then at the Company College of Haileybury, published a translation of Abu Talib's travelogue in 1810, soon after it was written in 1803 (O'Quinn, editor's introduction to *The Travels of Mirza Abu Taleb Khan*, 12). Stewart uses the term "Asiatic" to refer to Abu Talib (translator's preface to *The Travels of Mirza Abu Taleb Khan*, 57). For more on this text, see Garcia, "A Stranger's Love for Ireland."

65. Abū Ṭālib Isfahānī, *Masīr-i Ṭālibī*, 349.

66. Nasrin Askari has argued that the *Shahnama* was primarily read as a "mirror for princes" text (*Medieval Reception*). The text's purpose, however, is not a matter of either/or because, if we historicize the genre, we see that history was read for ethico-didactic purposes. For instance, Mirkhvand, in the introduction of *Rawzat al-Safa*, makes ethical instruction one of the primary "benefits" of history writing (*Rawzat al-Safā*, 1:11–15).

67. Abū Ṭālib Isfahānī, *Masīr-i Ṭālibī*, 349. In Stewart's English translation, Abu Talib understands a boundary of the Persianate world (*ʿajam*) but treats pre-Islamic Persianate history as fantastical and the history of the Greeks as the only reliable source.

To give such an impression, Stewart has selectively translated (and omitted most of) Abu Talib's discussion of pre-Islamic Persianate history.

68. Abū Tālib Isfahānī, *Masīr-i Tālibī*, 349. For more on the broader Islamic connotations around "the two seas," including their role in demarcating both difference and connection, see Pinto, *Medieval Islamic Maps*, 148–49.

69. This conflation is made again in describing parts of Istanbul described as "on the land of Asia, meaning the 'ajam" side of the Marmara. Abū Tālib Isfahānī, *Masīr-i Tālibī*, 355.

70. Radical difference is the basis of Said's analysis of European Orientalism and its image of "the Orient." Said, *Orientalism*, passim but especially, 1–2 and 45.

71. Āzar, *Ātashkadih*, 4:440.

72. Kaicker, "Unquiet City," 35.

73. Olsson, "The World in Arab Eyes," 489. Olsson seeks to complicate this model's simplicity by showing divergent understandings of climatic influences over peoples in various Arabic texts (491). Disagreement existed in Persian as well. Amin Razi, writing from late sixteenth-century Timurid domains, locates *'Iraq-i 'arab* in the third clime, under the larger heading of Iran. The third clime is marked by other Iranian regions, such as Fars and Kirman, alongside cities such as Farah and Ghazni in today's Afghanistan; Lahore, Panipat, Delhi, Agra, and Lucknow in the subcontinent; and Damascus and Aleppo in Sham. See Rāzī, *Tazkirih-y Haft Iqlīm*, 1:83–515.

74. Olsson, "The World in Arab Eyes," 503–4.

75. For Kashmir, see Āzar, *Ātashkadih*, 4:441. Balkh is listed under Turan but is in the fourth clime (4:241).

76. For instance, Khwārazm (Āzar, *Ātashkadih*, 4:282), Shirvan (1:148), and Ganja (1:204) are all in the fifth clime.

77. For Ghazni, see Āzar, *Ātashkadih*, 2:535; for Sistan (included as part of Khurasan), see 1:418; for *'Iraq-i 'arab*, see 3:921; for Fars, see 4:115. Yazd (4:101) is in the same clime as Delhi (4:423).

78. Āzar, *Ātashkadih*, 4:115.

79. On the clime system and its relation to humorial theory in medieval Arabic knowledge, see Olsson, "The World in Arab Eyes." For a view of the humors and the human body more specific to early modern Hindustan, see Chapter 2, drawing mainly on Alavi, *Islam and Healing*.

80. Hazīn, *Tārīkh va Safarnāma*, 165.

81. Ibid., 163.

82. Ibid., 165.

83. Ibid., 191.

84. Āzar, *Ātashkadih*, 4:520. On stereotypical characteristics associated with the inhabitants of particular Iranian cities in the work of the fourteenth-century satirist

Ubayd-i Zakani, see Brookshaw, "Have You Heard," 51–60. On Qomis as quarrelsome, see Brookshaw, 52.

85. Āzar, *Ātashkadih*, 4:495.

86. Bihbahānī, *Mir'āt al-Ahvāl*, 252–53.

Part II: Origin

1. Derrida, *Monolingualism of the Other*, 13.

2. Ibid., 10–11 and 14–15.

3. Ibid., 1.

4. Ibid., 14.

5. So much so that Derrida's problematizing self-identification can pose itself only with Maghrebian hyphenated to Franco, the impervious category of cultural national citizenship. For other observations of discrete analytic categories of belonging, see Jones, "Ethnicity."

6. On the problematic of Muslim origins, see Ahmed Asif, *A Book of Conquest*, 2–12, and Amin, *Conquest and Community*, 1–8. On colonial classification, see Dirks, *Castes of Mind*. Mamdani notes, "native does not designate a condition that is original and authentic"; rather, "the native is the creation of the colonial state: colonized, the native is pinned down, localized, thrown out of civilization as an outcast, confined to custom, and then defined as its product" (*Define and Rule*, 2–3). Mamdani links this category to indirect colonial rule, meaning the British Empire in the aftermath of the 1857 Indian uprising, then the template applied in other colonies (7–8). He notes, "governance of the native" was made "the prerogative of the native authority. As a form of governance, native administration claimed to be faithful to tradition and custom, which it defined in the singular, more or less unchanged since time immemorial." This singular, timeless essence of the native, its linkage to land and custom, makes it impervious to multiplicity and contingency. Modern colonial forms of knowing made natural the difference its rule purported to reflect, and was then marshaled as its justificatory premise.

7. Vernaculars are also Indic as derivations or siblings of Sanskrit, though Urdu as a Muslim expression of the vernacular is troubled by an assumed miscegeny, except perhaps by Marxist scholars for whom the masses are the locus of the nation. However, these scholars never question the conceptual ground of Indic as native-versus-Muslim-as-foreign binary, but merely shift the ground of the question. Habib, for instance, nativizes Indian Muslims as largely local converts marginal to both elite (native) Hindu urban society and (foreign) Muslim conquerors and migrants. A blood-based notion of (Indian) ethnicity, tied to land, anchors this conception of local authenticity, reinforcing the native-foreign binary (*Politics and Society*, 1:21–23, 116).

8. Even in contexts in which voluntary features of nationalism make membership more inclusive, a territory belongs to the nation because of its sanctification through blood-based genealogies (Porqueres, "Kinship Language," 137–40).

9. I have foregrounded South Asian studies in framing the problem, because Iranian studies, barring a programmatic intervention by Hamid Dabashi, has barely begun to question the proto-nationalist assumptions of its analytic categories (*Iran*, chapter 1). Another exception is the work of Arjomand in promoting a notion of the Persianate as a civilizational area, but which because of his emphasis on the early period is developed in Iran and Central Asia and subsequently spreads to regions such as India ("Review Essay," 315–16). He does point to important work, not yet translated into English, in Japanese Persianate studies showing reciprocal influence from traditions, such as Turkish, that fundamentally transform the Persianate in Iran and elsewhere (319). Even the most sophisticated works, such as Najmabadi's *Women with Mustaches*, take the political kingdom of Iran as their presumed arena for cultural transformations. Studies on earlier periods also do not question the validity of discrete political borders for cultural imagination. For instance, Babayan argues for "a cultural horizon common to Safavi[d] subjects," one in which India is a foreign land ("Topography of Travel," 26).

10. Ahmed argues against the limiting and anachronistic nature of Islam envisioned according to a Protestant notion of religion. He posits it more broadly to include cultural aspects that seemingly contradict a narrow view of Islam as the letter of its law (*What Is Islam?*). On the impossibility of secularism there is a vast literature, most pointedly noting its absence in modern Europe or, rather, as the invisible excess of Christianity; see, for example, Anidjar, *Blood*.

11. This is the case even with works that seek to challenge modern binaries, resulting in resolutely nationalist terms. For instance, Amin's study of Qazi Miyan offers answer to (Hindu nationalist) narratives of separate communities by giving a place to conflict in "India's vaunted syncretism," as the story of "the Indian people" (*Conquest and Community*, 6 and 8). The struggle to wrest history back from sectarian nationalists, but waged in nationalist terms, reinscribes its own limits, those of anachronistically understood categories of difference.

12. Jones, "Ethnicity," especially 324–25. These are concepts actively used in the social sciences and have had some critical engagement in fields such as anthropology, archaeology, and classics (for instance, respectively, Banks, *Ethnicity*; Jones, "Ethnicity;" Thomas, "Ethnicity, Genealogy, and Hellenism;" and Hall, *Hellenicity*). By comparison, scholarship in premodern Islamic or South Asian studies is small, and the concept itself is never questioned (see for instance, Akiner, "Islam, the State and Ethnicity"). An exception is Cooperson, writing about the meaning of Arab in relation to Iranian. He calls these terms "ethnonyms" and notes ways in which identities could be gained or lost by adopting language, religion, and political allegiances. Nevertheless, ethnicity's malleability was notable *in spite of* a descent still presumed as biological ("'Arabs' and 'Iranians'," 364–65).

13. Chandra, *Parties and Politics*, xviii. The same assumptions inform more recent work on this period (Alam, *Crisis of Empire*).

14. Chandra, *Parties and Politics* 15.

15. Mamdani observes that the political assumptions underpinning this created difference resulted in, for instance, "customary law privileging the ethnic native while discriminating against the ethnic migrant" (*Define and Rule*, 7).

16. Chandra, *Parties and Politics* 15.

17. Thus, in discussions of "Indo-Persian" literary culture, the transregionally celebrated Talib Amuli (d. 1626), Jahangir's poet laureate, is still an "Iranian expatriate in India" (Kinra, *Writing Self, Writing Empire*, 206).

18. Thomas, "Ethnicity, Genealogy, and Hellenism," 226.

19. Omi and Winant make this point about racial theory and instead call for a theory of racial formation that must "apply across historical time" ("Theoretical Status," 6–7). Absent, however, is any question of why certain formations should be called race and whether such labels are themselves objectivist assertions of modern race. Anidjar also raises this problem with respect to studies on Jews, which merely apply a reified, transhistorical category ("History of Race"). Jones notes that rigid categories are the heritage of ethnicity's relation to modern concepts of race and "ethnic groups remain firmly located at the empirical descriptive level" of analysis ("Ethnicity," especially 327–28, quote from 326).

20. Thomas, "Ethnicity, Genealogy, and Hellenism," 227.

21. Ibid., 217.

22. Hall, *Hellenicity*, 9.

23. Anidjar, *Blood*. Scholars of ancient Greece, such as Hall and Thomas, use these terms. Hall even cites Weber's understanding of an "objective blood relationship" without comment and reproduces its logic by arguing for kinship as having a "genetic reality," even if the operative kinship is "fictive" (*Hellenicity*, 15). Hall argues that ethnicity is distinct from other types of cultural identity (linguistic, religious, occupation) by "the fact that the symbols upon which it draws revolve around notions of fictive kinship and descent, common history, and specific homeland" (17).

24. This position is well developed in Alam's work, in which the actual experience of rule in India, or the "Indian" (and "Indic"), exert a teleological influence culminating in Akbar's rule, making the Timurids unique (*Languages of Political Islam*). Such reasoning often accompanies claims of Safavid "intolerance" and parochialism, continuing, for instance, in both Faruqui (*Princes of the Mughal Empire*) and Kinra (*Writing Self, Writing Empire*), whose sole basis for this claim seems to be the assumption that "pluralism" was a structural outcome of a large non-Muslim population, which forced Timurids to be "practical." Faruqui assumes that Timurids could therefore not be *ghāzīs* (warriors against non-Muslims), though claims to *ghazā* were for the purposes of bringing regions under Muslim rule, not widespread conversion (*Princes of the Mughal Empire*, 16–17).

25. For an excellent exposition of how lineages between the Deccan and in Iran were evoked transregionally, see Mancini-Lander, "Tales Bent Backward."

26. Kumkum Chatterjee has argued that "Persian tarikhs composed in eighteenth century Bengal also showed sensitivity to the immediate political and cultural contexts in which they were produced." Her study of "the provincial manifestations of an imperial political culture" demonstrates that Persianate culture had regional variations across Timurid domains, even as it partook of a larger imperial and transregional tradition (*Cultures of History*, 14–15).

27. By contrast, in Central and West Asia, the term meant a usually non-Muslim Mongol.

28. Lachmi Nara'in Shafiq uses this term to identify Persian poets, qualified by birth in Hindustan, whether Mughals or not. He notes that Persian dynasties (*salāṭīn-i Fārsī-gū*) ruled and created conditions for migration from Iran and Turan, the genesis for *Fārsī gūyān* existing in Hind, with those born in Hind as a particular subset of the larger term referring to Persians (Shafiq, *Gul-i Ra'nā*, f. 2a).

29. On interest in Sanskritic traditions suffusing Safavid intellectual culture at this time, see Sheffield, "Language of Heaven." On the ways in which the rise of occultism under the Timurids as a universal science from the fifteenth century also laid the ground for broader Persianate interest in non-Muslim traditions, see Melvin-Koushki, "Powers of One," and Binbaş, *Intellectual Networks*. On its prevalence in Central Asia, see Melvin-Koushki and Pickett, "Mobilizing Magic." On the Ilkhanids, see Berlekamp, "Administering Art, History, and Science."

30. Young argues that presumed cultural and ethnic categories operative in a postcolonial idea of hybridity are remarkably rooted in nineteenth-century colonial racism. Uncritically deployed, hybridity runs the risk of reifying what it seeks to challenge (*Colonial Desire*).

31. For the role of modern positivism in obscuring early modern Persian views of the world, see Kia, "Necessary Ornaments of Place."

32. Parkes, "Milk Kinship in Islam," 311.

33. For example, the first Nizam of Hyderabad, Asaf Jah, was born in Agra to an illustrious family in Timurid service. His paternal grandfather, a migrant from Samarqand in the last days of Shahjahan's reign, is described as a direct descendant of Shaykh Shahab al-Din Suhravardi (d. 1191) (Shafiq, *Gul-i Ra'nā*, f. 89a).

34. For instance, a common narrative circulated in eighteenth-century Persian commemorative texts connecting the origin of the Maratha Bhonsles to the Sassanian, Anushiravan the Just. Particulars of this relationship differ (as direct descendants or as clients linked by marriage), but the Bhonsles's origins were defined according to pre-Islamic Persian lineages of rule. On the former relationship, see Lachmi Nara'in Shafiq's 1799 Persian history of the Marathas written in Hyderabad (Shafiq, *Bisāt al-Ghanā'im*, f. 8b). I thank Dominic Vendell for this reference. On the latter relationship, see Ghulam Husayn Tabataba'i's 1780 history of the eighteenth century written in Bengal (*A Translation of the Seir Mutaqherin*, 4:11–12).

Chapter 4: Lineages and Their Places

Earlier versions of parts of this chapter were published in Kia, "Imagining Iran" and "Space, Sociality, and Sources of Pleasure."

1. Butler, *Gender Trouble*, 183. My thanks to Gil Anidjar for this reference.

2. On the rising ontological significance of writing, see Melvin-Koushki, "Of Islamic Grammatology."

3. Butler, *Gender Trouble*, 183. Emphasis in original.

4. Shafiq, *Gul-i Ra'nā*, f. 1b. The choice of this word is also an aesthetically appealing gesture to his teacher's proper name.

5. For more on structures of naming, see Schimmel, *Islamic Names*. Also see Chapter 6.

6. For more on Azad, see 'Abbās, *Ahvāl va Āsār*, and Ernst, "Reconfiguring South Asian Islam." For more on the *takiyyih* and its textual culture, see Green, "Uses of Books."

7. Shafiq, *Tazkirih-yi Gul-i Ra'nā*, 92–93.

8. The *hamd* in a Persianate text varies greatly according to the author's religious and sectarian affiliations. At the very least, all praise God, though the wording often reflects religious differences. For an overview of the structural elements in post-Timurid historiography, see Quinn, *Historical Writing*, 35–42.

9. This transcendence of strict sectarianism also appears in his pilgrimage and reverence for the Imami shrines in Mashhad and Iraq. If he was a Shi'a, his praise of the companions of the Prophet at least distinguishes him from orthodox Safavid Shi'ism (Stanfield-Johnson, *Ritual Cursing in Iran*).

10. Kashmiri qualifies this comparison by stating that he is just a lowly error-ridden person, unlike the great ancestor (Adam). This qualification allows him to talk about the tragedy of separation from Kashmir but avoid presumptuously equating himself with the first prophet (Kashmīrī, *Bayān*, 1).

11. Ibid., 5. *Hasab* and *nasab* "tended to split into contrasting concepts, *nasab* being defined as nobility by parentage and *hasab* as nobility in character and deeds." Together they demonstrate nobility or, in this case, its lack (Rosenthal, "Nasab").

12. Nadir rose from indigence to become stepson of the local chief. He was then made son-in-law through the merits of his perceptiveness and eventually succeeded his father-in-law as the chief of the Abivard Afshars (Kashmīrī, *Bayān*, 6. This great perceptiveness, manifested as Nadir's military prowess, precipitates his rise to power after the fall of the Safavids and subsequent invasions. For Kashmiri, this intelligence, without the ethical substance and refinement bestowed by lineage, results in great calamity for Iran (5–7). Also see Alam and Subrahmanyam, *Indo-Persian Travels*, 254.

13. Kashmīrī, *Bayān*, 6.

14. Faruqui, *Princes of the Mughal Empire*; and Lal, *Domesticity and Power*.

15. Hazīn, *Tarīkh va Safarnāma*, 145–46.

16. Ibid., 148.

17. For more on Emin, see Aslanian, *Dispersion History*; Kia, "Paradoxes of Circulation"; and Garcia, "Re-Orienting the Bluestockings." Fisher identifies his writing as like an Englishman ("Asians in Britain," 101–10).

18. This citation is in a letter republished along with his memoir, extrapolating on feelings of fondness at separation. Emin writes that these lines are the work of his son, and had been part of his education (*Life and Adventures*, 496–97).

19. Emin, *Life and Adventures*, 1–14.

20. Two forms of idealized manhood were the ethical warrior and the perfect man (*insān-i kāmil*). Their difference was the nature of the battlefield, the former material and the latter esoteric (Loewen, "Proper Conduct (*Adab*) Is Everything," 543).

21. Shūshtarī, *Tuhfat*. This text was widely circulated in Persian in both Hindustan and Iran. It was lithographed in 1847 in Bombay. Dalrymple seemed to think this lithograph is a rare text, in spite of multiple recent Tehran reprintings (*White Mughals*, xlii–xliii). Nevertheless, *White Mughals* provides helpful background for reading Shushtari's text, written in 1802 after a scandal that disgraced the family and placed them under house arrest. When reading Shushtari's disdaining tone toward Hindustan, these fallen fortunes amid the shifting politics of princely and Company rule must be kept in mind (Dalrymple, *White Mughals*, 129–39).

22. Shūshtarī, *Tuhfat*, 363–64.

23. Ibid., 364.

24. These roots likely predated Hajji Bayg Khan, since Shah Abbas I relocated the elites of Tabriz to Isfahan in response to Ottoman incursions in the early seventeenth century (Losensky, "Sā'eb Tabrizi").

25. Moral meanings also accrued to place through the dead, especially through the burial sites of those remembered as God's friends.

26. Shūshtarī, *Tuhfat*, 31. The text is dedicated to his paternal cousin and patron, Mir 'Alam, after whom it was named.

27. For the description of Shushtar, see Shūshtarī, *Tuhfat*, 32–95. For the description of the Nuriyyih sayyids, see 96–162. Shushtari's autobiography and travels are on 163–237. At the time of Abu Talib's narration, Shushtari's paternal cousins lived in Sabaghiya, near Basra (Abū Tālib Isfahānī, *Masīr-i Tālibī*, 452).

28. For more on Majlisi, see Momen, *Introduction to Shi'i Islam*, 127–28. For Khvansari's significance, see Momen, 117. These two prominent Safavid scholars were the intellectual forebearers of men with diverse genealogies of descent and itineraries of place throughout the Persianate world.

29. Abū Tālib Isfahānī, *Masīr-i Tālibī*, 452. This lineage's loftiness was not a perception particular to Abu Talib. Half a century earlier, Ghulam 'Ali Azad Bilgrami wrote similarly about Sayyid Riza ibn Nur al-Din "Aqdas," Shushtari's paternal uncle and Mir 'Alam's father. Azad mentions that Sayyid Riza's father, like his father before him, held

the position of Shaykh al-Islam of Shushtar. Born in 1715–16 AD/1128 AH, Sayyid Riza was, like some of Azad's other migrant friends from Iran, fleeing the disorders of post-Safavid times, but not before receiving extensive instruction from the luminaries in his own family and those of the two 'Iraqs (Āzād, *Sarv-i Āzād*, 223–24).

30. Abū Ṭālib Isfahānī, *Masīr-i Ṭālibī*, 7–8. Muhammad Bayg's fortunes were tied closely to Safdar Jang's, after whose death he was forced to flee to Bengal.

31. Āzād, *Sarv-i Āzād*, 223–24. Also see note 28.

32. Hākim, *Mardum Dīdih*, 149.

33. Abu'l-Fazl, *Akbarnāma*, 192–93.

34. Āzar, *Ātashkadih*, 1:37.

35. For instance, Azar includes sons of Sultan Husayn Mirza Bayqara' of Herat, such as Badi' al-Zaman Mirza (*Ātashkadih*, 1:48). For Akbar Shah, see 1:52.

36. For the entry, which lists only one line of poetry, see Āzar, *Ātashkadih*, 1:57–58. Shah Isma'il wrote in Turkish because this devotional poetry was aimed at his Qizil-bash followers. He named his sons Bahram, Sam, Alqas, and Tahmasp after figures in the *Shahnama*, tapping into its ideal of kingship as part of his political legitimacy. Like his contemporaries, Babur and the Ottoman Sultan Selim (who wrote Persian poetry), Isma'il was fluent in Persian and Turkish, a multilingualism that, like origins, was deployed according to context. On Shah Isma'il as a poet, see Minorsky, "The Poetry of Shah Isma'il I"; and Gallagher, "Shah Isma'il's Poetry."

37. For instance, see the entry on Shah Abbas I, Āzar, *Ātashkadih*, 1:76–77; the entry on Shah Tahmasp, 1:74; and the entry on Shah Isma'il II, 1:75.

38. Āzar, *Ātashkadih*, 1:100.

39. For instance, the Timurid ruler of Hindustan, Humayun (Āzar, *Ātashkadih*, 1:99–100).

40. The manuscripts differ on the word *tā'ifih*. One only has "*aslash az Rūmlū*," while three others use the word *tabagha* (a class or order of men) instead. See note 8 under the main entry in Āzar, *Ātashkadih*, 1:49.

41. Āzar, *Ātashkadih*, 1:64.

42. Ibid., 1:51.

43. Kashmīrī, *Bayān*, 6. Nadir was from the Kirklu branch of the Afshars, who were primarily in Khurasan. See Köprülü, "Afshār."

44. Āzar, *Ātashkadih*, 1:49. Though its veracity is not important to my argument, this detail is factually incorrect. Bayram Khan's Baharlu line was actually part of the Qaraquyunlu confederation that entered Timurid service in the mid-fifteenth century, when the Aqquyunlu took over Azarbayjan and eastern Anatolia. Bayram Khan followed his father in service to Babur and never switched loyalties. See Babur, *Baburnama*, 33, 473n71.

45. Azar's support for this claim is the praise bestowed on Rahim by many poets and those possessed of intellect. Azar erroneously refers to him as "Rahimi" (*Ātashkadih*, 1:59–60).

46. Khalīl, *Suhuf*, 59.

47. For more on women poets, see Brookshaw, "Odes of a Poet-Princess"; and Sharma, "From 'Ā'eshā to Nūr Jahān."

48. Āzar, *Ātashkadih*, 4:452.

49. Ibid., 4:448.

50. Ibid., 4:445. Azar notes a similar paucity of biographical information and availability of work for 'Ismati and 'Iffati (4:446).

51. Āzar, *Ātashkadih*, 4:449.

52. Steward notices that entries on women "share many features and conventions" of standard entries on men in a late seventeenth-century *tazkirih* of scholars written in Isfahan. Differences include lack of intimate student-teacher relations with nonrelated men, less information on their death dates and names, and more regular mention of husbands ("Women's Biographies," 123–25).

53. Āzar, *Ātashkadih*, 4:445.

54. Ibid., 4:448.

55. See entries on 'Ismati and 'Iffati (Ibid., 4:446). *'Iffat* is a common epithet of praise for women. See, for instance, Abu'l-Fazl on the Turco-Mongol ancestress Alan-qoa, whom he describes as "the queen of chastity (*masnad-nishīn-i 'iffat*)" (*Akbarnāma* 1:220–21).

56. Flatt, "Young Manliness," 155–59.

57. This final section opens with a twenty-page prose narrative of Azar's life as a way of introducing his contemporaries and is another way of defining himself (*Ātashkadih*, 4:455–83).

58. Reynolds et al. *Interpreting the Self*, 66–68.

59. Āzar, *Ātashkadih*, 4:446.

60. This equation of valorized behavior with manhood is common. Valih describes Lalih Khatun as "sitting on the throne of rule like a man" (*hamchūn mardān bar sarīr-i jahāndārī*) and her defense of the city as "Alexander-like" (Vālih, *Rīyāz*, 3:1940). Azar and Valih's entries are similar in both description and poetry selection. None of the other *tazkirih*s of this period produced in Hindustan mentions her. Valih also praises other female poets who write like men (meaning they write well) or defends their poetry as exceptional though they are women. See Sharma, "From 'Ā'eshā to Nūr Jahān," 155–57.

61. man ān zanam kih hamih kār-i man nikūkārī ast
    bih zīr-i maqna'ih-yi man basī kulah dārī ast
darūn-i pardih-yi 'ismat kih jā'īgāh-i man ast
    musāfirān-i sabā rā guzar bih dushvārī ast
jamāl-i sāyih-yi khūd rā dirīgh mīdāram
    az āftāb kih ān shahr gard va bāzār ast
nah har zanī bih dū gaz maqna'ih ast kadbānū
    nah har sarī bih kulāhī sazā'ī-yi sardārī ast (Āzar, *Ātashkadih*, 4:446).

62. Lalih Khatun, also known as Padshah Khatun of the Kutlugh Khans, ruled under the Ilkhanids in the thirteenth century. She and her mother are mentioned in Mernissi, *The Forgotten Queens of Islam*, 99–102. Mernissi's main source is Minorsky, "Kutlugh-khānids." Also see De Nicola, *Women in Mongol Iran*, 105–10. For more on the position and power of such Turkic women, see Togan, "Turkic Dynasties."

63. Scholarship on modern feminist claims to parity of access to education and public space using mastery of gendered norms has shown that such claims reinforce gendered hierarchies. See, for instance, Najmabadi, "Crafting an Educated Housewife."

Chapter 5: Kinship Without Ethnicity

Earlier versions of parts of this chapter were published in Kia, "Space, Sociality, and Sources of Pleasure."

1. Thus even studies of milk kinship have only biological and blood-based language with which to discuss extra-natal kinship. Peter Parkes contrasts "the blood of natal kinship" in "Christendom" and "in Islam" with the "adoptive kinship" of spiritual kinship in the former compared to milk kinship in the latter ("Fosterage, Kinship, and Legend," 587). Unjustified is the reason blood is the basis of natal kinship in *both* Christianity and Islam.

2. For a typology of political regimes in which distinctions are based on the unexplained "ethnic roots" and "ethnic ties" of rulers, see Sood, *India and the Islamic Heartlands*, 9–10. For an overview of anthropological positions, see Banks, *Ethnicity*. Even critical surveys like Banks's share the assumption of blood as the basis of allegiance because it is "seen as universal, as if all communities had to have been made of one substance, as it were, analogous to blood (this is said of the family, the class, the tribe and the race, and the nation too, except for the evolved or civilized ones that have emancipated themselves from blood)" (Anidjar, *Blood*, 43).

3. Anidjar, *Blood*, 50.

4. Ibid., 56.

5. Jones, "Ethnicity," 325. In premodern contexts, ethnicity (or ethnies as proto-ethnicity) is also presumed to be at least one of the building blocks of nationalism, especially after race fell out of fashion, and only partly immutable. The main proponent of this premodern proto-ethnicity is Anthony Smith. For an articulation of his arguments, see *The Nation in History*, especially 109–24.

6. Anidjar, *Blood*, 31–32. Well-developed arguments contest kinship as predicated on a "natural" biology, specifically identifying a relationship between the analytic binaries of nature and culture, posed as biological and social aspects of kinship (Carsten, *After Kinship*, 19–21, and chapter 1). Even work that argues kinship goes beyond nature or culture (as a "mutuality of being") still does not question the nature of biology/blood/birth as genealogy or the truth of biology, though it might not be kinship (Sahlins, *What Kinship Is*).

7. "Consanguinity, in other words, has a history, and it is briefer, more contained and specific, than commonly supposed." Since "it corresponds to a particular distribution (not yet a circulation) of blood within Western Christendom," its distinctions are "an *effect* of the historical movements we are still trying to grasp" (Anidjar, *Blood*, 58, emphasis in original). Anidjar's argument builds from a staggering literature on blood. Its centrality to medieval Christendom is widely recognized (for instance, Bildhauer, "Blood in Medieval Cultures"), but Anidjar shows this limited ascription to be a product of blood's continuing labor.

8. Thomas, "Ethnicity," 215. Representation of belonging emerged from a generative field that at any time consisted of "common but disputed currency" (227). These characteristics and habits were far from stable, and their circulations articulated everything from dispassionate observation to group strength.

9. Hall, *Hellenicity*, 17.

10. Ibid., 18.

11. In a study on early Islamic notions of Arab and Persian ethnicity, Cooperson argues that "ethnic identity is historically contingent" ("'Arabs' and 'Iranians'," 366). But his operative definition of ethnicity is the same modern halfway house between race and culture. From race it draws its immutable characteristics of "common ancestry." From culture it acquires mutable features such as language, faith, dress, and education. Cooperson holds that "ethnonyms do not refer to stable, primordial attributes of persons or communities." But presumably because "they are not constructed out of thin air, either . . . they represent an imposition of meaning upon contingent attributes of persons and communities, for particular purposes at a particular time" (367). While this definition is useful, the contingency of the attribute of descent is assumed to be a "biological heritage" (368). Writing about Kurds in premodern Arabic contexts, James similarly equates the perception of differences in collective groupings with "ethnic differentiation" ("Arab Ethnonyms, 683), going so far as to call *ethnos* "ethnicity or nation" (684). In neither case is ethnicity defined.

12. For a summary of critiques of kinship as biological fact in anthropological literature, see Clarke, *Islam and New Kinship*, 26–31; and Carsten, *After Kinship*, 6–23.

13. Carsten, *After Kinship*, 10.

14. Porqueres, "Kinship Language," 126.

15. Ibid., 127.

16. Butler, *Gender Trouble*. On the significance of gender for kinship studies, see Carsten, *After Kinship*, 57–66.

17. Anidjar, *Blood*, 32.

18. Ibid., 38.

19. Ibid., 31.

20. Ibid., 9.

21. Ibid., 23. This is the case throughout Sood's *India and Islamic Heartlands*, which

looks at ways individuals, embedded in associations, circulated across Islamic Eurasia. Among the most prominent was the family and then the larger "ethnic" collective (79–81, for instance). He assumes familial kinship established through "blood or marriage ties" (254).

22. Anidjar argues that "though *we* swim in a sea of blood, it has not been the case that blood has flown just everywhere," since "neither law nor politics, neither science nor kinship, not theology or literature are *universally* or *naturally* determined by or predicated on blood, on a figuration or an understanding of blood" (26, emphasis in original).

23. Recent attempts to adopt the notion of the king's two bodies from a European context to show simultaneity and similitude do not reckon with its Christological and European specificity. See, for example, Kinra, *Writing Self, Writing Empire*, 98–102. On its specificity, see Anidjar, *The Jew, the Arab*, 101–12; and *Blood*, 90–91.

24. Savant, *The New Muslims*, 11–12. James also outlines the relation of this concept to others in a changing system of meaning ("Arab Ethnonyms," 687).

25. Savant, *The New Muslims*, 17. I do not contest the particularity of Persian-ness in contrast to a universal Arab Islam, but I think this stark distinction breaks down later, when Persian had long been Muslim and had its own universal authority. That we have so much more scholarship on this earlier period is therefore a problem; its central issues, over time, are no longer a subject of debate.

26. Savant, *The New Muslims*, 12.

27. Ibid., 3.

28. The exception is Ho's work on genealogy, in which he reminds us, "genealogies may be incorporated into performative ritual texts such as mortuary chants, hagiographies, poetic narrations of scholarly pedigree, legal wills, and historical narratives. Viewed in such company, the old question of whether genealogies faithfully record the past or reflect contemporary interests ceases to be the most interesting one. Rather, a range of questions can be asked, about when genealogical discourses are energized, in what forms, and why" ("Precious Gift of Genealogy").

29. For studies of Persianate sacral kinship, see Moin, *Millennial Sovereign*. On the Ilkhanids, see Brack, "Mediating Sacred Kingship." For Timurid articulations of sacred kinship, see Binbaş, *Intellectual Networks in Timurid Iran*, 251–86. For the occult basis of these ideas, see Melvin-Koushki, "Astrology, Lettrism, Geomancy."

30. Bashir, "Origins and Rhetorical Evolution," 369.

31. Ibid., 366. Bashir marks the changing fortunes of the category but does not relate the term to its individual lines.

32. Binbaş has noted great variation in who was a Turk, how the eponymous ancestor Turk was identified, and how Turks related to and became other groups or subgroups, such as Uyghur, Tatar, Mongol, and Turcoman, especially after the fifteenth century ("Oğuz Khan Narratives").

33. I translate *sa'ādat* as virtuous well-being following Mottahedeh's logic ("Friendship in Islamic Ethical Philosophy," 229–30).

34. Āzar, *Ātashkadih*, 4:459–60.

35. That Azar foregrounds his Baygdili lineage and not his Shamlu heritage may be due to his family's high rank within the former and also to the fall of the Safavids themselves (notice Azar's declaration of dedication to the dynasty through Tahmasp II, the last ruling monarch).

36. Most scholarship on Muslim genealogy deals with Arabs in the early centuries of empire. Early Arab lineal progenitors became standardized and widely circulated in textual form. Later, families connected themselves to these "stems." See Szombathy, "Genealogy"; and Morimoto, "Formation and Development." I thank Soheb Niazi for bringing these works to my attention. For studies that include other peoples in early Islamic times, see the essays in Savant and de Felipe, *Genealogy and Knowledge in Muslim Societies*, particularly Savant's essay on attempts to reconcile pre-Islamic Persian with Qur'anic genealogies ("Genealogy and Ethnogenesis").

37. There is little consensus on its meaning, let alone critical engagement. Most words for tribe in the Qur'an overlap with lineage and family. Landau-Tasseron, "Tribes and Clans." With every definition, natal kinship is always accompanied by other forms of relation. This point is trenchantly made by Asad, "Kinship."

38. The *Akbarnama* makes reference to "the commanders and men" from the Chagatai *ulūs*, in the time of Chagatai Khan's sons. Only one generation removed from its eponymous ruler, the text applies the "Chagatai *ulūs*" as a group based on loyalty, defined by rule of a lineage rather than familial kinship (Abu'l-Fazl, *Akbarnāma*, 1:252–53).

39. Giladi, "Family."

40. For the distance between begetting a child and establishing paternity in early Islam, a period that functions as an Ur-context for Islamic practices, see Landau-Tasseron, "Adoption." Names (sing. *nisbat*) included families and social collectives of birth, adoption, and patronage (Landau-Tasseron, "Status of Allies," 15–19).

41. For more on nomadic Turco-Mongol groups and their relation to cities they ruled, mostly in the pre-Timurid era, see the essays in Durand-Guedy, *Turko-Mongol Rulers*.

42. Rosenthal, "Nasab."

43. Morimoto, "Formation and Development," 565.

44. Oral interviews and consultation of registers verified sayyid genealogies. Testimony of witnesses sufficed to authenticate an uncertain genealogy. When the family was uncertain about details, scholarly interpretation was adopted as social truth. These processes show genealogical construction to be a mutually symbiotic practice of truth (Morimoto, 564–69).

45. Morimoto notes that in canonical genealogical texts, "thorough descriptions of genealogies are only made up to a certain generation." These are the stems to which

later individuals or lineages connected themselves ("Formation and Development," 565). Szombathy has called this process "genealogical parasitism," yet these stems are socially solidified, uncontested genealogies upon which sometimes further connections are "forged" ("Genealogy," 5–6, and "Motives and Techniques").

46. This association was also made in the *Akbarnama*, which in addition made him a contemporary of the first Persian king, Gayomars (Abu'l-Fazl, *Akbarnāma*, 1:196–97). With Noah as the progenitor of all humankind, descent from this eponymous ancestor is not a particularly meaningful category of social distinction within the Persianate.

47. Golden, "Ġozz: i. Origins."

48. For Jamshid's significance, see Ferdowsi, *Shahnameh*, 6–8. Later, Azar compares Ughuz Khan's lineage to Faridun's line.

49. Abu'l-Fazl, *Akbarnāma*, 1:202–3. Bosworth says that though the name's "exact meaning has not yet been elucidated," the Ughuz were by the eleventh century "often designated in the sources as Turkmans" (Bosworth, "Ġozz: ii. Tribe."). For more on Ughuz Khan and his lineage, see the section on the "Muslim East" by Cl. Cahen, Deverdun, and Holt, "Ghuzz."

50. The relation with other groups, such as the Qipchaq, Tatars, Uyghurs, and Qarluqs, who are not considered Turks by the Ughuz in early modern times, is outlined in Binbaş, "Oğuz Khan Narratives." By contrast, the Seljuqs family was from one of the Ughuz tribes on the fringes of the Samanid domain (Bosworth, "Ġozz: ii. Tribe").

51. CL. Cahen, Deverdun, and Holt, "Ghuzz"; and Sela, "Rashīd al-Dīn's Historiographical Legacy." On later articulations of Timur's genealogy, see Woods, "Timur's Genealogy."

52. Neither Cl. Cahen, Deverdun, and Holt, "Ghuzz," nor Binbaş, "Oğuz Khan Narratives" discuss Abu'l-Fazl's later narrative.

53. Abu'l-Fazl, *Akbarnāma*, 1:208. Compare this posing of Tur as enemy with Abbasid-era Turkish writers, who associated Turan with Turkistan and Tur with Turk, translating Afrāsiyāb as Alp Er Tona, a storied Turkish hero (Golden, "'Eternal Stones'," 20–28).

54. Abu'l-Fazl, *Akbarnāma*, 1:208–13, quote from 210.

55. Ibid., 1:213–23.

56. For historical conceptions of false claims and forgery, see Szombathy, "Motives and Techniques."

57. We must presume multilingualism, with Turcomans knowing Persian well. The famous Chagatai man of letters, Mir 'Ali Shir Nava'i, in extolling the superiority of Turkish over Persian, claims that "Turks from notables to commoners and from slaves to lords are acquainted with the Persian language and speak it according to their particular stations. Turkish poets even write beautiful poems in Persian." We might dismiss this as polemic, but he admits, "Persian is more refined and profound than Turkish for the purposes of thought and science." Instead, he claims for Turks a mastery of social *adab*

in the form of "rectitude, honesty, and generosity" while conceding to Persians "the arts, sciences, and philosophy." Here a Turk is one in possession of the Turkish vernacular, lamented by even this great proponent of literary Turkish as lacking systematic development (Navā'ī, "Muhakamat al-Lughatain," excerpted in *Islamic Central Asia*, 185–86).

58. Historical scholarship still assumes that paternity (*istilḥāq*) "is based in principle on the pursuit of truth" and aimed "at establishing the identity of the true, i.e. biological father." In contrast, the *firāsh* principle bases paternity on the legal bond to the woman (Landau-Tasseron, "Adoption," 178). Historical sources reflect a truth deriving from law, such as Prophetic Traditions. Because God, not biology, does the creating, God's rules for deducing truth make them true. Landau-Tasseron's sources condemn knowingly making false claims, not a system of paternity lacking what we understand as biological truth or consistency ("Adoption," 178–79).

59. Abu'l-Fazl, *Akbarnāma*, 1:208–14. For another articulation of "generation to generation" as "*batn ba-batn*," see 1:216–17.

60. Kasmīrī, *Bayān*, 6.

61. Morimoto, "Formation and Development," 565–68.

62. Blood's location and role in Islamic thought, especially compared with bone and semen, is strikingly similar to its position in the Biblical-era Hebrew traditions (Anidjar, *Blood*, 44–49). For theories of conception in (largely Hanbali) thought, see Musallam, *Sex and Society*, 39–57.

63. Musallam, *Sex and Society*, 43. Ibn Sina reconciled various Greek theories. From Aristotle he adopted a gendered notion of semen, in which the female semen provides the matter and the male semen has "the principle of movement," meaning that it gives the form. These ideas held sway in natural philosophy but not in medical thought. His medical writings confirm that both men and women's semen accounted for resemblances of children to both parents (Musallam, 47–49).

64. Musallam, *Sex and Society*, 49–51.

65. Hadith cited in Musallam, *Sex and Society*, 52. Semen grows in the womb, in part, "because of the blood of its mother, which descends to the womb" (Ibn Qayyim, quoted and translated in Musallam, 56). Drawing on Hippocrates, he continues, "when the blood descends from the mother the foetus [sic] draws it and uses it for nourishment, and its flesh increases" (56).

66. The man who claims paternity can be a husband if the woman is free or a master if the woman is a slave (Landau-Tasseron, "Adoption.")

67. Hallaq, *Sharī'a*, 464. Indeed, "marriage (*nikāh*) was seen in Islam as the cornerstone of the social order and communal harmony, for as an institution it simultaneously regulated sexual, moral and familial relationships" (271).

68. Clarke, *Islam and New Kinship*, 47. Hallaq further notes the extent to which any claim of illegitimacy had to be supported by evidence that was "beyond any doubt" and

that "mere acknowledgement (*iqrār*) by the father that the child was his was deemed conclusive" (*Sharī'a*, 464).

69. For example, see Ahmad Bihbahani's use of "blood-thirsty" to describe social enmity in Kia, "Limning the Land," 64. Again, this usage is remarkably similar to the Jewish sources Anidjar consults (*Blood*, 44–49).

70. Landau-Tasseron, "Status of Allies," 19. Landau-Tasseron seems unable to reconcile the inclusion of allies, adopted members, and clients as part of a tribal group that simultaneously retain original *nisbat*s and membership in other groups.

71. Parkes, "Milk Kinship in Islam," 308–10.

72. Clarke, *Islam and New Kinship*, 45.

73. Ibid., 54; and Carsten, *After Kinship*, 228.

74. Gagan Sood outlines some of these obligations and privileges in *India and the Islamic Heartlands*, chapters 3 and 4.

75. Cooperson outlines an instance of a client also giving his son to be nursed and fostered by his Arab patron's family ("'Arabs' and 'Iranians'," 368–70).

76. Savant, *New Muslims*, 31.

77. Savant tells us that genealogies represent "the significance of blood ties for securing bonds within and among people" (*New Muslims*, 32).

78. Asad, "Kinship."

79. Chatterjee has noted the need to explore the "the polyvalence of familial terms in historical use" in South Asian contexts (editor's introduction to *Unfamiliar Relations*, 9–10, quote from 9).

80. Asad, "Kinship."

81. Sylvia Vatuk, "'Family' as a Contested Concept," 162.

82. Ibid.

83. Ibid., 163.

84. Sreenivasan, "Honoring the Family," 49.

85. Chatterjee, *Forgotten Friends*, 4–5, 127–29, and chapters 1–2.

86. Bashir, *Sufi Bodies*, 87–91; and Buehler, *Sufi Heirs*, 82–97. See Loewen, "Proper Conduct (*Adab*) Is Everything," on Va'iz Kashifi's (d. 1504–5 AD/910 AH) description of initiation in Sufi-based craft guild orders in *Futuvvatnama-yi Sultani*. Kashifi's repeated injunctions that initiates be Muslims indicate non-Muslim participation and confraternities. For a general overview of these orders, see Gevorgyan, "*Futuwwa* Varieties." For a study of futawwa practices encompassing non-Muslims in medieval Anatolia, see Goshgarian, "Opening and Closing."

87. Savant, *New Muslims*, 33.

88. Buehler, *Sufi Heirs*, 82–83.

89. Ibid., 82.

90. *Sīgha*, as language or form of offer (and its acceptance) in a contract, establishes rights and duties (Hallaq, *Sharī'a*, 239 and 273). Lachmi Nara'in Shafiq uses this

NOTES TO CHAPTER 5

term to describe his father's service above, as well as that of the migrant from Iran, Sayyid Riza "Aqdas" Shushtari in Bengal, whose relationship with Navvab Shuja'al-Dawlih he describes as "formal companionship (*sīghih-yi musāhibat)*" (Shafīq, *Shām-i Gharībān*, 44–45).

91. For more on "temporary marriage" in Iran, see Haeri, *Law of Desire.*

92. Adoption could happen through milk kinship, which was recognized in law, as well as other socially recognized practices, usually involving bodily intimacy and symbolized in exchange of clothing, (bread and) salt, or heterosocial integration. For more on milk kinship as a form of adoptive affiliation and a site of clientship, see Altorki, "Milk-Kinship;" Parkes, "Milk Kinship in Islam;" and Landau-Tasseron, "Adoption" and "Status of Allies." For the formal bond of obligations and privileges created through salt, see Gordon, "Babur," 83–84, and with the body through robes of honor, see Gordon, "Introduction," 1–11; and Hambly, "Emperor's Clothes."

93. Faruqi notes the importance of milk siblings to Mughal princes and emperors, with whom trust was far less fraught than with natal siblings (*Princes of the Mughal Empire*, 73–74). Also see Gordon, "Babur," 89–90 and 94–95. Texts of Persianate *adab* elaborated brothers and friends, as in 'Unsur al-Ma'ali's pronouncement, "it is best for a man to be without a brother than without a friend. When a sage was asked [if] it was better to have a friend or a brother, he said [that] a brother who is also a friend is best" (*Qābūsnāma*, 139).

94. Bihbahānī, *Mir'āt al-Ahvāl*, 206.

95. Ibid., 222.

96. Ibid., 223.

97. Vālih, *Rīyāz*, 3:1507–8. Mirza Hadi directs 'Alavi Khan's education by sending him to study with other teachers. These teachers carry the title of Mawlana or Akhund, indicating they had a specialization in the sciences (*'ulūm*), which could include astronomy, mathematics, medicine, law, or theology.

98. Vālih, *Rīyāz*, 3:1507–8.

99. Ibid., 2:1159.

100. Āzād, *Khizānih*, 1871, 368. Also repeated in Vālih, *Rīyāz*, 3:1679–82.

101. Vālih, *Rīyāz*, 1:337.

102. The sole exception is the late eighteenth-century Khalil Banarasi, who relates a possibility, unmentioned in earlier *tazkirih*s written by Umid's intimates (like Valih), that "they say that he is descended from the sons of the paternal uncles of Navvab Asad Khan, 'Alamgir Padshah's prime minister (*vazīr)*" (Khalīl, *Suhuf*, 60).

103. Āzād, *Sarv-i Āzād*, 221–22.

104. After the death of his father, Murshid Quli Khan went to Bengal to trade. He caught the attention of the Navvab of Bengal, Shuja' al-Dawlih, became his son-in-law, and spent many years as governor of Orissa. When "fate disposed him of his position," he entered into the service of the Nizam of Hyderabad until the end of his days. Over

his lifetime, Murshid Quli Khan was often simultaneously a poet, mystic, merchant, and statesmen and administrator (Āzād, *Sarv-i Āzād*, 221–22).

105. For more on this text, see Cole, "Mirror of the World;" Alam and Subrahmanyam, *Indo-Persian Travels*, 240–42; and Kia, "Limning the Land."

106. Bihbahānī, *Mir'āt al-Ahvāl*, 151–52.

107. Mottahedeh, *Mantle of the Prophet*, 180.

108. As students left the shrine cities to fan out across the Shi'a world, their reverence for their teacher and transmission of his ideas and texts popularized him as a *mujtahid*. The student could then collect funds on his teacher's behalf, enabling the teacher to gain the financial resources necessary to continue patronizing students and maintain his standing (Litvak, *Shi'i Scholars*, 24–29).

109. For a full list of his teachers, see Davvānī, editor's introduction to *Mir'āt al-Ahvāl*, 21.

110. Bihbahānī, *Mir'āt al-Ahvāl*, 151. The Tabataba'i are a huge, far-flung sayyid family descended from Ibrahim al-Tabataba, a fourth-generation descendent of the Prophet's grandson Hasan, the second Shi'a Imam (Momen, *Introduction to Shi'i Islam*, xxii).

111. Abbas Amanat, *Resurrection and Renewal*, 36–44.

112. Bihbahānī, *Mir'āt al-Ahvāl*, 152.

113. Litvak, *Shi'i Scholars*, 46. To ease this headache, see the genealogical table in Momen, *Introduction to Shi'i Islam*, 133–34. Amanat notes, "for more than half a century, close family ties, often with remote but vital genealogical links to the Majlisīs of Isfahan, guaranteed the domination of three families—Bihbahanis, Tabātabā'īs, and Najafis—over the clerical establishment" ("In Between the Madrasa and the Marketplace," 103–4).

114. Āzar, *Ātashkadih*, 4:650.

115. Ibid., 4:653.

116. Ārzū, *Majma'*, 3:1564.

117. Savant and de Felipe, "Introduction," 3.

118. Ibid., 2.

119. Āzar, *Ātashkadih*, 4:628.

120. Vālih, *Riyāz*, 3:1928.

Chapter 6: Naming and Its Affiliations

1. For a thorough detailing of Muslim names and their variations, see Schimmel, *Islamic Names*.

2. Cooperson, "'Arabs' and 'Iranians'."

3. Rosenthal, "Nasab."

4. Vālih, *Riyāz*, 1:338–39.

5. For more on the Qizilbash see Babayan, *Mystics, Monarchs and Messiahs*, 353–66; Haneda, *Le châh et les Qizilbāš*; and Savory, "Kizil-bāsh." For the changing meaning of

the term in in sixteenth- and seventeenth-century Persian sources, see Bashir, "Origins and Rhetorical Evolution."

6. Savory, *Iran Under the Safavids*, 20.

7. Ārzū, *Majmaʿ*, 1:85.

8. Vālih, *Riyāz*, 1:362–65.

9. Babaie, Babayan, and Baghdiantz-McCabe note that when Shah Abbas altered the Safavid state system and brought slave-elites into roles previously occupied by the Turkomen *uymāq*s these *ghulām*s continued to be called Qizilbash in chronicles (*Slaves of the Shah*, 34).

10. Hazīn, *Tārīkh va Safarnāma*, 265. Hazin also calls them the army (*lashkar*) of the Qizilbash, which is like saying the army of the Safavids (205). On the composition of Nadir's army, see Axworthy, *Sword of Persia*, 260–61.

11. Vālih, *Riyāz*, 1:338–39.

12. Hazīn, *Tārīkh va Safarnāma*, 206.

13. For an account of high-office holders under Timurid rule, see Ali, *Mughal Nobility*; and Subrahmanyam, "Iranians Abroad." Many other works on Timurid Hindustan casually mention the immediate entrance to imperial service of educated migrants from Iran (for instance, Faruqui, *Princes of the Mughal Empire*; and Kinra, *Writing Self, Writing Empire.*)

14. Shūshtarī, *Tuhfat*, 338. For the conflict's description, see 336–39.

15. Shūshtarī, *Tuhfat*, 339.

16. Such millenarian sentiments themselves were made possible by Safavid rule and flourished in its apocalyptic aftermath. See Babayan, *Mystics, Monarchs and Messiahs*, 485–87.

17. Amanat, "Introduction," 2–5.

18. On the importance for Qajars of representing themselves as legitimate successors to the Safavids, see Amanat, *Pivot of the Universe*, 2–8.

19. The critical edition mentions manuscripts produced in Iran and South Asia (Davvānī, editor's introduction to *Mir'āt al-Ahvāl*, 28–30).

20. Shūshtarī, *Tuhfat*, 359.

21. Ibid., 373.

22. Ibid., 371.

23. Tavakoli-Targhi, *Refashioning Iran*, 12–13; and Muvāhhid, editor's introduction to *Tuhfat*, 27–28.

24. For instance, Bihbahani mentions "'Ali Bayg Khan Kirmani who was the head of the Qizilbash community" in Hyderabad (Bihbahānī, *Mir'āt al-Ahvāl*, 231). No other *nisbat*s identify these individuals.

25. Bihbahānī, *Mir'āt al-Ahvāl*, 174.

26. This audience is made obvious through various textual mechanisms, such as the way in which Urdu words or Hindustani place names are rhymed with Persian words

to assist pronunciation. Constant explanations of things Hindustani and comparisons with Iran also assumed knowledge of Iran. We must be careful of assuming that those who needed help with Urdu words were outside of the subcontinent. As late as the mid-nineteenth century a book lithographed in Murshidabad explained Urdu poetic idioms to readers in Bengal written in Persian (Mirzā Jān Tapish, *Shams al-Bayān*).

27. Calmard, "Safavid Persia in Indo-Persian Sources," 375.

28. Shushtari was patronized by Fath 'Ali Khan, Valih's uncle and the grand vizier of Shah Sultan Husayn Safavid in the years before the Afghan invasion, and wrote a *qasīdih* in praise of him (Vālih, *Rīyāz*, 4:2212).

29. Vālih, *Rīyāz*, 1:632.

30. Fisher, *Counterflows to Colonialism*, 74.

31. Emin, *Life and Adventures*, 414–15. Per Persian language conventions, Emin narrates himself in the third person throughout his memoir.

32. Litvak, *Shi'i Scholars*, 31.

33. Aqa Ahmad refers to him as "Muhammad Baqir al-Isfahani, known as al-Bihbahani" (Bihbahānī, *Mir'āt al-Ahvāl*, 65).

34. Cole, *Roots of North Indian Shi'ism*, 32–34; Abbas Amanat, *Resurrection and Renewal*, 37–38; and Litvak, *Shi'i Scholars*, 14–15.

35. For the role of the state in creating permanent family surnames, see Scott, Tehranian, and Mathias, "Production of Legal Identities."

36. Wilson, "Introduction," 4. For more on naming as a strategy deployed in early colonial contexts, see Ghosh, "Decoding the Nameless," 297–316.

37. For an example of these efforts in early nineteenth-century British India, see Ghosh, *Sex and the Family*. For the frustrations the British faced in the Gulf, see Onley, *Arabian Frontier*. On negotiations possible with the state well into the twentieth century, see Sherman, "Migration, Citizenship and Belonging."

38. Axworthy, *Sword of Persia*, 5.

39. For instance, Dargah Quli Khan, the author of *Muraqqa'-i Dihli*, was from a Turkoman family of Shi'as originating from Khurasan who had migrated to Golconda in the mid-seventeenth century. See Āzād, *Khizānih* (2011), 315–188. On the Nizam's life and career, with a more sophisticated view of the relations within early eighteenth-century factionalism in high Mughal politics, see Faruqui, "At Empire's End."

40. Such factors were important in the sixteenth century, when Akbar was consolidating Mughal rule and sought to balance the power of Chagatai nobles with those of Irani and Rajput nobles (Richards, *The Mughal Empire*, 19–24). Such factional politics were specific to a time and place and not a primordial set of affiliations that can be applied to every period of Mughal rule.

41. "Colonialism taught Indians to identify themselves with the nation-state and to understand their freedom as citizens in terms of its history. Colonialism impressed on India's emerging historian-intellectuals a model of history-writing based on the positivist narratives

of the modern court of law, with its rules of evidence and apparatus for verification. . . . The coming of 'modern' history to India in this sense, as a profound change of consciousness and identification, signaled like nothing else the transforming power of colonialism and its imposition of a deep rupture with the past" (O'Hanlon, "'Premodern' Pasts," 108).

42. Balabanlilar, "Lords of the Auspicious Conjunction," 4. More generally, see Balabanlilar, *Imperial Identity*, prologue and chapter 2.

43. On shared idioms and practices of political universalism, see Moin, *Millennial Sovereign*; and Balabanlilar, *Imperial Identity*, chapter 5. On shared universal concepts, see Melvin-Koushki, "Astrology, Lettrism, Geomancy"; "Powers of One"; and "Early Modern Islamicate Empire." For these engagements, see Truschke, *Culture of Encounters*.

44. Quinn, "Timurid Historiographical Legacy." Succession practices based on the princely appanage system is one example of this shared political culture through the sixteenth century. Practices differed in the seventeenth century, but with the "shackling" of princes in the early eighteenth century, Timurid and Safavid practice realigned (Faruqui, *Princes of the Mughal Empire*). The ability to recite and compose poetry, ethics of rulership, and expectations of reciprocity in patronage were also shared notions among men of power (Balabanlilar, *Imperial Identity*, 11–13). Even Babur, from a far more peripatetic Turco-Mongol branch of the family and somewhat awed by his Herati cousins, could compose Persian verses (Schimmel, *Empire of the Great Mughals*, 23).

45. Balabanlilar, "Lords of the Auspicious Conjunction," 5; and *Imperial Identity*, 38–41. For the genealogical self-fashioning of Timur's successors in West and Central Asia, see Binbaş, *Intellectual Networks*, chapter 7.

46. For example, see Alam, *Crisis of Empire*, 278–79.

47. Balabanlilar notes that Babur's memoirs served as the lens through which the Mughals understood their Timurid heritage ("Lords of the Auspicious Conjunction," 6). Other Timurid texts circulating widely throughout Ottoman, Safavid, Uzbeg, and Mughal domains were also important. Among them are the fifteenth-century universal histories written under Timurid patronage, such as *Rawzat al-Safa* (see Chapter 1) and Sharaf al-Din 'Ali Yazdi's *Zafarnama*, a history of Timur's conquests (Quinn, "Timurid Historiographical Legacy").

48. Deccani court chronicles used "Mughal" as a term for Akbar and Jahangir at a time when Timurids threatened to swallow these regional powers whole. For example, see Fuzūnī-Astarābādī, *Futūhat-i Adil Shāhī* (Bijapur, c. 1640), 272b–274b. My thanks to Roy Fischel for alerting me to this usage and sharing examples.

49. Thackston, "Genghisid and Timurid Background," xlvi. On Timur, see Manz, *Rise and Rule of Tamerlane*. On the rule of Timur's son, Shahrukh (1409–1447), see Manz, *Power, Politics and Religion*. On the Herati-based Sultan Husyan Bayqara' (1469–1506), see Subtelny, *Timurids in Transition*. On the construction of Ilkhanid charismatic authority, see Brack, "Mediating Sacred Kingship."

50. Thackston notes that "[i]n Transoxiana and Cisoxiana (Khurasan and what is now Afghanistan) the Timurids inherited from the Mongols a bifurcated society—Turco-Mongolian and Persianate, two peoples existing side by side who had divided the responsibilities of government and rule into the military and civilian along ethnic lines" ("Genghisid and Timurid Background," xxxix).

51. Subtelny, "Symbiosis of Turk and Tajik," 45–61.

52. Shūshtarī, *Tuhfat*, 432 and 460 (for instance). Likely following him, Bihbahani calls the Hindustani imperial dynasty "*salātīn-i Bāburiyyih*" (Bihbahānī, *Mir'āt al-Ahvāl*, 190).

53. The Irano-centric Azar Baygdili (d. 1779) nevertheless calls Humayun a Gurkani (Āzar, *Ātashkadih*, 1:20).

54. Subhānī, *Nigāhī bih Tārīkh-i Adab*, 267. This diminished rendition is exemplified in Subhani's foregrounding the decisive battle of Panipat (1526) as the moment when "Hindustan came under the rule of the Gurkanis of Hind" (268). Gurkani and Gurgani are interchangeable, as the second line distinguishing gaf from kaf was often dropped in manuscripts. He also calls Babur's formal assumption of rulership in Delhi as "naming himself the emperor (*impurātūr*)," a title unknown in Babur's time (268). This ahistorical lineage renders Babur a petty ruler from Central Asia who seized the already constituted throne of Hindustan, which becomes the defining origin of the dynasty even as they are acquiring it.

55. *Muntakhab al-Lubab*, quoted in Mukhia, *Mughals of India*, 4.

56. *Ahkam*, cited in Chandra, *Parties and Politics*, 16, fn 18.

57. Ārzū, *Majma'*, 1:394.

58. Commemoration of maternally inherited sayyid descent was commonplace, showing *nasab* to be androcentric but not uniformly patrilineal. Other examples include the statesman 'Imad al-Mulk, whom the acknowledged Sayyid, Azad Bilgrami, names Mir Shahab al-Din, a title he acquires through his maternal grandfather, Mir Muhammad Fazil I'timad al-Dawlih Qamar al-din Khan, Muhammad Shah's Minister of State (*vazīr al-mamalik*). Mir Shahab al-Din's father was not a sayyid (Āzād, *Khizānih*, 2011, 73). Maternal sayyid status signified socially (though it could be contested), as seen in the poet Mir Muhammad Taqi "Mir"'s use of the common sayyid moniker as both title and pen name (Naim, translator's introduction to *Zikr-i Mir*, 11–12).

59. Shafiq, *Gul-i Ra'nā*, ff. 1b–2a, emphasis mine. For instance, Shahid's origin was from Tehran, his people are Turks, an ancestor came to Hind, and Shafiq considers him one of the poets of Hindustan (331b).

60. James argues for *jins* in reference to social collectives as ethnonym. He translates *jins* as "type" ("Arab Ethnonyms," 692, 695) but *jinsiyya* problematically as "ethnic solidarity" (711). Cooperson also calls terms such as *Arab*, *Iranian*, and *Persian* ethnonyms but notes that many traits were transferable, causing Arabs to align their designation more closely to *nasab* ("'Arabs' and 'Iranians'").

61. Āzād, *Khizānih*, 1871, 375.

62. Abū Tālib Isfahānī, *Masīr-i Tālibī*, 372.

63. Ibid., 7–8.

64. Ibid., 385–86.

65. Ibid., 387.

66. Ibid., 367.

67. Ibid., 355.

68. Alam, "Culture and Politics of Persian," 159.

69. Kashmīrī, *Bayān*, 166 and 170.

70. The celebrated mid-eighteenth-century poet Shams al-Din "Faqir" Dihlavi (1703–1769) is simply celebrated transregionally in *tazkirih*s as being "from the great ones of Delhi (*az akābir-zādih-hā-yi Dihlī ast*)," even as he was commemorated as descended from the Abbasids on his father's side and the sayyids on his mother's side. Faqir's lineage originated elsewhere, even as it constituted a great family of Delhi (Ārzū, *Majma'*, 2:1267.

71. This naming practice was similar to the way in which Turco-Mongol tribes were named after their leader's lineage. It is also the way the realm of Islam was defined, by a Muslim ruler and the governing order assumed by that rule, not by the dominant tradition of local inhabitants. This mistaken understanding of *ghazā*, waged against domains filled with non-Muslims rather than those ruled by non-Muslims, has been evoked as the cause of a supposed Indian exceptionalism (Faruqui, *Princes of the Mughal Empire*, 16–17).

72. Kashmīrī, *Bayān*, 166. Modern scholars seem confused about this term's meaning. Sarkar tells us that the core of these troops had arrived in Hindustan with Nadir's army and remained. He alternately calls them *Qizilbash* and then *Mughal*s (Sarkar, *Fall of the Mughal Empire*, 1:22–23). Cheema calls his force "*Qizilbash* cavalry" and notes that Safdar Jang "took great care that all the troopers and officers employed should be Mughals, for the most part Turkmans from Khurasan—hence the appellation Qizilbash" (*Forgotten Mughals*, 211). Regardless, in Kashmiri's text they are clearly troops under the command of Safdar Jang, himself a Mughal, a migrant from Iran and powerful figure at the Timurid court.

73. Thackston, "Genghisid and Timurid Background," xli–xliii. Before the establishment of the Hindustani-specific meanings, for someone like Babur, calling his family Mughals "would not have pleased him in the least" (xlvi).

Chapter 7: Commemorating Persianate Collectives, Selves

Earlier versions of parts of this chapter were published in Kia, "Imagining Iran."

1. Hāfiz Shirāzi, *Dīvān-i Hāfiz*, 62–63. These are the first two verses of the ghazal.

2. I follow Zaman in treating "auto/biographical" writing as an act crossing multiple generic boundaries, including "history" (*tārīkh*) and ethico-didactic texts (*akhlāq*), to which I add travel writing ("Instructive Memory," 679–80, quote from 679).

3. Shafir, "Art of Forgetfulness," 269. Shafir argues that in the seventeenth-century Ottoman context, memory became less central to morality as new forms of textual production and consumption led to different forms of learning and transmission of knowledge. Such developments, however, are relative. Persian sources from the eighteenth and early nineteenth centuries reflect a continued valorization of memory.

4. "[M]emory acts as a sentinel, keeping the base self from acting out and dragging humans into immorality. Forgetfulness creates a sort of vicious circle of morality in which each immoral act leads to memory loss, which in turn would further break down the capacity to act morally" (Shafir, "Art of Forgetfulness," 272). *Adab*, or collectively *ādāb*, is the proper form by which moral acts register. The aporetic continuum of *adab* reaches from the aesthetic (including forms of textual expression) to the social (as ethical behavior).

5. Zaman, "Instructive Memory," 684.

6. Ibid., 685.

7. See Chapter 4 for a discussion of Lalih Khatun. On early modern women's commemorative texts and the kind of figures they evoke, see Babayan, "'In Spirit We Ate Each Other's Sorrow'"; Bokhari, "Imperial Transgressions" and "Masculine Modes of Female Subjectivity"; and Zaman, "Instructive Memory." Bokhari and Zaman both look at royal women, whose social location afforded more enduring power to their commemorations. Babayan looks at the work of a mid-level chancellery scribe's widow, whose text was kept within the family archive until its publication in 1996. Undoubtedly, more women's commemorative texts are held in private collections.

8. Zaman, "Instructive Memory," 680.

9. For a lucid overview, see Losensky, "Biographical Writing," 19–38. Also see Naqavī, *Tazkirih Nivīsī*.

10. I follow Stefano Pellò's analysis of widely intelligible topoi, like that of the madman or the high and low urban figures of *shahr ashub* poetry in *tazkirih* biographies "to express moral, social and aesthetic judgements regarding the present time of poetic circles" ("Persian Poets on the Streets," 315; see also 316–17).

11. For a Sufi *tazkirih*, see *Farid ad-Din 'Attār's Memorial of God's Friends* and Jahanara Baygum's *Munis al-arvah* (in Begam, *Princess Jahān Ārā Begam*). For a *tazkirih* focused on imperial office holders, see Aurangabadi, *Ma'āsir al-Umarā*. For a *tazkirih* section commemorating the beneficiaries of a subimperial court, as part of a larger work, see Nahāvandī, *Ma'āsir-i Rahīmī*. For a study of a *tazkirih* of 'ulama, see Abi-Mershed, "Transmission of Knowledge."

12. For example, a late seventeenth-century *tazkirih* of Shi'a scholars in Iran, containing a section on women, was written in Arabic in Isfahan (Stewart, "Women's Biographies").

13. I use the term "imprint" instead of "effect" because I question the modern historical practice of narrating causality, which narrows our access to the range of possibilities at play, including those that later disappeared.

14. Davis notes in an early modern French context that "virtually all the occasions for talking or writing about the self involved a relationship; with God or God and one's confessor, with a patron, with a friend or a lover, or especially with one's family and lineage" ("Boundaries," 53.

15. Binbaş, *Intellectual Networks*, 7.

16. Date given in Shafiq, *Gul-i Ra'nā*, ff. 1b–2a.

17. Ibid., f. 1b–2a. The print edition of *Sham-i Ghariban* gives the date 1182 AH (Shafiq, *Shām-i Gharībān*, 15).

18. In *Sham-i Ghariban* he calls it "a *tazkirih* in memory of the versifiers of Hindustan (*dar zikr-i mawzūnān-i Hindūstān*)" (15).

19. On this work, see Dhavan and Pauwels, "Controversies," 641–44.

20. Shafiq, *Shām-i Gharībān*, 15.

21. Ibid., 16.

22. See, for instance, Rāzī, *Haft Iqlīm*, 1960, 1:30.

23. Shafiq, *Shām-i Gharībān*, 16. Other Muslim authors, such as Amin Razi, merely state Adam's place of arrival as *Sarandib* with no verification (Rāzī, *Haft Iqlīm*, 1960, 1:30).

24. Shafiq, *Gul-i Ra'nā*, f. 2a.

25. For more on Persian *tazkirih* writing by Hindu authors, see Pellò, "Drowned in the Sea of Mercy."

26. *Chamanistān*, 1.

27. For instance, Lala Jagat Rai was a Brahmin who converted to Shi'ism in the late seventeenth century and moved to Yazd. His story reached Shafiq by way of Tahir Nasrabadi's *tazkirih*, penned in Isfahan but heavily cited across the eighteenth-century Persianate (Shafiq, Tazkirih-yi *Gul-i Ra'nā*, 29).

28. For Sa'ib's entry, see Shafiq, *Shām-i Gharībān*, 158–61.

29. Browne, *Literary History of Persia*, 224.

30. Quinn's work serves as a major exception (see bibliography).

31. See Losensky, *Welcoming Fighānī*, 17–55; and Sharma, "Redrawing the Boundaries of 'Ajam."

32. See Pellò, "Persian Poets on the Streets," "Drowned in the Sea of Mercy," and "Persian as Passe-Partout"; and Schwartz, "The Local Lives of a Transregional Poet" and "The Curious Case of Carnatic."

33. Najmabadi, *Professing Selves*, 277. She challenges the triumph of "a psychic interiorized self" (9) in modern and even contemporary Iran (276).

34. For instance, Kinra contends that commemorative texts contain "alternative discourses" that were "often empirically unverifiable" and so "unlike their historical chronicle counterparts" (*Writing Self, Writing Empire*, 251).

35. Scholarship less shackled by uncritical acceptance of the historical discipline's positivist assumptions has noticed the considerable substantive and methodological

overlap across practices we identify as Persian chronicle, autobiography, hagiography, and biographical commemoration. See Losensky, "Biographical Writing," 37–38; Pellò, "Persian Poets on the Streets," 311–12; Reynolds, *Interpreting the Self*; and Zaman, "Instructive Memory." Biography was a method in all these types of writing.

36. For more on this episteme, see Kia, "Necessary Ornaments of Place."

37. Losensky has made this observation about the role of incorporating the present into a rewriting of the past to create tradition in "Biographical Writing," 27–33.

38. Hermansen and Lawrence, "Indo-Persian Tazkiras," 150. Though they propose to look at Timurid Sufi and poetic *tazkirih*s from the sixteenth to mid-nineteenth centuries, their discussion on poetic *tazkirih*s is limited to a post-1750 Urdu context (156–60). They note the proliferation of *tazkirih*s in the mid-to-late eighteenth century, and, puzzlingly, ascribe it to anticipation of British colonial domination and abolition of Persian as a language of power (156–57). See also Kinra, "Secretary-Poets," 367–437. For a persuasive argument that the victory at Plassey, let alone the British political domination that followed over the next century, was by no means inevitable, see Subrahmanyam, "*Un Grand Dérangement*."

39. Hermansen and Lawrence, "Indo-Persian Tazkiras," 150.

40. Malhotra and Lambert-Hurley, "Introduction," 8.

41. Shūshtarī, *Tuhfat*, 368.

42. Khalidi, *Arabic Historical Thought*, 85.

43. de Man, "Autobiography as De-facement," 919–20.

44. Derrida, *Monolingualism of the Other*, 28–29.

45. Ho, "Two Arms of Cambay," 348.

46. On the relationship of commemoration, circulation, and community, see Szuppe, "A Glorious Past."

47. Losensky notes the predominance of contemporary poets and a focus on the author's social relations that he calls an "author-oriented perspective" ("Biographical Writing," 34–35).

48. Kinra puzzles over the persistence of *naqlī* accounts of Chandar Bhan "Brahmi" and the heretical verse he supposedly recited to Shah Jahan (see Kia, "*Adab* as Literary Form," 291–95). Kinra notices that such accounts are related to their temporal contexts of composition and repetition but does not go so far as to connect this relationship to commemoration's labor in the world, that is, articulating community to figure the author in his present (*Writing Self, Writing Empire*, 259–77).

49. Āzād, *Khizānih*, 1871: 328–29.

50. Ibid., 368.

51. Ibid., 370. For the full account, see 370–73.

52. Simultaneously, the term invoked the connotation of interpretation. Reynolds, *Interpreting the Self*, 40–43. Stewart distinguishes *tarājim* from *tabaqāt* as texts whose biographies are alphabetical versus occupationally organized ("Women's Biographies," 108).

53. Azad claims that his account "is extremely correct" and that he "heard it from the tongue of Muhammad Salih Khan and Musavi Khan, the murderers of Nadir Shah" (Āzād, *Khizānih*, 1871: 372).

54. For a discussion of exclusion on the basis of violations of social *adab*, see Kia, "*Adab* as Literary Form," 298–300.

55. Hermansen and Lawrence, "Indo-Persian Tazkiras," 155. Being Muslim, however, was not enough; one had to display a particular *adab* to be manifest as Muslim.

56. This universalization occurred through the hegemony of the occult sciences in early modern Persianate contexts. See Melvin-Koushki, "Of Islamic Grammatology"; and Sheffield, "Language of Heaven." For discussions of non-Muslim use of esoteric language reflecting occult sensibilities (though not identified as such), see Kinra, *Writing Self, Writing Empire*, 191–98; and Pellò, "Persian as Passe-Partout" and "Drowned in the Sea of Mercy."

57. Pellò, "Drowned in the Sea of Mercy," 139.

58. For example, see *Haft Iqlim* or the *tazkirih* sections at the back of *A'in-i Akbari* (1596) and *'Alam Ara'i-yi 'Abbasi* (1628–29).

59. This relationality can also cast the author in a dissenting position, and we can contrast the figures put forth by 'Abd al-Qadir Bada'uni (*Muntakhab al-Tavarikh*) and Abu'l-Fazl (*Akbarnama*) in their chronicles of Akbar's reign. See also Zaman's discussion, "Instructive Memory," 694–96.

60. Chandra, *Parties and Politics*, 281. For a general overview of the financial problems behind the shrinking patronage opportunities at the Mughal court, see 29–39.

61. Butler Brown notes that 'Alamgir's abstention from music for pious reasons created a context in which patronage and stylistic cultivation of music were no longer determined by the royal court. With multiple sub-imperial sites of patronage, music production was much more polycentric ("Dargah Quli Khan's Strange Vision," 2).

62. On the proliferation of *tazkirih* writing, see Alam, "Culture and Politics of Persian," 175–77.

63. The standard entry seems remarkably similar to biographical dictionaries of *'ulama* two centuries earlier, at the other end of the Muslim world. See Abi-Mershed, "Transmission of Knowledge," 21.

64. Kinra notes that, for poets, "geographical location was far less important as a marker of identity than their location in time, vis-à-vis the canon of past masters whose works they so admired and struggled so hard to surpass" ("Secretary-Poets," 345). Yet Szuppe notes that post-Timurid texts "exhibit a marked attention to the individual and, especially, to contemporary society" ("A Glorious Past," 42). This view is echoed in Pellò's analysis of Indo-Persian *tazkirih*s, which calls a presentist focus "a generic protocol" ("Persian Poets on the Streets," 313). If we dispense with the need to articulate an argument in either/or terms, we can say that past poets authorized the commemoration of contemporary community.

65. Shafiq, *Shām-i Gharībān*, 282.

66. The text was lithographed twice in the nineteenth century with Hazin's *dīvān* and exists in numerous manuscripts (Browne, *Literary History of Persia*, 281). *Kulliyat-i Hazin* (The Complete Works of Hazin) was lithographed in Lucknow (1876) and in Kanpur (1893). Numerous subsequent *tazkirih*s of the period cite it. For example, see Khalīl, *Suhuf*, 156–57. Khalil actually reproduces Hazin's entries verbatim after his own preliminary information.

67. Gulchīn Ma'ānī, *Tārīkh-i Tazkirih hā-yi Fārsī*, 1:350. For more on this text, see 1:349–59.

68. Bland, "On the Earliest Persian Biography," 147–48.

69. Vālih, *Riyāz*, 4:2540.

70. For Isfahan, see Āzar, *Ātashkadih*, 3:922. For the whole of Iran, see 1:101. For Ardabil and Urdubad in Azarbayjan, see 1:102–3.

71. Schwartz, "Bâzgasht-i adabî," chapter 2.

72. Vālih, *Riyāz*, 4:2475.

73. The term is Tavakoli-Targhi's (*Refashioning Iran*, 8–15). For an instance of the problem, see Alam's study of the emergence of regional centers of power in early eighteenth-century north Hindustan. He uses Arzu's *Majma'* and Azad's *Khizanih*, but not Valih's *Riyaz* (Alam, *Crisis of Empire*). As someone who spent decades in Mughal service under the first two Navvabs of Awadh, Valih was close to relevant events and people. The long, historically embedded entries on Burhan al-Mulk and many other Mughal political, poetic, military, and mystical figures whom Valih knew, together with his participation in events such as the invasion of Nadir Shah, remain untapped. With manuscript copies of the *Riyaz* in most major collections in South Asia and its status as a source for almost all biographical dictionaries that came after it, the text is undoubtedly relevant.

74. In addition to his participation in debates over poetic idiom and style, Arzu was the first to establish a linguistic link between Persian and Sanskrit (Alam, "Culture and Politics of Persian," 175).

75. Zaman, "Instructive Memory," 696.

76. Zaman traces this indelible relationship between author, text, and commemorative subject in three accounts of the Timurid emperor Humayun ("Instructive Memory," 685–94).

77. Losensky, *Welcoming Fighānī*, 45. For a list of fifty manuscript copies that have survived in Iran, Pakistan, India, and various places in Europe, see Nājī Nasrābādī, editor's introduction to Vālih, *Riyāz*, 49–51.

78. See Ārzū, *Majma'*, 3:1509–18.

79. Ibid., 2:518. According to Valih, Rahib was born in Isfahan in 1706–7 (Vālih, *Riyāz*, 2:889). According to Mushtaq's chronogram, he died in 1752–53 (Hazīn, *Tazkirat al-Mu'āsirīn*, 376).

80. Āzād, *Khizānih*, 1871, 246–47.

81. Vālih, *Riyāz*, 2:884–89.

82. *See ibid.*, 3:1618 and 2:885.

83. Arzu includes three women, but two of them have one-line entries, and in the entry of the third he writes the disclaimer that women should not (rather than do not) participate in the poetic composition because they have not received prophecy. He further adds that women are suitable only to be sisters and mothers. Cited in Sharma, "From 'Ā'eshā to Nūr Jahān," 157–58.

84. Alam, "Culture and Politics of Persian," 184.

85. Ibid., 171.

86. Valih includes twenty-seven women poets, whose entries are incorporated into the main, alphabetically listed biographical notices (Sharma, "From 'Ā'eshā to Nūr Jahān," 155). Azar included only eight women, though with more substantial entries, and put them in a separate category at the back of the *Atashkadih* (Sharma, 158).

87. Schwartz, "Bâzgasht-i adabî," 40–44.

88. Vālih, *Riyāz*, 3:1879. Such statements challenge Alam's contention that Valih supported Arzu's position on the distinction between mastery of spoken versus written Persian ("Culture and Politics of Persian," 185).

89. A similar aside is in Valih's entry on Shaykh Faqirullah Afarin of Lahore (Vālih, *Riyāz*, 1:309–10). This was not, however, an idiomatic divergence specific to Iran and Hindustan. The perception that the idiom of a person from another region was nonsensical applied between ostensibly Iranian regions as well. Valih describes the unintelligibility of Baba Fighani Shirazi's verse to the Timurid court at Herat (Losensky, *Welcoming Fighānī*, 48). Also see Kinra, "This Noble Science," 362–64.

90. On the late Safavid ethos as articulated by Tahir Nasrabadi, see Schwartz, "Bâzgasht-i adabî," 37–40.

91. Ārzū, *Majma'*, 1:240–68. Arzu's entry explicitly corrects mistakes in previous *tazkirih*s, such as Tahir Nasrabadi's erroneous place of origin for Bidil as Lahore, and defends him against attacks by Irani poets and "their sycophants" in Hindustan. Arzu also includes twenty-seven pages of his poetry. For more on Bidil, see Keshavmurthy, "Bīdil's Portrait"; Pellò, "Persian as Passe-Partout"; Schwartz, "Local Lives of a Transregional Poet"; and Mikkelson, "Of Parrots and Crows."

92. For Valih's Bidil, see Vālih, *Riyāz*, 1:406–11.

93. Losensky, *Welcoming Fighānī*, 49–50. For Valih's entry on Fighani, see Vālih, *Riyāz*, 3:1616–24.

94. Vafa's paternal descent is from Sayyid Mirza Hashim Husayni, and his maternal descent is from Mawlana 'Abd al-Razzaq Qiyas Lahiji (Ārzū, *Majma'*, 3:1783).

95. Vafa seems to have been a lackadaisical student and prone to drink. Arzu mentioned that, though his poetry had potential, it could be great if only he studied more (Ārzū, *Majma'*, 3:1783).

96. Āzar, *Ātashkadih*, 4:681. Massumah was the sister of the eighth Shiʻi Imam, Riza and her tomb is a revered shrine.

97. Vālih, *Rīyāz*, 4:2474–75.

98. For instance, Azad Bilgrami's absence from the *Atashkadih* is curious, since he was a sayyid. The only post-sixteenth-century Timurid source Azar seems to have been able to access, however, was Valih's *Riyaz*, from which Azad was absent. Azar also dismisses poetic luminaries born in Iran, such as Zuhuri (*Ātashkadih*, 1:266–67) and Saʼib (1: 122–24), whose aesthetic style he abjures.

99. Āzar, *Ātashkadih*, 4:681.

100. See, for instance, the entry on ʻAli, whom Azar describes as a close friend and great painter who only "sometimes" composed poetry. This entry is longer than any contemporary poet with whom Azar did not have a personal relationship (Āzar, *Ātashkadih*, 4:628–29.

101. Āzar, *Ātashkadih*, 4:27.

102. For instance, in the late sixteenth century, Sharif went to Herat and then, upon the invasion of Abdullah Khan Uzbeg, to the Qutb Shahi court in Golconda (Āzar, *Ātashkadih*, 4:42). Hilmi went to Timurid domains and spent some time in the service of Prince Dara Shikoh, Shahjahan's eldest son (Āzar, 4:30).

103. Ārzū, *Majmaʻ*, 1:123–24.

104. Ibid., 1:124.

105. Ibid;, 3:1783.

106. Vālih, *Rīyāz*, 1:338–39.

107. Ironically, Azar also elides this life in Isfahan, pinning him to Hamadan (Āzar, *Ātashkadih*, 4:484).

108. Ārzū, *Majmaʻ*, 1:169.

109. For more on this popular courtly art, see Busch, *Poetry of Kings*, 153–63.

110. For more on this rivalry and Mir's *tazkirih*, see Pritchett, "A Long History," 866–70.

111. Qizilbash Khan is also featured in one of the *lat̤āʼif* (amusing tales) at the end of Mir's memoir (Mīr, *Zikr-i Mir*, 1999, 137–38). Shafiq's inclusion of Umid in *Chamanistan*, written in response to Mir's disparagement of Deccani *Rīkhta* poets, demonstrates that Umid was claimed even by contesting visions of *Rīkhta* community.

112. For an example of a bilingual poet, see the entry on Muʻizz Fitrat Musavi, a student of Arzu who also has an entry in the *Majmaʻ* (Mīr, *Nikāt*, 1979: 26).

113. Mīr, *Nikāt*, 23. Naim notes that the present version of the *Nikat* is a revision or abridgement of an earlier version that caused a great uproar in Delhi and spurred his contemporaries to write *tazkirih*s in response (translator's introduction to *Zikr-i Mir*, 8).

114. Mīr, *Nikāt*, 24–25.

115. See, for instance, Malik, "Muslim Culture and Reform."

116. Mīr, *Nikāt*, 28–29.

Coda: Memories and Multiplicity (Lost and Lingering)

1. This story was told to me by Hasan Behbehany (b. 1924), my mother's first cousin, who, beginning in the late 1930s, watched many of his generation migrate to Iran. Along with part of my maternal grandfather's family, he lived between Bengal and Burma until 1959, when he migrated to Pakistan and then, in 1980, to the United States. See also Behbehany, *Mother's Prayers*, 25–26.

2. Anderson, *Imagined Communities*, 6.

3. Ibid., 12.

4. For example, Chatterjee, *Nation and Its Fragments*, 3–13.

5. Ibid., 7. A good example of this shift in language is the early Bengali reformer Raja Rammohan Roy (1772–1833). In addition to his career in service to the East India Company's administration as a munshi, Roy is remembered primarily for his ideological founding of the *Brahmo Samaj* self-reform movement and his anti-Sati activism. His prolific output in newspapers and pamphlets included his *Mirat al-Akhbar* (1822), published in Persian. During the next decade, he went from writing in Persian to writing in Bengali and then in English, a progression indicative of larger epistemological shifts (Mani, *Contentious Traditions* 42–82).

6. For an initial foray, see Kia, "Indian Friends."

7. In addition, Safavid and Timurid paintings through the seventeenth century included rival rulers, each acknowledging the other yet portraying him as slightly subordinate (Koch, "How the Mughal *Pādshāhs* Referenced Iran").

8. I expand on the ways the non-Persianate and non-Muslim were given proximity (or not) in Kia, "Necessary Ornaments of Place."

9. On the meaning of this word, acquired in European struggles with the Ottoman Empire and a reflection of European conceptions of commonality, see Casale, "Ethnic Composition." In the course of arguing against the ethnic meaning of *Turk* in the early modern Ottoman context, Casale nevertheless accepts that there were (other) ethnicities (125).

10. Parkes, "Milk Kinship in Islam," 315. Parkes's critique of the anthropology of milk kinship is helpful in parsing these thoughts. This scholarship "always presupposes a concealed or 'implicit' somatic eugenics designed 'to prevent a deleterious mix of bodily substances'"—that is, insists on biological understandings of kinship that relate milk to blood (315).

11. Butler, *Gender Trouble*, 182.

12. Ibid., 182–83.

13. See Kia, "Moral Refinement and Manhood."

14. Schwartz, "Transregional Persianate Library." Schwartz's selection of *tazkirih*s is limited to those described in catalogs, encyclopedic works on *tazkirih*s, or published texts. It is further limited by other features (such as having a date and title). Texts that fall outside this purview, such as a *tazkirih* on women poets largely focused on Qajar

women (1849), also referenced Hindustani poets (Anonymous, *Tazkira-yi Ashʿār-i Zanān*, ff. 11–14). Inclusion of Hindustani poets continued through the early twentieth century (Ansarī Isfahānī, *Biographical Dictionary*, for example 6, 54, and 88).

15. Akhūndzādih, *Maktūbāt*. For more on this text, see Kia, "Indian Friends," 401–3.

16. Kia, "Indian Friends."

17. This observation is not particularly original. In Indian Ocean studies, discussion of the long and storied history of Gujarati merchants has proposed that we think of social, economic, and cultural ties to East Africa and West Asia as integral to Gujarat as its hinterlands. See, for instance, Alpers, *The Indian Ocean*, 88–89, 115–16; and his classic "Gujarat and the Trade of East Africa."

Bibliography

Primary Sources

Abu'l-Fazl, *The History of Akbar [Akbarnāma]*. Edited and translated by Wheeler M. Thackston. 5 volumes [and counting]. Cambridge: Harvard University Press, Murty Classical Library of India, 2015–2019.

———. *Akbarnāma*. Manuscript, British Library, London, n.d. Or. 12988.

Aftabachi, Jawhar. "Tazkirat al-Vaqiʿāt." In *Three Memoirs of Homayun*, vol. 1, edited and translated by Wheeler M. Thackston, 118–29. Costa Mesa, CA: Mazda, 2009.

Ākhūndzādih, Fath ʿAlī. *Maktūbāt-i Mīrzā Fath ʿAli Ākhundzādih*. Tehran[?]: Intishārāt-i Mard-i Imrūz, 1985.

Amīr Khusraw Dihlavī, *Dībāchih-yi Dīvān-i Ghurrat al-Kamāl*. Edited by Vazīr al-Hasan ʿĀbīdī. Lahore: National Committee, 1975.

Anonymous, *Majmūʿih*. Manuscript. British Library, London, n.d. IO Islamic 379.

Anonymous, *Tazkira-'i Ashʿār-i Zanān-i Vilāyat-i Īrān Va-ghayruhu Musammá Ba-Javāhir al-ʿAjāyib*. Manuscript. Houghton Library, Harvard University, 1849. MS Persian 92. Available online at https://iiif.lib.harvard.edu/manifests/view /drs:13506141$11 (accessed March 11, 2019).

Ansarī Isfahānī, Shaykh Hasan ibn ʿAlī Jabirī. *Biographical Dictionary of Selected Women Poets*, Majlis Library, Museum and Document Center, Tehran, n.d. MS 13890. Available online at http://www.qajarwomen.org/en/items/1018A4.html (accessed January 29, 2013).

Ārzū, Sirāj al-Dīn ʿAlī Khān. *Tazkirih-yi Majmaʿ al-Nafāʾis*. Edited by Zib al-Nissāʾ ʿAlī Khān, Mihr Nūr Muhammad Khān, and Muhammad Sarfarāz Zafar. 3 vols. Islamabad: Markaz-i Tahqīqāt-i Fārsī-i Īrān va Pākistān, 2004–2006.

'Attār, Farīd al-Dīn. *Farid ad-Din 'Attār's Memorial of God's Friends: Lives and Sayings of Sufis*. Translated by Paul Losensky. New York: Paulist Press, 2009.

Aurangābādī, Shāhnavāz Khān. *Ma'āsir al-Umarā*. Edited by Mawlavī 'Abd al-Rahīm. 3 vols. Calcutta: Asiatic Society of Bengal, 1888–1892.

———. *The Maāthir-ul-Umarā: Being Biographies of the Muhammadan and Hindu Officers of the Timurid Sovereigns of India from 1500 to About 1780 A.D.* 2nd ed. Translated by H. Beveridge. Edited by Baini Prashad. 3 vols. Patna, India: Janaki Prakashan, 1979.

Āzād Bilgrāmī, Ghulām 'Alī. *Khizānih-yi 'Āmirih*. Kānpūr, India: Munshī Naval Kishur, 1871.

———. *Daftar-i Sānī-yi Ma'āsir al-Kirām, Mawsām bih Sarv-i Āzād*. Edited by 'Abdullah Khān and Mawlavī 'Abd al-Haqq. Lahore: n.p., 1913.

———. *Khizānih-yi 'Āmirih*. Edited by Nāsir Nīkūbakht and Shakīl Aslam Bayg. Tehran: Pizhūhishgāh-i 'Ulūm-i Insānī va Mutāla'āt-i Farhangī, 2011 AD/1390 SH.

Āzar Baygdilī, Lutf 'Alī ibn Āqā Khān. *Ātashkadih*. 1336–1378 AH. Edited by Hasan Sādāt Nāsirī and Mīr Hāshim Muhaddas. 4 vols. Tehran: Amīr Kabīr, 1957–1999.

Babur, Zahiruddin Muhammad. *The Baburnama: Memoirs of Babur, Prince and Emperor*. Translated by Wheeler M. Thackston. New York: Modern Library, 2002.

Begam, Qamar Jahān. *Princess Jahān Ārā Begam: Her Life and Works*. Karachi: S. M. Hamid Ali, 1991.

Behbehany, Hasan. *Mother's Prayers: The Autobiography of Hasan Behbehany*. Albany, OR: LifeWriter Personal Histories, 2016.

Bihbahānī, Āqā Ahmad ibn Muhammad 'Alī. *Mir'āt al-Ahvāl-i Jahān Numā*. Edited by 'Alī Davvānī. Tehran: Markaz-i Farhangī-yi Qibla, 1993 AD/1372 SH.

Davvānī, Jalāl al-Dīn. *Akhlāq-i Jalālī*. 1391 AH. Edited by 'Abdullah Ma'sūdī Ārānī. Tehran: Intishārāt-i Ittilā'at, 2011.

Emin, Joseph. *The Life and Adventures of Joseph Emin, an Armenian, Written in English by Himself*. 2nd ed. Edited by Amy Apcar. Calcutta: Baptist Mission Press, 1918.

Ferdowsi, Abolqasem. *Shahnameh: The Persian Book of Kings*. Translated by Dick Davis. New York: Penguin, 2007.

Fuzūnī Astarābādī, Mīr Muhammad Hāshim. *Futūhat-i 'Ādil Shāhī*. Manuscript. British Library, London, n.d. Add. 27,251.

Hāfiz Shīrāzī, Shams al-Dīn Muhammad. *Dīvān-i Hāfiz, az nuskhih-yi Ghanī-yi Qazvīnī, ba-khatt-i Mas'ūd Mahdīkhānī*. Tehran: Intishārāt-i Mihr-i Īrān, 2002 AD/1381 SH.

Hākim, 'Abd al-Hakīm. *Tazkirih-yi Mardum Dīdih*. Edited by Sayyid 'Abdullah. Lahore: Panjābī Adabī Akaydaymī, 1961.

Hazīn Lāhījī, Shaykh Muhammad 'Alī. *The Life of Sheikh Mohammed Ali Hazin*. Translated by F. C. Belfour. London: Oriental Translation Fund, 1830.

———. *Tārīkh va Safarnāma-yi Hazīn*. Edited by 'Alī Davvānī. Tehran: Markaz-i Asnād-i Inqilāb-i Islāmī, 1996 AD/ 1375 SH.

———. *Tazkirat al-Mu'āsirīn*. Edited by Ma'sūmih Sālik. Tehran: Nashr-i Sāyih, 1996 AD/ 1375 SH.

———. *Dīvān-i Hazīn-i Lāhījī*. Edited by Zabīhullah Sāhibkār. Tehran: Nashr-i Sāyih, 2005 AD/ 1384 SH.

Isfahānī, Abū Tālib Khān ibn Muhammad. *Masīr-i Tālibī yā, Safarnāma-yi Mīrzā Abū Tālib Khān*. 4th ed. Edited by Husayn Khadīvjam. Tehran: Shirkat-i Intishārāt-i 'Ilmī va Farhangī, 2004 AD/1383 SH.

Kashmīrī, 'Abd al-Karīm. *Memoirs of Khojeh Abdulkurreem, Who Accompanied Nadir Shah on His Return from Hindostan to Persia, from Whence He Travelled to Baghdad, Damascus and Aleppo, and After Visiting Medina and Mecca, Embarked at Jeddeh and Sailed to Hooghly in Bengal; Including the History of Hindostan, from 1739 to 1749*. Translated by Francis Gladwin. London: J.S. Barr, 1793.

———. *Bayān-i Wāqi': Sarguzasht-i Ahvāl-i Nādir Shāh va Safarhā-yi Munnasif-i Khwājih 'Abd al-Karīm ibn Khwājih 'Āqibat Mahmūd Kashmīrī*. Edited by K. B. Nasim. Lahore: Research Society of Pakistan, 1970.

Khalīl Banārasī, 'Alī Ibrāhīm Khān. *Suhuf-i Ibrāhīm: Bakhsh-i Mu'āsirān*. Edited by Mīr Hāshim Muhaddis. Tehran: Anjuman-i Āsār va Mufākhir-i Farhangī, 2006 AD/1384 SH.

Ludī, Shīr 'Alī Khān. *Tazkirih-yi Mir'āt al-Khayāl*. Edited by Bihrūz Safarzādih. Tehran: Rawzanih, 1998 AD/1377 SH.

Maftūn, Hājjī 'Ali Mīrzā. *Zubdat al-Akhbār fī Savānih al-Asfār: Safarnāma-yi Īrān, Qarn-i Nuzdahum-i Mīlādī*. Edited by Zakera Sharif Qasemi. New Delhi: Islamic Wonders Bureau, 2003.

Mīr, Mīr Muhammad Taqī. *Zikr-i Mīr, Ya'nī Hazrat-i Mīr Taqī Mīr ki Khūd Nivisht Savānih 'Umrī*. Edited by 'Abd al-Haqq. Aurangabad, India: Anjuman-i Taraqqī-yi Urdū, 1928.

———. *Nikāt al-Shu'arā*. Edited by 'Abd al-Haqq. Karachi: Anjuman-i Taraqqī-yi Urdū-yi Pākistān, 1979.

———. *Zikr-i Mir: The Autobiography of the Eighteenth Century Mughal Poet Mir Muhammad Taqi "Mir."* Translated by C. M. Naim. New Delhi: Oxford University Press, 1999.

Mīr Khvānd [MirKhond], Muhammad ibn Khāvandshāh ibn Mahmud. *History of the Early Kings of Persia: From Kaiomars, the First of the Peshdadian Dynasty, to the Conquest of Iran by Alexander the Great*. Translated by David Shea. London: Printed for the Oriental Translation Fund of Great Britain and Ireland, 1832.

———. *Tārīkh-i Rawzat al-Safā fī Sīrat al-Anbiyā' va al-Mulūk va al-Khulafā'*. Edited by Jamshīd Kiyānfar. 15 vols. Tehran: Asātīr, 2001 AD/1380 SH.

Muhammad Rabīʿ ibn Muhammad Ibrāhīm. *Safīnih-yi Sulaymānī: Safarnāma-yi Safīr-i Īrān bih Sīʾām*. Edited by ʿAbbās Fārūqī. 2nd ed. Tehran: Muʾasasih-yi Intishārāt va chāp-i Dānishgāh-i Tehran, Pāʾīz, 1999 AD/1378 SH.

Nahāvandī, ʿAbd al-Bāqī. *Maʾāsir-i Rahīmī*. Vol. 3. Edited by ʿAbd al-Husayn Navāʾī. Tehran: Anjuman-i Āsār va Mufākhir-i Farhangī, 2002 AD/1381 SH.

Nasrābādī, Muhammad Tāhir. *Tazkirih-yi Nasrābādī*. Edited by Ahmad Mudaqqiq Yazdī. Yazd, Iran: Dānishgāh-i Yazd, 1999 AD/1378 SH.

Navāʾī, ʿAbd al-Husayn, ed. *Shāh Tahmāsb Safavī, Majmūʿ-yi Asnād va Mukātibāt-i Tārīkhī Hamrāh bā Yāddāsht-hā-yi Tafsīlī*. Tehran: Bunyād-i Farhang-i Īrān, 1971 AD/1350 SH.

Navāʾī, Mir ʿAli Shir. "Muhakamat al-Lughatain." In *Islamic Central Asia: An Anthology of Historical Sources*, edited by Scott C. Levi and Ron Sela, 184–87. Bloomington: Indiana University Press, 2010.

Qazvīnī, ʿAbd al-Nabī Fakhr al-Zamānī. *Tazkirih-yi Maykhānih*. Edited by Ahmad Gulchīn Maʿānī. Tehran: Iqbāl, 1984 AD/1363 SH.

Rāzī, Amin ibn Ahmad. *Haft Iqlīm*. Edited by Javād Fāzil. 3 vols. Tehran: Kitābfurūshī-yi ʿAli Akbar ʾIlmī va Kitābfurūshī-yi Adabīyyih, 1960.

———. *Tazkirih-yi Haft Iqlīm*. Edited by Muhammad Rizā Tāhirī. 3 vols. Tehran: Surūsh, 1999 AD/1378 SH.

Saʿdī, Shaykh Mushrifuddin of Shiraz. *The Gulistan (Rose Garden) of Saʿdi: Bilingual English and Persian Edition with Vocabulary*. Translated by Wheeler M. Thackston. Bethesda, MD: Ibex, 2008.

Safarnāma-yi Manzūm-i Hajj. Edited by Rasul Jafarian. Qum, Iran: Sāzmān-i Jughrāfiyā-yi Nīrūhā-yi Musallah, 2007 AD/1386 SH (originally 1996).

Sarkhvush, Muhammad Afzal. *Kalimāt al-Shuʿarā*. Edited by ʿAlī Rizā Qazvah. Tehran: Markaz-i Pizhūhish-i Kitābkhānih, Mūzih va Markaz-i Asnād-i Majlis-i Shūrā-yi Islāmī, 2011 AD/1389 SH.

Shafiq Aurangābādī, Lachmī Naraʾin. *Bisāt al-Ghanāʾim*. Manuscript. British Library, London, 1799. Add. 26, 274.

———. *Tazkirih-yi Gul-i Raʾnā*. Part 2. Hyderabad: ʿAhd-i Afarīn, 1900 AD/1223 SH.

———. *Chamanistān-i Shuʿarā*. Edited by ʿAbdul Haqq. Aurangabad: Anjuman-i Taraqqī-yi Urdū, 1928.

———. *Shām-i Gharībān*. Edited by Muhammad Akbar al-Dīn Siddīqī. Karachi: Anjuman-i Taraqqī-yi Urdū, 1977.

———. *Gul-i Raʾnā*. Manuscript. British Library, London, n.d. IO Islamic 3692.

Shūshtarī, Mīr ʿAbd al-Latīf Khān. *Tuhfat al-ʾĀlam va Zīl al-Tuhfih*. Edited by Samad Muvahhid. Tehran: Kitābkhānih-yi Tahūrī, 1984 AD/1363 SH.

Stewart, Charles. Translator's preface. In *The Travels of Mirza Abu Taleb Khan in Asia, Africa, and Europe: During the Years 1799, 1800, 1801, 1802, and 1803*, translated by

Charles Stewart, edited by Daniel O'Quinn. Peterborough, ON: Broadview Press, 2009.

Tabataba'i, Ghulam Husayn. *A Translation of the Seir Mutaqherin; or View of Modern Times.* Translated by Nota-Manus. 4 vols. Calcutta: R. Cambray & Co., 1926 (original 1786).

Tapish, Mirzā Jān. *Shams al-Bayān* [The Illuminating Sun of Explanation: A Collection of Urdu Idioms Explained in Persian with Quotation from the Poets]. Murshidabad, India: n.p., 1848 AD/1265 SH.

Tūsī, Nāsir al-Dīn. *Akhlāq-i Nāsirī.* Edited by Mujtabā Mīnu'ī and 'Alīrizā Haydarī. Tehran: Khawrazmī, 1984 AD/1364 SH.

'Unsur al-Ma'ālī Kaykāvūs ibn Iskandar ibn Qābūs. *Qābūsnāma.* Edited by Ghulām Husayn Yūsufī. Tehran: Intishārāt-i 'Ilmī va Farhangī, 1989 AD/1368 SH.

Vā'iz Kāshifī, Husayn. *Akhlāk-i Muhsinī, The Morals of the Beneficent.* Hertford, UK: Stephen Austin, 1850a.

———. *Akhlāk-i Muhsinī; or, The Morals of the Beneficient.* Literally translated from the Persian of Husain Vāiz Kāshifī by the Rev. H. G. Keene. Hertford: Stephen Austin, 1850b.

———. *Akhlāq-i Muhsinī.* Tehran: Bunyād-i Farhang-i Īrān, 1913 AD/1331 AH.

Vā'iz Kāshifī, Mawlāna Husayn. *Futuvvatnāmih-yi Sultānī.* Edited by M. J. Mahjūb. Tehran: Bunyād-i Farhang-i Īrān, 1971 AD/1350 SH.

Vālih Dāghistānī, 'Alī Qulī. *Tazkirih-yi Rīyāz al-Shu'arā.* Edited by Muhsin Nājī Nasrābādī. 5 vols. Tehran: Asātīr, 2005 AD/1384 SH.

Secondary Sources

'Abbās, Hasan. *Ahvāl va Āsār-i Mīr Ghulām 'Ali Āzād Bilgrāmī.* Tehran: Bunyād-i Mawqūfāt-i Duktur Mahmūd Afshār, 2005.

Abi-Mershed, Osama. "The Transmission of Knowledge and the Education of the 'Ulama in Late Sixteenth Century Maghrib: A Study of the Biographical Dictionary of Muhammad ibn Maryam." In *Auto/biography and the Construction of Identity and Community in the Middle East,* edited by Mary Ann Fay, 19–36. New York: Palgrave, 2002.

Abisaab, Rula Jurdi. *Converting Persia: Religion and Power in the Safavid Empire.* London: I.B. Tauris, 2004.

Ahmadi, Wali. "The Institution of Persian Literature and the Genealogy of Bahar's 'Stylistics'." *British Journal of Middle Eastern Studies* 31, no. 2 (2004): 141–52.

Ahmed Asif, Manan. *A Book of Conquest: The Chachnama and Muslim Origins in South Asia.* Cambridge: Harvard University Press, 2016.

Ahmed, Shahab. *What Is Islam?: The Importance of Being Islamic.* Princeton, NJ: Princeton University Press, 2016.

Akiner, Shirin. "Islam, the State and Ethnicity in Central Asia in Historical Perspective." *Religion, State, and Society* 24, nos. 2–3 (1996): 91–132.

Alam, Muzaffar. *The Crisis of Empire in Mughal North India: Awadh and the Punjab, 1707–48.* Delhi: Oxford University Press, 1986.

———. "The Culture and Politics of Persian in Precolonial Hindustan." In *Literary Cultures in History: Reconstructions from South Asia*, edited by Sheldon Pollock, 131–98. Berkeley: University of California Press, 2003.

———. *The Languages of Political Islam: India, 1200–1800.* Chicago: University of Chicago Press, 2004.

Alam, Muzaffar, and Sanjay Subrahmanyam. "The Deccan Frontier and Mughal Expansion, c. 1600: Contemporary Perspectives." *Journal of the Economic and Social History of the Orient* 47, no. 3 (2004): 357–89.

———. *Indo-Persian Travels in the Age of Discoveries, 1400–1800.* Cambridge: Cambridge University Press, 2007.

———. "Of Princes and Poets in Eighteenth-Century Lucknow." In *India's Fabled City: The Art of Courtly Lucknow*, edited by Stephen Markel, 187–97. Los Angeles: Los Angeles County Museum of Art, c. 2010.

———, Eds. *The Mughal State: 1526–1750.* New Delhi: Oxford University Press, 1998.

Alavi, Seema. *Islam and Healing: Loss and Recovery of an Indo-Muslim Medical Tradition, 1600–1900.* New York: Palgrave Macmillan, 2008.

Ali, M. Athar. *The Mughal Nobility Under Aurangzeb.* Rev. ed. Delhi: Oxford University Press, 1997.

Alpers, Edward A. "Gujarat and the Trade of East Africa, c. 1500–1800," *The International Journal of African Historical Studies* 9, no. 1 (1976): 22–44.

———. *The Indian Ocean in World History.* Oxford: Oxford University Press, 2014.

Altorki, Soraya. "Milk-Kinship in Arab Society: An Unexplored Problem in the Ethnography of Marriage." *Ethnology* 19, no. 2 (1980): 233–44.

Amanat, Abbas. "In Between the Madrasa and the Marketplace: The Designation of Clerical Leadership in Modern Shi'ism." In *Authority and Political Culture in Shi'ism*, edited by Said Amir Arjomand, 98–132. Albany: State University of New York Press, 1988.

———. *Resurrection and Renewal: The Making of the Babi Movement in Iran, 1844–1850.* Ithaca, NY: Cornell University Press, 1989.

———. *Pivot of the Universe: Nasir al-Din Shah Qajar and the Iranian Monarchy, 1831–1896.* Berkeley: University of California Press, 1997.

———. "The Kayanid Crown and Qajar Reclaiming of Royal Authority." *Iranian Studies* 34, nos. 1–4 (2001): 17–30.

———. "Introduction: Apocalyptic Anxieties and Millennial Hopes in the Salvation Religions of the Middle East." In *Imagining the End: Visions of Apocalypse from the Ancient Middle East to Modern America*, edited by Abbas Amanat and Magnus Bernhardsson, 1–19. London: I.B. Tauris, distributed by St. Martin's Press, 2002.

Amin, Shahid. *Conquest and Community: The Afterlife of Warrior Saint Ghazi Miyan.* Chicago: University of Chicago Press, 2016.

Anderson, Benedict. *Imagined Communities: Reflections on the Origin and Spread of Nationalism.* Rev. ed. London: Verso, 1991.

Anidjar, Gil. *The Jew, the Arab: A History of the Enemy.* Stanford, CA: Stanford University Press, 2003.

———. *Blood: A Critique of Christianity.* New York: Columbia University Press, 2014.

———. "The History of Race, the Race of History." *The Jewish Quarterly Review* 105, no. 4 (Fall 2015): 515–21.

Antrim, Zayde. *Routes and Realms: The Power of Place in the Early Islamic World.* Oxford: Oxford University Press, 2012.

Arjomand, Said Amir. "The Salience of Political Ethic in the Spread of Persianate Islam." *Journal of Persianate Studies* 1 (2008): 5–29.

———. "The Conception of Revolution in Persianate Political Thought." *Journal of Persianate Studies* 5 (2012): 1–16.

———. "Review Essay: A Decade of Persianate Studies." *Journal of Persianate Studies* 8, no. 2 (2015): 309–33.

Asad, Talal. "Kinship." In *Encyclopaedia of the Qur'ān*, General Editor: Jane Dammen McAuliffe. Washington, DC: Georgetown University, n.d. Available online at http://dx.doi.org/10.1163/1875-3922_q3_EQSIM_00250 (accessed March 14, 2017).

Asher, Catherine B., and Cynthia Talbot. *India Before Europe.* Cambridge: Cambridge University Press, 2006.

Askari, Nasrin. *The Medieval Reception of the Shāhnāma as a Mirror for Princes.* Leiden: Brill, 2016.

Aslanian, Sebouh David. *Dispersion History and the Polycentric Nation: The Role of Simeon Yerevantsi's Girk Or Koci Partavacar in the 18th Century National Revival.* Venice: S. Lazarus, 2004.

———. *From the Indian Ocean to the Mediterranean: The Global Trade Networks of Armenian Merchants from New Julfa.* Berkeley: University of California Press, 2011.

Ateş, Sabri. *The Ottoman-Iranian Borderlands: Making a Boundary, 1843–1914.* New York: Cambridge University Press, 2015.

Auer, Blain H. *Symbols of Authority in Medieval Islam: History, Religion and Muslim Legitimacy in the Delhi Sultanate.* London: I.B. Tauris, 2012.

Avery, Peter. "Foreword: Hāfiz of Shīrāz." In *Hafiz and the Religion of Love in Classical Persian Poetry*, edited by Leonard Lewisohn. London: I.B. Tauris, 2010.

Axworthy, Michael. *The Sword of Persia: Nader Shah, from Tribal Warrior to Conquering Tyrant.* London: I.B. Tauris, 2006.

Babaie, Sussan, Kathryn Babayan, and Ina Baghdiantz-McCabe. *Slaves of the Shah: New Elites of Safavid Iran*. London: I.B. Tauris, distributed by Palgrave Macmillan, 2004.

Babayan, Kathryn. "The Safavid Synthesis: From Qizilbash Islam to Imamite Shi'ism." *Iranian Studies* 27, no. 1/4 (1994): 135–61.

———. *Mystics, Monarchs and Messiahs: Cultural Landscapes of Early Modern Iran*. Cambridge: Harvard Center for Middle East Studies, distributed by Harvard University Press, 2002.

———. "'In Spirit We Ate Each Other's Sorrow': Female Companionship in Seventeenth-Century Safavi Iran." In *Islamicate Sexualities: Translations Across Temporal Geographies of Desire*, edited by Kathryn Babayan and Afsaneh Najmabadi, 239–74. Cambridge, MA: Center for Middle Eastern Studies of Harvard University, distributed by Harvard University Press, 2008.

———. "The Topography of Travel in Early Modern Persianate Landscapes," *Harvard Library Bulletin* 23, nos. 1–2 (2012): 25–34.

Balabanlilar, Lisa. "Lords of the Auspicious Conjunction: Turco-Mongol Imperial Identity on the Subcontinent." *Journal of World History* 18, no. 1 (2007): 1–39.

———. *Imperial Identity in the Mughal Empire: Memory and Dynastic Politics in Early Modern South and Central Asia*. London: I.B. Tauris, 2012.

Banks, Marcus. *Ethnicity: Anthropological Constructions*. London: Routledge, 1996.

Bashir, Shahzad. *Sufi Bodies: Religion and Society in Medieval Islam*. New York: Columbia University Press, 2011.

———. "On Islamic Time: Rethinking Chronology in the Historiography of Muslim Societies." *History and Theory* 53, no. 4 (2014): 519–44.

———. "The Origins and Rhetorical Evolution of the Term Qizilbāsh in Persianate Literature." *Journal of the Economic and Social History of the Orient* 57, no. 3 (2014): 364–91.

———. "A Perso-Islamic Universal Chronicle in Its Historical Context." In *History and Religion: Narrating a Religious Past*, edited by Otto Bernd-Christian, Susanne Rau, and Jrg Rpke, 209–26. Berlin; Boston: Walter de Gruyter, 2015.

Bayly, C. A. *Origins of Nationality in South Asia: Patriotism and Ethical Government in the Making of Modern India*. New Delhi: Oxford University Press, 2003 (originally 1998).

Berlekamp, Persis. "Administering Art, History, and Science in the Mongol Empire." In *Pearls on a String: Artists, Patrons, and Poets at the Great Islamic Courts*, edited by Amy S. Landau, 53–85. Baltimore: Walters Art Museum, 2015.

Beveridge, A., and Beatrice Forbes Manz. "Mīrkhwānd." In *Encyclopaedia of Islam*, 2nd ed., edited by P. Bearman, Th. Bianquis, C. E. Bosworth, E. van Donzel, and W. P. Heinrichs. Brill Online, available at https://referenceworks.brillonline.com /entries/encyclopaedia-of-islam-2/mirkhwand-SIM_5224 (accessed June 21, 2019).

Bildhauer, Bettina. "Blood in Medieval Cultures." *History Compass* 4, no. 6 (2006): 1049–59.

Binbaş, Ilker Evrim. "Oğuz Khan Narratives." In *Encyclopedia Iranica*, online edition, 2010. Available online at http://www.iranicaonline.org/articles/oguz -khan-narratives (accessed February 26, 2017).

———. *Intellectual Networks in Timurid Iran: Sharaf al-Dīn 'Alī Yazdī and the Islamicate Republic of Letters.* Cambridge: Cambridge University Press, 2016.

Bland, N. "On the Earliest Persian Biography of Poets by Muhammad Aufi and On Some Other Works of the Class Called Tazkirat ul Shuara." *Journal of Royal Asiatic Society of Great Britain and Ireland* 9 (1848): 111–76.

Blow, David. *Shah Abbas: The Ruthless King Who Became an Iranian Legend.* London: I.B. Tauris, 2009.

Bokhari, Afshan. "Imperial Transgressions and Spiritual Investitures: A Begam's 'Ascension' in Seventeenth Century Mughal India." *Journal of Persianate Studies* 4, no. 1 (2011): 86–108.

———. "Masculine Modes of Female Subjectivity: The Case of Jahanara Begum." In *Speaking of the Self: Gender, Performance, and Autobiography in South Asia*, edited by Anshu Malhotra and Siobhan Lambert-Hurley, 165–202. Durham, NC: Duke University Press, 2015.

Bonakdarian, Mansour. *Britain and the Iranian Constitutional Revolution of 1906–1911: Foreign Policy, Imperialism, and Dissent.* Syracuse, NY: Syracuse University Press, with the Iran Heritage Foundation, 2006.

Bosworth, C. Edmund. "Mawara' al-Nahr." In *Encyclopedia Iranica*, online edition, 2011. Available online at http://www.iranicaonline.org/articles/mawara-al-nahr (accessed August 21, 2014).

———. "Ḡozz: ii. Tribe." In *Encyclopedia Iranica*, online edition, 2002. Available at http://www.iranicaonline.org/articles/gozz#tribe (accessed February 26, 2017).

Brack, Jonathan Z. "Mediating Sacred Kingship: Conversion and Sovereignty in Mongol Iran." PhD diss., University of Michigan, 2016.

Browne, Edward G. *A Literary History of Persia.* Vol. 4, *Modern Times, 1500–1924.* Rev. ed. Bethesda, MD: Iranbooks, 1997.

Brookshaw, Dominic Parviz. "Odes of a Poet-Princess: The *Ghazal*s of Jahān-Malik Khātun." *Iran* 43 (2005): 173–95.

———. "Have You Heard the One About the Man from Qazvin? Regionalist Humor in the Works of Ubayd-i Zākānī." In *Ruse and Wit: The Humorous in Arabic, Persian, and Turkish Narrative*, edited by Dominic Parviz Brookshaw. Boston: Ilex, distributed by Harvard University Press, 2012.

Buehler, Arthur F. *Sufi Heirs of the Prophet: The Indian Naqshbandiyya and the Rise of the Mediating Sufi Shaykh.* Columbia: University of South Carolina Press, 2008.

Burbank, Jane, and Frederick Cooper. *Empires in World History: Power and the Politics of Difference.* Princeton, NJ: Princeton University Press, 2008.

Busch, Allison. *Poetry of Kings: The Classical Hindi Literature of Mughal India.* New York: Oxford University Press, c. 2011.

Butler, Judith. *Gender Trouble: Feminism and the Subversion of Identity.* New York: Routledge, 1999 (original 1990).

Butler Brown, Katherine. "Dargah Quli Khan's Strange Vision: Mughals, Music and the Muraqqaʻ-i Delhī," Centre of South Asian Studies, University of Cambridge, Occasional Paper, no. 4 (2003): 1–20.

Cahen, Cl., G. Deverdun, and P. M. Holt. "Ghuzz." In *Encyclopaedia of Islam*, 2nd ed., edited by P. Bearman, Th. Bianquis, C. E. Bosworth, E. van Donzel, and W. P. Heinrichs. Brill Online, available at https://referenceworks.brillonline .com/entries/encyclopaedia-of-islam-2/ghuzz-COM_0240 (accessed June 21, 2019).

Calmard, Jean. "Safavid Persia in Indo-Persian Sources and in Timurid-Mughal Perception." In *The Making of Indo-Persian Culture: Indian and French Studies*, edited by Muzaffar Alam, Francoise 'Nalini' Delvoye, and Marc Gaborieau, 351–92. New Delhi: Manohar, 2000.

Carsten, Janet. *After Kinship: New Departures in Anthropology.* Cambridge: Cambridge University Press, 2004.

Casale, Giancarlo. "The Ethnic Composition of Ottoman Ship Crews and the 'Rumi Challenge' to Portuguese Identity." *Medieval Encounters* 13, no. 1 (2007): 122–44.

Chandra, Satish. *Parties and Politics at the Mughal Court, 1707–1740.* 4th ed. New Delhi: Oxford University Press, 2002.

Chatterjee, Indrani. Introduction. In *Unfamiliar Relations: Family and History in South Asia*, edited by Indrani Chatterjee. New Brunswick, NJ: Rutgers University Press, 2004, 3–45.

———. *Forgotten Friends: Monks, Marriages, and Memories of Northeast India.* New Delhi: Oxford University Press, 2013.

———. "Connected Histories and the Dream of Decolonial History." *South Asia: Journal of South Asian Studies* 41, no. 1 (2018): 69–86.

Chatterjee, Kumkum. *The Cultures of History in Early Modern India: Persianization and Mughal Culture in Bengal.* New Delhi: Oxford University Press, 2009.

Chatterjee, Partha. *The Nation and Its Fragments: Colonial and Postcolonial Histories.* Princeton, NJ: Princeton University Press, 1993.

Cheema, G. S. *The Forgotten Mughals: A History of the Later Emperors of the House of Babar, 1707–1857.* New Delhi: Manohar, 2002.

Clarke, Morgan. *Islam and New Kinship: Reproductive Technology and the Shariah in Lebanon.* New York: Berghahn Books, 2009.

Cohn, Bernard S. *Colonialism and Its Forms of Knowledge: The British in India* (Princeton, NJ: Princeton University Press, c. 1996).

Cole, Juan R. I. *Roots of North Indian Shi'ism in Iran and Iraq: Religion and State in Awadh, 1722–1859.* Berkeley: University of California Press, 1988.

———. "Mirror of the World: Iranian 'Orientalism' and Early 19th-Century India," *Critique: Critical Middle Eastern Studies* 5 (1996): 41–60.

———. "Iranian Culture and South Asia, 1500–1900." In *Iran and the Surrounding World: Interactions in Culture and Cultural Politics*, edited by Nikki R. Keddie and Rudi Matthee, 15–35. Seattle: University of Washington Press, 2002.

Cooperson, Michael. "'Arabs' and 'Iranians:' The Uses of Ethnicity in the Early Abbasid Period." In *Islamic Cultures, Islamic Contexts: Essays in Honor of Professor Patricia Crone*, edited by Behnam Sadeghi, Asad Q. Ahmed, Adam Silverstein, and Robert Hoyland, 364–87. Leiden: Brill, 2015.

Csirkés, Ferenc. "'Chaghatay Oration, Ottoman Eloquence, Qizilbash Rhetoric': Turkic Literature in Safavid Persia," PhD diss., University of Chicago, 2016.

Dabashi, Hamid. *Iran: A People Interrupted.* New York: New Press, 2007.

Dadlani, Chanchal. "The 'Palais Indiens' Collection of 1774: Representing Mughal Architecture in Late Eighteenth-Century India." *Ars Orientalis* 39 (2010): 175–97.

Dadvar, Abolghasem. *Iranians in Mughal Politics and Society, 1606–1658.* New Delhi: Gyan, 1999.

Dale, Stephen Frederic. *Indian Merchants and Eurasian Trade, 1600–1750.* Cambridge: Cambridge University Press, 1994.

Dalrymple, William. *White Mughals: Love and Betrayal in Eighteenth-Century India.* London: HarperCollins, 2002.

Daniel, Elton L. "The Rise and Development of Persian Historiography." In *Persian Historiography*, edited by Charles Melville. Vol. X, *A History of Persian Literature*, 101–54. London: I.B. Tauris, 2012.

Darwish, Mahmoud. Acceptance speech for the Prince Claus Award in Amsterdam, December 1, 2004, Prince Claus Fund for Culture and Development. Available online at https://talinedv.com/2010/08/09/darwish-the-amsterdam-speech (accessed July 12, 2018).

Davis, Natalie Zemon. "Boundaries and the Sense of Self in Sixteenth-Century France." In *Reconstructing Individualism: Autonomy, Individuality, and the Self in Western Thought*, edited by Thomas C. Heller, et al., 53–63. Stanford, CA: Stanford University Press, 1986.

Davvānī, ʿAlī. Editor's Introduction. In *Mirʾāt al-Ahvāl-i Jahān Numā* [1372], by Āqā Ahmad ibn Muhammad ʿAlī Bihbahānī, 3–40. Tehran: Markaz-i Farhangī-yi Qiblih, 1993 or 1994.

————. Editor's Introduction. In *Tārīkh va Safarnāma-yi Hazīn* by Muhammad ʿAlī Hazīn Lāhījī, 16–140. Tehran: Markaz-i Asnād-i Inqilāb-i Islāmī, 1996 AD/1375 SH.

de Man, Paul. "Autobiography as De-facement." *MLN* 94, no. 5 (December 1979): 919–30.

De Nicola, Bruno. *Women in Mongol Iran: The Khātūns, 1206–1335*. Edinburgh: Edinburgh University Press, 2017.

Derrida, Jacques. *Aporias: Dying—Awaiting (One Another at) the "Limits of Truth" (Mourir—S'attendre Aux "Limites De La Vérité")*. Stanford, CA: Stanford University Press, 1993.

————. *Monolingualism of the Other, or, The Prosthesis of Origin*. Translated by Patrick Mensah. Stanford, CA: Stanford University Press, 1998.

Dhavan, P., and H. Pauwels. "Controversies Surrounding the Reception of Vali 'Dakhani' (1665?–1707?) in early *Tazkiras* of Urdu Poets." *Journal of the Royal Asiatic Society*, 25, no. 4 (2015): 625–46.

Dirks, Nicholas B. *Castes of Mind: Colonialism and the Making of Modern India*. Princeton, NJ: Princeton University Press, 2001.

Durand-Guedy, David, ed. *Turko-Mongol Rulers, Cities and City Life*. Leiden; Boston: Brill, 2013.

Eaton, Richard M. *The Rise of Islam and the Bengal Frontier, 1204–1760*. Berkeley: University of California Press, 1996.

Eaton, Richard M., and Philip B. Wagoner. *Power, Memory, Architecture: Contested Sites on India's Deccan Plateau, 1300–1600*. New Delhi: Oxford University Press, 2014.

Ernst, Carl W. "Reconfiguring South Asian Islam: From the 18th to the 19th Century." *Comparative Islamic studies* 5, no. 2 (2011): 247–72.

Faruqi, Shamur Rahman. "Unprivileged Power: The Strange Case of Persian (and Urdu) in Nineteenth Century India." *The Annual of Urdu Studies* (1998): 3–30.

Faruqui, Munis D. "At Empire's End: The Nizam, Hyderabad and 18th-Century India." *Modern Asian Studies* 43, no. 1 (2009): 5–43.

————. *The Princes of the Mughal Empire, 1504–1719*. Cambridge: Cambridge University Press, 2012.

Fay, Mary Ann, ed. *Auto/biography and the Construction of Identity and Community in the Middle East*. New York: Palgrave, 2002.

Fisher, Michael. "Asians in Britain: Negotiations of Identity Through Self-Representation." In *A New Imperial History: Culture, Identity, and Modernity in Britain and the Empire, 1660–1840*, edited by Kathleen Wilson, 91–112. Cambridge: Cambridge University Press, 2004.

————. *Counterflows to Colonialism: Indian Travellers and Settlers in Britain 1600–1857*. Delhi: Permanent Black, distributed by Orient Longman, 2004.

Flatt, Emma. "Young Manliness: Ethical Culture in the Gymnasiums of the Medieval

Deccan." In *Ethical Life in South Asia*, edited by Anand Pandian and Daud Ali, 153–73. Bloomington: Indiana University Press, 2010.

Floor, Willem, and Hasan Javadi. "The Role of Azerbaijani Turkish in Safavid Iran." *Iranian Studies* 46, no. 4 (2013): 569–81.

Foltz, Richard C. *Mughal India and Central Asia*. Karachi: Oxford University Press, 1998.

Gallagher, Amelia. "Shah Isma'il's Poetry in the *Silsilat al-Nasab-i Safawiyya*," *Iranian Studies* 44, no. 6 (2011): 895–911.

Garcia, Humberto. "A Stranger's Love for Ireland: Indo-Irish Xenophilia in *The Travels of Mirza Abu Taleb Khan* (1810, 1814)." *Common Knowledge* 23, no. 2 (2017): 232–53.

———. "Re-Orienting the Bluestockings: Chivalric Romance, Manliness, and Empire in Joseph Emin's Letters." *Huntington Library Quarterly* 81, no. 2 (2018): 227–55.

Gevorgyan, Khachik. "*Futuwwa* Varieties and the *Futuwwat-nāma* Literature: An Attempt to Classify *Futuwwa* and Persian *Futuwwat-nāmas*." *British Journal of Middle Eastern Studies*, 40, no. 1 (2013): 2–13.

Ghosh, Durba. "Decoding the Nameless: Gender, Subjectivity, and Historical Methodologies in Reading the Archives of Colonial India." In *A New Imperial History: Culture, Identity and Modernity in Britain and the Empire, 1660–1840*, edited by Kathleen Wilson, 297–316. Cambridge: Cambridge University Press, 2004.

———. *Sex and the Family in Colonial India*. Cambridge: Cambridge University Press, 2006.

Giladi, Avner. "Family." In *Encyclopaedia of the Qur'ān*, General Editor: Jane Dammen McAuliffe. Washington, DC: Georgetown University, n.d. Available online at http://dx.doi.org/10.1163/1875-3922_q3_EQSIM_00148 (accessed March 14, 2017).

Golden, Peter. "Ǧozz: i. Origins." In *Encyclopedia Iranica*, online edition, 2002. Available online at http://www.iranicaonline.org/articles/gozz#origins (accessed February 26, 2017).

———. "'Eternal Stones': Historical Memory and Notions of History Among the Early Turkish People." In *Turks in the Indian Subcontinent, Central and West Asia: The Turkish Presence in the Islamic World*, edited by Ismail K. Poonwala, 3–63. New Delhi: Oxford University Press, 2017.

Gordon, Stewart. "Introduction: Ibn Battuta and a Region of Robing." In *Robes of Honor: Khil'at in Pre-Colonial and Colonial India*, edited by Stewart Gordon, 1–30. New Delhi: Oxford University Press, 2003.

———. "Babur: Salt, Social Closeness and Friendship." *Studies in History* 33, no. 1 (2017): 82–97.

Goshgarian, Rachel. "Opening and Closing: Coexistence and Competition in Associations Based on *Futuwwa* in Late Medieval Anatolian Cities." *British Journal of Middle Eastern Studies* 40, no. 1 (2013): 36–52.

Gould, Rebecca. "The Geographies of 'Ajam: The Circulation of Persian Poetry from South Asia to the Caucasus." *The Medieval History Journal* 18, no. 1 (2015): 87–119.

Green, Nile. "The Uses of Books in a Late Mughal Takiyya: Persianate Knowledge Between Person and Paper." *Modern Asian Studies* 44, no. 2 (2010): 241–65.

———. *Making Space: Sufis and Settlers in Early Modern India*. New Delhi: Oxford University Press, 2012.

Grigor, Talinn. "Persian Architectural Revivals in the British Raj and Qajar Iran." *Comparative Studies of South Asia, Africa and the Middle East* 36, no. 3 (2016): 384–97.

Gulchīn Ma'ānī, Ahmad. *Tazkirih-yi Paymanih*. 1359. Mashhad, Iran: Intishārāt-i Dānishgāh-i Mashhad, 1981.

———. *Tārīkh-i Tazkirih hā-yi Fārsī*. 1363. 2 vols. Tehran: Kitābkhānih-yi Sanā'ī, 1984.

———. *Kāravān-i Hind*. 2 vols. Mashhad, Iran: Āstān-i Quds-i Razavī, 1990 AD/1369 SH.

Habib, Mohammad. *Politics and Society During the Early Medieval Period: Collected Works of Professor Mohammad Habib*. Edited by K. A. Nizami. 2 vols. New Delhi: People's Publishing House, 1974–1981.

Haeri, Shahla. *Law of Desire: Temporary Marriage in Shi'i Iran*. Syracuse, NY: Syracuse University Press, 1998.

Haidar, Navina Najat, and Marika Sardar. *Sultans of Deccan India, 1500–1700: Opulence and Fantasy*. New Haven, CT: Yale University Press, 2015.

Hall, Jonathan M. *Hellenicity: Between Ethnicity and Culture*. Chicago: University of Chicago Press, 2002.

Hall, Stuart. "The Work of Representation." In *Representation: Cultural Representations and Signifying Practices*, edited by Stuart Hall, 15–30. London: Sage, in association with the Open University, 1997.

Hallaq, Wael B. *Shari'a: Theory, Practice, Transformations*. Cambridge: Cambridge University Press, 2009.

Hambly, Gavin. "The Emperor's Clothes: Robing and 'Robes of Honor' in Mughal India." In *Robes of Honor: Khil'at in Pre-Colonial and Colonial India*, edited by Stewart Gordon, 31–49. New Delhi: Oxford University Press, 2003.

Haneda, Masashi. *Le châh et les Qizilbāš: le système militaire safavide*. Berlin: K. Schwarz, 1987.

———. "Emigration of Iranian Elites to India During the 16th–18th Centuries," *Cahiers d'Asie centrale* 3/4 (1997): 129–43.

Hemmat, Kaveh Louis. "Children of Cain in the Land of Error: A Central Asian Merchant's Treatise on Government and Society in Ming China." *Comparative Studies of South Asia, Africa and the Middle East*. 30, no. 3 (2010): 434–48.

Hermansen, Marcia K., and Bruce B. Lawrence. "Indo-Persian Tazkiras as Memorative Communications." In *Beyond Turk and Hindu: Rethinking Religious Identities in Islamicate South Asia*, edited by David Gilmartin and Bruce B. Lawrence, 149–75. New Delhi: India Research Press, 2002.

Hinz, W. "Farsakh." In *Encyclopaedia of Islam*, 2nd ed., edited by P. Bearman, Th. Bianquis, C. E. Bosworth, E. van Donzel, and W. P. Heinrichs. Brill Online, available at https://referenceworks.brillonline.com/entries/encyclopaedia-of -islam-2/farsakh-SIM_2299 (accessed June 21, 2019).

Ho, Engseng. "The Precious Gift of Genealogy." In *Emirs et présidents. Figures de la parenté et du politique en islam*, edited by P. Bonte, E. Conte, and P. Dresch, 79–110. Paris: CNRS Editions, 2001.

———. "The Two Arms of Cambay: Diasporic Texts of Ecumenical Islam in the Indian Ocean." *Journal of the Economic and Social History of the Orient* 50, nos. 2–3 (2007): 347–61.

Hodgson, Marshal G. S. *The Venture of Islam: Conscience and History in a World Civilization*. 4 vols. Chicago: University of Chicago Press, 1974.

d'Hubert, Thibaut. "Living in Marvelous Lands: Persianate Vernacular Literatures and Cosmographical *Imaginaires* Around the Bay of Bengal." In *The Persianate World: Rethinking a Shared Sphere*, edited by Abbas Amanat and Assef Ashraf, 84–104. Leiden: Brill, 2019.

Husain, Afzal. *The Nobility Under Akbar and Jahāngīr: A Study of Family Groups*. New Delhi: Manohar, 1999.

Jabbari, Alexander. "The Making of Modernity in Persianate Literary History." *Comparative Studies of South Asia, Africa and the Middle East* 36, no. 3 (2016): 418–34.

Jabbari, Hooshang. *Trade and Commerce Between Iran and India During the Safavid Period, 1555–1707*. Delhi: Indian Bibliographies Bureau, 2004.

Jackson, Peter. *Studies on the Mongol Empire and Early Muslim India*. Farnham, UK: Ashgate/Variorum, 2009.

———. *The Mongols and the Islamic World: From Conquest to Conversion*. New Haven, CT: Yale University Press, 2017.

James, Boris. "Arab Ethnonyms ('Ajam, 'Arab, Badū and Turk): The Kurdish Case as a Paradigm for Thinking About Differences in the Middle Ages." *Iranian Studies* 47, no. 5 (2014): 683–712.

Jones, Sian. "Ethnicity: Theoretical Approaches, Methodological Implications." In *Handbook of Archaeological Theories*, edited by R. Alexander Bentley, Herbert D. G. Maschner, and Christopher Chippindale, 321–32. Lanham, MD: AltaMira Press, 2008.

Kaicker, Abhishek. "Unquiet City: Making and Unmaking Politics in Mughal Delhi, 1707–39." PhD diss., Columbia University, 2014.

Kamola, Stefan. "History and Legend in the Jami al-Tawarikh." *Journal of the Royal Asiatic Society* 25, no. 4 (2015): 555–77.

Kashani-Sabet, Firoozeh. *Frontier Fictions: Shaping the Iranian Nation, 1804–1946.* Princeton, NJ: Princeton University Press, 1999.

Keshavmurthy, Prashant. "Bīdil's Portrait: Asceticism and Autobiography." *Philological Encounters* 1, nos. 1–4 (2016): 313–46.

Khalidi, Tarif. *Arabic Historical Thought in the Classical Period.* Cambridge: Cambridge University Press, 1994.

Khan, Pasha Mohammad. "Marvellous Histories: Reading the *Shāhnāmah* in India." *The Indian Economic and Social History Review* 49, no. 4 (2012): 527–56.

Khan, Yar Muhammad. *Iranian Influence in Mughal India.* Lahore: Yar Muhammad Khan, 1978.

Khatak, Sarfaraz Khan. *Shaikh Muhammad 'Ali Hazin: His Life, Times and Works.* Lahore: M. Ashraf, 1944.

Khera, Dipti. "Marginal, Mobile, Multilayered: Painted Invitation Letters as Bazaar Objects in Early Modern India." *Journal* 18 1 (2016). doi:10.30610/1.2016.4.

Kia, Mana. "Paradoxes of Circulation and Hybridity: Joseph Emin's Cultural Idioms of Self and Nation." Paper presented at the Sixth Biennial Conference on Iranian Studies, London, United Kingdom, August 2006.

———. "Accounting for Difference: A Comparative Look at the Autobiographical Travel Narratives of Muhammad 'Ali Hazin Lahiji and 'Abd al-Karim Kashmiri." *Journal of Persianate Studies* 2 (2009): 210–36.

———. "Muhammad 'Ali 'Hazin' Lahiji (1692–1766), *Tazkirat al-ahval* (1742)," Accessing Muslim Lives, 2012. Available at http://www.accessingmuslimlives.org /images/pdfs/HazinTazkirat.pdf.

———. "Limning the Land: Social Encounters and Historical Meaning in Early 19th-Century Travelogues Between Iran and India." In *On the Wonders of Land and Sea: Persianate Travel Writing,* edited by Roberta Micallef and Sunil Sharma, 44–67. Boston: Ilex, distributed by Harvard University Press, 2013).

———. "Imagining Iran Before Nationalism: Geocultural Meanings of Land in Azar's *Ātashkadah.*" In *Rethinking Iranian Nationalism and Modernity,* edited by Kamran Aghaie and Afshin Marashi, 89–112. Austin: University of Texas Press, 2014.

———. "*Adab* as Literary Form and Social Conduct: Reading the *Gulistan* in Late Mughal India." In *"No Tapping Around Philology": A Festschrift in Celebration and Honor of Wheeler McIntosh Thackston Jr.'s 70th Birthday,* edited by Alireza Korangy and Daniel J. Sheffield, 281–308. Wiesbaden, Germany: Harrassowitz, 2014.

———. "Moral Refinement and Manhood in Persian." In *Civilizing Emotions: Concepts in Nineteenth Century Asia and Europe,* edited by Margrit Pernau et al., 146–64. (Oxford: Oxford University Press, 2015).

———. "Indian Friends, Iranian Selves, Persianate Modern." *Comparative Studies of South Asia, Africa and the Middle East* 36, no. 3 (2016): 398–417.

———. "Space, Sociality, and Sources of Pleasure: A Response to Sanjay Subrahmanyam." *Journal of the Economic and Social History of the Orient* 61, nos. 1–2 (2018): 252–72.

———. "The Necessary Ornaments of Place: Similarity and Alterity in the Persianate Imaginary." *Comparative Islamic Studies* (forthcoming).

Kinra, Rajeev. "Secretary-Poets in Mughal India and the Ethos of Persian: The Case of Chandar Bhan Brahman." PhD diss., University of Chicago, 2008.

———. "Infantalizing Bābā Dārā: The Cultural Memory of Dārā Shekuh and the Mughal Public Sphere." *Journal of Persianate Studies* 2 (2009): 165–93.

———. "Master and Munshī: A Brahman Secretary's Guide to Mughal Governance." *The Indian Economic and Social History Review* 47, no. 4 (2010): 527–61.

———. "Make It Fresh: Time, Tradition, and Indo-Persian Literary Modernity." In *Time, History, and the Religious Imaginary in South Asia*, edited by Anne C. Murphy, 12–39. London; New York: Routledge, 2011.

———. "This Noble Science: Indo-Persian Comparative Philology, c. 1000–1800 CE." In *South Asian Texts in History: Critical Engagements with Sheldon Pollock*, edited by Yigal Bronner, Lawrence McCrea, and Whitney Cox, 359–85. Ann Arbor, MI: Association for Asian Studies, 2011.

———. *Writing Self, Writing Empire: Chandar Bhan Brahman and the Cultural World of the Indo-Persian State Secretary*. Oakland: University of Californa Press, 2015.

Kleinberg, Ethan, Joan Wallach Scott, and Gary Wilder. *Theses on Theory and History*, https://www.versobooks.com/blogs/3893-theses-on-theory-and-history (accessed May 31, 2018).

Koch, Ebba. "How the Mughal *Pādshāh*s Referenced Iran in Their Visual Construction of Universal Rule." In *Universal Empire: A Comparative Approach to Imperial Culture and Representation in Eurasian History*, edited by Peter Fibiger Bang and Dariusz Koodziejczyk, 194–209. Cambridge: Cambridge University Press, 2012.

Köprülü, M. Fuad, "Afshār." In *Encyclopaedia of Islam*, 2nd ed., edited by P. Bearman, Th. Bianquis, C. E. Bosworth, E. van Donzel, and W. P. Heinrichs. Brill Online, available at https://referenceworks.brillonline.com/entries/encyclopaedia-of -islam-2/afshar-SIM_0349?lang=en (accessed June 21, 2019).

Kumar, Sunil. *The Emergence of the Delhi Sultanate, 1192–1286*. New Delhi: Permanent Black, distributed by Orient Longman, 2007.

Lal, Ruby. *Domesticity and Power in the Early Mughal World*. Cambridge: Cambridge University Press, 2005.

Landau-Tasseron, Ella. "Adoption, Acknowledgement of Paternity and False Genealogical Claims in Arabian and Islamic Societies." *Bulletin of the School of Oriental and African Studies, University of London* 66, no. 2 (2003): 169–92.

———. "The Status of Allies in Pre-Islamic and Early Islamic Arabian Society." *Islamic Law and Society* 13, no. 1 (2006): 6–32.

———. "Tribes and Clans." In *Encyclopedia of the Qur'ān*, General Editor: Jane Dammen McAuliffe. Washington, DC: Georgetown University, n.d. Available online at http://dx.doi.org/10.1163/1875-3922_q3_EQSIM_00427 (accessed March 14, 2017).

Levi, Scott C. *The Indian Diaspora in Central Asia and Its Trade, 1550–1900.* Leiden: Brill, 2002.

Lewisohn, Leonard, ed. *Hafiz and the Religion of Love in Classical Persian Poetry.* London: I.B. Tauris, 2010.

Litvak, Meir. *Shi'i Scholars of Nineteenth-Century Iraq: The Ulama of Najaf and Karbala.* Cambridge: Cambridge University Press, 1998.

Lockhart, Laurence. *Nadir Shah: A Critical Study Based Mainly Upon Contemporary Sources.* London: Luzac, 1938.

Loewen, Arley. "Proper Conduct (*Adab*) Is Everything: The *Futuwwat-namah-i Sultani* of Husayn Va'iz-i Kashifi." *Iranian Studies* 36, no. 4 (December 2003): 543–70.

Losensky, Paul E. *Welcoming Fighānī: Imitation and Poetic Individuality in the Safavid-Mughal Ghazal.* Costa Mesa, CA: Mazda, 1998.

———. "Sā'eb Tabrizi." In *Encyclopaedia Iranica*, online edition, July 20, 2003. Available at http://www.iranicaonline.org/articles/saeb-tabrizi.

———. "Sāqi-nāma." In *Encyclopedia Iranica*, online edition, 2009. Available at http://www.iranicaonline.org/articles/saqi-nama-book (accessed on August 8, 2014).

———. Translator's Introduction. In *Farid ad-Din 'Attār's Memorial of God's Friends: Lives and Sayings of Sufis*, translated by Paul E. Losensky, 1–37. New York: Paulist Press, 2009.

———. "'Square Like a Bubble:' Architecture, Power, and Poetics in Two Inscriptions by Kalim Kāshāni." *Journal of Persianate Studies* 8, no. 1 (2015): 42–70.

———. "Zuhūrī Turshīzī." In *Encyclopaedia of Islam*, 2nd ed., edited by P. Bearman, Th. Bianquis, C. E. Bosworth, E. van Donzel, and W. P. Heinrichs. Brill Online, available at https://referenceworks.brillonline.com/entries/encyclopaedia-of-islam -2/zuhuri-turshizi-SIM_8206?s.num=26&s.start=20 (accessed June 21, 2019).

———. "Biographical Writing: *Tadhkere* and *Manāqeb*." In *A History of Persian Literature.* Vol. 5, *Persian Prose*, edited by Bo Utas. New York: I.B. Tauris, forthcoming.

Malhotra, Anshu, and Siobhan Lambert-Hurley, "Introduction: Gender, Performance, and Autobiography in South Asia." In *Speaking of the Self: Gender, Performance, and Autobiography in South Asia*, edited by Anshu Malhotra and Siobhan Lambert-Hurley, 1–30. Durham, NC: Duke University Press, 2015.

Malik, Jamal. "Muslim Culture and Reform in 18th Century South Asia." *Journal of the Royal Asiatic Society* 3rd ser., 13, no. 2 (2003): 227–43.

Mamdani, Mahmood. *Define and Rule: Native as Political Identity.* Cambridge, MA: Harvard University Press, 2012.

Mancini-Lander, Derek J. "Memory on the Boundaries of Empire: Narrating Place in the Early Modern Local Historiography of Yazd." PhD diss., University of Michigan, 2012.

———. "Tales Bent Backward: Early Modern Local History in Persianate Transregional Contexts." *Journal of the Royal Asiatic Society* 28, no. 1 (2018): 23–54.

Mani, Lata. *Contentious Traditions: The Debate on Sati in Colonial India* (Berkeley: University of California Press, c. 1998).

Manz, Beatrice Forbes. *The Rise and Rule of Tamerlane*. Cambridge: Cambridge University Press, 1989.

———. *Power, Politics and Religion in Timurid Iran*. Cambridge: Cambridge University Press, 2007.

Marashi, Afshin. *Nationalizing Iran: Culture, Power, and the State, 1870–1940*. Seattle: University of Washington Press, 2008.

Matthee, Rudi. *Persia in Crisis: Safavid Decline and the Fall of Isfahan*. London: I.B. Tauris, 2012.

Maurya, Anubhuti. "Of Tulips and Daffodils: *Kashmir Jannat Nazir* as a Political Landscape in the Mughal Empire." *Economic & Political Weekly* 52, no. 15 (April 15, 2017).

Meisami, Julie Scott. "The Past in the Service of the Present: Two Views of History in Medieval Persia." *Poetics Today* 14, no. 2 (Summer 1993): 247–75.

———. "Places in the Past: The Poetics/Politics of Nostalgia." *Edebiyât* 8 (1998): 63–106.

———. *Persian Historiography to the End of the Twelfth Century*. Edinburgh: Edinburgh University Press, 1999.

———. "History as Literature." In *Persian Historiography*, edited by Charles Melville. London: I.B. Tauris, 2012.

Melville, Charles. "The Early Persian Historiography of Anatolia." In *History and Historiography of Post-Mongol Central Asia and the Middle East: Studies in Honor of John E. Woods*, edited by Judith Pfeiffer and Sholeh A. Quinn, 135–66. Wiesbaden, Germany: Harrassowitz, 2006.

———. Introduction. In *Persian Historiography*, edited by Charles Melville, xxv–lvi. London: I.B. Tauris; New York: Distributed in the U.S. and Canada exclusively by Palgrave Macmillan, 2012.

Melvin-Koushki, Matthew. "Astrology, Lettrism, Geomancy: The Occult-Scientific Methods of Post-Mongol Islamicate Imperialism." *Medieval History Journal* 19, no. 1 (2016): 142–50.

———. "Of Islamic Grammatology: Ibn Turka's Lettrist Metaphysics of Light." *Al-'Usūr al-Wustā* 24 (2016): 42–113.

———. "Early Modern Islamicate Empire: New Forms of Religiopolitical Legitimacy." In *The Wiley-Blackwell History of Islam*, edited by Armando Salvatore,

Roberto Tottoli, Babak Rahimi, Fariduddin Attar, and Naznin Patel, 351–75. Hoboken, NJ: John Wiley & Sons, 2017.

———. "Powers of One: The Mathematicalization of the Occult Sciences in the High Persianate Tradition." *Intellectual History of the Islamicate World* 5, no. 1 (2017): 127–99.

———. "Imperial Talismanic Love: Ibn Turka's *Debate of Feast and Fight* (1426) as Philosophical Romance and Lettrist Mirror for Timurid Princes." *Der Islam* 96, no. 1 (2019).

Melvin-Koushki, Matthew, and James Pickett. "Mobilizing Magic: Occultism in Central Asia and the Continuity of High Persianate Culture Under Russian Rule." *Studia Islamica* 111, no. 2 (2016): 231–84.

Memon, M. U. "Amīn Ahmad Rāzī." In *Encyclopedia Iranica*, online edition, n.d. Available online at http://www.iranicaonline.org/articles/razi-amin-ahmad (accessed December 30, 2012).

Mernissi, Fatima. *The Forgotten Queens of Islam*. Translated by Mary Jo Lakeland. Minneapolis: University of Minnesota Press, 1993.

Mikkelson, Jane. "Of Parrots and Crows: Bīdil and Hazīn in Their Own Words." *Comparative Studies of South Asia, Africa and the Middle East* 37, no. 3 (2017): 510–30.

Minorsky, V. "The Poetry of Shah Isma'il I." *Bulletin of the School of Oriental and African Studies*, University of London (1942): 1006a–1053a.

———. "Kutlugh-khānids." In *Encyclopaedia of Islam*, 2nd ed., edited by P. Bearman, Th. Bianquis, C. E. Bosworth, E. van Donzel, and W. P. Heinrichs. Brill Online, available at https://referenceworks.brillonline.com/entries/encyclopaedia -of-islam-2/kutlugh-khanids-SIM_4588?lang=en (accessed June 21, 2019).

Mitchell, Colin P. *The Practice of Politics in Safavid Iran: Power, Religion and Rhetoric*. London: I.B. Tauris, 2009.

———. "Am I My Brother's Keeper?: Negotiating Corporate Sovereignty and Divine Absolutism in Sixteenth-Century Turco-Iranian Politics." In *New Perspectives on Safavid Iran: Empire and Society*, edited by Colin P. Mitchell, 33–58. New York: Routledge, 2011.

Moin, A. Azfar. *The Millennial Sovereign: Sacred Kingship and Sainthood in Islam*. New York: Columbia University Press, 2012.

Momen, Moojan. *An Introduction to Shi'i Islam: The History and Doctrines of Twelver Shi'ism*. New Haven, CT: Yale University Press, 1985.

Morimoto, Kazuo. "The Formation and Development of the Science of Talibid Genealogies in the 10th and 11th-Century Middle East." *Oriente Moderno* 18 (79), no. 2 (1999): 541–70.

Mottahedeh, Roy P. *The Mantle of the Prophet: Religion and Politics in Iran*. New York: Pantheon, 1985.

———. "The Idea of Iran in Buyid Dominions." In *Early Islamic Iran*, edited by Edmund Herzig and Sarah Stewart, 153–60. London: I.B. Tauris, 2012.

———. "Friendship in Islamic Ethical Philosophy." In *Essays in Islamic Philology, History, and Philosophy: A Festschrift in Celebration and Honor of Professor Ahmad Mahdavi Damghani's 90th Birthday*, edited by Alireza Korangy, Roy P. Mottahedeh, William Granara, and Wheeler M. Thackston, 229–39. Berlin: De Gruyter, 2016.

Mozaffari, Ali. *Forming National Identity in Iran: The Idea of Homeland Derived from Ancient Persian and Islamic Imaginations of Place*. London: I.B. Tauris, 2014.

Mukhia, Harbans. *The Mughals of India*. Malden, MA: Blackwell, 2004.

Musallam, Basim F. *Sex and Society in Islam: Birth Control Before the Nineteenth Century*. Cambridge: Cambridge University Press, 1983.

Muvāḥḥid, Samad. Editor's Introduction. In *Tuhfat al-ʿālam va zīl al-Tuhfah*, by Mīr ʿAbd al-Laṭīf Khān Shūshtarī, 11–28. Tehran: Kitābkhānih-yi Tahūrī, 1984 AD/1363 SH.

Naim, C. M. Translator's Introduction. In *Zikr-i Mir: The Autobiography of the Eighteenth Century Mughal Poet Mir Muhammad Taqi "Mir,"* 1–21. New Delhi: Oxford University Press, 1999.

Nājī Nasrābādī, Muhsin. Editor's Introduction. In *Tazkirih-yi Riyāz al-Shuʿarāʾ*, by ʿAlī Qulī Vālih Dāghistānī. Vol. 1, 19–58. Tehran: Asātīr, 2005 AD/1384 SH.

Najmabadi, Afsaneh, ed. *Women's Autobiographies in Contemporary Iran*. Cambridge, MA: Harvard University Press, 1990.

———. "Crafting an Educated Housewife in Iran." In *Remaking Women: Feminism and Modernity in the Middle East*, edited by Lila Abu-Lughod, 91–125. Princeton, NJ: Princeton University Press, 1998.

———. *Women with Mustaches and Men Without Beards: Gender and Sexual Anxieties of Iranian Modernity*. Berkeley: University of California Press, 2005.

———. *Professing Selves: Transsexuality and Same-Sex Desire in Contemporary Iran*. Durham, NC: Duke University Press, 2014.

Naqavī, ʿAlīrizā. *Tazkirih Nivīsī-yi Fārsi dar Hind va Pākistān*. Tehran: ʿIlmī, 1964.

Nasim, K. B. Introduction. In *Bayān-i Wāqiʿ: Sarguzasht-i Ahvāl-i Nādir Shāh va Safarhā-yi munnasif-i Khwājih ʿAbd al-Karīm ibn Khwājih ʿĀqibat Mahmūd Kashmīrī*, by ʿAbd al-Karīm, Kashmīrī, ix–xvii. Lahore: Research Society of Pakistan, 1970.

O'Hanlon, Rosalind. "'Premodern' Pasts: South Asia." In *A Companion to Global Historical Thought*, edited by Prasenjit Duara, Viren Murthy, and Andrew Sartori, 107–21. Malden, MA: John Wiley & Sons, 2014.

Olsson, J. T. "The World in Arab Eyes: A Reassessment of the Climes in Medieval Islamic Scholarship." *Bulletin of the School of Oriental and African Studies* 77, no. 3 (2014): 487–508.

Omi, Michael, and Howard Winant. "The Theoretical Status of the Concept of Race." In *Race, Identity and Representation in Education*, 2nd ed., edited by Cameron McCarthy, 3–12. New York: Routledge, 2005.

Onley, James. *The Arabian Frontier of the British Raj: Merchants, Rulers, and the British in the Nineteenth-Century Gulf.* Oxford: Oxford University Press, 2007.

O'Quinn, Daniel. Editor's Introduction. In *The Travels of Mirza Abu Taleb Khan in Asia, Africa, and Europe: During the Years* 1799, 1800, 1801, 1802, *and* 1803, translated by Charles Stewart, edited by Daniel O'Quinn. Peterborough, ON: Broadview Press, 2009.

Parkes, Peter. "Fosterage, Kinship, and Legend: When Milk Was Thicker Than Blood?" *Comparative Studies in Society and History* 46, no. 3 (2004): 587–615.

———. "Milk Kinship in Islam: Substance, Structure, History." *Social Anthropology* 13, no. 3 (2005): 307–29.

Pellò, Stefano. "Drowned in the Sea of Mercy." In *Religious Interactions in Mughal India*, edited by Vasudha Dalmia and Munis D. Faruqui, 135–58. Delhi: Oxford University Press, 2014.

———. "Persian as Passe-Partout." In *Culture and Circulation: Literatures in Motion in Early Modern India*, edited by Thomas de Bruijn and Allison Busch, 21–46. Leiden: Brill, 2014.

———. "Persian Poets on the Streets: The Lore of Indo-Persian Poetic Circles in Late Mughal India." In *Tellings and Texts: Music, Literature and Performance in North India*, edited by Orsini Francesca and Schofield Katherine Butler, 303–26. Cambridge, UK: Open Book, 2015.

———. "A Linguistic Conversion: Mīrzā Muhammad Qatīl and the Varieties of Persian (c. 1790)." In *Borders: Itineraries on the Edges of Iran*, edited by Stefano Pellò, 203–40. Venice: Edizioni Ca' Foscari, 2016.

Pernau, Margrit, et al., eds. *Civilizing Emotions: Concepts in Nineteenth Century Asia and Europe.* Oxford: Oxford University Press, 2015.

Perry, John R. *Karim Khan Zand: A History of Iran,* 1747–1779. Chicago: University of Chicago Press, 1979.

———. "The Historical Role of Turkish in Relation to Persian of Iran." *Iran & the Caucasus* 5 (2001): 193–200.

———. "Turkic-Iranian Contacts i. Linguistic Contacts." In *Encyclopedia Iranica*, online edition, August 15, 2006. Available at http://www.iranicaonline.org/articles/turkic-iranian-contacts-i-linguistic.

Pinto, Karen C. *Medieval Islamic Maps: An Exploration.* Chicago: University of Chicago Press, 2016.

Pollock, Sheldon I. *The Language of the Gods in the World of Men: Sanskrit, Culture, and Power in Premodern India.* Berkeley: University of California Press, 2006.

———. Introduction. In *Forms of Knowledge in Early Modern Asia: Explorations in the Intellectual History of India and Tibet,* 1500–1800, edited by Sheldon Pollock, 1–16. Durham, NC: Duke University Press, 2011.

———. "The Languages of Science in Early Modern India." In *Forms of Knowledge in Early Modern Asia: Explorations in the Intellectual History of India and Tibet, 1500–1800*, edited by Sheldon Pollock, 19–48. Durham, NC: Duke University Press, 2011.

Porqueres i Gené, Enric. "Kinship Language and the Dynamics of Race." In *Race, Ethnicity and Nation: Perspectives from Kinship and Genetics*, edited by Peter Wade, 125–44. New York; Oxford: Berghahn Books, 2007.

Power, Timothy. *The Red Sea from Byzantium to the Caliphate: AD 500–1000*. Cairo: American University in Cairo Press, 2012.

Pritchett, Frances W. "A Long History of Urdu Literary Culture, Part 2: Histories Performances, Masters." In *Literary Cultures in History: Reconstructions from South Asia*, edited by Sheldon Pollock, 864–911. Berkeley: University of California Press, 2003.

Quinn, Sholeh A. *Historical Writing During the Reign of Shah 'Abbas: Ideology, Imitation and Legitimacy in Safavid Chronicles*. Salt Lake City: University of Utah Press, 2000.

———. "Timurid Historiographical Legacy: A Comparative Study of Persianate Historical Writing." In *Society and Culture in the Early Modern Middle East: Studies on Iran in the Safavid Period*, edited by A. J. Newman, 19–31. Leiden: Brill, 2003.

———. *Shah Abbas: The King Who Refashioned Iran*. New York: Oneworld, 2015.

Rahman, T. "Decline of Persian in British India." *South Asia* 22, no. 1 (1999): 47–62.

Ray, Rajat Kanta. *The Felt Community: Commonalty and Mentality Before the Emergence of Indian Nationalism*. New Delhi: Oxford University Press, 2003.

Ray, Sukumar. *Humayun in Persia*. Calcutta: The Royal Asiatic Society of Bengal, 1948.

Rehatsek, Edward. *Catalogue Raisonne of the Arabic, Hindostani, Persian and Turkish MSS in the Mulla Firuz Library*. Bombay: Managing Committee of the Mulla Firuz Library, 1873.

Reynolds, Dwight, et al. *Interpreting the Self: Autobiography in the Arabic Literary Tradition*. Berkeley: University of California Press, 2001.

Richards, John F. *The Mughal Empire*. Cambridge: Cambridge University Press, 1995.

———. "The Formulation of Imperial Authority Under Akbar and Jahangir." In *The Mughal State: 1526–1750*, edited by Muzaffar Alam and Sanjay Subrahmanyam, 126–67. New Delhi: Oxford University Press, 1998.

Robinson, Francis. "Perso-Islamic Culture in India from the Seventeenth to the Early Twentieth Century." In *Turko-Persia in Historical Perspective*, edited by Robert L. Canfield, 104–31. Cambridge: Cambridge University Press, 1991.

———. *The 'Ulama of Farangi Mahall and Islamic Culture in South Asia*. New Delhi: Permanent Black, 2001.

Rosenthal, Franz. "The Stranger in Medieval Islam." *Arabica* 44, no. 1 (1997): 35–75.

———. "Nasab." In *Encyclopaedia of Islam,* 2nd ed., edited by P. Bearman, Th. Bianquis, C. E. Bosworth, E. van Donzel, and W. P. Heinrichs. Brill Online, available at https://referenceworks.brillonline.com/entries/encyclopedie-de-l-islam/nasab-SIM_5807 (accessed June 21, 2019).

Sahlins, Marshall David. *What Kinship Is, and Is Not*. Chicago: University of Chicago Press, 2013.

Said, Edward W. *Orientalism*. New York: Vintage, 1978.

———. *Culture and Imperialism*. New York: Knopf, distributed by Random House, 1994.

Sardar, Marika. "The Bahmanis and Their Artistic Legacy." In *Sultans of Deccan India, 1500–1700: Opulence and Fantasy*, edited by Navina Najat Haidar and Marika Sardar, 29–34. New York: Metropolitan Museum of Art, 2015.

Sarkar, Jadunath. *Fall of the Mughal Empire*. 4 vols. Calcutta: M.C. Sarkar & Sons, 1932–1950.

Savant, Sarah Bowen. *The New Muslims of Post-Conquest Iran: Tradition, Memory and Conversion*. Cambridge: Cambridge University Press, 2013.

———. "Genealogy and Ethnogenesis in al-Mas'udi's Muruj al-dhahab." In *Genealogy and Knowledge in Muslim Societies: Understanding the Past*, edited by Sarah Bowen Savant and Helena de Felipe. Edinburgh: Edinburgh University Press, 2014.

Savant, Sarah Bowen, and Helena de Felipe. Introduction. In *Genealogy and Knowledge in Muslim Societies: Understanding the Past*, edited by Sarah Bowen Savant and Helena de Felipe. Edinburgh: Edinburgh University Press, 2014.

Savory, Roger M. *Iran Under the Safavids*. Cambridge: Cambridge University Press, 1980.

———. "Kizil-bāsh." In *Encyclopaedia of Islam*, 2nd ed., edited by P. Bearman, Th. Bianquis, C. E. Bosworth, E. van Donzel, and W. P. Heinrichs. Brill Online, available at https://referenceworks.brillonline.com/entries/encyclopaedia-of-islam-2/kizil-bash-SIM_4415 (accessed June 21, 2019).

Schimmel, Annemarie. *Islam in the Indian Subcontinent*. Leiden: Brill, 1980.

———. *Islamic Names*. Edinburgh: Edinburgh University Press, 1989.

———. *The Empire of the Great Mughals: History, Art and Culture*. Translated by Corinne Attwood. Edited by Burzine K. Waghmar. London: Reaktion Books, 2004.

Schwartz, Kevin L. "Bâzgasht-i adabî (Literary Return) and Persianate Literary Culture in Eighteenth and Nineteenth Century Iran, India, and Afghanistan." PhD diss., University of California, Berkeley, 2014.

———. "The Curious Case of Carnatic: The Last Nawâb of Arcot (d. 1855) and Persian Literary Culture." *The Indian Economic & Social History Review* 53, no. 4 (2016): 533–60.

———. "The Local Lives of a Transregional Poet: 'Abd al-Qâdir Bîdil and the Writing of Persianate Literary History." *Journal of Persianate Studies* 9 (2016): 83–106.

———. "A Transregional Persianate Library: *Tadhkira* Production and Circulation in the 18th and 19th Centuries." *International Journal of Middle East Studies*. Forthcoming.

Scott, James C., John Tehranian, and Jeremy Mathias. "The Production of Legal Identities Proper to States: The Case of the Permanent Family Surname." *Comparative Studies in Society and History* 44, no. 1 (January 2002): 4–44.

Scott, Joan W. "History-Writing as Critique." In *Manifestos for History*, edited by Keith Jenkins, Sue Morgan, and Alun Munslow, 19–38. New York: Routledge, 2007.

Sela, Ron. *The Legendary Biographies of Tamerlane: Islam and Heroic Apocrypha in Central Asia*. New York: Cambridge University Press, 2011.

———. "Rashīd al-Dīn's Historiographical Legacy in the Muslim World." In *Rashīd al-Dīn: Agent and Mediator of Cultural Exchanges in Ilkhanid Iran*, edited by Anna Akasoy, Charles Burnett, and Ronit Yoeli-Tlalim, 213–22. London: The Warburg Institute; Turin: Nino Aragno Editore, 2013.

Sen, Sudipta. *Distant Sovereignty: National Imperialism and the Origins of British India*. New York: Routledge, 2002.

Shafīʿī Kadkanī, Muhammad Riżā. *Shāʿirī dar Hujūm-i Muntaqidīn: Naqd-i Adabī dar Sabk-i Hindī*. Tehran: Āgāh, 1996 AD/1375 SH.

Shafir, Nir. "The Art of Forgetfulness—Abd al-Ghani al-Nabulusi on Memory and Morality." In *Early Modern Trends in Islamic Theology: ʿAbd al-Ghanī al-Nābulusī and His Network of Scholarship*, edited by Lejla Demiri and Samuela Pagani, 263–76. Tübingen, Germany: Mohr Siebeck, 2018.

Sharma, Sunil. *Persian Poetry at the Indian Frontier: Masʿud Saʿd Salmon of Lahore*. Delhi: Permanent Black, 2000.

———. "The Land of Darkness: Images of India in the Works of Some Safavid Poets." *Studies on Persianate Societies* 1 (2003): 97–110.

———. "From ʿĀeshā to Nūr Jahān: The Shaping of a Classical Persian Poetic Canon of Women." *Journal of Persianate Studies* 2, no. 2 (2009): 148–64.

———. "The Nizamshahi Persianate Garden in Zuhuri's *Sāqīnāma*." In *Garden and Landscape Practices in Pre-Colonial India: Histories from the Deccan*, edited by Daud Ali and Emma J. Flatt, 159–71. London: Routledge, 2012.

———. "Redrawing the Boundaries of ʿAjam in Early Modern Persian Literary Histories." In *Iran Facing Others: Identity Boundaries in a Historical Perspective*, edited by Abbas Amanat and Farzin Vejdani, 49–62. New York: Palgrave Macmillan, 2012).

———. "The Production of Mughal *Shāhnāma*s: Imperial, Sub-imperial, and Provincial Manuscripts." In *Ferdowsi's Shāhnāma: Millennial Perspectives*, edited by Olga M. Davidson and Marianna Shreve Simpson, 86–103. Boston: Ilex, distributed by Harvard University Press, 2013.

———. *Mughal Arcadia: Persian Literature in an Indian Court*. Cambridge, MA: Harvard University Press, 2017.

Sheffield, Daniel J. "The Language of Heaven in Safavid Iran: Speech and Cosmology in the Thought of Āzar Kayvān and His Followers." In *"No Tapping Around Philology": A Festschrift in Celebration and Honor of Wheeler McIntosh Thackston Jr.'s 70th Birthday*, edited by Alireza Korangy and Daniel J. Sheffield, 161–83. Wiesbaden, Germany: Harrassowitz, 2014.

Sheikh, Samira. *Forging a Region: Sultans, Traders, and Pilgrims in Gujarat, 1200–1500.* New Delhi: Oxford University Press, 2010.

Sherman, Taylor C. "Migration, Citizenship and Belonging in Hyderabad (Deccan), 1946–1956." *Modern Asian Studies* 45 (2011): 81–107.

Smith, Anthony D. *The Nation in History: Historiographical Debates About Ethnicity and Nationalism.* Hanover, NH: University Press of New England, 2000.

Sohrabi, Naghmeh. *Taken for Wonder: Nineteenth Century Travel Accounts from Iran to Europe.* Oxford: Oxford University Press, 2013.

Sood, Gagan. *India and the Islamic Heartlands: An Eighteenth-Century World of Circulation and Exchange.* Cambridge: Cambridge University Press, 2016.

Sreenivasan, Ramya. "Honoring the Family: Narratives and Politics of Kinship in Precolonial Rajasthan." In *Unfamiliar Relations: Family and History in South Asia*, edited by Indrani Chatterjee, 46–72. New Brunswick, NJ: Rutgers University Press, 2004.

Stanfield-Johnson, Rosemary. *Ritual Cursing in Iran: Theology, Politics and the Public in Safavid Persia.* London: Tauris Academic Studies, 2015.

Stewart, Devin. "An Episode in the 'Amili Migration to Safavid Iran: Husayn b. 'Abd al-Samad al-'Amili's Travel Account." *Iranian Studies* 39, no. 4 (December 2006): 481–508.

———. "Women's Biographies in Islamic Societies: Mīrzā 'Abd al-Isfahānī's Riyāz al-'ulamā'." In *The Rhetoric of Biography: Narrating Lives in Persianate Societies*, edited by Louise Marlow, 106–39. Boston: Ilex, distributed by Harvard University Press, c. 2011.

Subhānī, Tawfīq. *Nigāhī bih Tārīkh-i Adab-i Fārsī dar Hind.* Tehran: Intishārāt-i Dabīrkhānah-i Shūrā-yi Gustarish-i Zabān va Adabīyāt-i Fārsī, 1998 AD/1377 SH.

Subrahmanyam, Sanjay. "Persians, Pilgrims and Portuguese: The Travails of Masulipatnam Shipping in the Western Indian Ocean, 1590–1665." *Modern Asian Studies* 22, no. 3 (1988): 503–30.

———. "Iranians Abroad: Intra-Asian Elite Migration and Early Modern State Formation." In *Merchant Networks in the Early Modern World*, ed. Sanjay Subrahmanyam, 72–95. Aldershot, UK: Valorium, 1996.

———. *"Un Grand Dérangement*: Dreaming an Indo-Persian Empire in South Asia, 1740–1800." *Journal of Early Modern History* 4, nos. 3–4 (2000): 337–78.

———. "Persianization and Mercantilism in Bay of Bengal History, 1400–1700." In

Explorations in Connected History: From the Tagus to the Ganges, 45–79. Delhi: Oxford University Press, 2005.

Subtelny, Maria E. "The Symbiosis of Turk and Tajik." In *Central Asia in Historical Perspective*, edited by Beatrice F. Manz, 45–61. Boulder, CO: Westview Press, 1994.

———. "A Late Medieval Persian *Summa* on Ethics: Kashifi's *Akhlāq-i Muhsinī*." *Iranian Studies* 36, no. 4 (2003): 601–14.

———. *Timurids in Transition: Turko-Persian Politics and Acculturation in Medieval Iran*. Leiden: Brill, 2007.

Szombathy, Zoltán. "Genealogy in Medieval Muslim Societies." *Studia Islamica*, no. 95 (2002): 5–35.

———. "Motives and Techniques of Genealogical Forgery in Pre-Modern Muslim Societies." In *Genealogy and Knowledge in Muslim Societies: Understanding the Past*, edited by Sarah Bowen Savant and Helena de Felipe, 24–36. Edinburgh: Edinburgh University Press, 2014.

Szuppe, Maria. "A Glorious Past and Outstanding Present: Writing a Collection of Biographies in Late Persianate Central Asia." In *The Rhetoric of Biography: Narrating Lives in Persianate Societies*, edited by Louise Marlow, 41–88. Boston: Ilex, distributed by Harvard University Press, c. 2011.

Tāhirī, Muhammad Rizā. Preface. In *Tazkirih-yi Haft Iqlīm* edited by Muhammad Rizā Tāhirī. 3 vols. Tehran: Surūsh, 1999 AD/1378 SH.

Tavakoli-Targhi, Mohamad. *Refashioning Iran: Orientalism, Occidentalism and Historiography*. London: Palgrave, 2001.

Thackston, Wheeler M. "The Genghisid and Timurid Background of Iran and Central Asia." In *The Baburnama: Memoirs of Babur, Prince and Emperor*, translated and edited by Wheeler M. Thackston, xxxv–xlvii. New York: Modern Library, 2002.

Thomas, Rosalind. "Ethnicity, Genealogy, and Hellenism in Herodotus." In *Ancient Perceptions of Greek Ethnicity*, edited by Irad Malkin, 213–33. Washington, DC: Center for Hellenic Studies, distributed by Harvard University Press, 2001.

Togan, Isenbike. "Turkic Dynasties: 9th to 15th Century." In *Encyclopedia of Women & Islamic Cultures*, edited by Suad Joseph. Brill Online. Available at http://www.brillonline.nl/subscriber/entry?entry=ewic_COM-0005 (accessed December 227, 2010).

Trausch, Tilmann. "Ghazā and Ghazā Terminology in Chronicles from the Sixteenth-Century Safavid Courtly Sphere." *Journal of Persianate Studies* 10 (2017): 240–68.

Travers, Robert. *Ideology and Empire in Eighteenth Century India: The British in Bengal*. Cambridge: Cambridge University Press, 2007.

Truschke, Audrey. "Cosmopolitan Encounters: Sanskrit and Persian at the Mughal Court." PhD diss., Columbia University, 2012.

———. *Culture of Encounters: Sanskrit at the Mughal Court*. New York: Columbia University Press, 2016.

Tuan, Yi-Fu. *Space and Place: The Perspective of Experience*. Minneapolis: University of Minnesota Press, 2014.

Tucker, Ernest S. *Nadir Shah's Quest for Legitimacy in Post-Safavid Iran*. Gainesville: University Press of Florida, 2006.

Vasilyeva, Olga V., and Olga M. Yastrebova. "The Muraqqaʻ Album of the Zand Period (PNS 383) in the National Library of Russia." In *Ferdowsi, the Mongols and the History of Iran: Art, Literature and Culture from Early Islam to Qajar Persia, Studies in Honor of Charles Melville*, edited by Robert Hillenbrand, A.C.S. Peacock, and Firuza Abdullaeva, 359–69. London: I.B. Tauris, 2013.

Vatuk, Sylvia. "'Family' as a Contested Concept in Early-Nineteenth-Century Madras." In *Unfamiliar Relations: Family and History in South Asia*, edited by Indrani Chatterjee, 161–91. New Brunswick, NJ: Rutgers University Press, 2004.

Vejdani, Farzin. "Contesting Nations and Canons." *International Journal of Turkish Studies* 20, nos. 1–2 (2014): 49–66.

———. *Making History in Iran: Education, Nationalism, and Print Culture*. Stanford, CA: Stanford University Press, 2014.

———. "The Place of Islam in Interwar Iranian Nationalist Historiography." In *Rethinking Iranian Nationalism and Modernity*, edited by Kamran Scot Aghaie and Afshin Marashi, 205–18. Austin: University of Texas Press, 2014.

———. "Indo-Iranian Linguistic, Literary, and Religious Entanglements: Between Nationalism and Cosmopolitanism, ca. 1900–1940." *Comparative Studies of South Asia, Africa and the Middle East* 36, no. 3 (2016): 435–54.

Wagoner, Phillip B. "'Sultan Among the Hindu Kings': Dress, Titles, and the Islamicization of Hindu Culture at Vijayanagara." *Journal of Asian Studies* 55, no. 4 (November 1996): 851–80.

Walker, J., and P. Fenton. "Sulaymān b. Dāwūd." In *Encyclopaedia of Islam*, 2nd ed., edited by P. Bearman, Th. Bianquis, C. E. Bosworth, E. van Donzel, and W. P. Heinrichs. Brill Online, available at http://referenceworks.brillonline.com/entries/encyclopaedia-of-islam-2/sulayman-b-dawud-SIM_7158 (accessed June 21, 2019).

Wick, Alexis. *Red Sea: In Search of Lost Space*. Berkeley: University of California Press, 2016.

Wilson, Kathleen. "Introduction: Histories, Empires, Modernities." In *A New Imperial History: Culture, Identity and Modernity in Britain and the Empire, 1660–1840*, edited by Kathleen Wilson, 1–26. Cambridge: Cambridge University Press, 2004.

Woods, John E. "Timur's Genealogy." In *Intellectual Studies on Islam: Essays Written in Honor of Martin B. Dickson*, edited by Michel M. Mazzaoui and Vera B. Moreen, 85–125. Salt Lake City: University of Utah Press, c. 1990.

———. *The Aqquyunlu: Clan, Confederation, Empire*. Salt Lake City: University of Utah Press, 1999.

Yeroushalmi, David. "Emrani." In *Encyclopedia Iranica*, online edition. Available online at http://www.iranicaonline.org/articles/emrani (accessed August 13, 2016).

Yildiz, Sara Nur. "Ottoman Historical Writing in Persian, 1400–1600." In *Persian Historiography*, edited by Charles Melville, 436–502. London: I.B. Tauris, 2012.

Young, Robert. *Colonial Desire: Hybridity in Theory, Culture, and Race*. London: Routledge, 2005.

Zaman, Taymiya R. "Instructive Memory: An Analysis of Auto/Biographical Writing in Early Mughal India." *Journal of the Economic and Social History of the Orient* 54, no. 5 (2011): 677–700.

Zarinebaf, Fariba. "From Istanbul to Tabriz: Modernity and Constitutionalism in the Ottoman Empire and Iran." *Comparative Studies of South Asia, Africa, and the Middle East* 28, no. 1 (2008): 154–69.

———. "Rebels and Renegades on the Ottoman-Iranian Frontier." In *Iran Facing Others: Identity Boundaries in a Historical Perspective*, edited by Abbas Amanat and Farzin Vejdani, 79–98. London: Palgrave, 2012.

Zia-Ebrahimi, Reza. "An Emissary of the Golden Age: Manekji Limji Hataria and the Charisma of the Archaic in Pre-Nationalist Iran." *Studies in Ethnicity and Nationalism* 10, no. 3 (2010): 377–90.

———. *The Emergence of Iranian Nationalism: Race and the Politics of Dislocation*. New York: Columbia University Press, 2016.

Index

Abbas I (Safavid), Shah, 88

Abbas II (Safavid), Shah, 72

'Abdullah Khan Uzbeg, 119

Abu Talib. *See* Isfahani, Mirza Abu Talib Khan

adab (proper aesthetic and ethical form): and aporia, 11; as core of Persianate belonging, 5, 9; fall of Safavid empire and, 181; Hazin on, 95; and character, Bihbahani on, 96; Islam and, 14; and memory, 164; as mode by which Persians identify, 174; and moral substance, 199–200; of naming, 146, 199; and Persianate inclusion, 145, 174, 176; protection of people through proper forms, 164; and refiguring Iran after Safavid fall, 198; role in commemorative texts, 164, 167–68; role in kinship relations, 102–3, 139, 144, 200; role in Persianate origin accounts, 98, 100, 101–2, 104–5, 106; and self-definition through *tazkirih*s, 171–76, 202; shared language as indication of *jins* (type) and, 160; as social and aesthetic

form, 199–200; *tazkirih*s and, 163, 165, 166, 171, 174, 183

adab literature, Franz Rosenthal on, 32

Adam, Shafiq on, 168–69

adoption, as kinship, 139–40, 249n92; and adoptive clients (*mawālī*), 137

affiliations, premodern, ethnicity as term inapplicable to, 6, 11, 113–14, 122–23, 199

Afsah (Mir Muhammad 'Ali "Afsah"), 114–15

Ahmadnagar: Razi on, 78–79; Zuhuri on, 80

Ahmad Shah (Durrani), 46

Ahmed, Shahab, 14, 211n51, 235n10

'A'isha Samarqandi, 119

'ajam: as basis of type (*jinsiyat*), 60, 66, 159–60; as geocultural line, 66; line separating from Europe (*farang*), 91–92; as term for place, 160–61; as term for speakers of Persian, 101, 152, 160. See also *'Iraq-i 'ajam*

Akbar Shah (Timurid): and Irani and Turani factions, 161; Kashmiri on, 68, 227n58; lineage of, 127; modern narratives on, 69

71; life of, xix, 31; on Hindustan,
66–70; lineage claimed by, 107–9;
on Nadir Shah, 37, 44; on patrilin-
ear kinship, 135; as second generation of represented authors, 22–23;
similarities and differences with
Hazin's *tazkirih*, 56; textual corpus
referred to, 45, 219n42; as traveler with Nadir Shah's Army, xix,
31, 56; use of *mamlakat* term, 40;
works by, xix. *See also Bayan-i Vaqi'*
(Kashmiri)
Kayanids, Shushtari on, 151
Kayfi-yi Naw Musalman, 145
Khafi Khan, 158
Khalil (Navvab 'Ali Ibrahim Khan
"Khalil" Banarasi), xix, 117, 158,
249n102
Khayr al-Nissa, 74
Khizanih-yi 'Amirih (Azad), xvi, 175
Khurasan: as *mamlakat*, 40; Persian
migrants to Turkestan, 16; Razi on,
78; as Safavid province, 12, 20; and
transregional Persianate culture, 37
Khusraw Dihlavi, Amir, 192, 217n5
Khusraw and Shirin (Nizami), 45
Kinra, Rajeev, 258n48, 259n64
kinship: ethnicity as term inapplicable to
premodern affiliations, 6, 11, 113–14,
122–23, 199; modern blood-connection models of, 123–26, 135–36,
242n2, 242n6
kinship, Persianate understanding
of: adoption as, 139–40, 249n92;
ambiguity of terms describing
legal or social terms for, 137; lack
of Qur'anic term for, 137; range of
legal and social forms of, 100, 102–3,
122, 200, 237nn33–34; role of *adab*
in, 102–3, 139, 144, 200; and role
of marriage in, 108; spectrum of
extra-legal forms of, 137–41. *See also*
ethnicity

knowledge, mix of local and transregional, in Kashmiri's *Bayan-i Vaqi'*,
87–91

Lahore: Azar on, 93; and Hindustan,
relation to, 38
Lalih (Padshah) Khatun, 119–20
Lambert-Hurley, Siobhan, 172–73
language: and culture, 97; and experience
of self, as aporetic, 105; and lineages,
Persianate understanding of, 113–14,
133; nationalism's transformation
of, 196
Lawrence, Bruce B., 171–72, 176,
258n38
lineage: Arab, 245n36; and concept of
ethnicity, 124; blood-connection
model of, 123–26, 136–37; other
than biological, in South Asia cultures, 137–38; Timurid, 127. *See also*
kinship, Persianate understanding of
lineages, Persianate understanding of: as
cause of immoral behavior, 107–8,
238n12; connections created by, 113,
114–15; criteria for sorting lineages
by type, 159–60; crossing of modern
conceptual boundaries by, 201–2;
family ancestry and, 106–7, 109, 110,
112, 129, 134, 200, 249–50n104,
249–50n104; "fictive" elements
in, 102, 133; labor performed by,
141–45; language and, 113–14, 133;
learning/education and, 105–6,
108–9, 111–13, 140, 142–43; legally-
defined forms of, 134–37; moral
virtue and, 110, 133; multiple overlapping forms of, 97–98, 100, 140,
142, 143, 144; names as indicators
of, 144, 146–47; in nineteenth-
century works, 110; nobility and,
127; *vs.* origin, 133–34; place and,
104, 105, 107, 109–14, 120, 199;
poetic lineages, 140–41, 144–45; and